Ours To Hold It High
The History of the 77th Infantry Division in World War II

By
Men Who Were There
Edited by Max Myers

Thierry Keith Tedford

Elistment = Apr 13 1944
discharge Feb 22, 1946

Co. I, 306 Inf. Regt.

Purple Heart
Bronze stars

First published by The Infantry Journal Press, in 1947.

Copyright © Max Myers.

This edition published in 2019.

To Those Who Did Not Return

They shall not grow old as we that are left grow old:
Age shall not weary them, nor the years condemn,
To the going down of sun and in the morning
We shall remember them.

Table of Contents

FOREWORD	6
THOSE WHO HANDED US THE TORCH	7
PART I: BUILDING A COMBAT DIVISION	11
CHAPTER 1: ACTIVATION AND TRAINING	12
CHAPTER 2: LOUISIANA MANEUVERS	31
CHAPTER 3: THE SANDS OF HYDER	35
CHAPTER 4: FROM WEST VIRGINIA TO CHESAPEAKE BAY	42
CHAPTER 5: TRAINING IN PINEAPPLE LAND	48
PART II: THE LIBERATION OF GUAM	52
PART III: THE LIBERATION OF LEYTE	123
CHAPTER 13: NO REST FOR THE WEARY	124
CHAPTER 14: EAST LEYTE: 23 NOVEMBER TO 5 DECEMBER	125
CHAPTER 15: THE END RUN TO ORMOC	131
CHAPTER 16: COGON, VALENCIA, TAGBONG RIVER AND LIBUNGAO ROAD JUNCTION	144
CHAPTER 17: THE ROAD TO PALOMPON	169

PART IV: KERAMA RETTO	193
CHAPTER 18: GETTING READY FOR THE NEXT ONE	194
CHAPTER 19: FIVE ASSAULT LANDINGS ON L-6 DAY	198
CHAPTER 20: LATER LANDINGS	207
PART V: IE SHIMA: IMPORTANT LITTLE ISLAND	211
CHAPTER 21: DODGING A DIVINE WIND	212
CHAPTER 22: ASSAULT THROUGH THE BACK DOOR	217
CHAPTER 23: IEGUSUGU YAMA	226
PART VI: OKINAWA: FINAL BLOW TO DAI NIPPON	242
CHAPTER 24: THE ESCARPMENT	243
CHAPTER 25: THE JAPS STRIKE BACK	257
CHAPTER 26: BREAKING OF THE SHURI LINE	271
CHAPTER 27: THE LAST THREE HILLS	314
PART VII: MOPPING UP AFTER THE WAR	327
CHAPTER 28: CEBU: REHABILITATION AND THE JAP SURRENDER	329
CHAPTER 29: THE OCCUPATION OF HOKKAIDO	339
CHAPTER 30: MISSION ACCOMPLISHED	349
A NOTE TO THE READER	351

Foreword

Soldiers of the 77th Infantry Division:

I have repeatedly said, a division to be good, must be good in every department. The pages following do not contain the saga of each unit. Nevertheless, our superb record was made possible by the superior performance of Reconnaissance, Headquarters, Signal, Military Police, Quartermaster, Ordnance, Engineer, Medical, and Service units of the Division, and of the habitually attached Antiaircraft, Amphibious, Chemical Warfare, Engineer, Hospital, Intelligence, Jasco, Ordnance, Quartermaster, and Tank units as well as by the outstanding performance of the basic Infantry-Artillery combination.

I have repeatedly said that I take great pride in our combat accomplishments; but I treasure the memories of the self-discipline, cleanliness, orderliness, cooperation, sense of humor, ability to do a job, and inherent courtesy of the tough guys — in combat — of the "Liberty Division" who actually liberated thousands of the oppressed, who said the Liberty Torch was "Ours to Hold it High," who kept the mental flag of their country flying before them.

I have repeatedly said, "I am Proud to Belong."

Andrew D. Bruce
Major General, U. S. Army
Commanding

Those Who Handed Us the Torch

THIS is the story of a proud and efficient fighting team. It trained, it fought and it decisively defeated the Japanese on Guam, Leyte, Kerama Retto, Ie Shima and Okinawa.

It is believed desirable, now, before the facts become distorted by frequent retelling, to narrate the part of the 77th Infantry Division in World War II as the events were seen by the soldiers who participated in them. This is a history written by men who were there rather than the work of a historian who delved among dusty records. If, perhaps, this narrative is somewhat less orderly, the operations seem more involved, the results attained less clear cut and the participants appear more confused than in a story written years after the events, well, the war at first hand was like that.

This story began at Fort Jackson, South Carolina, in March 1942. There in less than 40 days were assembled the men of the reborn 77th. However, behind these recruits was the "old" 77th which in World War I had likewise been a proud, efficient fighting team which had left a splendid record and an inspiring tradition. Its record and its tradition were ever present with the "new ' Division during its training and combat. The veterans of Argonne Forest passed on much of their gallant spirit and determination to the men who became veterans of Ormoc Valley and Okinawa.

At Fort Jackson in 1942 most of us, brash and busy, were not greatly impressed by such intangibles as patriotism, comradeship and tradition. Now, in 1946, we, those of us who returned, can appreciate these things. We have witnessed selfless patriotism; we have lived for months and years in the closest comradeship, and we have helped to build a tradition. Now we can understand what experienced military leaders knew prior to the Division's activation, that those organizations fight best which have behind them a long and proud history of battle achievement. We can appreciate the influence of the "old" 77th in the building of the "new".

In order that readers whose memories do not reach back to the days of the A.E.F. may know something of the "old" 77th, a little will be told here concerning its accomplishments.

The 77th Division, National Army, was organized at Camp Upton, New York, in September 1917. It called itself the "Metropolitan" Division because its personnel came almost entirely from the sidewalks of New York. It was an aggregation of about 23,000 Manhattan taxi drivers, Bronx tailors, Brooklyn factory hands, Wall Street executives, with a generous sprinkling of professional men from the entire city.

The first commander was Major General James Franklin Bell. Under him the men trained for seven months on the wind-swept sand dunes and snow-covered marshes of Long Island. Their objectives were discipline, hardening and the development of combat efficiency. The time was desperately short but the objectives were attained to a degree evidenced by the subsequent record of the Division.

Only six months after activation the 77th, under command of Brigadier General Evan M. Johnson, departed for France. The infantry and engineers went to Pas-de-Calais, the artillery to Camp de Souge for training with battle-experienced British troops.

On June 21, 1918 the 77th entered the front lines in the Baccarat sector which was relatively quiet but provided opportunities for local actions and front line training. August 12th found the Division along the Vesle River near Bazoches. Following the German withdrawal to the Aisne River, the 77th advanced on September 4th and occupied the ridges north of the Vesle. The following day the plateau between the Vesle and the Aisne was secured. It was in the bitter, though relatively unpublicized fighting and hard living along the Vesle that the 77th was forged into a combat machine. Major General Robert Alexander took command from Major General George B. Duncan, and the Division was relieved from this sector on September 16, 1918.

It was in the Meuse-Argonne Offensive that the 77th Division attained its greatest fame. Its mission was to smash through a heavily-defended, almost impregnable forest area. The deep gullies and tangled underbrush caused this region to be compared with the Virginia "Wilderness" of Civil War fame. The 77th attacked through the forest on September 26th and overran German positions to a depth of two kilometers. Again on September 28th a gain of two kilometers was made. Thereafter until October 3rd excellent daily progress was made against bitter German resistance.

It was during this drive that the "Lost Battalion" of the 308th Infantry made its heroic stand. Major Charles S. Whittlesey, under orders to move forward as far as possible, led six companies through a gap in the German lines. Units on the right and left were unable to advance and Major Whittlesey's troops were cut off and surrounded by Germans. From October 3rd to 6th while the remainder of the Division tried desperately to relieve them, these men beat off repeated German attacks. This battalion could not get food or water and could not evacuate its casualties. The Germans sent over a note urging surrender, but Major Whittlesey's answer was "Come and get us". On October 7th the Germans began to withdraw from the forest, the Division was able to advance and relieve the isolated force by nightfall.

The 77th continued its advance, reached the Aire River on October 10th, and was relieved on October 16th with its mission completed. On November 1st it went into action again in the general attack of the First Army north of St. Juvin. Fighting was especially bitter for two days but by November 6th the assault battalions had reached the Meuse River and the 77th held a line along the river at the time of the Armistice, 11:00 A. M. November 11th, 1918. The Division during its 68 days of combat fought in four campaigns — Baccarat, Oise-Aisne, Aisne-Marne, and Meuse-Argonne. It had done its job well, but at a cost of 2,275 men killed or missing and 4,934 wounded.

It went to the Ninth Training Area in France and eventually to Camp Miller and then Camp Upton, Long Island, New York, closing at Upton on May 6th, 1919. There it was inactivated at the age of approximately 19 months, of which the greater portion had been spent overseas.

In 1921, the 77th became a reserve division. To it were assigned reserve officers and a few non-commissioned officers, many of whom had served with the Division in France, who were to constitute a nucleus around which to build a division in case of need. These reservists held weekly sessions during which tactical and administrative lessons were studied. From 1924 to 1940 the Division furnished officers for the summer camps of the Citizens Military Training Camps at Plattsburg, N. Y. Other officers attended maneuvers and army schools, to maintain themselves in a state of readiness. Although the 77th Reserve Division was never activated as such and these officers were scattered to many types of assignments at the outbreak of World War II, it played a part in the history of the 77th.

Therefore, when the men who were to form the "new" 77th Infantry Division gathered at Fort Jackson, South Carolina in the Spring of 1942, they were a new generation picking up the chain of history and tradition of the "old" Division. They had much in common with the veterans of the previous generation in that they came mostly from the metropolitan area and with the same purpose. The national and regimental colors of the old outfits were brought out of retirement and given with appropriate ceremonies to the new. In each orderly room was to be found a copy of the history of the old organization. To each organization came delegations of old-timers to greet the new men and give them encouragement, advice and best wishes. Members of the "old" 77th followed with intense interest and pride the development and later the battles of the re-activated division. They maintained at 28 East 39th Street, New York City, the 77th Division Association Headquarters and Club, so that the 77th always had a U. S. office even when fighting far out on the Pacific. Now that World War II is ended and the 77th for the second time reverts to shadow form, similarity of experiences within a common organization will bind closer still those two generations of fighting men.

This book is volume two in the history of the 77th Division. There is, unfortunately, little in the present world situation to definitely assure us that this volume closes the series.

Part I: Building a Combat Division

BRIEF: The 77th Infantry Division was re-activated on 25 March 1942 as one of the first three reserve divisions to be re-born in preparation for World War II. Under the leadership of a cadre of officers and non-commissioned officers, the selectees, mostly men from New York, New Jersey, and Pennsylvania, shed much sweat and a little blood on the drill fields and training areas of Fort Jackson, South Carolina. In January 1943 a hardened and partly trained team entrained for the Louisiana maneuver area where for eight weeks the 77th learned war with its sister division, the 90th.

Then in March the 77th moved west to Hyder, a water-stop in the heart of the Arizona desert on the Southern Pacific Railroad, built a tent camp, called Camp Hyder, and learned to get along on less of everything. The elements of the Division were in the field almost constantly. Most of July was spent in maneuvers in the adjoining California desert with a daily temperature well past the 100 degree mark. The August and September training exercises near Camp Hyder were equally strenuous.

The next move was back to the east coast. Distributed between Camp Pickett, Virginia; Indiantown Gap, Pennsylvania; Elkins, West Virginia; the A. P. Hill Military Reservation, Virginia; Camp Bradford, Virginia; Solomons Island, Maryland; and Fort Pierce, Florida, the officers and men learned the detailed technique of amphibious warfare, how to fight in the mountains in the winter, and reviewed their marksmanship and small unit tactics. Early in March 1944, troop trains carried the Division a third time across the continent to Camp Stoneman, California, where it embarked for the Hawaiian Islands.

Three busy months were spent on .Oahu. Here, individual, small unit and amphibious training was reviewed. New combat equipment was issued and the Division Commander and his staff planned operations against far off and very secret targets with names like Saipan, Guam and Babelthuap.

On July 1, 1944 the advance elements of the 77th Infantry Division sailed west to fight. The objective was Guam.

Chapter 1: Activation and Training

A COMBAT DIVISION is an organism and a complex entity. It is conceived and born after incredible planning, but not without, confusion and a certain amount of suffering; it passes through periods of semi-helplessness and of awkwardness. Finally it learns by experience, attains coordination and confidence, and becomes a mature, competent body with an individual personality and abilities.

In December 1941 the world was aflame. The need was imperative. A great Army was created on paper, and plans called for three divisions to be re-activated on 25 March 1942. These were the 77th, 82nd, and the 90th, all three of which had made distinguished combat records in 1918.

During what might be called the gestation period of the 77th Infantry Division, Major General Robert L. Eichelberger was designated as its commanding general. War Department orders dated 10 February 1942 were terse: "Announcement is made of the assignment of Major General Robert L. Eichelberger, 0-2624, United States Army, to command the 77th Infantry Division, Fort Jackson, South Carolina, effective upon its activation". General Eichelberger had a distinguished professional military career already behind him and was ready and qualified to train and lead the new Division into action. He had served in Panama, on the Mexican Border, in Siberia, and in the Philippines, and had held command and staff assignments in all echelons including the War Department. He came to Fort Jackson from a tour of duty as Superintendent of the United States Military Academy at West Point, New York.

The order directing the activation of the 77th Infantry Division was dated 14 February 1942. However, prenatal development had occurred prior to this time. General Eichelberger and sixteen staff officers had attended a short course at the Command and General Staff School for new Division Commanders and their staffs. At the same time approximately two hundred line officers who had been selected from existing army organizations were at various service schools taking quick refresher courses. Elsewhere nearly four hundred additional officers were being selected "for duty with a combat division to be activated at Fort Jackson." In the 8th and 30th Divisions, whose members had already experienced a degree of field service in the Carolina Maneuvers of the previous fall, enlisted men were being selected for places in the cadre of the 77th, and harassed commanders were unhappily filling this requisition for 1,178 competent non-commissioned officers.

Thus, the 77th Division became a reality before its first member set foot on Fort Jackson. It was a rumor which spread through the Army Latrineogram: "A new Division at Jackson in the Spring . . . combat outfit . . . 77th." It existed in the minds of officers watching demonstrations at Fort Benning: "They're going to the 77th . . . one of three new divisions ... to be built from the ground up . . . don't envy them that job ..." It was, to be quite frank, a symbol of fear which hung over certain training officers at Replacement Centers: "The Old Man got orders to furnish ten officers from the battalion for the 77th Division ... I just rented a house and brought my family here . . . sure hope they send those new reserve officers who came in last week . . . let's talk to the exec . . It was a word of hope to others: "That outfit will see action ... I wonder if it would do any good to ask for a transfer . . . ?"

The 77th Division was named in thousands of letters, orders, messages, notes, phone calls, and memoranda which traveled various ways in order that a camp and its facilities, hundreds of officers and noncommissioned officers, thousands of selectees, hundreds of vehicles, trainloads of supplies and essential items of equipment might be poured into one place almost simultaneously with a minimum of confusion.

Above all, the 77th and its two sister divisions were a challenge and a question in high American and Allied military circles: "Can it be done? Can new and effective combat divisions be built with only a handful of experienced officers? Can it be done soon enough?" In the background of the thoughts of those men in high places was the greatest worry of all: "Will the American selectees work and learn and fight?" The outcome of the war hinged upon the answer to that unspoken question.

General Eichelberger and his sixteen staff officers arrived at Fort Jackson by 18 February 1942 and started to work. The planning necessary for the tasks of quartering and feeding, classifying, assigning, and clothing fifteen thousand strangers was in itself enough to keep dozens of officers busy. In addition, someone had to amplify the War Department training program and directives for units and organizations from squads to regiments. Someone had to organize schools for drivers, typists, radio men, cooks, and dozens of other types of specialists. What is more, this had to be done all at once. No one could foresee the exact deadline on training except, perhaps, our enemies, the Germans and the Japanese. The Division might have time to finish seventeen weeks basic training, as well as the subsequent fourteen weeks of unit and combined training, and be ready for action by the end of 1942. But it might be called sooner, and without much notice. There was so little time, and experience was spread so thin.

A distinguished and competent group of senior officers was assigned to assist General Eichelberger. Brigadier General Roscoe B. Woodruff, Assistant Division Commander, was a veteran of the Mexican Border and of the 2d Division's campaigns in France in 1918. He had served with troops and with the War Department General Staff. Brigadier General John E. McMahon, Division Artillery Commander, had likewise had a long, varied career. The commanders of the 305th, 306th and 307th Infantry Regiments were Colonel Louis K. Underhill, Colonel James N. Peale, and Colonel William H. Craig. The Division Staff included Colonel Clovis E. Byers, Lieutenant Colonels Cecil W. Nist, George B. Peploe, Hugh S. Cort, and Major Frank S. Bowen. These officers, and some few others were experienced regulars who were to be the hard, purposeful core around which the Division was to be formed. To them fell the tremendous task of changing the thinking of more than fifteen thousand officers and men from civilian attitudes to military points of view. If the Division was to succeed in combat against veteran enemy troops, they must rapidly infuse into the civilian psychosis, the stiffness and discipline necessary to overcome the terrors of the battlefield and push on, with skill, into the very teeth of the worst the enemy could throw at them.

The two hundred officers who were to lead the regiments, battalions, and companies arrived 25 February, surveyed their little kingdoms and planned the organizational work to be done. During the period 3 to 5 March, four hundred officer "fillers" reported. These were mostly reserve lieutenants fresh from civil life whose only experience in soldiering had been gained at Reserve Officer Training Corps schools and at a six-weeks' camp. On the 5th, also, the cadre of twelve hundred noncommissioned officers moved to their new quarters and duties.

Three major tasks faced these officers and men prior to the arrival of the selectees. In three weeks they must get acquainted with each other and construct the framework around which functioning units could be built; they must make ready the physical plant to handle the Division; and they must prepare themselves to train the new men. Furthermore, while accomplishing these three tasks this skeleton force must maintain itself even though lacking men and equipment.

The first task more or less took care of itself in the rush of working together at the barracks and preparing themselves for the training job which was just ahead. The officers and men began to know each other; commanders found subordinates who were reliable and others who were not, and began to gauge the respective speeds and talents of all. Six strange officers and twelve strange non-commissioned officers would engage in the rush job of scrubbing barracks space and come away from the task as "K" Company. Here were the beginnings of loyalties which paid off at places like Barrigada and "Chocolate Drop".

General Eichelberger had directed that from the start the Division would maintain superior standards of discipline, police, and dress. He had also ordered that when the new men arrived at Fort Jackson, they should find clean quarters, hot showers, hot food, and clean beds already made up for them. This meant a great deal of dirty, undignified work for the officers and non-commissioned officers. The camp area was drab and the soil badly eroded. The buildings, though sound, were in some cases, filthy. Cots and bedding were in warehouses in another part of the camp. Company and battery commanders faced the task of policing and preparing about two acres of grounds, four large barracks, a kitchen and mess hall, an orderly room, and a day room, all to accommodate about two hundred men. For this they had four or five officers, twelve non-commissioned officers, no vehicles, no tools and no funds. The work must be done between and after school periods; so, for three weeks, the unbelievable occurred. Officers scrubbed floors, painted walls, carried cots, and made beds. They worked side by side with their non-commissioned officers. Sergeants walked guard at night, attended schools and scrubbed floors by day. Both officers and non-commissioned officers complained more than a little; but they did the work and they learned to work together.

Preparation for training the selectees was the most difficult task. The 77th Division was to be the "guinea pig" for the new training program. Furthermore, the training was to be done by inexperienced instructors. Most of the company grade officers were unfamiliar with the new drill regulations, had not had adequate training with recently developed weapons, and were not even familiar with the sources of training information. The cadre sergeants, most of whom had only a few months service had been recently promoted to unfamiliar positions. Training aids were scarce and so were funds with which to obtain materials to make them. For several hours each day the officers and non-commissioned officers listened and saw and practiced and sweated, in an attempt to crowd years of learning and experience into a few days. Although this goal was not reached, the results attained were invaluable to the junior officers and sergeants when their men arrived.

By mid-March, the men who were destined to wear the Statue of Liberty patch were pouring into Induction Centers and gathering in Reception Centers at Fort Devens, Fort Niagara, Camp Upton, Fort Dix, and Fort George Meade. They represented the white, yellow, red, and brown races, and almost one third were either foreign born or of more or less recent immigrant descent. There were even a few from very wealthy families who later, as privates, maintained apartments, expensive cars, and valets in Columbia, S. C. As a group they were not young; their average age was close to thirty-two; there were some in their forties, and a few past fifty. Aaron Miller, a volunteer, was fifty-seven. These were the older men, in some cases the established family men, who were gathered by Selective Service Boards toward the end of the first draft. Ordinarily they would not have been sent to a combat division, and certainly not to infantry; but this was March 1942, and the need was great.

Their trains rolled south loaded with bewildered, uncomfortable, somewhat resentful, but resigned men, not yet accustomed to Army clothes or Army ways. There were, however, a few among them who had been through all this before, in World War I, and had volunteered to see it through again. These were men like Otto Becker, (age 53), Leo J. McHugh, (age 49), and Joseph L. Donner, (age 52). The first train load of selectees reached Fort Jackson on 25 March, the day that the 77th Division was reborn. Other groups continued to arrive until the 12th of April.

As the tired, disheveled men poured from the trains, they were loaded into trucks and sent to regimental and battalion areas. There, the milling mob of heavy-laden individuals was quickly and arbitrarily divided into groups, each of which was led to a barracks and a mess hall by a company officer. The hot meals, the hot baths, and clean beds ordered by the Division Commander were ready. These men were casuals; they did not belong to the company whose barracks they occupied, but were simply lodgers until the Division Classification Section assigned them to permanent organizations. Each company entertained several hundred of these casuals for an average of two days, before all were sorted and assigned. More than entertainment was involved; these men received training in basic subjects such as military courtesy, infantry drill, and hygiene. Every bit of instruction which could be given prior to the initiation of the training program was that much gained. Actually, the casual had anything but a casual time. Some had a turn at kitchen police and others walked guard carrying clubs or unloaded rifles.

While Private Joe was undergoing, though not necessarily enjoying the hospitality of "B" Company, the battle of the cards was going on. For the first time in the history of the Army a classification system was being tried out on a division-scale. As each newly inducted man passed through a Reception center, he was interviewed and a large yellow card was filled out and punched according to a machine code. This card, bearing a record of his civilian and military experience, as well as a great deal of other information, arrived at the Division with him. At Fort Jackson, all cards went to Captain John J. Sigwald and a crew of assistants who had been training for a month for this sorting and classifying task. The cards were machine sorted and cross-sorted in the Division Headquarters. The cards of truck drivers came out in one pile and those of typists in another. The cards of the men with high test scores came to the top of the piles. Then, with the Tables of Organization at hand, the classification experts assigned the men. Within two days of his arrival Private Joe shouldered his barracks bag and moved to the 77th Signal Company. At the time he did not know how it happened and perhaps did not care.

This classification and assignment of recruits was a long way from being perfect. Many men ended up in the wrong niches, or found there was no place for their particular talent in an Infantry Division. Such errors were unavoidable but were held to a minimum and usually corrected later. After all, there was a war on and everything had to be done double time.

Two days after the Division was officially re-born, Brigadier General Mark W. Clark, Chief of Staff of the Army Ground Forces, came to inspect the activities of the new Division and to witness the presentation of the colors which the old 77th Division had carried in World War I. As General Clark, his staff, and new men looked on, Lieutenant Colonel Paul Knight, the only officer present who had served with the 77th in World War I, presented the Colors to General Eichelberger. General Clark's party then toured the camp to observe how the young soldiers were being cared for.

On 7 April, the training program officially started. By that time each unit had been organized and the men assigned to specific jobs. The new men had familiarized themselves with the camp and with the routine of living in barracks. They had received some instruction in the more fundamental subjects by means of conferences, training films, and demonstrations. They had been busy from the start, but now the real work commenced. Their daily schedule began before dawn with a reveille formation, followed by a hurried toilet, breakfast, and policing of their quarters and area. They then had almost ten crowded hours of training, after which, until taps, their time was their own, unless there were fatigue details or night classes. Sunday was a day of light duty, but hardly a day of rest. Life became a steady, weary grind of classes, drills, and duties under driving taskmasters.

The willing attitude of the officers and men of the Division was remarkable. All hated war, and almost all thoroughly disliked the restrictions and subordination of the individual inherent in Army life. Many of the officers and most of the men had been ordered to active service contrary to their personal inclinations, and were being subjected to an almost impossible training schedule. They were expected to absorb knowledge at a rate which no civilian educational institution would have considered possible or desirable. A few were not yet convinced that the United States should have any part in the war, and many had relatives in Axis countries. Despite all this, they pitched in and worked. They wore themselves out and kept on working. They not only obeyed orders, but inquired as to the reasons and asked for more. Experienced officers commented that they had never known men to learn as rapidly as these recruits.

There was griping, of course, and a little of it was justified. There were a few unpleasant occurrences, sometimes not without cause. An outsider eavesdropping at the latrines, or in the dayrooms or officers' clubs might have gained the entirely erroneous impression that the task was hopeless and that everyone was being overworked to no purpose. The important fact was that having blown off steam, the gripers went out and as they had been taught efficiently made the "goddam march" or dug the "lousy holes."

The men could not help seeing that the officers were working on a longer, tougher schedule than the one they were following. This was particularly true in the companies and batteries. Most of the platoon leaders, at the start, knew very little more than the men, and less than some of the cadre sergeants; but the officers had responsibilities. By Division order, every company officer was required to spend eight to ten hours with his unit on the training field. Most of that time he was teaching what he had probably learned only the night before. Also, by Division order, each officer attended a two-hour school three or four nights a week. In addition, there was the ever-present administrative and paper work; all of it must be done or checked by an officer, because the standards in the Division were perfection in administration as well as in training. Officers must supervise and check the feeding, quartering, supply, and recreation of their men. Then too, there were courts and boards and inspection committees. Finally, sometime between 10:00 p.m. and 6:00 a.m. the officers must learn, or at least review, the subjects to be taught the following day. It was no wonder that absent wives received few letters, and those living in Columbia rarely saw their husbands. It is understandable that at least one capable sergeant refused to go to Officer Candidate School because he "would not put up with the hell my lieutenants are getting here."

The officers took it as did the men, griping a little but carrying on. Both learned to work under pressure, to expect little and to get the job done well and quickly. They all tightened their belts over shrinking waist lines and worked. General Eichelberger told them on 11 May: "This will be no joy ride or picnic. Time is precious and we cannot afford to waste it. We shall have thorough training and hard work, the methods used by all successful armies; for there is no substitute for hard work. If you think you are working too hard, remember what our enemies are doing." All knew that the Division was going to war soon and that their own survival would depend, to a large extent, on their performance in training. Spurred on by such considerations and working under great pressure, these men helped to prove that America, given adequate time, could convert its men as well as its machines to war.

As the rigorous training program progressed, the obvious misfits were weeded out or reassigned. Some of the older men were shifted to assignments which required less physical endurance. A few men who had been selected by careless draft boards, or passed by casual medical examiners turned out to be inept or to possess chronic disabilities: they had to be discharged whatever their good intentions. In addition, each unit had the task of correcting unsanitary or unpleasant habits of a few of its members. There were, for example, men who through shyness or because of natural aversion to water as a cleansing agent, were reluctant to make use of the available community showers. Such cases were usually corrected by the men themselves, led by some barracks-wise non-commissioned officer who administered to the reluctant one a thorough scrubbing with yellow soap and a GI brush.

Inspections were frequent. Every man in the Division, because he was part of a large-scale training experiment, was on show every hour of the day. By sad experience they learned to report properly to high ranking visitors, to answer questions, to continue with their work as if inspections were a daily occurrence, which they soon became.

On 16 May, when many of the men had received less than five weeks' training, Lieutenant General Ben Lear, commanding the Second Army, made a thorough and searching inspection of the Division. He and his staff were not looking for men who knew or even appeared to know the answers. They questioned the dullest appearing men they could select to find if these were learning. Legend has it that one alert company commander avoided recrimination by instructing only those men who did not know the answer to hold up their hands. The inspectors searched for those who did not have the full allowance of underdrawers or tent pins, and when such shortages were found the officer responsible was made uncomfortable. But General Lear found little to criticize and was pleased with the progress made.

Despite the strenuous training and the stiff and bruised muscles from bayonet drill and obstacle courses, the men found time and energy for outside activities. Helped by local organizations in Columbia and neighboring towns, each unit furnished its day room where men could read, write letters, play cards, or just loaf. The Post Exchanges were popular and crowded. Each unit organized athletic teams which competed for organization championships. The Division Band provided talent for orchestras which became popular locally and on radio programs. Professor Coleslaw (Private Paul Kuhlthau) and his toy piano were in demand.

The chaplains soon became friends and backers of their men and the neat frame chapels scattered over the camp became centers of religious activity, under a program directed by Lieutenant Colonel William F. O'Brien, Division Chaplain.

Men on pass went to Columbia and neighboring towns where they found that Southern hospitality had been only slightly lessened by the strain of having sixty thousand soldiers as neighbors. However, officers and men alike found Main Street on Saturday afternoon a nightmare for those who conscientiously attempted to observe saluting rules.

Late in May, after hours of practicing sighting and aiming, positions, trigger squeeze, and rapid fire, the regiments began taking their men to the Leesburg Rifle Range where they fired live ammunition and felt the recoil of Army weapons. The 305th Infantry first marched the fourteen odd miles to the range camp, and while there set some high scores for those who came later to match. The spring weather was pleasant, the range camp was comfortable though primitive, and the work was interesting and noisy. During June the remainder of the organizations of the Division took their turn at the range. It was used to capacity and the competition was keen. So keen, in fact, that methods used by some units in firing and scoring would scarcely have been approved at official matches; but the men did learn to handle and to fire their weapons with accuracy.

General Eichelberger was transferred to the Command of the I Army Corps and on 5 June Brigadier General Woodruff moved up from Assistant Division Commander to Commanding General of the 77th Division. General Woodruff and his jeep had become familiar to the officers and men and they had full confidence in him. He was promoted to Major General later in the month and Brigadier General Harris M. Melasky was assigned as Assistant Division Commander.

Numerous parades and reviews were included in the training schedules of organizations. On 8 June the Division participated in its first large ceremony. The entire I Corps was assembled on the dry, dusty, Anchrum Ferry Field just outside of Fort Jackson, to be reviewed by an unnamed visitor. For hours the 8th and the 30th Divisions, and the troops and vehicles of the eight-week-old 77th moved and formed on the field. The day was very hot and canteens were soon empty. It required real stamina to stay there and take it. The newspaper reports did not mention that, because of careful planning, routing and discipline, the 77th Division did not have men fall out overcome by the heat, but this made a vivid impression on those who took part.

When the distinguished visitors, riding in jeeps, passed around the motionless ranks, the men began to identify them. The officer in white was Lord Mountbatten; his picture had been on a recent "Time" cover. There was General Marshall, and the other Britisher was General Sir John Dill. These and many other Allied officials were on the reviewing stand during the one and one-half hours it took the troops and equipment to move past — three divisions in mass formations. Though not yet through basic training the men of the 77th marched like old-timers, their lines straight and their step firm and correct.

Lord Mountbatten later wrote to General Woodruff: "Although I tried to express in some small measure, the other day, my admiration and astonishment at the way in which the 77th Division turned out in the review of the First Army Corps, I feel I must write and tell you once more that of all the many interesting and encouraging things I have come across during my visit to the United States, none has made me feel more certain of our victory than the efficiency which your Division displayed at the end of only eight weeks training. If the United States can go on turning out divisions like that, victory will be ours much sooner than I had thought possible."

A comment made by General George C. Marshall, Chief of Staff of the United States Army, hinted at the worry, now dispelled, which had been present in high places concerning the possibility of training a citizen Army capable of modern war: "The training shown by these new soldiers has lifted a weight off my shoulders equalled only by the winning of the recent battle in the Pacific."

Sixteen days later on 24 June, Winston Churchill, Prime Minister of Great Britain, stepped from a train at Fort Jackson to see for himself the troops his subordinates had complimented. With him were Secretary of War Henry L. Stimson, veteran of the 77th in World War I, General George C. Marshall, General Sir John Dill, Lieutenant General Lesley J. McNair, General Sir Alan Brooke, and others. The Guard of Honor was the 3rd Battalion of the 306th Infantry, commanded by Lieutenant Colonel Alexander Adair. Every man was proud to be present and anxious to appear determined and steady. As the great leader of the British Empire passed down the line that is the impression he received. He remarked: "The faces of the men gave me the greatest and everlasting memory of the day. I have never been more impressed than I was with the bearing of the men whom I saw. The undemonstrative, therefore grim determination of the newly drafted bodies bodes ill for our enemies."

Mr. Churchill witnessed a composite review of one Regimental Combat Team from each of the three divisions of the I Corps; the 307th Combat Team represented the 77th Division. During his stay at Fort Jackson, he made a rapid inspection of every phase of training.

The reviews continued. On 14 July the 306th Infantry paraded for Lieutenant General E. K. Smart and Lieutenant General T. R. Blarney of the Australian Army. On the 23rd the 307th Regimental Combat Team represented the 77th Division in a composite I Corps review for Lieutenant General Ben Lear who caused Major Aubrey Smith's 3rd Battalion of that Regiment to be moved to the reviewing line to receive the review with him, because, as he said later, "I thought they were the best-looking battalion I had ever seen in ranks."

In the rush of training and reviews the Fourth of July slipped by without much celebration. Parades, however, were only incidental to the continuous routine of training. Each day found new subjects which busy S-3s had extracted from Mobilization Training Programs and Field Manuals, and included in training schedules. The marches along the narrow, sandy trails which criss-crossed Fort Jackson's scrub oak and pine-covered slopes became longer and hotter. Men, who at the start, had handled poison oak and picked up live rattlesnakes from ignorance rather than from bravado, learned about life away from the city sidewalks. Specialists devoted less time to basic drills and more to learning their specialties, such as communications, motor maintenance, typing, care of the wounded, and many others. The men of the 302d Engineer Battalion learned to build bridges and to use explosives to make loud, destructive noises. In August they threw a ponton bridge across the Wateree River in the record time of two hours and fifteen minutes.

Army vehicles began to be used somewhat more. During the early months, gasoline was rationed at one gallon per vehicle per day, which meant that if the essential supply vehicles were kept operating, tactical vehicles must be deadlined most of the time. During those months the infantry travelled on foot. There were many men and some junior officers who spent two months in the Division without riding in any army vehicle. However, as field training increased, the gasoline restrictions were relaxed and jeeps and other trucks came out of motor pools. They were driven by men who had practiced and earned drivers' permits over the roughest terrain at Fort Jackson. The crews of the half-tracks and jeeps of the hard-driving 77th Reconnaissance Troop explored all side roads for miles around.

Promotions were constant and plentiful. There were many non-commissioned grades open from the start, and others developed as soldiers were transferred to schools or out on cadres. Alert, willing men were given positions of responsibility almost over night. For example, Private John F. Moran became a sergeant after thirty-six days in the Division. Private

Horace J. Hoolihan jumped five grades to Technical Sergeant after four months' service, and Private David P. Zink became Master Sergeant Zink in less than six months.

Officers likewise profited by changed insignia and increased pay checks. There were vacancies at the start and more constantly developed, but always there was a candidate waiting to take over the job in the belief that he could do it well. Several of the senior officers were transferred to other assignments. Lieutenant Colonel Hugh Cort replaced Colonel Clovis E. Byers as Chief of Staff. Colonel Lincoln F. Daniels and Lieutenant Colonel Alexander Adair succeeded Colonel Lewis K. Underhill and Colonel James M. Peale as commanders of the 305th and 306th Regiments, respectively.

A steady stream of officers and a few key non-commissioned officers were sent away to schools for short periods, and then returned, to pass on their specialized knowledge to others. Such schools included The Infantry School at Fort Benning, Georgia; the Field Artillery School at Fort Sill, Oklahoma; the Engineer School at Fort Belvoir, Virginia; and the Command and General Staff School at Fort Leavenworth, Kansas.

Two large-scale emigrations from the Division took place during its early months. The first was the departure of a cadre for the new 94th Division. About two hundred officers and twelve hundred men were selected and trained to form the nucleus of this new Division. The requirements were high and commanding officers had the difficult task of filling their quotas without, at the same time, seriously crippling their own organizations. This cadre left in July carrying with it the best wishes of the Division. It included among its numbers many a March selectee now facing the task of training others. Later in the summer, smaller cadres of officers were furnished to assist in the organization of the 99th and 100th Divisions.

The second exodus was to the Officer Candidate Schools. These quotas were large and the same intelligent, reliable sort of men who were doing so well as non-commissioned officers were in demand for conversion to second lieutenants. About one thousand officer candidates left the Division during the summer.

There were, of course, a few who refused to become parts of the team, or who lacked the moral responsibility to discipline themselves. So there were a few brawls in town, a few AWOLs, and a few cases of venereal disease; but surprisingly few considering the number of men in the Division. The age and steadiness of the great majority contributed materially to the maintenance of discipline. The first few hesitant AWOLs were treated somewhat too leniently and as more began to take unauthorized vacations, it was necessary to resort to courts martial to discourage the practice.

On 7 August another veteran of the 77th Division of World War I came to visit. This was Under Secretary of War Robert P. Patterson who in World War I had been Captain Patterson of F Company, 306th Infantry, and later commander of the 2d Battalion of that regiment. In his honor the 306th Regimental Combat Team and a combat team each from the 8th and 30th Divisions passed in review. Mr. Patterson also witnessed camouflage demonstrations, and a tank attack.

As each step of training was completed there were tests of proficiency by Division or organization staffs, followed by higher headquarters' tests to determine how the new training program was progressing. For the most part these tests were practical and were applied to sample individuals or units. The I Corp tests, given at the end of individual and small unit training, were particularly comprehensive. For several days testing teams spread over the training areas, asking questions and posing problems. The training, however, had been thorough and the Division came through with such success that Lieutenant General Ben Lear, who had observed the tests, remarked drily to the assembled officers, "You of the 77th Division have a flair for showmanship. You display yourselves well."

During August the infantry battalions conducted three-day field exercises, designed to develop tactics, technique, and teamwork. These were followed by regimental exercises. As the exercises lengthened the men began to look on Fort Jackson as a place to spend weekends. The pine groves of South Carolina became their homes.

Several strenuous tests of physical ability and stamina were successfully passed. The most trying of these was a twenty-five mile march in eight hours. Successful completion by regimental combat teams required sustained marching at a rate faster than the normal two and a half miles per hour, and careful planning for handling of those who fell by the wayside. Not all of the troops accomplished the twenty-five miles in the prescribed time, but a very few failed to finish even though exhausted and, in some cases, marching on bleeding, blistered feet.

In September, the entire Division Artillery and the 1st Battalion of the 307th Infantry entrained for the Field Artillery School at Fort Sill, Oklahoma, to serve for six weeks as School troops. This was the first of the many large-scale troop movements the Division was to make. It was an uncomfortable experience because only old and dirty day coaches were provided. Despite lack of washing facilities the men stepped off the train spick and span in clean uniforms. Student artillery officers watched the infantry and artillery work together as a modern battle team. They saw demonstrations of infantry and its supporting units, and of the effectiveness of artillery fire. The Division Artillery fired some 100,000 rounds of ammunition during its six weeks at Fort Sill. It was later announced that it had broken all records for the proficiency of School Troops at Fort Sill.

These men found some free time to roam about the neighboring country and some got as far, on week ends, as Oklahoma City and Wichita Falls. They also made the acquaintance of the deep, sticky Oklahoma mud which dried to a bricklike hardness on shoes and equipment. Despite it they made long marches, climbed hills and conducted field exercises until late in October when they returned to Fort Jackson in Pullman comfort.

About 20 September the United States Military Academy, in a departure from its usual procedure, sent sixty cadets for a short tour of duty with the Division. These were given temporary assignments as platoon leaders under the supervision of more experienced officers and, after a few days, they returned to West Point with a better knowledge of the problems of training a citizen army. On 27 September two simultaneous celebrations marked the twenty-fifth anniversary of the 77th Division. In New York City six hundred veterans of the "old" 77th marched up Fifth Avenue in a drizzling rain, assembled in Central Park Mall and listened to General Woodruff, commander of the "new" Division tell them about it. "From the very first," he said "we emphasized that the new 77th was to be a fighting outfit in keeping with its proud heritage ... for us there can be no eight hour day, no five day week. We have worked our men and officers hard. It would be no kindness to the men of the Division to permit any relaxation in the rigorous training . . . the big test lies ahead. . . ." Meanwhile, at Fort Jackson, the "new" 77th was assembled and Colonel Hugh S. Cort, its Chief of Staff, outlined the record of the Division in World War I, and spoke of the unfinished tasks ahead.

As September ended, plans were made for a Division review in honor of another unnamed guest. By a process of elimination the troops deducted that this time the "Top Man" was coming. Their opinion was reinforced by the assignment of most of the 307th Infantry to guard the railroads, the station, and the routes to the review field. It was, therefore, really no surprise when one of the open topped cars in the caravan which toured the post on 30 September contained the Commander-in-Chief, Franklin D. Roosevelt, President of the United States. From this same open car the confident but rather care-worn President watched the 77th pass in review.

On 6 October the 302d Engineers made their loudest and most satisfying noise when they efficiently demolished a large, condemned, steel bridge over the Wateree River near Camden, South Carolina. Nearly two thousand troops witnessed the destructive force of 2,500 pounds of explosives.

The Division took on an international aspect when, on 16 October, five Latin-American officers from Argentina, Colombia, Ecuador and Guatemala were attached for periods of from one to three months.

Late in October the Division prepared exhibits at the South Carolina State Fair which attracted much attention. Each organization had a part in a carefully planned, integrated display of all types of divisional equipment, from trucks and guns to medical laboratories and teletype machines.

A portion of the troops took part in the Armistice Day parade in Columbia, and the ranks of marching men with fixed bayonets made a forceful impression on the large crowds which lined the streets.

By mid-November the Division had progressed from individual training, through field training of units and organizations to readiness for larger operations. As the combined training phase started, involving tactical exercises for the Division acting as a complete force, General Woodruff assembled all officers and men for one of his brief, pointed talks. Holding aloft a rifle with a fixed bayonet he said, "With an awful lot of help it is the man who drags this around with him who wins wars." He added that the 77th was no longer a recruit division; that the "old" 77th, with a corresponding period of time devoted to training, had already been at the front in France. He pointed out that success in large-scale exercises hinged upon the same attention to small details of performance, discipline, and personal health that had been true in small problems: that the job was tough and going to get tougher, and the Division had to get ready to meet an unsportsmanlike enemy and beat him at his own game.

During this phase of training most of the time was spent in the woods and fields around Fort Jackson, the men returning to barracks only occasionally for a welcome chance to wash up and get warm all over. The weather became definitely cold; rain and snow were frequent. To men making long night marches and sleeping on the ground, this meant acute discomfort. Thanksgiving dinner, complete with turkey and trimmings, was served in the field, and services were held under the pines.

During those cold night marches, with sudden unexplained motor movements, and maneuvering through the underbrush, the big team began to function, its members to trust and rely on each other. Somehow the supplies did arrive, the battalions reached the proper places at the appointed times, and all the supporting troops cooperated with their infantry teammates. Out in the nasty weather the troops developed a "know how" for living in the field. The few "woods-wise" men taught the others where to find dry tinder during a rain, how to reflect the heat of a fire into a tent, and how to make beds of leaves and boughs. The inventiveness and knack for improvisation possessed by the ordinary American began to really assert itself. The men developed self-reliance and an attitude of "just leave us alone and don't ask too many questions and we'll take care of ourselves."

During the second and third weeks of December the entire Division was given a practical field test by the XII Corps. This exercise proved that the 77th was well along in its training. Brigadier General Floyd Parks, Chief of Staff of the Army Ground Forces, toured the area and commented: "The men of the 77th displayed a fine spirit and enthusiasm in playing the game. When I saw them they had been all night on the problem. They waded through water waist deep during freezing temperatures — hardships comparable to actual battle. Yet they were going through with the problem, maintaining communications and pushing forward with a zeal that was highly commendable. I was very much impressed with their training."

Deward Brittain, writing for the Columbia Record said of his tour with the troops: "I am not a blasphemous man but I cussed. That jeep . . . cold as a Siberian barn. The good captain looked at my tweed trousers and sympathetically handed me his overcoat as protection against the freezing sunlight . . . too cold to eat . . . the men were so busy I don't believe they even bothered to look at the thermometer . . . if the rest of the Army is like the 77th Division, it's a tough, hardened outfit."

It was during this type of exercise that Colonel Alexander Adair, Commander of the 306th Infantry, keynoted the rugged attitude of the men by refusing to take himself and his broken ankle (result of a slip during an icy river crossing) to the hospital, but stayed with his regiment and continued the maneuver on crutches.

During December more selectees began to arrive to replace the men who had gone to other divisions and to schools. Organized into a training regiment under the command of Lieutenant Colonel Stephen S. Hamilton of the 307th Infantry, these new soldiers entered willingly into the task of learning everything all at once, that they might catch up with the rest of the Division.

The holiday season of 1942 was crowded into a schedule already filled with field training, but somehow there were plenty of holiday activities. Archbishop Francis Joseph Spellman visited Fort Jackson: there was Christmas music, special church services, and a turkey dinner which most of the men ate in their own mess halls. The 77th Division held open house for all of the men of the post. Lieutenant Winthrop Rockefeller, commanding Company H, 305th Infantry, changed his grandfather's custom and gave each man in his company, not a dime, but a silver dollar. The 307th Infantry adopted three Columbia youngsters for a day, gave them a tour of the post, a dinner with the soldiers, and sent each one home with a $75.00 war bond and a new personal wardrobe. During this winter season many men obtained eagerly awaited furloughs and passes for short visits home.

On 7 January 1943 Brigadier General Harris M. Melasky, the Assistant Division Commander, departed to take command of the 86th Division. He was tendered a farewell Retreat parade.

On 12 January the Division witnessed arid took part in a series of realistic demonstrations of air-power in support of infantry. Bombing, pursuit, and attack planes took part. The artillery and infantry fired service ammunition in a demonstration of coordinated combat firing. For the first time most of the men heard bombs whistle close and artillery shells wing overhead.

On 13 January the Division was reviewed by Major General W. H. Simpson, Commanding General of the XII Corps. The troops passed in review singing "Over There," "The Old Grey Mare" and "Marching to Victory." The songs, though an indication of the spirit of the men, could not temper the cold wind which drove the spectators to shelter. But the soldiers, inured to anything, just took it and marched.

By mid-December the barbers in Columbia were telling the 77th Division soldiers that the Division would leave for Louisiana in January and would not return. Eventually the soldiers learned from official sources that this particular rumor was true. Throughout the Division camp preparations were made for the train movement. Everyone was to go except the Training Regiment out at North Camp and that was to follow later. During January the trains made up in the railroad yards and rolled westward filled with lean, hardened men.

Chapter 2: Louisiana Maneuvers

THE 77th Division detrained at Many, Louisiana late in January 1943. Here it assembled, bivouacked, and prepared for the first phase of the eight-week maneuvers. These maneuvers were under the direction of Major General Daniel I. Sultan, Commanding General of the VIII Corps of the Third Army. The maneuvers were conducted with the 77th on one side, operating against its twin, the 90th Motorized Division, on the other.

Though nominally a free maneuver, it was closely supervised by many umpires who adjusted the situation to keep the troops within the bounds of the area and to insure that each phase followed the desired pattern. In addition, each division, from among its own officers, furnished the other with a large group of organization and unit umpires, and each division prepared to try every tactic not forbidden by the Umpire Manual. By a set method of evaluating constructive fire power, and by close front-line umpiring, actual physical contact was usually prevented.

Phase One was fought north and south over Peason Ridge, and back and forth through many little Louisiana villages. To most of the men the maneuvers consisted almost entirely of marching by night and moving across country by day. At intervals the strafing A-24s would drive mem off the roads. Occasionally they would get a glimpse of the "enemy," then blank ammunition would be fired, white umpire flags would go up, the umpires would confer, and one side would have to withdraw. The communication units and supply agencies, however, found many problems to solve in keeping up with the fast moving troops. Phase One demonstrated that both divisions had learned their training lessons well, that there were many small details to be corrected, and that life in the field during a Louisiana winter could be strenuous and uncomfortable.

Phase Two found the 77th with superior force, shoving the 90th westward and back against the swampy Sabine River. It included river crossings which no one who was there will forget, and cold weather skirmishes on the Texas hills to the west. It ended, as the Corps commander had intended it should, with an umpire-abetted, wild breakthrough by the 90th.

In Phase Three, the 77th was on the receiving end and defended first the rivers, and then successive positions against a numerically superior "enemy." It involved withdrawing by day and by night in a series of delaying actions. Into the midst of this last struggle dropped a regiment of reckless paratroopers who neither knew nor respected umpire rules, but who cooled down somewhat after a few fist fights, a little enforced quiet behind barbed wire, and some hot food.

Throughout the maneuvers both divisions attempted, sometimes successfully, tricks and ruses. The 90th's larger reconnaissance elements staged some embarrassing raids. The 77th once tapped the 90th's main telephone line and for two days listened sympathetically to the troubles of the "enemy" headquarters. Master Sergeant Clarence Taylor, of the 77ths G-2 Section, spent several profitable hours in a concealed observation post behind the "enemy" lines. Lieutenant Wright Powers joined an "enemy" column on the march one rainy night and picked up information of value. Scouts and patrols from the regiments of both divisions swam the rivers and waded the swamps to get behind "enemy" lines where they prowled, cut telephone lines, sneaked into command posts, "borrowed" jeeps, and caused as much consternation and confusion as possible. The 77th even permitted a Field Order to be captured by the 90th, although the messenger carrying it had a very difficult time getting himself captured. Acting on information gleefully extracted from this phony order, the 90th found itself backed in some confusion against the Sabine River, with its bridges blown behind it. Admittedly, much that happened during the maneuvers was what General Sultan termed "Boy Scout stuff," and contributed little to the tactical development of either side, but the initiative and alertness engendered by these tricks were of some benefit, and the occasional humorous situation tended to counteract the miserable weather. The mobility, sustained movement and effort demanded in these exercises were often greater than that required in actual combat.

The maneuvers served the important purpose of shaking down the Division into a fighting, self-reliant team which could go anywhere and take care of itself under almost any condition. They taught individuals to work for long periods without sleep or food. They further seasoned and hardened both officers and men. Both learned to read maps correctly or they missed many meals. It was as simple as that.

Those who quickly forgot, if they ever knew, the exact problems or the names of the towns through which they passed or the rivers they crossed will, nevertheless, remember many of the minor occurrences and sights which, from day to day, provided humor and topics for conversation. These included the following: The bivouacs in the pine woods on the rare occasions when fires were permitted and the smell of burning pitch drifted for miles . . . the razor-back pigs which considered every pup tent an opportunity for looting and rooting . . . the rather bewildered local residents, white and colored, standing by their pine-cone fires in the early morning chill to watch the army trucks roll by . . . the Signal Company using "skip-wave" to communicate, quite illegally, with the rear echelon at Fort Jackson which was far beyond the normal range of the Divisions radios . . . night moves into bivouac areas covered with mud, and attempts to sleep notwithstanding . . . that all-night movement through continuous rain over rutted, swampy trails to the Sabine River, followed by the miserable work of launching boats, building bridges, and spading down thirty foot banks of gooey red clay . . . those breaks between problems when it was permissible to go to Alexandria or Leesville and obtain, at not much more than double prices, at least half as much fun and entertainment as was desired . . . the hard-boiled, inspiring leadership of Lieutenant Colonel Stephen S. Hamilton, new commanding officer of the 307th Infantry . . . the misery of waiting for hours without blankets or rations on some cold hillside until trucks which, by mistake, had been sent to the wrong rendezvous were found and returned . . . General Sultan roaming through various command posts and making very plain his opinions concerning everything in sight . . . the actual danger and risks, usually disregarded but occasionally emphasized by accidents . . . that truck that crashed into the log pile . . . the car which skidded through the bridge guard rail . . . or the man wearing the full field equipment who almost swam the river . . . Brigadier General George Griner's friendly spoken tours through the bivouacs of the 77th, of which he was now Assistant Division Commander . . . the trick of burying a glowing pine log and sleeping warm, if all went well, on those nights when the situation was tactical and fires taboo . . . and finally, the three-day job of "policing up" the maneuver areas.

Almost exactly a year from the date of its re-activation the 77th Division assembled in bivouac on the outskirts of Camp Polk, near Leesville, Louisiana. The men of the 306th Infantry named their bivouac on the grassy knolls "Camp Doolittle" and the name applied equally well to the entire area. Emphasis was on re-equipping the organizations, resting the men, and spreading rumors as to the next destination of the Division.

The troops were convinced that they were ready for combat and likely to be sent. Word had circulated that the Division had orders to Camp Edwards, Massachusetts. This rumor, straight from Headquarters and as a matter of fact temporarily true, caused some officers to ship household goods to Massachusetts. But it was soon cancelled by an equally authentic rumor that the destination was the Desert Training Center. This rumor won out. About the 25th of March advance parties entrained for the west.

Chapter 3: The Sands of Hyder

THE Division Advance Party reached Hyder, Arizona, on 1 April 1943. To the men who stared disgustedly at the landscape it was truly April Fool's Day, and they were convinced that the joke, such as it was, was on them. The little yellow railroad station, the siding shimmering in the sun, the five or six squat, dusty buildings, and the low water tanks — those were Hyder. That flat expanse of brush-covered, dusty, desolate desert; that pile of folded tents, those few survey stakes would be Camp Hyder after they built it. The raw, sun-blackened, naked mountain just behind the little settlement was Hyder Mountain: they would come to know it well but not affectionately.

As the advance party started to lay out the camp, troop trains were en route from Louisiana. On those trains the rumors were heartening. The 77th would stay only twelve weeks at a good camp in the desert; would do two weeks of maneuvers and then ship for overseas. It was a pleasant trip in comfortable, clean, Pullman cars. The good food, clean sheets, and time for loafing were welcome after maneuver life. On one of the trains of the 305th Infantry were photographers from Life Magazine, and the pictorial record of a troop movement by rail appeared, without identifying the organization, beginning on page 77 of the issue of 28 June 1943.

One by one the trains slowed to a halt at Hyder, and one by one the soldiers had the shock of looking out upon an arid, barren waste which, as scenery, might have some beauty in its own way, but was certainly not like Brooklyn to live in. The Division Band met most of the trains and welcomed the troops with such well chosen tunes as "This is the Army" and "There'll Be a Hot Time." Each successive company slogged through the powdery, ankle-deep dust to its new camp site, and went to work.

'As usual, the 302d Engineers bore the brunt of the construction, although all units were busy. The nearest water was six miles away at Agua Caliente and it was, as the name indicated, hot water. The roads soon disappeared in powdered silt. The Engineers sprinkled and finally paved them with rock blasted from the mountain. They drilled a deep well near camp where the Southern Pacific Railroad had repeatedly found no water, and struck a flow of 120,000 gallons a day. They established there a water point and built a huge shower facility.

Camp Hyder became a city of tents extending two miles across the dusty desert. Each company had a double row of pyramidal tents and in each tent were six cots, six straw ticks, twelve barracks bags, and several lizards and scorpions. Division Headquarters was a semicircular row of pyramidal tents. But Camp Hyder eventually did obtain one building when the officers of the 306th Infantry built an adobe club. Later the 305th Infantry also went into the mud-brick business and erected a larger club. All units had an equal share of dust, heat, snakes, cacti, ground squirrels and lizards.

Training got underway slowly because it was necessary for the men to become acclimated. A firing range and an infiltration course were started. However, it was found necessary to police the firing line each morning to remove the rattlesnakes. Columns made practice marches across the greasewood flats and discovered that deep arroyos cut across the desert with irritating frequency, adding to the difficulties of travel.

To develop leadership in junior officers each infantry platoon was sent out alone on a six-day exercise which called for compass marches by day and by night in the desert mountains. Platoons would pick up caches of water and rations at points designated on the map, if they read their maps and compasses correctly. Several narrow escapes and instances of real hardship developed from these treks, but no lives were lost.

Previously, several armored divisions had trained in the American desert, but the 77th was the first infantry division to maneuver in that oppressive place. Still serving as a "guinea pig" outfit it was called on to test desert formation wherein the entire Division would maneuver on a broad front as do ships at sea. For several days the desert was churned to clouds of rolling dust as 13,000 men and hundreds of vehicles advanced and wheeled and halted, guiding on colored captive balloon markers. The arroyos hindered and diverted though they did not stop the movement of troops.

At the same time the Division was testing drinking water requirements of foot soldiers in the desert. The infantry proved the hard way what any old desert prospector could have told them — that with searing temperatures of a hundred and twenty degrees in non-existent shade one quart of drinking water per man per day was far below their body losses. The men quickly learned, however, how to make shade by tossing a shelter half atop a greasewood brush or a sparse palo verde tree, how to put a wet sock around their canteens and how to use sweating desert bags to keep water cool. A very few even began to like the desert, but their comrades attributed this attitude to a touch of the sun.

On 22 May General Woodruff was suddenly ordered to assume command of the VII Corps. On the 27th Major General A. D. Bruce assumed command of the Division. General Bruce had served with distinction in the 2d Division in World War I, rising in combat from lieutenant to lieutenant colonel. He received high decorations from both the United States and French Governments, including the American Distinguished Service Cross and the French Legion of Honor. During the years between the two wars he had graduated from The Infantry School, the Field Artillery School, the Command and General Staff School, the Army War College, and the Naval War College. During World War II, prior to joining the 77th, General Bruce had served on the War Department General Staff and had organized, built, and commanded the Tank Destroyer Center at Camp Hood, Texas. With characteristic aggressiveness he set out to continue the training of the Division and to ready it for whatever combat duties might be in store.

At about the same time Brigadier General Griner was called away to assume command of another Division. A little later his place as Assistant Division Commander was taken by Brigadier General Edwin H. Randle who had served in France in World War I with the 5th Division. In World War II as a Colonel he had commanded a regimental combat team of the 9th Infantry Division which made an assault landing and captured Safi, French Morocco on 8 November 1942. His combat team fought at El Guettar where General Randle was awarded the Distinguished Service Cross, and captured Bizerte, Tunisia, in May 1943 at the close of the African campaign. He was then promoted and assigned to the 77th Division.

Later in June the Division moved by motor convoy along sweltering, dusty desert roads to an assembly area near Palo Verde, California. Here, among the mesquite trees at the edge of the California desert it prepared for an advance to the north. The maneuvers were under the direction and control of the IX Corps. The 77th's teammates were the 7th Armored Division, the 4th Cavalry, and several Tank Destroyer Battalions. The "enemy," the 8th Motorized Division, heavily reinforced, was on the defensive somewhere to the north.

In the first phase, the Blue forces moved north, found the "enemy" in Palen Pass, slowly pushed him out of his positions and started in pursuit.

Then the Blue force was ordered south to Ogilby, California for a brief rest. In Phase Two the maneuver was repeated, but this time the Blues moved eighty miles in a single hectic night to surprise the "enemy" at Palen Pass. This time the pursuit continued north over the sun-baked desert and white-crusted salt flats almost to Needles. Just as the Blue forces had the retreating "enemy" almost trapped, the maneuver terminated.

This was a maneuver of supply and movement. The emphasis was on ammunition, water, gasoline, and rations. For the troops it meant only scorching, dusty, endless, miles of marching or riding: it meant temperatures of 130 degrees and no shade, and never quite enough water. There was nothing new in that, or in cutting barbed-wire entanglements, dodging simulated land mines, or operating observation posts atop those barren, heat-baked ridges. But the officers and men responsible for supply learned how to function without roads from supply bases fifty to one hundred miles distant.

Another group which received valuable training was the second string unit commanders. All commanding officers of regiments, battalions, and companies were deliberately placed on umpire duty with the "enemy," and the seconds-in-command carried the ball. Although this sometimes resulted in less efficient performances it helped many of the officers who later had to take over in the midst of combat.

The 77th Division established some records and proved that infantry could move fast and far, even in the desert in July; but it was not a pleasant task and when, late in the month, after a twenty-four hour motor movement the rows of tents appeared over the horizon, even Camp Hyder looked somewhat inviting.

Another bitter disappointment was in store for officers and men. They had expected to leave the desert immediately after the maneuvers. Now they found they were to remain another two months. This, combined with a feeling of having gone stale, a rather drastic shakeup among the officer personnel, the discomforts of the terrific heat and primitive living conditions, and the almost total absence of recreational facilities noticeably lowered the morale and effectiveness of the Division.

Nevertheless, training and a great deal of work in making the camp more livable were carried on. General Bruce brought Lieutenant Colonel Gordon F. Kimbrell, a graduate of British Commando training, to establish near the camp his "Bull Dog School." There, under the most realistic conditions possible, with lavish use of service ammunition and demolitions, all company and battery officers, and many non-commissioned officers of the Division practiced small unit tactics, hand to hand fighting, firing small arms and light machine guns from the hip, infiltration under rifle and machine gun fire, and village fighting. A week at this school of hard knocks was guaranteed to sweat pounds from any man and to add to his skill, alertness and self-confidence. He had to crawl across open ground swept by the fire of expert riflemen who placed warning shots close if he made errors. He took part in patrols and small unit attacks against "enemy" who fired live ammunition. He manufactured and used demolition charges and booby traps until he came to consider TNT a commonplace commodity. He fired all infantry weapons under all conditions. He lived hard and dangerously, for despite precautions, men were hurt and one officer was killed. He finished the course with a much better idea of what was ahead, and a confidence in his own ability to take it.

Such rugged, dangerous training made, by comparison, the life of a garrison prisoner in the stockade seem relatively pleasant. So, for those offenders, there was established at a place even more remote, a Training Company where life was even more rigorous than at the Bull Dog School. There were, however, relatively few members of this company. Any incipient plans for absence without leave were discouraged by the tragic fate of one who tried it: his buzzard-torn remains and empty canteen were found covered with alkali dust in a waterless arroyo.

During the last week of maneuvers, Colonel Alexander Adair had been transferred from the division. His place as commanding officer of the 306th Infantry was filled, temporarily, by Lieutenant Colonel Cecil Nist, then by Lieutenant Aubrey D. Smith. Shortly thereafter, Colonel William McChesney Chapman was assigned to the 77th and given command of the 306th Infantry.

At Camp Hyder, despite a Desert Training Center prescription which put salt in the lukewarm drinking water, greasy C rations and powdered eggs on the menu, life did have a few brighter spots. A limited amount of beer and soft drinks and even an inadequate amount of ice to cool them found their way into the Post Exchanges. There were nightly movies and a few courageous Hollywood troupes toured the cactus circuit, although the performers always departed with a touch of heat exhaustion and remarks about foreign service pay. Athletic programs got under way and baseball and boxing teams represented the organizations in competition. The Engineers found time to rebuild the swimming pool at Agua Caliente and many men spent pleasant hours at this one place where water seemed abundant though hot.

Those few queer characters who grew to like the desert found opportunities to study the strange plant and animal life of this forgotten, sun-baked land. They learned to find bitter yellow water in "tanks" in the mountains, sampled the edible fruits of the cacti and explored old mining claims.

Best of all were the visits to Phoenix. This city, one hundred miles to the east, was a recreation spot for the dehydrated soldiers, and its hospitality was appreciated. In its modern hotels and homes they scrubbed off desert dust and drank cool liquids. Its parks contained green grass and trees. Here in the city the wives of the 77th found houses, apartments, and cabins. Some footloose individuals obtained passes to travel further, even to Palm Springs, the Grand Canyon, and Los Angeles.

The Division newspaper reappeared 26 August after a lapse in publication since Fort Jackson days under sponsorship of the Division Special Service Office. Both the name, "The Liberty Torch" and the sub-title "Ours to Hold it High" had been suggested by the anything but sentimental soldiers.

In August a great and surprising natural phenomenon took place. It rained. Not only once but several times. But a great deal of wind and terrific dust clouds always presaged the rain drops. In two or three storms, on successive nights, whole rows of tents were ripped and flattened, and sudden floods washed away parts of the camp. During these August days clerks learned to put heavy rocks on every loose paper, otherwise they were likely to be snatched away by a whirlwind and filed in a greasewood bush.

Lieutenant General Lesley J. McNair, who had visited the 77th during both the Louisiana and Desert Maneuvers, came again on 27 August to inspect the Division. He found the regimental combat teams engaged in strenuous six-day exercises in the mountainous terrain east of Hyder. These involved long marches, night motor movements along narrow winding mountain roads, and camouflage training under difficult conditions. Reconnaissance and intelligence personnel were undergoing practical tests which included dangerous and extended patrol missions over strange terrain.

Following the six-day problems the regiments received air-ground training and were given tests which included aircraft recognition, air-ground communication and close air-support coordination. It was on 15 September, at the conclusion of an air-support demonstration witnessed by most of the men of the Division, that General Bruce announced that the 77th would soon entrain for Indiantown Gap Military Reservation in Pennsylvania. The news was received with cheers.

With a small advance party General Bruce left at once for the east. In New York he had the pleasure of addressing the 77th Division Association on 26 September. General McMahon, Division Artillery Commander, also departed, but for a new assignment. As the troop trains were loaded, confusion developed concerning their destination. Several new orders were received. The A. P. Hill Military Reservation in Virginia was named, and then Camp Pickett, Virginia. No one knew where the movement would end but at least all of the suggested destinations were near the east coast, and they were bound to be more desirable than Camp Hyder. So, each day, train loads of men shook from themselves the dust of Hyder and departed eastward with rumors flying.

The Division spent six months in the desert. It lost some men there, a few actual casualties and many who could not endure the combination of climate and rugged training. It had been in fighting trim when it arrived: it came out leaner, tougher, and a little bitter, ready to cause trouble for someone, as the Japanese found to their distress several months later. But the men were still able to laugh in that dry way in which experienced soldiers laugh, mostly at themselves. It was this sort of humor which conceived the Hyder Campaign Medal, which will probably never be recognized by the War Department. In the words of one junior officer who lost thirty pounds during the desert summer, "The Hyder ribbon is a strip of sandpaper on which is mounted a broken thermometer. If you fought at Palen Pass you can wear on it one salt tablet, and if you climbed Fourth of July Butte you are eligible to wear on it a small bronze cactus lobe."

Chapter 4: From West Virginia to Chesapeake Bay

BY VARIOUS routes all elements of the 77th Division reached the eastern seaboard and were scattered among widely separated training areas. The Division Headquarters and Special Troops were established at Camp Pickett, Virginia. The training program called for each regimental combat team to receive three weeks each of mountain training, amphibious training, and marksmanship and combat exercises. The 306th Regimental Combat Team proceeded at once to the West Virginia Training Area near Elkins; the 305th moved to Indiantown Gap, Pennsylvania, to use the ranges there; and the 307th first moved to Indiantown Gap and then to Camp Pickett where it began amphibious training, and later continued it at Camp Bradford, Virginia and Solomons Island, Maryland. Subsequently, the combat teams of the Division rotated among the areas in order to receive each type of training.

Most of these camps provided such long-denied conveniences as real barracks, beds, hot showers, and mess halls. The Division had been in the field so long that there was some question as to whether or not the men were house-broken, but they managed without undue strain to re-adjust themselves to a degree of civilization.

Mountain training in West Virginia required strenuous maneuvering in that rugged country. Later, when the weather became really cold, winter training was provided as an extra dividend, officers and men fresh from the heat of the desert learned to use arctic sleeping bags, to sleep in the snow, and on occasion to anchor themselves to trees in order to wake up on the same slope on which they had retired. Even so they sweated under heavy packboards as they marched up mountain trails in freezing temperatures. They found that vehicles and weapons needed different treatment under cold-weather conditions. Meanwhile, selected men from each unit received practical instruction from experts in the various techniques of mountain climbing.

At Indiantown Gap and later at Camp Pickett new "Bull Dog Schools" were established. The name for these schools had been selected by General Bruce because one of the principal characteristics of the men of the Division seemed to be tenacity. Junior officers and men fired all types of weapons on all sorts of ranges, including a village with dummies which ingeniously appeared at windows and crossed streets; where explosive charges detonated, throwing up geysers of mud and water as the attackers approached. Tank hunting and destruction, attacks against fortified positions, night attacks, mines and booby traps and many other specialties were included in the curriculum.

Under Secretary of War Robert P. Patterson made a return visit to the Division at Indiantown Gap on 13 November 1943. He inspected the Honor Guard from Company F, 306th Infantry, and lunched with this, his World War I outfit. He made a whirlwind tour of training activities and ended by witnessing a realistic attack on a fortified position by a reinforced battalion of the 305th Infantry, now under the command of Colonel Vincent J. Tanzola.

Amphibious training began with lectures about boats, ships, shipboard life, and landing technique; then progressed through climbing down cargo nets suspended from platforms, to drills with real landing boats at Camp Bradford, Virginia. The troops were taught that a floor was a "deck," a latrine a "head," and a kitchen a "galley." Officers learned the mysteries of combat loading ships with the most possible materiel in the smallest possible space, the mysteries of master boat employment plans, boat assignment tables and landing diagrams. Life Magazine photographers returned for an article on landing craft and their uses. The 77th was not mentioned this time either, but the Division markings on the vehicles were visible in the published photographs.

The final stage in amphibious training was a cruise up the Chesapeake Bay to Solomons Island, Maryland. Transports were combat loaded with transportation, equipment, and dummy ammunition; and the battalion landing teams and regimental combat teams made practice landings, unloaded their equipment and supplies over the beaches, and advanced inland across country to seize or capture beachheads. At times these landings were conducted under severe weather and sea conditions. The 305th Regimental Combat Team made its final landing through rough water and in a temperature below freezing. The men, stiffened from a cold, wet ride in the landing craft, and with icicles forming on their helmets, waded ashore wet to the waist. Although those soaked and chilled were almost immediately evacuated to the ships as practice "casualties," many who were more than damp moved inland for a cold day and a bitter night of simulated warfare under tactical conditions which permitted no fires. Such occurrences were considered inherent in the training.

There were other features of the multi-ringed, Divisional training circus. Up at the A.P. Hill Military Reservation the .50 caliber machinegun crews practiced on aerial targets. The 77th Reconnaissance Troop and selected Infantry scouts went to Fort Pierce, Florida, to receive instructions in Amphibious Reconnaissance and the use of rubber boats. There they had additional physical conditioning and became experts with their ungainly, pneumatic craft.

The Division Artillery, now commanded by Brigadier General Isaac Spalding, participated in nearly all of the training with the infantry, and also had to pass the Army Ground Force Artillery tests conducted by the XIII Corps. These firing tests were started in West Virginia but were called off because of weather conditions. The tests were eventually successfully completed at Camp Butner, North Carolina.

There were many other tests. The Division was "hot" for overseas shipment and higher headquarters carefully scrutinized all of its activities including supply, administration, discipline, physical condition of officers and men, intelligence training and combat readiness. All officers were required to pass a practical test in map and compass reading. Officers and men considered for any reason unsuitable or unready for combat were transferred to other organizations. Some of these had literally worn themselves out in training the Division, just as a few had given their lives without ever leaving the United States. The 77th as it prepared for overseas shipment owed much to many officers and men who were no longer with it.

As the separate companies, separate battalions, and regiments of the Division moved between Pennsylvania, Virginia, Maryland and North Carolina, the men wearing the Liberty patch were in evidence in almost every village and town. This was heightened by the large number who obtained leaves, furloughs, and passes to get home for brief visits. The months back east did a great deal to raise the morale of the troops and prepare them for what lay ahead.

Throughout its training, the Division had come to take pride in building a reputation for leaving its camp and maneuver areas clean and thoroughly policed. As organizations departed from Camp Hyder, competition to receive a rating of "superior" on their abandoned areas was keen. The same was true as organizations left Indiantown Gap. Buildings and areas were inspected just prior to their departure by organization commanders, then by representatives of the Division, and finally by staff members of the post commander. The latter was very complimentary. The Solomons Island maneuver area consisted of leased civilian property. When the Division finally completed its training there, several days were spent in removing cans and rubbish from the beaches where children would play, thoroughly cleaning buildings, policing woods and fields, repairing farm fences, and filling fox holes throughout the entire area. The result was that not a single claim for damages was presented to the Claims Board. Also, the Division received a letter of commendation from the Commanding General, Third Service Command, citing it for the superior condition in which the area was left. A similar commendation was received from the War Department. All this, of course, was an indication of steadily increasing pride and discipline.

Other qualities which began to be quite marked at this time were the innate courtesy and the consideration for others which were widespread among the men. They had passed through the boisterous, exhibitionist stage common to all recruits, and had developed the common courtesy and reserved characteristics of trained soldiers. But fortunately, their completely American sense of humor had not lessened. The motto on the coat of arms of the 307th Infantry was "Clear the Way." The men of that regiment, after having to do most of the final policing of the Solomons Island beaches and maneuver area, suggested changing the regimental insignia to crossed brooms, but leaving the motto unrevised.

A full program of outdoor and indoor sports was somehow fitted into the training schedule, and the facilities for sports and recreation at Camp Pickett were utilized to capacity. The 1943 volley ball champions came from Headquarters Company, 305th Infantry, and that regiment also won the basketball crown. The 306th Infantry developed the outstanding boxing squad, and the 307th produced the winning officers' basketball team. The 902d Field Artillery Battalion won the Softball championship. Dances, concerts and parties were given by various organizations during this period and from the Band came talented orchestras to suit any occasion.

It was about this time that General Bruce, because of his insistence that the troops wear leggings, helmet liners, and carefully police barracks and areas on leaving them, was given the affectionate nickname of "Old Man Leggings, Liners, and Landscape." It can now be disclosed that he took no little pride in this sobriquet.

By February the entire Division was assembled at Camp Pickett and struggling to master the requirements of POM (Preparation for Overseas Movement). There were "show-down" inspections to determine what clothing and equipment were lacking, and then more "showdowns" just to prove that what had recently been issued had not yet been lost. Everything had to be done at once; shots, shipment home of radios, cameras, and electric razors, 'writing of final non-censored letters, last-minute crawling through the mud of infiltration courses, dental checks, physical inspections, study of enemy weapons, and final farewell parties on and away from the post.

Of course, the whole movement was very "hush-hush," but railroad men living in near-by towns could have told and did tell when and where the trains would be made up, and where they would go. It was generally known that the 77th was again headed west and that its fighting would be against the Japanese. Nevertheless, there was an air of mystery and suspense about the whole movement which was increased toward the end of February by the sudden, silent departure of an advance party.

The Division, now thoroughly familiar with the technique of transcontinental rail movements, efficiently and smoothly loaded out of Camp Pickett during the period 8-13 March. The troops were seasoned travelers and the trains were comfortable, so the five days of the trip across the American continent proved to be a pleasure jaunt. As the trains carrying unidentified troops paused along the routes, cities and towns which heretofore had been only names on maps came to mean Red Cross women and volunteer workers with coffee and doughnuts and cookies.

Most of the Division was processed through Camp Stoneman, California, near San Francisco, although a few supply elements took the northern route to Seattle, Washington. There was no lingering on the west coast. A fortunate few wangled short passes in San Francisco and had a quick look at Market Street, Chinatown and the Top of the Mark. But as fast as trains came in the troops received their final checking over, a few suggestions about censorship, and a day or two of light work. Then they marched to a steamer on the near-by Sacramento River for a short trip to the transports tied up at the docks in the city.

Nearly everyone was impressed, to a greater or lesser degree, by the signs on the Camp Stoneman dock; "Through These Portals Pass the Best Damn Soldiers in the World." And "The Army Ground Forces Trained You, the Services of Supply Equipped You, the Air Force Watches Over

You. Now its up to You." As they stood on the decks of the river steamer the Band played "The Sidewalks of New York" and, as the vessel pulled out into the stream, "Over There."

It was corny and it was sentimental and some made sarcastic remarks about it, but there was a lump in the throat of each soldier.

Chapter 5: Training in Pineapple Land

THE DEPARTURE from San Francisco was anti-climactic after that at Camp Stoneman. The troops simply moved off the river steamer, filed across a covered dock, grabbed Red Cross coffee and doughnuts en route, and were checked aboard grey Navy transports which, in most cases, remained overnight at their piers. The following day the transports passed under the Golden Gate Bridge, moved slowly out of the bay, and plowed westward. That was all there was to it, except that the ocean just off the Golden Gate became distinctly restless.

The voyage was made in escorted convoys and the ships were totally blacked out at night. Troop compartments were crowded, dimly lighted, and not too well ventilated. This, however, was to be a customary condition for the many wartime voyages of the 77th Division, so the men got used to it. Otherwise, the trip was restful.

Honolulu from the sea appeared just like the post-card pictures of Honolulu from the sea except that the activities of a Pacific War crowded the harbors. General Bruce, who had flown ahead by Clipper, was waiting on the dock to watch the troops file down the gangplanks and board waiting trucks and miniature railway cars for runs to the camps on the windward (northeast) side of Oahu.

Division Headquarters, the 306th Regimental Combat Team, Headquarters Division Artillery, Special Troops, the 706th Tank Battalion, the 1118th Engineer Group Headquarters and the 292d Joint Assault Signal Company settled down at Fort Hase, on a peninsula which forms Kaneohe Bay. The 305th Regimental Combat Team and the 7th Anti-Aircraft Artillery Battalion were quartered at Pali Camp in the eastern foot-hills of the precipitous, rocky up-lift which divides the island. To the 307th Regimental Combat Team and the 504th Anti-Aircraft Artillery Battalion (Gun) went the task of improving a camp on the red clay hills and among the sugar-cane fields at Kahuku, near the northeast corner of Oahu.

As soon as opportunity permitted, the troops familiarized themselves with the terrain and the situation. This necessarily included off-duty patrols to near-by small towns such as Kailua and Kahuku, and missions in force to Honolulu and the beach of Waikiki. Trips were organized to both of these celebrated places, and to other superb bathing beaches. Early reconnaissance confirmed reports of the friendly character of the local residents and many officers and men investigated the native version of a barbecue, known as luau. While most of the insular cuisine met with high favor, there were no reported instances of anyone developing a taste for the sour-smelling paste-like poi.

One of the many unique and valuable attachments to the Division was a team of Nisei interpreters who joined about this time. In five operations they proved themselves excellent soldiers and splendid Americans.

Training on Oahu featured the Unit Jungle Training Center. There the troops learned how to live in the jungle and how to make it provide them with food. They practiced stream crossing and first aid, reviewed all of the dirty tricks of hand-to-hand fighting, and repeated hip firing, village combat and how to attack pillboxes. This training center was very much like the "Bull Dog School" except that there were more opportunities to be surprised, startled, plunged into streams and, if men were not wary, actually injured. The 77th, drawing on its experience in the desert and at Indiantown Gap, adjusted itself to the jungle and left an outstanding record at the Jungle Center. There were comments on the steady and casual attitude of the men working with live ammunition and high explosives; but one observer who had witnessed their training in the United States replied: "These men have been shot at, shot over, blasted at and blown up so much and so often that nothing like this bothers them in the least."

Amphibious techniques were reviewed at three areas on Oahu. This culminated in an assault, firing service ammunition, on barren Makua Pocket. Although a review of training previously received in Virginia, it provided an opportunity, in delightfully warm water, to correct minor deficiencies. Here, too, the troops were, for the first time, introduced to the new amphibious chariots they were to use so frequently. These were the LVTs (Landing Vehicle, Tracked) which had been designed for the sole function of carrying fighting men across the coral reefs surrounding Japanese-held islands.

While training progressed the Division staff was busy. Additional weapons, vehicles, and items of equipment best adapted to the Pacific Theatre of Operations were selected and obtained. A planning board, headed by Brigadier General Randle, prepared and published a complete standing operating procedure for all organizations of the Division, both organic and attached, and for all phases of an amphibious assault. The great value of these SOP's was proven in all of the amphibious operations of the Division, and they became standard references for other Divisions which followed the 77th to the Pacific.

Before the troops were completely established on Oahu, planning started for a combat mission. The 77th was included in the Marianas Operation as land reserve: i.e., to remain on Oahu prepared to embark and move to the Marianas on short notice. Top-secret documents accumulated at Headquarters and the G-2 Section prepared detailed terrain studies and estimates of the situation for Saipan, Tinian, and Guam. General Bruce and the G-3 Section prepared plans for the employment of the Division on any of those islands. The G-4 Section and the Transport Quartermasters accumulated and palletized rations, water, ammunition and other supplies, obtained ships' characteristics and calculated the necessary assault shipping.

Since the 77th might not be needed in the Marianas, another planning mission was assigned — Babelthuap Island in the Palau group. The tremendously detailed intelligence, operational and supply ponderings were repeated for this target.

During June the 77th watched with more than casual interest the reports of the tough fighting on Saipan. The two Marine Divisions ashore had been reinforced by the floating reserve, the 27th Infantry Division. The battle still progressed slowly. The question in the minds of everyone at Headquarters was "Will they commit the Guam Task Force, or will they call for the 77th?" As it turned out neither alternative was necessary, but the Guam operation was postponed and the 77th was alerted. About this time Lieutenant Colonel Aubrey Smith was transferred from his assignment as G-3 of the Division to command the 306th Infantry replacing Col. William McChesney Chapman.

Late in June loading commenced. The 305th Regimental Combat Team, and an advance Division Headquarters under General Randle, were loaded on a hastily assembled Transport Division of five ships which sailed from Honolulu on 1 July 1944. The remainder of the Division loaded as soon as Transport Divisions arrived from Saipan.

The advance convoy pushed west at seventeen knots, zigzagging all the way to avoid enemy torpedoes. A few days out it met two empty Transport Divisions steaming eastward to pick up the remainder of the 77th. All that General Randle and his staff knew was that they were to receive instructions at Eniwetok; so en route they worked on plans for landings on

Tinian because the assault on Saipan and Guam had already been planned in detail. All that the men of the 305th Regimental Combat Team knew was that there was a very nasty war on and they were sailing right into the midst of it.

At Eniwetok orders were awaiting. Saipan was under control and the 77th was attached to the III (Marine) Amphibious Corps, consisting of the 3rd Marine Division and the 1st Provisional Marine Brigade. The target was Guam, the first populated American territory to be recovered from the Japanese.

Part II: The Liberation of Guam

BRIEF: On 21 July 1944 the 305th Regimental Combat Team of the 77th Division landed with the 1st Provisional Marine Brigade in the assault on Guam. The remainder of the Division, after a hurried voyage from Oahu via Eniwetok, went ashore during the next three days and carried on its share of the task of liberating the first populated United States possession to be wrested from the Japanese.

The first mission given the Division was to hold and expand the southern beachhead line. This, coupled with aggressive combat patrolling, reconnaissance of southern Guam, and the capture of Mount Tenjo occupied the troops until 30 July. On the 31st the Division struck east across the island. Despite the absence of roads and despite great supply difficulties, the regiments quickly seized positions in readiness for the main attack to the north.

At Barrigada on 2 and 3 August the 305th and 307th Infantry Regiments encountered and defeated determined Japanese forces. This was followed by an energetic pursuit through dense and almost trackless jungle.

The Japanese made their final stand at Yigo in northern Guam on 7 August. The combined fire power of the infantry and the artillery blasted them out. After that it was mopping up, dirty, bitter, and dangerous, but against a disorganized enemy.

The 77th killed 2,741 Japanese and took 36 prisoners on Guam, liberated thousands of native Chamorros, and learned what jungle fighting was like. It cost the Division 265 killed, 876 wounded, and two missing.

After the fighting the 77th spent two rainy, uncomfortable months in primitive Camp McNair on the hills above Agat. There, operations against Yap, Ulithi, and Leyte were planned: but only the last was ever executed. From Guam the Division loaded-out for the rest camps of New Caledonia, but en route was diverted to Leyte, Philippine Islands.

The 77th's campaign on Guam consisted of many small unit actions. Therefore, these are described in detail, a method which cannot be accommodated in the descriptions of subsequent campaigns. It is believed essential to include these descriptions in order to depict more accurately what the individual soldier witnessed throughout the Pacific War.

Chapter 6
Objective Guam

THE INVASION of the Marianas in June and July of 1944 brought to a climax a twenty-month advance across nearly 3,000 miles of Pacific waters by amphibious forces of the United States. For the first time American forces now would possess bases from which an attack on the Japanese homeland could be made. On 23 February a strong task force, including hundreds of carrier-based aircraft, attacked Saipan and near-by Tinian; a small raid was made on Guam. During the following months air attacks against these islands intensified. On 11 June the carrier-based aircraft of a large task force attacked Guam, Rota, Tinian and Saipan. On the 13th battleships and cruisers steamed in and shelled Saipan and Tinian.

As these blows developed, the pattern of American conquest in the Central Pacific became clear. United States forces, in possession of most of the Gilberts and Marshalls, would by-pass the Carolines and strike directly at the island chain which, beginning with Guam, stretches to Japan itself.

The largest and most southern of the Marianas, Guam was indeed a prize. The island afforded a harbor for small and medium vessels; the Japanese had built a mile-long air strip and there were other sites for large fields. From these, planes would be able to attack enemy supply lines west and south of Guam, and the new B-29s could reach the heart of Japan.

Guam had been a United States possession prior to its capture by the Japanese on 12 December 1941. The pride of the American people was touched when the enemy overwhelmed the few score Marines, who put up what resistance they could. The Japanese took over the naval installations, the cable facilities, and the barracks. They recruited slave labor from the natives and dealt cruelly with those who dared to resist. They used the island as a base for further penetration to the south and east. Guam became a major bastion in the Japanese inner fortress.

The island of Guam lies 3,320 airline miles from Pearl Harbor, 1,499 miles from Manila, and 1,595 miles from Tokyo. Truk in the Carolines is only 562 miles to the southeast. Guam is 34.5 miles in length and varies from 5 to 9 miles in width, with an area of 228 square miles. The southern and central portions are chiefly rolling hills, culminating in a few rugged mountains. The occasional villages, plantations and clearings are surrounded by dense woods and jungle. The northern part of the island is heavily jungled. An unbroken fringing reef surrounds the entire island.

There were about 22,000 native Chamorros on Guam, over half of whom lived in the capital city, Agana. Many of the natives were descendants of the Spaniards who had formerly occupied the island, but others bore the blood of Americans, British, Chinese and Japanese who came later. The Chamorros were mostly Catholic and almost all could speak some English. Generally friendly and docile, they had grown increasingly restive under the Japanese but the extent of their opposition was not known.

The enemy on Guam was strong and the attack on Saipan had put him on guard. On 17 June the G-2 of the 77th Division estimated that the Japanese had between 9,000 and 10,200 Army and Navy combat troops on Guam, and 1,100 to 2,585 Navy construction troops. This total was believed to represent a forty per cent increase since the beginning of April, and it seemed likely that many reinforcements had been brought in. The air strength on Guam on 12 June was estimated at 48 cargo planes, 58 light and medium bombers, 6 float planes, and 2 flying boats. Some of these 114 planes had been lost in action since 12 June, but replacements had probably been flown in.

Recent intelligence and the bloody fighting on Saipan indicated that the Guam assault would be, if anything, more difficult than the one on Saipan. By the end of June the estimates of enemy strength had been raised to a probable 20,000 and a possible 36,218. Documents captured on Saipan and interrogation of prisoners of war suggested that the Japanese Army, rather than the Navy, had the over-all responsibility for the defense of Guam. Intelligence indicated that the Army forces present consisted of the 29th Division less two regiments, and the 6th Expeditionary Force, recently organized from several disassociated units. A large amount of mobile artillery was believed to be on Guam. Some tanks were definitely known to be on the island.

Guam itself presented formidable obstacles to invading forces. The unbroken fringing reef around the island was a distinct handicap because it would force a transfer of troops from boats to tracked vehicles, or it would necessitate the troops wading 300 to 800 yards across the reef to the beach in water as much as five feet deep at low tide. The Japanese could find concealment and cover at all landing points. Observation from the mountain peaks in the central and south was excellent. The high cliffs around much of the island reduced the number of possible landing places to be defended and enabled the enemy to group his forces more advantageously. The hill masses dominating the beaches, the inadequate road system and the rugged terrain all favored the defenders.

Captured documents indicated that the enemy considered his most vulnerable landing beaches to be those along the center of the west side of the island, from the beaches just below Agana south to below the town of Agat, excluding the Orote Peninsula. These areas were heavily defended and the approaches to the beaches were barred by artificial obstacles on the reef. The area of most interest to the 77th Division, since it seemed to be its most likely landing place, was the stretch of beach just south of the village of Agat. The whole Agat sector was, because of poor roads, comparatively isolated from the more populated areas to the north; the 38th Japanese Infantry defended this area and its commander was to a degree independent of the rest of the island command.

The enemy planned to hold his fire until landing attempts were actually under way; he would make no real effort to resist the invasion until our forces were committed. A Chamorro woman, who was employed at the headquarters of the enemy 29th Division, later stated that a Japanese staff officer told her the Guam garrison would profit from the experience on Tarawa where the defenders, waiting inland, killed 5,000 Marines when they tried to land. The Japanese planned to take full advantage of the terrain, especially of the difficult reefs. "While the enemy is advancing from the line of coral reefs to the shore" a Japanese order read, "the combined infantry and artillery fire power will be developed. In particular when they reach the water obstacles, oblique and flanking fire will be employed to establish a dense fire net and thus annihilate them on water. Every company will make a sudden attack with its fire power . . ."

Only the general disposition of the enemy was known as American forces neared the island. Many questions remained whose answers were important to the high command and the front-line infantryman alike. How much would the fringing reef impede the landing? What sort of beach obstacles would there be? Would the enemy attempt a counter landing once the troops were ashore? Would he counterattack us on the beaches or further inland? What would be the attitude of the natives?

Whatever advantages the enemy possessed in terrain and disposition, the American invaders of the Marianas were somewhat superior in numbers, and tremendously so in equipment and experience. Both the naval and ground commanders of the Southern Attack Force were highly experienced in amphibious operations. The commander of the Force was Rear Admiral Richard L. Conolly, United States Navy. The III Amphibious Corps was under Major General Roy S. Geiger of the United States Marine Corps. The two Marine units of the Corps were the 3d Marine Division commanded by Major General Allen H. Turnage, and the 1st Provisional Marine Brigade, commanded by Brigadier General Lemuel C. Shepherd, Jr. The Marines were veteran Pacific atoll and jungle fighters. The 3rd Division had fought in the Solomons and the Brigade was a consolidation of such well known organizations as Carlson's Raiders, Liversedges' Raiders, and the Marines who had served under Brigadier General Merritt C. Edson.

The Army element of the III Amphibious Corps was the 77th Division, reinforced. The attack on Guam would be the debut of New York's "Statue of Liberty Division" in World War II.

On 30 June Admiral Conolly and General Geiger flew from Guadalcanal to Saipan to confer with Vice-Admiral Richmond Kelly Turner and Lieutenant General Holland Smith, United States Marine Corps, overall commanders of the combined Marianas attack forces. It was decided: (1) to set 21 July as W-Day; (2) to attach the 77th Infantry Division to the III Amphibious Corps; (3) to make one regimental combat team of the 77th available on W-Day, and the remainder of the Division not later than W plus 2 Day.

The plan of attack which the III Amphibious Corps had developed during the previous months remained substantially unchanged. The blow would be a double envelopment from the sea of the Orote Peninsula, with its air strip and military installations, Apra Harbor and the populous areas near the base of Orote.

No landings were to be made on the peninsula itself for it was partly surrounded by cliffs and rip-tides and was strongly defended. It was to be pinched off by landings to the north and to the south and then attacked from inland. Relatively good landing beaches to the north were at Asan, between Apra Harbor and Agana; and south of the peninsula at Agat. Once in control of these beachheads the Orote Peninsula would be isolated and attacked from landward. The next phase would be an advance to the north, where the remaining Japanese were expected to group for their final stand. The sector north of Orote Peninsula was assigned the 3d Marine Division which would land on the beaches between Adelup Point and the mouth of the Tague River, turn southwest and capture the area east of Apra Harbor, meanwhile holding a final beachhead on the hills inland parallel to the coastline. The 1st Provisional Marine Brigade, landing on the beaches between Agat and Bangi Point, would turn north into the base of the Orote peninsula and attack and clear the peninsula of the enemy. The 305th Regimental Combat Team of the 77th Division, attached to the 1st Provisional Brigade, would land on W-Day on orders of the Brigade commander. The remainder of the Division would initially be in Corps reserve.

The landings in the Agat area would be over a fringing coral reef varying in width from 300 to 700 yards, to narrow sandy beaches. The Provisional Brigade was equipped with LSTs (Landing Ships, Tank) loaded with LVTs (Landing Vehicles, Tracked) for its assault battalions, but it was believed that subsequent waves could use landing boats in favorable weather at high tide. Inland from the beaches were fringes of palm trees and light scrub growing in rich black soil. Behind them, rolling terrain and foothills led up to the mountains. Before the Brigade could strike at Orote the high ground beyond the beachhead must be captured and held.

The postponement of the attack on Guam from the date originally set, as a result of the slow and costly fight on Saipan, had one highly significant effect on the operation. The original plan called for only two days of preliminary naval bombardment. The delay made possible a much longer, heavier and more thorough softening-up than would otherwise have been possible. The heavy bombardments by battleships, cruisers and destroyers were coordinated with air strikes and the intense preparation greatly weakened the ability and the will of the enemy to resist. They also gave new evidence of the tremendously powerful effect which battleship, cruiser and carrier support could give to landing operations.

The Advance Division Headquarters and the 305th Regimental Combat Team, which had been waiting with all of the Marine elements of the III Amphibious Corps in the heat of the Eniwetok Lagoon, sailed on 18 July and arrived off Guam before daylight on the 21st. The remainder of the 77th from Oahu, paused briefly at Eniwetok, and arrived off Guam later on the 21st. En route, the troops had listened to final exhaustive briefings. They had pored over maps which portrayed in detail the roads, towns and the enemy installations. Terrain models of the island showed graphically the natural characteristics of the hilly, wooded island. The men had given their weapons a last check. H-Hour was 0830.

Chapter 7
The Fight for the Beachhead

AT 0530 on 21 July 1944 the thunder of 16-inch guns shattered the early morning quiet of Guam. Between the heavy salvos of the battleships, sharper reports of 8-inch, 6-inch, and 5-inch guns echoed across the beaches of western Guam and into the mountains beyond. Six battleships, four heavy cruisers, five light cruisers, and seven destroyers moved slowly, paralleling the beaches inshore of the transport areas, all guns trained on the dark mass of the tropical island. Bursts of flame lighted the dawn as shells exploded along the beaches and among the inland hills.

To the deeply entrenched Japanese the firing meant another day of nerve-shaking naval and air bombardment which had devastated their installations along the coast. Heavy air strikes had begun on 5 July and naval bombardment three days later. Aircraft from the Fast Carrier Forces had bombed and strafed Guam daily for sixteen days. On 18 July the tempo of the air strikes had increased, reaching a peak on the 20th when carrier planes made 614 strafing runs and dropped 486 tons of bombs on the battered island.

The naval bombardment had been intense and destructive. On 8 July the cruisers Wichita, Minneapolis, New Orleans, and San Francisco had opened a three-day bombardment, pouring 5,500 8-inch and 5-inch shells on Guam. From the 12th through the 16th the battleships New Mexico, Idaho, Pennsylvania, and Colorado fired over 3,000 16-inch and 14-inch shells. During the next four days they were joined by two more battleships, the Tennessee and the California, and six cruisers; and over 16,000 more shells of all sizes blasted the island. The heavier ships stood off-shore and poured a deluge of steel and high explosives on suspected defensive areas; the smaller ships closed in and knocked out guns and pillboxes at point-blank range. Destroyers screened the large ships and delivered harassing fire at night.

At 0803 on W-Day there was a change in the pattern of the bombardment. The slow deliberate shelling of installations and suspected areas changed to the rolling thunder of exploding projectiles on the landing beaches. LVTs crowded with Marine assault units jockeyed into position on the Line of Departure a few thousand yards off shore. Soon after, these low-silhouetted landing vehicles surged forward. From a distance came the roar of carrier planes as they wheeled into position for strafing runs against the beaches.

At 0822 the bombardment rose to a furious crescendo. Guns bearing on the landing beaches increased their tempo, some firing every six seconds. Forty-eight planes strafed the beaches. When the leading waves of Marines were a thousand yards off-shore, hundreds of rockets streamed from rocket boats and smashed into the beaches with terrific explosions. When they had closed to within three hundred yards, supporting fires were lifted from the beaches to the flanks and inland; the planes shifted their attacks inland.

On the left the leading waves of the 1st Provisional Brigade hit the beaches at 0828, and on the right three minutes later. The bombardments had knocked out virtually all of the enemy positions; a few Japanese machine guns fired from small caves, but were soon overcome. Enemy mortars nestled in the hills beyond placed scattered fire on the early waves. The Brigade, south of Orote Peninsula, made its landings with such aggressiveness that by 0900, thirty minutes after H-Hour, tanks were ashore and in action.

Just as the initial waves of the 1st Provisional Brigade reached the beaches, the 2d Battalion of the 305th Regimental Combat Team, commanded by Lieutenant Colonel Robert D. Adair, and the artillery liaison team of the 305th Field Artillery Battalion, commanded by Lieutenant Colonel E. B. Leever, were debarking from their transport into LCVPs (Landing Craft, Vehicle-Personnel). Orders prescribed that this battalion be on call at the line of departure as soon as the assault elements of the Brigade had cleared. The battalion was not called for four hours and during that time its boat teams milled and circled, but the artillery liaison team landed during the morning and selected positions on the south flank of the Brigade.

At 1300 Lieutenant Colonel Adair received a message from General Shepherd to proceed to the beach. As the Division had no LVTs and those of the Brigade which were still operative were engaged in bringing in ammunition and taking out casualties, the troops waded across the reef. Some fell into pot-holes and were completely submerged. Weapons could be kept dry only by following a narrow coral ridge where the water was sufficiently shallow for the men to keep their heads and shoulders above the surface. By so doing, however, they lost their dispersed formation. Fortunately little fire was received as the enemy was occupied by the Marines now a half mile inland.

Although boat teams managed to keep together while wading the reef, platoons and companies became intermingled. The battalion found White Beach 1 littered with charred and broken palm trees and a maze of sand heaps and craters. Units quickly reorganized, and company assembly areas were established. The battalion moved several hundred yards inland to an area designated by General Shepherd and organized a defensive position for the night.

Colonel Vincent J. Tanzola waited on his headquarters ship, the U.S.S. Lamar, for orders to land the remainder of his combat team. At 1530 he received a message from General Shepherd to land the remainder of it at 1530. The message had been delayed one hour in transit. Colonel Tanzola replied that he had only sufficient boats to land the 1st Battalion and that he would send in the 3d Battalion as soon as those returned which had been used by Colonel Adair's Battalion. When Lieutenant Colonel Adair's boats returned at about 1615, the boat teams of the 1st Battalion started descending the nets and within an hour five waves were boated. Further delay occurred when the Navy Control Officer insisted he had no instructions at that time to dispatch waves to the beach. It was 1730 when the 1st Battalion was permitted to proceed.

With the approach of darkness Colonel Tanzola grew increasingly disturbed. At 1725 he notified General Shepherd "Cannot complete unloading of teams before dark . . . suggest suspension of unloading ..." A reply came promptly, "Land your combat team at once . . ."

The Provisional Brigade needed the 305th ashore. The long previous bombardment and the naval gunfire and air support preparations had enabled it to land almost unopposed. As the Marines pushed inland, however, they came under some enemy mortar and artillery fire. Two small but spirited counterattacks were beaten off, but they indicated the enemy might be able to launch a strong attack during the night. The recent disastrous blow against a division on Saipan was uppermost in the minds of all. By dusk the Brigade had pushed inland 2,000 yards on a 4,500 yard front. Its call for all of the 305th was a summons for more assistance to hold this area and to expand it the following day. Poor shore-to-ship communications caused the long delay in Colonel Tanzola's receipt of the orders.

The landing of the 1st Battalion encountered the same difficulties the 2d Battalion had met earlier, with darkness added. Ahead, the troops could see the outlines of the hills where skirmishes between Marines and the enemy were marked by bright flashes and by the dull, red glow of burned-out positions. The officers and men of the 1st Battalion also waded the wide reef in water up to their chests. Desperately trying to keep their weapons dry, stepping off into pot-holes, sometimes swimming, the troops slowly made their way to the beach.

In the confusion, Lieutenant Colonel James E. Landrum, commanding the 1st Battalion, waded in on the left of his first wave although, for better control, he had planned to be in the center. On the beach troops were milling about in the darkness. The Battalion had landed perilously close to enemy terrain after veering too far to the south. Colonel Landrum dispersed his men just behind the beach. With his staff and guides he located the battalion assembly area and by 2130 the bulk of the battalion was in it.

Because of too few boats, the 3d Battalion, under Lieutenant Colonel Edward Chalgren, Jr., was unable to land simultaneously with the 1st Battalion, While awaiting boats, its transport was suddenly ordered to sea because of a reported imminent submarine attack. The ship steamed out ten or fifteen miles and then returned to the transport area, arriving at 2120. Debarkation began and continued as rapidly as boats arrived.

The 3d Battalion did not begin landing over the reef until 0330 the 22d. Some boats became lost and landed their troops to the south, but most of the Battalion arrived on the same part of White Beach 1 on which the 1st Battalion had landed. Men were wet and tired after their long wait in the small boats, and some were seasick. Fearing that the Marines might fire on them if they moved about in the dark, they dug in for the night on the beach. The last elements arrived at 0600.

Colonel Tanzola and his staff started ashore at 2330 when the 3d Battalion was boated. On reaching the edge of the reef they debarked and waded, sometimes even swimming, until an empty rubber boat was found floating nearby. Colonel Tanzola reached the beach in it.

The 305th Field Artillery Battalion was equipped with DUKWs (2K-ton amphibious trucks), which could negotiate the fringing reef. Late in the afternoon of the 21st when Battery A was ordered ashore, its movement was complicated by the lack of a marked channel across the reef, and the presence of many coral "niggerheads" on it. After landing, the Battery remained on the beach throughout the night. An all-around defense was established and the men were able to dig in well. They were not disturbed by Japanese infiltrators, but were aroused when an enemy soldier threw a hand grenade at a near-by vehicle, missing it but blowing up a large pile of Japanese land-mines which had been removed from the beaches. The detonation was terrific but the Battery suffered no casualties. The remainder of the Battalion landed without incident and during the next morning occupied positions on the south flank near Bangi Point which had been selected by the liaison teams.

FIRST HOURS ON GUAM

With two battalions ashore by midnight and the 3d on the way, the 305th could take stock of its situation. Looming above White Beach was Mount Alifan. The enemy still occupied it, although the Marines had fought their way over a mile inland. Mount Alifan formed the highest elevation of a range opposite the southern beachhead, and its control by the enemy gave him command and observation of all of the Brigade area.

The Brigade was highly vulnerable to counterattack with the enemy on three sides of the rectangular beachhead. It was not a night for sleeping. Fire fights kept breaking out between the Marines and the Japanese. Small groups of the enemy infiltrated through the front lines to the battalion areas of the 305th. The most harassed by these was the 1st Battalion, which was farther inland than the other elements of the regiment. The troops had made an effort to dig in but they had landed too late to do an effective job.

Early in the morning heavy firing broke out just outside the 1st Battalion assembly area. The men were surprised and confused. It was impossible to discover the location of the enemy; sentinels who challenged when they heard movements received a burst of fire. A small attack was launched against the Battalion. Several Japanese broke through to the Battalion command post, but an automatic rifle team held its position and killed them before they could inflict serious damage. Companies A and B lost seven men killed and ten wounded during the night. Although fire discipline was good, considering that the troops were green, some of the casualties were caused by the fire of friendly troops. The 1st Battalion counted twenty dead Japanese the next morning.

The 2d Battalion, nearer the beach, had less trouble during the night except for one savage skirmish. A Japanese charged into its position, wildly brandishing his saber. He slashed at Private Alvin Fisher of Company F, who grappled with him. Two more of the enemy rushed in behind a barrage of grenades. Private August B. McLees dispatched one with a butt stroke and the other was shot at close range. Men near Fisher tried to help him by grabbing the Japanese saber, only to cut their hands. In the darkness Staff Sergeant Carmino Guimara tried to make out the lurching figures and shouted, "which is which?" Finally in desperation Staff Sergeant Robert Livingstone smashed the Japanese over the head with his carbine. Grenades were still coming in, but the men discovered the source and killed a lone enemy soldier.

The Marines on the front lines beat off a small but determined counterattack. One enemy attack during the night, supported by tanks and artillery, was launched against the southern flanks of the Brigade, but it was counterattacked and beaten off. The Japanese lost five tanks.

During this first restless night ashore and subsequent hectic days, mutually cordial relations were established and maintained with the Marines. The men of the 1st Brigade nicknamed the 305th Infantry "the 305th Marines." Marines, most of whom had never voted, referred to the 77th's fast slogging oldsters as "the old bastards." Equipment and supplies were traded between the services; staff relations were friendly and efficient. There was a job to be done and no time for bickering.

THE STRUGGLE FOR ELBOW ROOM

The 22d of July dawned with the 1st Provisional Brigade fighting to reach its final beachhead line which ran along the foothills but did not include the 1,500-foot Mount Alifan. After evacuating their casualties of the previous night, the battalions of the 305th reorganized and checked their supplies and equipment. A good deal of equipment, especially communications materiel, had been lost or damaged in the landing, or had not yet come ashore from the transports. Some arms and ammunition had also been lost. But their realistic training had prepared the troops for just such difficulties. General Shepherd granted time for the regiment to reorganize and ordered it to attack to the northeast at 1030 with the battalions abreast.

The mission of the 1st Battalion was to swing around the northern base of Mount Alifan, and capture the high ground over which the Harmon

Road passed to the east. The 3d Battalion on the left of the 1st was to conform generally to it and capture the high ground on the north of the 1st Battalions objective. The objectives assigned to the 305th would help give the Brigade elbow room and cover for its wheeling movement toward the base of the Orote Peninsula.

The 1st Battalion encountered very difficult going more from the eroded and brush-covered hills rather than from the enemy. So steep and thickly wooded were the hills in its zone of advance that supplies had to be manhandled. Just before reaching their objective at 1700 the troops observed a Marine signalling from Mount Alifan. The Brigade had seized the peak but there were still many Japanese on the long ridge itself.

The 3d Battalion made rapid progress over fairly open terrain. Company K finished off one Japanese strongpoint, which had already been partly destroyed by shell fire. The troops found enemy positions so devastated by shells and bombs that they encountered very little resistance and dug in for the night on a red clay ridge facing north, at right angle to the left of the 1st Battalion.

The 2d Battalion of the 305th, which had been the first organization of the 77th Division to go ashore, remained in Corps reserve on the 22d. The enemy seemed to have this Battalion located, for it was harassed by artillery and mortar fire during this day and throughout the night. Japanese snipers were still active in the area. The 2d Battalion, reverting to regimental control on the 23rd, moved up and helped its sister battalions hold the high ground to the north and south of the Harmon Road, and beyond Mount Alifan.

During the following week the 305th Infantry defended this line while other elements of the Division supported the Brigade in its attack on the Orote Peninsula. It was not a passive defense. The very fact that the 305th held such a long frontage forced it to maintain an aggressive defense in order to disrupt Japanese groups which might try to slip through the gaps. Constant patrolling in enemy territory and a continual extension was necessary.

At 1226 on 22 July General Geiger ordered the remainder of the 77th Infantry Division, less one regimental combat team, to land over White Beaches the following day: the 77th then to relieve the 1st Provisional Brigade on its entire Final Beachhead Line so the Brigade could reorganize and prepare for its attack up the Orote Peninsula. One regimental combat team was to remain afloat in Corps reserve, prepared to land on order.

Shortly before noon on the 23d the 306th Regimental Combat Team, commanded by Colonel Aubrey D. Smith, started landing across White Beach 2 to relieve the 4th Marine Regiment in the south' and southeast. The regimental and battalion commanders had the previous day reconnoitered the sectors and arranged with the 4th Marines for the relief. The 306th also had to wade across the broad reef which so delayed its landing that only the 3d Battalion was that day able to complete the relief in its sector. It took over the sector between Mount Taene and the shore; the 1st and 2d Battalions occupied assembly areas near the beach.

During the course of the relief by the 3d Battalion, Company K was attacked by about fifty Japanese. The Marines had just left the position and as the men of Company K started to improve their foxholes the Japanese began to advance through a coconut grove to the front. Although fatigued from wading the reef and the fast march to the position, the company was immediately stimulated by this first sight of the enemy and met the attack with heavy fire. Captain William Geissert, Company Commander, reported the attack to his Battalion Commander, Lieutentant Colonel Gordon T. Kimbrell, and requested artillery fire. The battalion artillery liaison officer, Captain John C. Coine communicated with the Marine Artillery and quickly adjusted fire on the coconut grove. The enemy was forced to retreat in haste, leaving several dead behind. The remainder of the night was spent without incident.

At 0800 on 24 July Colonel Smith assumed responsibility for the sector and by 1400 the last elements of the regiment were in position. During the day there were a few small skirmishes with enemy patrols and the regiment cleared caves and dugouts in its sector. During the early hours of darkness an attempt was made to infiltrate into the position but all were driven off and no casualties suffered.

On 24 July the 307th Regimental Combat Team under Colonel Stephen S. Hamilton debarked and landed on White Beach 2. A storm at sea raised heavy ground swells and imperiled the landing. One company suffered two casualties when men fell from the nets of the rolling transport. The LCVPs circled for several hours and many men became seasick. At least part of their misery came from the realization that they were losing the last good navy food with which they had stuffed themselves before debarking.

The boats finally made the run to the reef, the ramps went down and officers and men began the long wade to the beach, searching for footing on the treacherous coral bottom and wrestling with their equipment;

sometimes to their necks in water. The men were top heavy with equipment; the average soldier was burdened with a steel helmet, gas mask, light pack, life belt, rifle and bayonet, grenade launcher, ammunition, rations, a pouch of hand grenades, two canteens of water and a machete. Heavy-weapons company men carried most of this equipment and in addition part of a mortar or heavy machine gun.

But for the most part the men were in good spirits. "Have you dubbined your shoes?" they asked each other as they slowly pushed through the deep water. Some of them realized for the first time how it must feel to wade the reef and contend with enemy fire at the same time. Good order was maintained and reorganization was effected rapidly once the beach was reached. The 307th, still in reserve, moved to assembly positions and established all-around defenses for the night. Foxholes were dug in the shape of an inverted V, with the apex pointed out; these were connected by slit trenches, making it possible for two men to sleep while a third remained on the alert. Company F was ordered to the left of the 305th Infantry to occupy a gap.

By the evening of the 24th the 1st Provisional Brigade had isolated the peninsula by seizing its narrow neck in preparation for the attack up this important terrain feature.

"THE TOUGHEST REEF IN THIS WAR"

The reef which had so delayed the landing of troops had even more serious effect on the supply program. No matter what the tide, LCVPs and LCMs could not cross the reef. Amphibious tractors (LVTs) and DUKWs could, but there were not enough of them to transport thousands of tons of supplies. The G-4 plan was disrupted. It had envisaged that at high tide landing craft could reach the beaches and pallets of supplies would be hooked to a bulldozer or tractor and dragged out of the boats directly to dumps. The only solution was to transfer supplies, by means of cranes at the reef edge, from boats to DUKWs and LVTs which could negotiate the reef. Vehicles, medium artillery, medium tanks, M-10 tank destroyers, with which Antitank companies were equipped, as well as heavy engineer equipment were also a problem; they had to be landed at the reef edge and driven or dragged to the beach. This could only be done at low tide, and even then some motors were drowned out in spite of deep water fording equipment and waterproofing.

The 1st Provisional Brigade was charged with responsibility for supply during the first three days of the action. The fact that virtually all ammunition and supplies of the Army and the Marine Corps were identical, simplified the task. Although the beaches were unusually crowded, the Shore Parties of the two services worked together with little difficulty. White Beach 1 was turned over to the Division on the 23rd of July and White Beach 2 a short time later.

Despite these and many other difficulties, the vital work of keeping the assault troops supplied was carried on successfully. After watching unloading operations a naval officer who had been at Guadalcanal, Attu, Tarawa, Kwajalein, and Saipan Wrote General Bruce, "Your people have landed and supplied themselves over the toughest reef yet worked by any outfit in this war."

At 1700 on 25 July General Geiger postponed the attack up the Orote Peninsula until 0700 26 July. The 1st Provisional Brigade needed the additional time to prepare. During the 25th, heavy resistance developed in its front at the base of the peninsula and it became apparent that the main enemy positions on Orote had been encountered. During the day the Brigade moved all elements into position and completed preparations for the next day's attack. To the north the 3d Division had met continual heavy resistance since it had landed and was still pressing its attack on the 25th all along the line to capture its Final Beachhead Line.

Although the mission of the 77th Division during the Orote attack was to hold the FBL, elements of the Division were preparing to support the Brigade on the peninsula. The 305th Field Artillery Battalion had landed on 21-22 July with the 305th Regimental Combat Team. The remainder of the Division Artillery landed during the next two days, except for the 306th Field Artillery Battalion (155mm howitzers) which came ashore on 25-26 July. Initially the mission of the Division Artillery, commanded by Brigadier General Isaac Spalding, was to support the defense of the FBL, but during the drive up Orote it was to add its fire power to that of the Corps Artillery, in an effort to pulverize the earth and concrete positions of the enemy.

DIVISION ARTILLERY SUPPORTS OROTE ATTACK

At daybreak on 26 July the 77th Division Artillery opened fire on the Orote defenses. The 305th, 306th, and 902d Field Artillery Battalions joined in the opening concentrations, although howitzers of some of the batteries were not yet in position. Some batteries fired at the rate of two rounds per minute until the attack was launched. Naval gun fire and air strikes added to the inferno. Even the 90mm antiaircraft guns on Cabras Island were used in this effort to destroy the most concentrated defense on Guam. The hard coral surface of the peninsula gave perfect ricochet air bursts and this type of fire was used extensively and with excellent results.

At 0700 the attack of the 1st Provisional Brigade was launched. Dense undergrowth and jungle covering the base of the peninsula slowed its progress. Many Japanese had survived the bombing, shelling, and strafing and fiercely resisted with mortars, machine guns, and small arms. The narrow neck of the peninsula hampered the Brigade in the effective employment of its forces, but it pressed on. By the evening of the 26th favorable terrain had been captured from which to launch the next day's attack.

During the 26th and the next three days, the 77th Division's artillery battalions were grouped with the 3d Amphibious Corps Artillery, but operated under Division Artillery control. The massing of all battalions made possible intense and sustained fire. On one occasion a preparation was laid down by the equivalent of seven battalions on a one thousand yard front. The Marines moved up slowly behind it and reported that they advanced 500 yards before encountering a live enemy.

The Division Artillery maintained a flash observation post on the high ground between Mount Alifan and Mount Tenjo. No sound ranging apparatus was available and the flash observation was made less effective because of the rain and mist. However, the artillery had excellent observation of the peninsula from its high positions. From some battery positions howitzer crews could see the bursts of their own shells. On one occasion the Marines, emphasizing the need for close support, asked for a concentration one hundred yards in front of their forward elements, evidently with the expectation that this would bring the fire within several hundred yards of their lines. When the concentration from the 305th Field Artillery Battalion began falling precisely one hundred yards in front of their positions, they requested an increase in range of two hundred yards.

Enemy artillery fire was negligible. An old and well known Japanese ruse was observed early in the operation. Battery A of the 305th was firing a harassing mission when the Brigade Artillery Officer reported that rounds were falling short. The staff of the 305th Field Artillery Battalion, however, had observed enemy artillery firing from the mountains. On closer examination the enemy was discovered to be firing into the troops coincidentally with the volleys of Battery A, to induce the Marines to believe that friendly artillery fires were falling short.

While the 1st Provisional Brigade was attacking the enemy on the Orote Peninsula, the 3d Marine Division north of the peninsula continued to press its attacks against bitter resistance over difficult terrain. At dawn on 26 July the Japanese threw a determined counterattack against its center. Heavy fighting developed. The Japanese 18th Regiment (less one battalion), and elements of the 48th Independent Mixed Brigade attacked behind artillery and mortar fires with such force that the front lines were penetrated.

Those who had broken through were killed in savage hand-to-hand fighting, and the counterattack was beaten off and badly disorganized after sustaining heavy casualties.

ARMY TANKS LEAD THE MARINES

The Japanese continued a stubborn resistance on Orote Peninsula on 27 July. General Shepherd requested tanks from the 77th Division. The Marines had used their own medium tanks in their advance, but several had been lost by enemy fire and mines. A platoon of Company D (light tanks) of the 706th Tank Battalion was dispatched.

Commanded by 2d Lieutenant Charles J. Fuchs, the platoon reported early in the afternoon of 28 July and was attached to Company I, 4th Marine Regiment. The attack was scheduled to be resumed at 1600. The units on the flanks of Company I had been reinforced by the two platoons of Marine medium tanks. Lieutenant Fuchs's platoon was to strengthen the center. Just before the attack two medium tanks from Headquarters Company of the 706th joined the platoon.

When the attack was launched the light tanks moved through the Marines at fifty-yard intervals, against a series of pillboxes. One log and concrete position withstood the 37mm fire from the lights but the mediums quickly demolished it with their heavier guns. The Marines, following closely, mopped up over-run positions, grenaded Japanese in their foxholes and protected the tanks. The latter advanced cautiously over the shell-torn terrain and the fighting was so concentrated that they fired at targets at a range of only ten or fifteen yards. At such close range the 37mm gun-fire was effective. When high explosive shells did not blast apart the logs of pillboxes, the light tanks poured fire through the crevices. Small arms fire was received but not enough to stop the steady advance of the tanks and the Marines.

Within two hours the forward elements of Company I, with adjacent units, had come abreast of the 22d Marine Regiment on the right. The tank platoon had fired over 10,000 rounds of .30 calibre ammunition, 100 rounds of high explosives, and twenty rounds of canister. They had destroyed four pillboxes, numerous dugouts, and killed about 250 Japanese. There were no casualties in the tank platoon and few among Company I. The advance on this day reached the airfield. Heavy resistance continued around the field and in the vicinity of Sumay.

On 29 July Lieutenant Fuchs supported the 1st Battalion of the 4th Marine Regiment in a drive along the south side of the airfield. Captain Leonard H. Seegar of Company D led an improvised formation of two medium tanks and three light tanks on the right of Lieutenant Fuchs.

At 1000 an attack was launched to capture the airfield. Under small arms and mortar fire the tanks and the Marines pushed on. Japanese were killed defending pillboxes, dugouts, and even a ruined airplane hangar. Less than five hours after the attack started the tank-Marine combination had cleared the way to the far end of the field.

It was about this time that two heretofore silent Japanese guns, located in the rocky face of the southern edge of the peninsula, opened up on a group of LVTs engaged in reconnoitering the base of the peninsula from the sea. The exact location of the pieces could not be determined by the artillery observer although the latter was less than a thousand yards distant. They were spotted, however, by the artillery liaison officer on Mount Alifan, over 10,000 yards away; he adjusted fire by radio and silenced them. Two of the amphibious vehicles were damaged by the Japanese fire, but none was sunk.

The area between the airfield and the tip of Orote Peninsula was quickly cleared. Between 1500 and 1700 Marines and tanks pushed out over the jungle trails and reached the ocean. A few more Japanese were killed, but it was clear that most of the enemy on the peninsula had elected to die in their positions defending the airfield. At 1700 the tanks of the 706th were relieved. As they returned over the captured air strip, the crews saw the American flag rising over the remnants of the Marine barracks which had been captured by the enemy thirty-two months before.

3d BATTALION 307th LINKS TWO BEACHHEADS

There was still a gap between the beachheads of the 3d Marine Division to the north and the 77th Division on the south, even after the opening of the attack on the Orote Peninsula. Patrols had operated in the gap during the daytime, but the enemy also took advantage of it. Most of this area was high ground commanding the peninsula and some of the coast. On 26 July General Geiger ordered the 3d Battalion of the 307th Infantry, commanded by Lieutenant Colonel John W. Lovell, to relieve elements of the 3d Marine Division near Sasa, and then sweep south along the Old Agat Road toward Mount Tenjo.

That afternoon the 3d Battalion made the long march north between the beachheads, from Agat to Piti. On the 27th it organized a defensive position along the Sasa River east of the Old Agat Road, and early the next morning relieved the 3d Battalion, 9th Marine Regiment. To the west the position was anchored on the swamps inland from Apra Harbor and extended east to the hills where it tied in with the 3d Division. At 1045 on the 28th the battalion reversed itself and returned to the south with its objective the unimproved road extending east from the Old Agat Road, and lying 1,500 yards distant.

The maneuver was an unusual one since the 3d Battalion was combing through an area over which it had marched to Piti two days earlier, and which was actually a no-man's-land. To cover the wide area the 3d Battalion advanced with a three-company front. After traversing about six hundred yards, contact was made with the 3d Battalion, 9th Marine Regiment on the left. The advance continued and patrols met patrols of the 305th Infantry which were operating northwest of Mount Tenjo. Mortar fire was especially effective in destroying the grass huts from which scattered groups of the enemy tried to hold up the advance. By 1800 the battalion had reached its objective, occupied positions along the unimproved road, and tied in with the 305th Infantry. North and south beachheads were one.

During 29 July the 3d Battalion held its position. The battle for the Orote Peninsula was drawing to a close and the desperate Japanese were attempting to escape by swimming to the beaches near the 3d Battalion. Permitting them to come in close, machine gun and mortar teams killed twenty-seven during the day. "It was like a day at a shooting gallery back home" one of the men recalled later. The following day the Battalion was relieved from its attachment to the 3d Marine Division and moved southeast to the vicinity of Mount Tenjo, which had been captured two days earlier.

THE CAPTURE OF MOUNT TENJO

The precipitous slopes of Mount Tenjo rose steeply from the soggy fields east of the face of the Orote Peninsula. It, and its sister, Mount Alif an, opposite and to the south, were like two huge gate-posts between which the Harmon Road passed over a ridge and into the open valley to the east. Mount Tenjo was an objective which had been assigned to the 3d Marine Division, but because of the rugged terrain and heavy enemy resistance encountered by that organization, it had not yet been reached. The mountain rose 1,022 feet and control of it would give observation over large areas and clinch the linking of the northern and southern beachheads.

On the afternoon of 27 July General Bruce requested and received permission from General Geiger to feel out with patrols the enemy strength on the mountain in the 3d Marine Division sector and to capture it if the patrols found it only lightly held. Although little activity had been observed on Tenjo, Japanese prisoners of war had declared there were 3,000 troops in its vicinity.

Orders were issued to the 305th Infantry to have one company at daylight the next morning reconnoiter the mountain from the southeast. The 2d Battalion, 307th Infantry, commanded by Lieutenant Colonel Charles F. Learner, was directed to march to the base of the mountain at daylight to capture it, should reconnaissance by the 305th find it only lightly held.

Moving out before dawn on the 28th, Company A of the 305th Infantry, commanded by Captain Arthur G. Curtin, labored up the precipitous slopes and by 0830 had reached the summit. He had been directed by General Bruce to advance from the rear of the mountain instead of the forward slopes. Enemy opposition consisted of only scattered sniper fire. A real crisis, however, came after the company had reached the top. Friendly planes suddenly appeared and began to strafe and bomb the troops. Desperately the men tried to dig in. As the planes came in for another run, Private First Class Benno Levi seized his platoon's signal panels, ran into the open and displayed them to the zooming aircraft. They veered off and Company A consolidated its hold on the mountain. Miraculously no casualties had been sustained. At 1500 the 2d Battalion of the 307th reached the summit and relieved Company A. The next day men of the Division heard a broadcast from the United States that Mount Tenjo had been captured by the 3d Marine Division. This error was corrected in a statement made by General Geiger.

The capture of Mount Tenjo was the final link in forging a single continuous beachhead which was held by the 3d Marine Division and the 77th Infantry Division. The 306th Infantry, the 305th Infantry, and the 2d Battalion, 307th Infantry, from right to left, occupied a line extending from the ocean south of Bangi Point up to Taene Mountain, along Mount Alifan and the adjoining ridge line to Maanot Reservoir at Road Junction 370. The line then continued northeast, still following the ridges, crossed Inalas Mountain and continued to and including Mount Tenjo, where the 77th Division tied in with the 3d Marine Division. The 307th Infantry, less the 2d Battalion, was in Division reserve a few hundred yards inland from Agat.

AN AGGRESSIVE DEFENSE

During the operations on Orote the 77th Division faced the major problem of holding a long defensive line on rugged terrain. Thousands of well equipped Japanese were just beyond the line; it would be easy for them to move about in the jungle and group for a major attack on our thinly held line. To prevent such developments our plan called for aggressive defense. Elements of the 77th extended their lines, improved their fields of fire, and sent out strong reconnaissance patrols. These patrols kept the enemy off balance by threats of large-scale attack, and they brought back information on enemy movements. The typical infantry reconnaissance formation was a platoon strength combat patrol. These patrols were assigned objectives 1,000 to 2,000 yards beyond our lines with orders to clean out any small defensive positions or snipers encountered along the way. The patrols burned shacks and high grass to smoke out well camouflaged pockets, and occasionally called for mortar and artillery fire. So effective were these tactics that the enemy did not launch a single attack in force during the daytime.

The Japanese were quick, however, to organize countermeasures. On several occasions, they attempted to set up ambushes for our patrols, and one such on 29 July developed into a small but fierce fire fight. The 3d Platoon of Company B of the 305th was returning from a patrol when they spotted movement in high grass in a ravine fronting a small knoll directly to the left of the leading men. The 2d squad was sent directly to the ravine, while the 1st squad moved forward and then cut in to the left, and the 3rd stayed back in reserve. As the squads approached, the Americans saw two Japanese climbing trees in the ravine and shot them down.

As the men of the 2d Squad climbed down into the ravine through the high grass, rifle fire broke out from the other side. The enemy was invisible in the thick growth. The men tried to get cover, but they were pinned against the steep side of the ravine and completely exposed to the fire. They were virtually helpless. Within a few seconds two men were killed and three others wounded.

The 1st Squad, moving in from the right shot up a distress flare; the flare was observed by the 305th which sent reinforcements from the 1st Battalion. Approaching from the direction of the American lines, the 1st Platoon or Company B deployed along the knoll on the other side of the ravine from the helpless 2d Squad. It was still impossible to locate the Japanese position.

1st Sgt. Donald L. Hathaway of Company B (who had been a rear echelon commissioned officer in the last war and was "looking for action" in this one) decided to reconnoiter the enemy position personally. He climbed down into the ravine with two other men on the right of the trapped squad. At the same time he dispatched the 1st Squad of the 1st Platoon down into the ravine to approach from the opposite direction to his own move. Hathaway's plan was to conduct a boxing-in maneuver, along with the 3d Squad 3d Platoon, which was trying to cut in from up the draw but meeting difficulty in the high grass.

Working down the steep slope in the tall grass was a slow process for Hathaway. He could hear the enemy fire in the ravine but he could not locate the exact source. As he neared the bottom, Pfc. Albert Bogdanowski next to him was shot through the throat. Hathaway fell the rest of the way, landing on a dead Jap at the bottom of the ravine. He still could not locate the source of the fire, so he made his way painfully back up the bank. Bogdanowski was bleeding heavily and died while Hathaway crouched at his side.

The enemy fire, however, was gradually becoming more scattered. Although the 1st Squad of the 1st Platoon also got bogged down in vegetation as it tried to come up the draw and had to be content with throwing grenades into the approximate position of the enemy, the infantrymen on top of the knoll and even the trapped squad on the other side of the draw were able to pour a good deal of rifle and BAR fire on the enemy. The members of the 2d Squad managed to work their way out. The next day when American dead were recovered 14 dead and 1 wounded Japanese were found in the center of the ravine.

However active our defense was during the day, with aggressive patrols operating out in front of the lines, it was passive at night, and then the Japanese assumed the initiative. The infantry companies on the FBL organized at night into battalion defense positions on high points along the line. Automatic fire covered lower areas. Although fields of fire were cleared where possible, and dominating positions were held, the enemy made use of his skillful infiltration tactics to move up the slopes. Hardly a night passed without these groups attempting to harass or pass through.

The Japanese seemed to follow no standard plan in attempts at infiltration. They used a variety of weapons — mortars, small arms, sabers, even hatchets. Sometimes our first notice of the enemy was a grenade thrown in from the outer darkness. Sometimes an enemy soldier in plain sight would walk slowly toward the American lines; fire from all directions easily knocked him down, but this gave our positions away. Sometimes heavy fire and grenades landed in the defense positions, followed by small enemy groups trying to move in where confusion had been created. Enemy mortar fire was especially effective, although it was not frequently used at night.

At first the inexperienced American troops caused most of the confusion by their movement and firing during the night and were embarrassed to discover little evidence of the enemy the next day. But on succeeding nights the men grew more crafty. They learned to stay immobile in their slit trenches, never venturing outside no matter how severe their diarrhea. They learned to hold their fire until they had a definite target, to prevent the enemy from discovering their position. They set up their own booby traps and caught a few Japs that way. They devised ingenious trip flares which shot up and illuminated the whole area when the enemy tangled with them. They learned to kill Japanese by night as well as by day.

SEARCHING OUT THE ENEMY

During the fight for the Orote Peninsula and the aggressive defense of the Final Beachhead Line, the Division staff was working on plans for the next phase of the operation. Only a small part of the island had been captured and less than half of the enemy strength encountered. Before General Bruce could crystallize his plans for the next phase, more detailed information was needed as to where the enemy was, and, almost equally important, where he was not.

By 28 July there were indications that the Japanese would withdraw to the north of the island to make their last stand. It was believed that they had supply dumps, an emergency headquarters, radio equipment capable of communicating with Tokyo, and prepared positions in that region. There, too, were potential sites for large air fields which the enemy would be reluctant to give up. While the terrain, both north and south, had defensive advantages, the northern part of the island, because of its jungle and a few tactically important mountains, would afford the enemy good observation and be especially difficult to attack. Moreover, intelligence reports on 27 July indicated a northward movement by the Japanese.

But more precise intelligence was needed before final commitments could be made. Even though the bulk of the Japanese appeared to be moving to the northern part of the island, were there any organized troops remaining in the South? Could the Division, having cut the island in two, safely turn its back on the southern half of the island, or would troops have to be left behind to cover its rear and protect its communications? To the 77th Division Reconnaissance Troop fell the task of collecting this important information. Because of the dense vegetation which covered most of the island, reconnaissance planes and observation posts were not sufficient. The only way to obtain accurate information was for patrols to move on foot, scour the area, and question friendly Chamorros.

On 28 July five small patrols from the Reconnaissance Troop departed on long range scouting missions. Two of these were to cross the island to the east coast and return. Three others were to move directly south. General routes were prescribed but the patrols could depart from them when it seemed desirable. They were to report by radio every few hours and they could call for artillery support if it was needed. Native guides were attached to each patrol and map codes were prearranged.

The sending out of these small patrols represented a calculated risk of twenty or more men against the value of the information needed. To the men who went represented a trip of two or three days into an unknown land populated by hostile Japanese. But they went and they obtained information. Patrol Easy, led by Sgt. Barnes Compton, Jr., of Yonkers, New York, for example, reached Umatac on the southwest coast and learned that there was little enemy activity and that the Chamorros there were friendly.

The most successful of these five patrols was led by 2d Lieutenant Jack B. Miller and included Sgt. Clifford Austin, Sgt. Richard De Ponto and T/4 Joseph Bogdzio. It left at daybreak 28 July from near the Maanot Reservoir. Guided by a native, Tony Cruz, the four-man patrol moved eastward to cross the island and reconnoiter Talofofo and Togcha Bays, on the east coast. It had proceeded hardly a mile when five Japanese were seen in the open ahead. The enemy also saw the patrol: each group sought cover and by-passed the other. The patrol continued on and reached high ground overlooking Talofofo Bay, but saw no enemy activity. By this time it was late in the afternoon and the men spent the night in a cave near Talofofo.

The next morning Lieutenant Miller and his patrol reconnoitered Togcha Bay and found no enemy activity there. By radio, he received orders to move to Ylig Bay and reconnoiter. Approaching Ylig the patrol encountered a small group of Chamorros who greeted the Americans with joy. The natives reported that many Japanese troops were to the north and that only small groups of ten to fifteen were still in the southern area. Tracks and other indications of movement to the north were observed.

Lieutenant Miller and his men reported back with their information, which when added to that gained by the other patrols, confirmed the view that the enemy would organize his final stand to the north and that only a few disorganized stragglers remained in the south.

On 29 July a patrol from Company I, 306th Infantry reached Cetti Bay on the west coast. No Japanese were encountered but two natives reported that several thousand Chamorros were gathered at Merizo, at the extreme southern end of the island, and that many were in need of medical attention. Staff Sergeant Harry Kolata of the 3d Battalion Medical Section, volunteered to make the fourteen mile trip with a company aid man to help the natives. Guided by two Chamorros Sergeant Kolata and his companion arrived at Merizo. After receiving a joyous welcome they spent the night assisting the sick and wounded, and next day, led over 2,000 natives back to the American position.

Patrols on foot had checked the areas to the south and to the east of the Division sector, but there was a large region to the southeast which must be reconnoitered before the Division could feel secure in turning its back on that district and concentrating its efforts to the north. At noon on 30 July a four-man patrol commanded by 2d Lieutenant John R. Stringer was directed to proceed first to Talofofo Bay, and then move south along the high ground west of the shore road and reconnoiter Inarajan and Agfayan Bay at the very southeast tip of Guam. It was to report by radio every two hours.

Preceded by the invaluable native guide, Tony Cruz, the patrol moved out from Maanot Reservoir. Except for an occasional straggler no enemy activity was observed. With dusk, the patrol located a jungle area near the Talofofo River and spent the night in it. The next morning, approaching Inarajan, several Chamorros were enountered on the trail. Excitedly the natives reported that eight Japanese soldiers, former guards of a concentration camp, were preparing to flee to the north in a truck. Proudly they related that the native "underground" had plans to kill them and all other stragglers, using stolen Japanese arms and ammunition. After that the Chamorros would go north and offer their services to the Americans. Dramatically, the leader exclaimed, "American soldier, we strike tonight!"

In the meantime, however, word had preceded the patrol to the village that it was on the way and the Japanese guards hurriedly made off. Two of them blundered into the patrol and were killed. As Lieutenant Stringer and his men reached the village the natives turned out and gave them a joyful welcome. "It looked like Armistice Day," one of the men related later. The Japanese had converted Inarajan into a concentration camp and labor pool. Packed into a small area, the people were made to load and unload ships, clear fields, and work on fortifications. Sometimes they were paid, more often not. "We have waited two and a half years for you," they told Lieutenant Stringer. The Chamorros spent most of the night entertaining their visitors.

The weary members of the patrol returned to Division Headquarters at 0700, 31 July, with the information that the southeastern area was clear of the enemy and that the Chamorros had the situation well in hand. These reconnaissances enabled the Division Commander to decide to leave only a small security detachment in the rear when the Division turned north, and not an entire regimental combat team as he had previously estimated would be necessary.

THE BATTLE OF THE BEACHES

Behind the Division another desperate battle was being fought to unload from the transports and land the supplies and heavy equipment of the 18,000 men of the 77th. The broad fringing reef which had made the landing of the assault troops so difficult was an even more serious impediment in getting ashore during the following days the tremendous bulk of supplies and equipment. White Beach 1 was congested. Although the Marines had departed, much of their equipment remained, and the beach dump area contained a battalion or artillery, emplaced and firing, and an LVT repair pool. Beach roads were poor and the many muddy rice paddies restricted traffic.

The sixty DUKWs of the Division were pooled and operated under the control of G-4 Lieutenant Colonel Guy V. Miller. Supplies were even floated ashore from transports on ship's life rafts and ten-man rubber boats belonging to the Reconnaissance Troop. Six crane barges were used at the seaward edge of the reef for transferring cargo from boats to DUKWs and LVTs, and on each an officer supervised operations and maintained communication by radio with the Shore Party. When some special type of supplies or equipment was urgently needed, Shore Party Headquarters on the beach informed the officers on the crane barges or G-4 on the Control Boat, who had lists of cargoes of all transports, and the requested supplies or equipment were sent to the beach with top priority.

With the supplies and equipment safely on shore, all difficulties were not yet overcome. Vehicles sometimes took as long as three hours to make a return trip from the beach to the dumps; a distance of usually not over 600 yards. Tropical rains and constant, grinding traffic churned the roads into a sea of mud. Wheeled vehicles repeatedly bogged down and had to be pulled out by tractors. The dump areas were soggy rice paddies. Shore party personnel and equipment were diverted to maintain beach roads and dump areas.

Very early in the operation it became clear that the transports of the Division could not be unloaded in a reasonable time on a dawn-to-dark basis only. Fortunately, since the enemy was unable to bomb or place artillery fire on the beaches, it was possible to illuminate them at night. Flood lights powered by generator units enabled work to proceed on a twenty-four hour basis and the APAs (Assault Transports) were 80 percent unloaded by the end of the fifth day.

Landing supplies and equipment on a twenty-four hour basis imposed a tremendous strain on the officers and men of the 1118th Engineer Group who comprised the Shore Party and worked the beaches, reefs, and beach dumps. The men worked with little rest or sleep. They were aided by men from the 302d Engineer Battalion, the 7th Antiaircraft Battalion, which worked and patrolled but found no Jap planes, and of Division Troops including the Division Band.

Despite almost unsurmountable difficulties, cargo arrived on the beach and was disposed of. By the time the Orote Peninsula had been captured and the southern part of the island reconnoitered, sufficient supplies were on shore to support the movement across the island and to the north. A combination of exhausting work and intelligent application of many expedients kept the unloading and supply program on schedule for the battle ahead.

While the battle of the beaches was in progress, unit by unit the men of the 77th came to the realization that they were personally involved in a shooting war. Even the officers and men of the Division Command Post had this quite unexpectedly impressed upon them. On their second night ashore they took to their foxholes as a Japanese antiaircraft gun below them on the Orote Peninsula shelled the command post, wounding two clerks. A few nights later a destroyer of the Navy accidentally dropped a five-inch shell into the CP. Fortunately it failed to explode. The next morning Major Bert Mendlin, of Division Artillery Headquarters, looked at the dud and answered his telephone, "Major Mendlin; by the grace of God, and a five-inch dud."

Chapter 8
To Pago Bay: The Fight for Food

THE STRENGTH of the 77th Division had been relatively slightly impaired during its first ten days on Guam. By 30 July, including attached units, it had lost 2 officers and 54 enlisted men killed in action, 8 officers and 152 enlisted men wounded in action, and 1 man missing. The Division had killed 479 Japanese and taken 2 prisoners. Most of the enemy casualties occurred during small skirmishes with patrols and attempted night infiltrations.

For the next phase of the operation it had been planned that the 77th Division and the 3d Marine Division attack abreast to the north, with the 77th on the right; the 1st Provisional Brigade in Corps reserve. Before this attack could be launched it would be necessary for the 3d Division to pivot to the north and extend to the east, and for the 77th to strike out toward the east coast and seize areas from which the drive to the north could be launched. For the attack across the island, the boundary between the two Divisions ran from a point about half way between Mount Tenjo and Alutom Mountain, eastward along the Sigua River to its junction with the Pago River; for the attack to the north this boundary turned northeast and bisected the upper half of Guam. At a conference between General Bruce and General Turnage while still at Eniwetok, General Bruce had recommended that the boundary be moved to the west in order that responsibility for certain terrain features would not be divided and, as the 77th was making the main effort of the Corps, to give it more maneuver space. This change was later approved by General Geiger.

Early on the morning of 31 July the 307th Infantry, with the 3d Battalion of the 305th attached, moved out from near Mount Tenio and led the advance east to the Pago River. The 307th Infantry advanced in column of battalions in the order 1st, 3d, and 2d, with the 3d Battalion echeloned to the right rear. Reconnoitering on the right front of the advancing infantry was a patrol from the 77th Reconnaissance Troop, commanded by Corporal John W. Ringer and guided by a native, Jesus Castro. The remainder of the Reconnaissance Troop patrolled and protected the south flank.

The march was a most difficult one and almost entirely across country. The troops initially scaled steep slopes or slid down into narrow gorges. The route then took them along the steep ridges and over the foothills southwest of the central mountain mass of Guam. Vehicles were able to follow part way, but soon the terrain became too rough even for the hardy jeeps. As one infantryman, W. F. Connolly, wrote later:

The distance across the island is not far, as the crow flies, but unluckily we can't fly. The nearest I came to flying was while descending the slippery side of a mountain in a sitting position. After advancing a few yards you find that the handle of the machine gun on your shoulder, your pack and shovel, canteens, knife, and machete all stick out at right angles and are as tenacious in their grip on the surrounding underbrush as a dozen grappling hooks. Straining, sweating and swearing avails you nothing so you decide on a full-bodied lunge — success crowns your efforts as all the entangling encumbrances decide to give up the struggle simultaneously. Just before you hit the ground a low swinging vine breaks your fall by looping itself under your chin, almost decapitating you and snapping your helmet 15 yards to the rear, narrowly missing your lieutenant's head. He glares at you as though he suspected you threw it. What a suspicious nature. You untangle your equipment, retrieve your helmet, and move on. The flies, the mosquitos have discovered your route of march and have called up all the reinforcements including the underfed and undernourished who regard us as nothing but walking blood banks. We continue to push on . . .

Originally, the plan had allowed two days for the movement but because of the complete absence of enemy resistance, and the ability of the infantry to move rapidly despite the rugged route and their heavy burdens, it became apparent by mid-day that the lower Pago River could be reached that night. Orders to press on to the Pago were dropped to the 307th from an artillery liaison plane. Late in the afternoon the 1st and 3d Battalions of the 307th occupied the high ground on the southwest bank of the Pago River, and elements of the 3d Marine Division moved into positions across the river on the left. No serious resistance had been encountered during the day and it was expected that the rapid advance would throw the enemy off balance.

LIBERATION

The "Liberty" Division lived up to its name on this day. While approaching the Pago River, Company L of the 307th came across several Chamorros who told of a native concentration camp near Asinan. The natives guided patrols to the camp where 2,000 Chamorros were found and freed without delay.

The Chamorros were almost beside themselves with joy. Not sure of whether to kiss their liberators, bow to them, or shake hands, they tried to do all three at once. Many produced tiny American flags they had hidden from the Japanese until the day of liberation. "We wait long time for you to come," was frequently repeated; but their faith in the return of the Americans had seemingly never faltered. "We were told by the Japanese that the U.S.A. was being defeated, that Japan had control of the Hawaiian Islands, and the Americans had only one ship left, as the rest had been sunk," one reported scornfully.

The weary troops were immensely moved by the jubilant natives as they passed through the lines. Men who had been complaining because rations with more cigarettes had not come up, now eagerly passed out what few they had. Soldiers with packs watched with awe as children carried huge baskets and women trudged along happily with half their household possessions on their backs. Most of the women were shy, but one remarked to a digging infantryman, "Jap soldier dig much deeper hole than American soldier." Although many of the native men were suffering from malnutrition, torture, and the hardships of the concentration camp, they begged to be allowed to accompany the troops. Others requested permission to dig foxholes for the soldiers. As the natives passed more troops coming up, the good cheer spread; at times men had to be prodded on when they stopped to hear about life under the Japanese. For the first time most of the men realized the meaning of the often heard expression, "Liberation of enslaved peoples," for they themselves were taking part in the liberation.

SKIRMISH AT YONA

Attached to the 307th Infantry and echeloned to its right during the movement across the island, the 3d Battalion of the 305th advanced toward Pago Bay. This battalion, on the outer flank in the turn to the north, had an even longer distance to cover than the 307th. It was 1730 and almost dark on 31 July when Company I reached the high ground overlooking Pago Bay. This was the objective and an important one, for from Yona an improved road crossed the island to Agana. Japanese troops from the southern part of Guam had made Yona a rendezvous point.

Because of the late hour and the need to find a secure position for the night, Company I, commanded by Captain Lee P. Cothran, moved rapidly along the trail which ran down from the northwest and then curved to enter the town from the southwest. The dense vegetation on both sides of the trail made deployment difficult so the company pushed on in column of platoon columns. The men moved silently, not knowing what they would find.

About 200 yards from a clearing, the leading scouts of the 2d platoon saw two Japanese run across the trail. Just beyond were the grass huts of Yona. The 2d squad was in the lead and opened fire. As the platoon moved forward, small arms fire broke out from the village. A few Japanese could be seen running among the huts. Crawling up the trail the 2d squad reached the clearing in the face of scattered fire from the huts and from pillboxes which were now visible. The 1st squad came up on the right and the 3d on the left.

The Japanese evidently were surprised by the attack. Some of them ran out of the buildings half dressed, and made off for the brush. Others fired from dugouts and buildings, and then waited stolidly to be killed. One jumped out of a dugout and started to run, but he got tangled up in his gas mask and Private Edward Stiltner shot him "right where his galluses would have crossed."

As the 2d Platoon moved through the village the men went about their work systematically, grenading buildings and shooting down their occupants. The Japanese would not surrender. Staff Sergeant Chester P. Opdyke, Jr., flushed two natives from a dugout and one reported that two Japanese soldiers were still in it. Opdyke ran to the entrance and shouted: "come out with your hands up and your clothes off!" He waited a few moments, then in rapid succession threw in two grenades.

The remainder of Company I joined quickly. The 1st Platoon moved toward the highway on the right to protect the flank and rear of the troops in the village. The 3d went to the left (north) of the 2d. The Weapons Platoon mounted its light machine guns in the forward slope of a small knoll and, shortly after, the heavy machine guns attached from Company M opened fire.

Company K followed Company I directly into Yona and, with this support, the latter pushed rapidly through the village. Small arms and machine gun fire poured into the flimsy huts from which the Japanese could offer only the slightest resistance. As the troops reached the far side of the village, enemy soldiers fled into the jungle just beyond. They left behind a considerable supply of hand grenades, small arms, and ammunition. One of the buildings had obviously been used as a barracks. The natives stated that Yona had been a supply center and garrison for several hundred soldiers.

It was now dark and the 3d Battalion of the 305th had to push on quickly and seize a position for the night. About a half mile toward Pago Bay a defensive position was organized on a hill overlooking the bay. It was late, the hard coral made it almost impossible to dig adequate fox holes, and a wide gap lay between the battalion and the 307th. The troops spent an uneasy night.

THE REAR ECHELON

While the 307th Infantry Regiment moved across the island and prepared for the attack to the north, intense activity went on all the way back to the beaches. The Division was now entering a critical phase and would require complete support from all services behind the lines.

There was no road across the island in the Division zone and the construction of a main supply route extending from south of Mount Tenjo to Yona and Pago Bay had been planned. Companies A and C of the 302d Engineer Battalion started reconnoitering a route for this road even in advance of the troops. Other Engineers worked on roads within the beachhead. These soon became deeply rutted and required maintenance day and night.

All nature seemed to combine against the construction of a main supply route across the island. Heavy rains contributed to make completed sections of it a quagmire. It was almost impossible to find crossings over some of the deep, narrow, rocky ravines, and finally one such gorge was encountered which was impossible to bridge, go around, or cut approaches through in the time available. A few "jeeps" got through, dragged by bulldozers, but it was obvious that by the time the road could be made to take loaded 2 1/2-ton trucks and artillery, the need for it would have ceased to exist.

Fortunately, a solution was at hand. Arrangements were made with the 3d Division to use its main supply route up the west coast to Agana and then east over the road which crossed the island to Pago Bay.

General Bruce said later of this use of one road by two Divisions: "Some books would say it can't be done, but on Guam it was done — it had to be." First, the eastern section of the road across the island in the zone of the 77th had to be captured and cleared of the enemy. After that was accomplished on 1 August, supply and evacuation were carried on by using all available transportation and keeping it on the move day and night.

In sniper-infested country vehicles ground over the road at night with their lights on. The absence of air attacks and the extremely poor use by the enemy of his available artillery made this possible.

The Engineers had other work besides the highly important one of building and maintaining roads. On 26 July they had established their first water point on the Harmon Road along a four-inch pipe line which ran to Agat from a large reservoir in the hills. Another water point was established along the same pipe line about 300 yards north of the first, and produced as high as 25,000 gallons daily. These points were adequate as long as the troops remained on the west side of the island.

The medical troops had been busily engaged in carrying on their functions. Company aid men had landed with their companies; battalion and regimental medical sections and collecting platoons were ashore soon after. All aid station equipment and supplies needed during the first few days had been carried in on packboards. Medical vehicles were slow in arriving on the beach, however, and this had hindered the evacuation of casualties during the first few days of the operation. When the "jeep" ambulances did arrive, casualties were evacuated directly from battalion aid stations and were usually in a place of definitive treatment thirty to ninety minutes after being wounded.

Within a week the Clearing Company of the 302d Medical Battalion, and the attached 95th Portable Surgical and 36th Field Hospitals were all in operation. However, the loss of supplies and equipment on the beach seriously affected their operations. The 302d Medical Battalion had lost twenty percent of its supplies. The clearing company lost 94 out of 150 cots, mainly from looting on the beach, and the Portable Surgical Hospital lost 61 out of 75. X-ray and laboratory equipment and one washing machine were also missing. Here again field expedients were made to serve.

The chaplains of the 77th kept busy at the front and in the rear alike. Some had the distasteful job of working with the Graves Registration units at the cemetery at Agat, and later at Agana. Others worked at the hospitals, ministering to the sick and wounded. Most of the chaplains, however, were with the troops and lived with them in the jungle, the rain, and the mud, sharing their discomforts and dangers. The chaplains soon realized that they were no more immune to Japanese attacks than any other soldiers, especially at night. One chaplain wrote:

On watch . . . each one of us is responsible for the lives in our area and we must be ready to defend them. I wonder what your thoughts would be if you could see me crouched each night in my hole, with a gun in one hand, extra clips by my side, and knife in the other, the latter to be used in close combat. I assure you I had no qualms about using either weapon if necessity warranted it.

PURSUIT TO THE NORTH

Where was the enemy?

Apart from the resistance at Yona, the Division had met only small disorganized groups of Japanese during its advance across the waist of the island. Intelligence officers expected to find well defended installations on the north side of the Pago River, but patrols returned with negative reports. Intelligence reports indicated that the enemy 38th Infantry Regiment (less

3d Battalion) and all naval organizations on Orote Peninsula had been destroyed. Elements of other Japanese units on the island had been wiped out in the preliminary bombardment or in later fighting. It was clear, nevertheless, that many Japanese troops remained and were assembling in the northeast. Where would the enemy make a stand?

Information was coming in from many sources. Interrogation of natives and negative reports from patrols indicated that the enemy must be preparing his stand farther north, probably near the town of Barrigada in the 77th's zone of advance. If the capture of Orote and the fast movement across the island had thrown the Japanese off balance, as seemed likely, then he must be kept off balance. From a tactical point of view, the situation on the night of 31 July changed from an attack to a pursuit. The enemy must not be given time to organize and prepare defenses in the northern part of the island. The initiative must remain in American hands.

There was another almost equally important reason for a rapid advance at this stage. The supply situation could become critical. The attempt to open a main supply route across the country had to be given up. It was imperative to capture the Agana-Pago Bay Road without delay so that all types of supplies could be brought up on the Agat-Agana-Pago Bay Road.

At daylight on 1 August the 1st and 3d Battalions of the 307th Infantry crossed the Pago River on a broad front, advanced across country and reached the Agana-Pago Bay Road before noon. Company K captured the bridge over the Pago and sent a platoon over it to the far side. The bridge was mined with four 250 pound aerial bombs, but the wire running from the heads of the bombs had been broken. Companies K and I continued to the north, the former leaving one platoon with heavy machine guns to guard the bridge. When a soldier was seen by Staff Sergeant Donald Simmons coming up the road he shouted, "Keep moving!" the figure kept moving, but now he had a rifle pointed at Sergeant Simmons who gave him a burst from the hip and the Japanese soldier ran off into the brush.

As usual, the infantrymen were unaware of the fact that they were now in pursuit, and of other tactical aspects of the advance but they were very much aware of their hunger, thirst, and general weariness. As usual, they pushed on and, as usual they worked out their field expedients. Lacking pure water, they drank coconut milk. Halazone tablets made the brackish water of the creeks at least drinkable, if not pleasant. The canned salmon abandoned by the retreating Japanese helped keep them going.

Rear elements of the 305th, passing through Yona during the day, made a lucky find. In some huts were cigarettes, sake, and — reportedly — some Canadian Club. The sake was not very palatable, but the thirsty men quickly worked out a good recipe: they mixed a pint of it with three packages of synthetic lemon powder and two lumps of sugar from their K rations and had what tasted like a wartime Tom Collins. Strawberry gumdrops tasted good, but the canned octopus was not very popular. Carrying out the idea of pursuit, as soon as the news of the capture of the Agana-Pago road was flashed to Division Headquarters, artillery, tanks and supplies were started by the roundabout Agat-Agana route through the 3d Marine Division sector. The military police of both divisions working side by side at each key point kept vehicles moving in accordance with agreed priorities. Lieutenant Colonel Henry O'Brien, Division Quartermaster, personally led the first convoy of supply trucks eastward from Agana to meet the advancing troops and establish advance supply dumps.

Instead of trying to maintain a wire line across jungle country which had not been mopped up it was decided to also abandon that project with the road project and start wire from a new Division Command Post. The Division Commander, too, had to be forward in the pursuit.

There wasn't time to establish a new Command Post that day. Consequently he, with Major Koepcke, Assistant G-3, Major Meyers, Assistant G-2 and Major Davis, S-3 of the Division Artillery with a small communications detail, were among the first to use the new route through Agana and to proceed east along a road which it was hoped that the 307th had captured. En route they met Colonel Hamilton and while discussing the situation found that he had been refusing all day to be evacuated for illness. The Division Commander found him too ill to go on and ordered his evacuation despite his protests and placed Lieutenant Colonel Thomas B. Manuel in command of the 307th Infantry.

Continuing on, the Divisional party went on the road running north toward San Antonio and Barrigada in the 305th Infantry zone of action. En route "pursuit" decisions for hasty artillery positions, a site for the clearing company and areas for elements of the 306th Infantry in Division reserve were made to gather up the Division for another push the next day.

Arriving at the command post of the 305th Infantry on the evening of 1 August, the Divisional party found that the 1st and 2d Battalions, 305th Infantry, occupied positions a mile and a half northeast of RJ 171 and the 307th extended its left in a northerly direction. General Bruce decided to spend 'the night by the Command Post of the 305th Infantry and the party started to dig foxholes for their "visit." Later it was reported there were no suitable trails to get rations to the forward elements of the 307th Infantry. The men had started their march across the island with light rations to save weight on an arduous trip and now were out of rations. Permission was asked for a delay in the advance the next day in order to hand-carry rations up to the front. General Bruce pointed out that the pursuit must go on, and that it would be quicker and less labor to bring rations by trucks on a road in the 305th zone that led to Barrigada and curved in front of and not far from the front lines of the 307th. He ended the conference by saying in effect, "Attack, capture that road, and you'll get your breakfast."

Chapter 9
Barrigada: The Fight for Water

THE 307th on the 2d of August captured their road and during the reorganization period rations and water arrived and the men had their breakfast. Meanwhile, more "pursuit" decisions were made soon after daylight by the Division Commander's party during the reconnaissance of the forward areas. For example, the Division CP site was selected about 300 yards from the existing front line and a dump site for supplies was selected 150 yards from the line so that as the pursuit progressed they would not be too far behind when they were established that day.

The Division had its own special reasons for wishing to press the pursuit and to capture the village of Barrigada quickly. In the center of the settlement was a deep well and pump. The 20,000 gallons of water which this well could supply daily to the thirsty troops was badly needed. Since leaving the water points near Agat, the men had individually purified water taken from muddy streams. But the northern half of Guam had very few streams; its sub-surface coral quickly absorbed the heaviest rainfalls.

TANK RECONNAISSANCE
Meanwhile, early in the morning the light tanks of Company D, 706th Tank Battalion moved rapidly up the road toward Barrigada and drew

small arms fire from the outskirts of the village. It was difficult to discover the source of the fire, but the tanks machine-gunned suspected areas and withdrew. General Bruce promptly ordered them forward again. Reaching Barrigada by 0840, the twelve light tanks according to plan turned left toward Finegayan, passing an empty pill-box at the road junction. Five hundred yards up the road, where it entered thick jungle, the Japanese had erected a flimsy road block, but the tanks easily by-passed this and kept on, sweeping the jungle with machine gun and canister fire. When almost abreast of Mount Barrigada on their right, they encountered three enemy trucks blocking the road with several Japanese behind them. The leading tanks poured machine gun and 37mm fire into the trucks, demolishing them and killing the Japanese.

Returning to the village, they turned northwest. The jungle was very dense and they were completely roadbound. A few hundred yards from the road junction one tank hung up on a stump, stopping the rest of the column. At once the jungle on each side of the road seemed to come alive and the fire from 20mm guns and machine guns lashed the sides of the tanks while Japanese soldiers crawled forward with grenades.

The tanks protected each other. Enemy soldiers were able to throw grenades from the dense vegetation along the road, but when one tried to climb a tank, the tank behind shot him off. Heavy fire was poured into the jungle and the enemy fire began to decrease. Meanwhile, the tank on the stump worked itself free. Over the radio the company commander, Captain Leonard H. Seegar asked:

"Can I come home?"

"Why?" demanded G-2.

"Damn-it-to-hell," yelled the captain, "there are a hundred and fifty Japs trying to climb on my tanks. They've got grenades, machine guns, and a 20mm gun. Can I come home?"

"Come home," the answer came back.

THE INFANTRY MOVES UP

During the tank reconnaissance, the 3d Battalion of the 305th was approaching the southern edge of the village of Barrigada. In the lead was Company I with Sergeant Opdyke's squad of the 2d Platoon as point. Two scouts, Privates John Andzelik and Salvatore Capobianco, preceded the point. Following, in squad columns, was the remainder of the company with its attached heavy machine guns in the center. Several hundred yards behind, the battalion followed.

About 0930, as the point came out on open ground the men saw the buildings of the village only 300 yards to the left. A long reservoir and a two-story temple were clearly visible, but only the roofs of the other buildings could be seen as the ground sloped down toward the woods beyond. All was quiet, but Andzelik saw three Japanese soldiers cross a trail 300 yards ahead. Sergeant Opdyke halted his point and sent men to investigate and check to the right. They had moved only a few yards when fire broke out from ahead and Private Andzelik was killed instantly; Capobianco was struck in the arm and leg.

The fire increased and seemed to come from the left front and the front. It was difficult to determine its source. Sergeant Opdyke started off toward the shack on the right, only to be stopped by a bullet in his arm. Others of the point were hit as they ran to cover. The two squads of the advance party came up on each flank of the point and formed a skirmish line in a slight defilade. Captain Lee Cothran, commanding Company I, came forward and moved up the 1st Platoon to the right in a more covered area, but it had trouble deploying because of the heavy fire.

Second Lieutenant Edward C. Harper, commanding the 1st Platoon, now attempted to advance his men across a small open draw to get around the enemy's flank. Some managed to advance and others were starting when machine gun fire broke out from the left. Private Arthur Haberman almost reached the other side when he was killed. Staff Sergeant William Hunt fell mortally wounded. Private George McKilroy almost got back out of the draw when he was dropped with a bullet through his heart. Company I was stopped. Snipers seemed to be all around. Taking the place of a wounded machine gunner, Private Edwin O'Brien picked up the smoking gun, cradled it in his arm, and poured fire into a tree almost directly above him. Down tumbled the sniper who had shot the gunner. Other companies of the battalion made slow progress moving up on the right because of the enemy fire and the difficult terrain. The 307th was moving up on the left.

THE CASE OF THE WRONG AZIMUTH

The 307th had reorganized a mile from Barrigada and resumed its advance at 1030 with the two battalions abreast. On the far left, keeping contact with the right of the 3d Marine Division, was Company A, which tied in with Company L to its right. Between Company L and the 305th was Company K.

The direction of advance, an azimuth of 45 degrees, would bring Companies L and K directly against the village and place the 1st Battalion in position to flank it from the west. Rifle fire held up Company A southwest of Barrigada. Company C found its zone clear and moved beyond and to the northwest of the village. Company A got started again but veered too far to the right.

Contact with Company C was never regained that day. That company ended up in the woods northwest and north of the village, harassed by snipers and friendly artillery fire. By closing in on the 3d Battalion, Company A collided with Company L, which in turn gave way toward the 305th. Company L succeeded in maintaining most of its front, but at the expense of Company K to its right rear which was squeezed out. These three companies were crowded into a frontage insufficient for two, and their full strength and fire power were never brought to bear.

But most dangerous of all was the gap which was created between Company C, far to the left, and Company A. It was a thousand yards wide and opposite some of the strongest enemy positions, positions which all day continued to place deadly flanking fire on the attacking troops.

Taking advantage of a very slight defilade, the squads of Company A reached a line along the pumphouse and temple. As members of the 2d Platoon moved around to the right of the temple they ran into men of Company L, which was advancing by a series of rushes. The leader of its 1st Platoon, Lieutenant Michael J. Sterling, fell with several bullet wounds.

Having lost contact with his battalion commander, Lieutenant Colonel Joseph B. Coolidge, who had accompanied Company C, Major Gerald G. Cooney, the Battalion Executive Officer, assumed command. His left flank lay dangerously open and Company A and the 3d Battalion to his right had been stopped. Major Cooney committed Company B on his left. Its 2d Platoon, under Lieutenant Willis J. Munger, was moving up on the left rear of Company A. Its advance would take it diagonally across a large field stretching toward the Finegayan-Barrigada Road. Lieutenant Munger's objective was a two story green house with a concrete base, and it appeared to be a good position. By short rushes of two or three men at a time the platoon crossed the field. The men were starting across the road when an enemy machine gun opened up from the woods just beyond the green house.

At this time the machine gunners and mortar observers near the temple finally located a target — a grass shack from which fire had been coming. They opened fire, the shack burst into flames, and a Japanese medium tank crawled out and sped down the road toward the troops. Three Japanese riding on top were quickly knocked off as machine guns, automatic rifles and rifles opened up. But the tank itself gained speed and raked with its machine gun and cannon everything it passed. At the road junction it turned right and stopped. Ahead of it and in plain view was the 2d Platoon of Company B. Several men made a dash for the green house while others lay prone to escape both enemy and friendly fire. One man was killed and two others wounded. The tank turned back and headed toward a heavy machine gun at the corner of the temple. It crashed into the building, slowed to a stop, changed gears, and forced its way through the side of the structure. Private John E. Raley, the machine gunner, stuck to his post and the tracks of the tank missed him by a foot. It emerged, blinded by a piece of thatch over its vision slit, but continued on and overran another machine gun position.

The tank was in the midst of the battle and receiving concentrated fire from every weapon which could be brought to bear. Stalled on a coconut log its tracks kept revolving and its guns firing. It backed off, shook off the thatch, and raced down the road where it ran through a battalion aid station, a battalion command post, and the 307th Regimental Command Post in rapid succession, its guns still firing.

The tank left a chaotic situation behind it. Formations were more disorganized than ever. Fortunately the enemy failed to follow up his lone tank attack with an infantry advance.

Worst off of all at the moment, were the men of Company B who had sought refuge in the green house. From a pillbox twenty yards away and from other positions in the woods, bursts of fire tore through the upper part of the structure. The men were cut off. One automatic rifleman was shot as he fired through a window. The concrete walls around the lower part of the building stopped small arms fire, but the men realized that they had no protection against mortars or artillery.

"Anyone who wants to go can leave: I wouldn't blame you," Lieutenant Munger said, "but I'm sticking." Sergeant Charles J. Kunze volunteered to go back for assistance. He sprinted from the house to the road, dived into the ditch, crawled through a culvert, and ran across the exposed field to Captain Frank L. Vernon who commanded Company B. He poured out his story and made the perilous trip back to the besieged men. They were to withdraw and Company A would cover them.

Just as Sergeant Kunze returned, several heavy explosions rocked the house. The men dashed out, dropped into ditches, and then plunged on. As he crossed the open field for the fourth time that day, Sergeant Kunze was hit. Lieutenant Munger was killed as he dashed from the house.

Almost all of Company A, covering the withdrawal of the men from the green house, fell back in the face of artillery fire; but Privates Alfred A. Pucci and Stanley J. Mrowka, an automatic rifle team, remained in their position despite shells falling; within twenty feet. Machine gunner John E. Raley was hit, but he continued to fire so that litter bearers could evacuate the wounded over the open ground. As the last wounded man was carried to the rear, Private First Class Raley started back and was killed.

TANK SUPPORT ON THE RIGHT

With the bloody repulse of Company B, the nature of the enemy defense was becoming clearer. Nests of machine guns, riflemen, and at least one 20mm gun covered the road running east from Barrigada. It was these which had caused the light tanks trouble in the morning, and which later had stopped the attack in the center. Another series of enemy positions were along the woods on the northeast side of the Finegayan Road. It was fire from these positions which had stopped Company B on the left. Over to the right the 305th was still engaged with machine guns and snipers. Everywhere the Japanese were superbly concealed and camouflaged.

The positions the troops had stumbled into were far from advantageous. Three companies — A, L and K of the 307th — were jammed together in the center where the enemy was the strongest. To the left was a huge gap. Beyond the gap was Company C, out of contact and unaware of the situation of any other unit.

At 1330 Company K, 305th Infantry attacked on the right of Company I. Attached to Company K were five light tanks. They were used because the medium tanks were still moving up along the Agat-Agana route. The mediums had had difficulty in moving out of their muddy area near Mount Tenjo and had found it necessary to check all bridge capacities before using them. Company K advanced until it was parallel with the lower end of the draw where Company I had been stopped in the morning. Cautiously the tanks crawled across the draw. Each tank had infantrymen around it for close-in protection; directly behind were two platoons of Company K. Four tanks and part of Company K crossed the draw without incident. Just as the last tank was crossing, machine gun and artillery fire opened up from the left. Bullets and shell fragments ricocheted off the side of the tank. Sergeant Dexter W. Berry was killed and two others were wounded. The men beyond the draw kept out of the line of fire by lying in the brush but Private Glendon C. Gray continued advancing and was killed. The tanks returned the fire but it was hard to find a target and their shots did not seem to have much effect. Soon they pulled back to a less exposed position but the foot soldiers remained, not daring to move either forward or back. Lieutenant Colonel Edward Chalgren, Jr., commanding the 3d Battalion of the 305th held a hurried conference. Lieutenant Harper of Company I, whose platoon had been stopped in the draw that morning, volunteered to direct a tank to a position from which fire was coming. He had previously crawled under fire close to the position and reconnoitered it.

Lieutenant Harper climbed into Lieutenant Charles J. Fuchs's tank and it moved up the draw. The tank got to within five yards of the position and poured machine gun fire into it through the leaves and brush. Then an enemy gun opened up. In rapid succession it scored hits on the trailing idler, the drive shaft, and one through the side which missed Lieutenant Harper by six inches. The tank could not move forward; when it backed up the track dropped off. Lieutenant Harper and the crew tumbled out and ran back to cover.

Another advance had been stopped in the draw. The enemy seemed able to absorb any amount of fire. The men across the draw were ordered back, but Private Robert Slauson was mortally wounded during the withdrawal. It was impossible to adjust artillery fire because the situation was so confused, no one knew where other units were in the jungle.

Help was on the way in the form of a platoon of medium tanks. These finally arrived on the scene after the long trip from Mount Tenjo. Again Lieutenant Harper volunteered to conduct them. The tanks moved out four abreast, their cannon and machine guns pounding and tearing into the Japanese positions. A 75mm shell knocked off a bit of camouflage and squatting in the underbrush was a Japanese tank.

"Is that a tank?" an excited crew member shouted over the radio.

"Hell yes!" was the answer.

"Ours?"

"No!"

Gun fire quickly destroyed it.

It was now dusk and too late to follow up the attack. Off to the right Companies A and B of the 305th came up late in the afternoon. With the aid of medium tanks they had made steady progress in a wide enveloping movement, but darkness closed in before they could capitalize on it by an attack on the main enemy positions near the road leading northeast from the village. Company L of the 305th reconnoitered the jungle between the regiment and the east coast without encountering the enemy in any strength.

LAST TRY ON THE LEFT

While the 1st and 3rd Battalions of the 307th were fighting at Barrigada, the 2d Battalion was approaching from the southwest with Company G in the lead. The Japanese tank which had broken free advanced rapidly on Company G, its guns still spitting fire. A "bazooka" shell struck it but failed to explode, rifle fire had no effect. The tank kept on down the road with two light tanks in close pursuit. Company G approached the left rear of Company A. The men from Company B were withdrawing from the green house. To the left lay the large open field between the Finegayan and Agana roads.

Lieutenant Colonel Joseph B. Coolidge, commanding the 1st Battalion of the 307th, had returned to his command post late in the afternoon. He had made the long trip back from Company C to find his battalion stopped before Barrigada. Word came from the Regimental Command Post that the 2d Battalion was moving up to attack on the left of the 1st Battalion and close the gap between it and Company C. Soon after, Lieutenant Colonel Charles F. Learner, commanding the 2d Battalion, appeared at the 1st Battalion command post and Lieutenant Colonel Coolidge informed him that he was about to send tanks to the green house to cover the evacuation of the wounded. The latter offered to send men from Company G to protect the tanks. After the tanks reached the road junction they turned left toward the green house and opened fire on the woods beyond.

Lieutenant Robert C. Smith, commanding the 2d Platoon of Company G was ordered to move his platoon up on the left and Captain Vernon pointed out to him the area to which Company G was to move. By a series of squad rushes Lieutenant Smith worked his platoon up the protected side of a low rise in front of him. At the top it received rifle fire. A messenger from company headquarters told Lieutenant Smith he was to follow the tanks in. He moved his platoon toward the tanks by a series of rushes under heavy fire. One squad worked its way to the right where the tanks were firing on the green house and the woods beyond. The fire seemed to silence the enemy beyond the house. On the left Sergeant William J. Ganter was killed while directing his squad.

The 1st Platoon of Company G was also in action now. Its leader, Lieutenant Whitney, had been ordered by Captain Gannon to move up on the left of the 2nd Platoon. Just as it started to cross the open field, the tanks began to pull back. Their departure was a signal for the Japanese. From the woods across the field to the left, machine guns and rifles opened fire. Some of Lieutenant Whitney's men hit the ground, others tried to reach the Finegayan road, but they never made it. Finally they groped for cover in the open field; some found shell holes but most lay in the short grass, exposed to the fire.

The same fire hit Lieutenant Smith's platoon. A machine gun opened up from beyond the green house and two men volunteered and were directed into the house. Four men tried to go around the right and were hit. Captain Gannon, while following the platoon in its advance, was wounded in the leg and dragged to cover. Staff Sergeant Edward E. Whittemore volunteered to go back across the open field for help, just as Sergeant Kunze had done earlier in the day. The 3d Platoon of Company G, under Lieutenant Walter E. Seibert, Jr., advanced rapidly across the field. After crossing the road on the left of the green house it received heavy fire from the woods on the left.

Under Sergeant Whittemores direction heavy machine guns from Company H moved forward under fire to give support. He also ordered 81mm mortar fire on the woods from which the enemy had all day flanked the troops, but the fire order was countermanded because battalion headquarters still did not know the location of Company C.

Despite the heavy fire from his left, Lieutenant Seibert was afraid to fire on the woods across the field because he had no idea where the 1st Platoon had gotten to. He did not know that it was being annihilated by Japanese fire from those very woods.

Lieutenant Garret V. Richards had assumed command of Company G. When informed by Sergeant Whittemore that the 2d Platoon had suffered heavy casualties he obtained tanks from the battalion commander to cover the evacuation of the wounded. Lieutenant Smith received orders to withdraw and the Japanese sprayed the depleted platoon with small arms fire, but there were few casualties. All of the wounded men were brought back except one who could not be located and lay all night near the green house.

Over on the left the 1st Platoon was in desperate straits. It was deployed across the field and the enemy was entrenched in positions dug into a bank just inside the woods on its left flank. The enemy could see every move and had the platoon enfiladed perfectly. The only men who escaped being hit were those who found some sort of a hole in the field. But over half of the men lay there helpless. One by one they were picked off. Finally tanks arrived, covered them from the right, and sprayed the woods. The tanks beat down some of the fire while those who were wounded were evacuated and the few who were not, withdrew. Lieutenant Colonel Coolidge was hit while directing the evacuation, as were several others. The platoon had suffered 26 casualties, most of them killed. Its 1st squad alone lost 8 killed and one wounded out of 13 men. Lieutenant Whitney was dead. During the day the 307th had suffered 22 killed and 63 wounded, while the 305th had lost 7 killed and 35 wounded.

As darkness closed, Company E of the 307th pulled out to the far left, found the road from Finegayan which ran south to Barrigada and started down it to take the enemy from the rear; but darkness and sniper fire held it up.

All along the line of the 307th and the 305th units dug in for the night. The 2d of August had been a day of frustration. Few men had even seen the enemy, so well concealed were his positions. Throughout the day great courage but little tactical skill had been demonstrated. The night was quiet. The capture of Barrigada the next day was anticlimactic. The Japanese had had enough. Very few had been seen or located but the troops had covered the area with very heavy fire and the enemy was badly hurt. During the night of 2-3 August he evacuated his dead and wounded and withdrew. The next morning our troops passed through the quiet village. The 302nd Engineers arrived, jacked up a jeep for a power plant, improvised a belt from Japanese fire hose, and started the precious water flowing.

Chapter 10
Pursuit Through the Jungle

THE NEXT four days were trying ones for the Division. Tropical downpours occurred every day and never before had the wet, muddy, infantrymen encountered such brush and jungle. Trails faded out; others represented on the map were never found; new ones had to be cut through the trees, vines, and roots. Steaming heat alternated with the drenching rains. At night, when the men most needed warmth, they sat in flooded foxholes, their teeth chattering; during the day their mud-encrusted uniforms remained wet with sweat. Mosquitoes tormented them at night and flies took over with the coming of dawn. And always the mud: helmets, uniforms, equipment, and their skins took on the color of Guam's soil — a dirty red.

The village of Barrigada had been captured, and the 3d Marine Division had taken the Tiyan air strip on the same day — 2 August. The precious water was in our hands, the Japanese had overlooked blowing up the pump or destroying the well. Officers and men began to worry about a night Banzai attack. They had heard of the wild charge of over 5,000 frenzied Japanese on Saipan. The Japanese on Guam, squeezed into the northern end of the island, were now in a somewhat similar plight. G-2 estimated that the enemy had around 4,500 effective troops left. Each night the wet and weary infantrymen in their foxholes said, "This will be it."

The vegetation was so dense that advancing columns often had only a general idea of their location. As a result, coordination with adjacent units and with the artillery was extremely difficult. The maps were not accurate and the few aerial photographs seemed to have been taken when clouds obscured most of the important areas. An excessive number of patrols had to be kept out constantly in an attempt to maintain contact. Columns veered to the right and to the left as they hacked their way through the almost trackless jungle.

Front-line units were often hundreds of yards from where they reported themselves and it was necessary to check their location by artillery fire. Smoke rounds would be placed close to a point which could be seen by the observer. Location of this round would be computed in the artillery fire direction center and sent to the infantry. The registering of night defensive fires, after an all day advance through the jungle, in some instances corrected locations of infantry units as much as 2,000 yards.

There was an unceasing pressure from above to drive on. The troops were again in pursuit and the Corps and Division Commanders demanded that all organizations move rapidly to keep the enemy off balance, even if it meant pushing the men to just short of exhaustion. For the infantry this pressure often meant organizing their night defensive areas too late to dig properly. It meant lack of time to clear lanes of fire through the jungle in order to stop lurking Japanese before they could close to grenade range. Yet the men kept driving ahead, determined to get the job over and realizing that the quicker it was over the better.

The jungle tremendously limited the maneuverability of the Division, the development of its terrific fire power and the opportunities for air strikes. Once the beachheads were won, air support played a very limited role in the operations on Guam. From 22-29 July an average of 212 sorties were flown and an average of seventy-nine tons of bombs were dropped daily. From 30 July through 8 August the daily sorties averaged only fifty and the weight of bombs dropped fell to twenty tons. The destruction of the enemy on Guam became chiefly an infantrymans fight.

During the period 3-6 August the Division advanced on a wide front, following such roads and trails as existed, by-passing scattered groups of the enemy in its search for organized resistance. The 3d Marine Division continued to advance on the left. Because of the jungle there was not a continuous front, but a number of columns pushing forward. The fighting became a series of isolated actions in which small groups of Americans and Japanese became locked in fierce fire fights and bloody hand-to-hand encounters.

CAPTURE OF MOUNT BARRIGADA

Mount Barrigada lay one mile northeast of the village. The Finegayan Road ran to the west of it, and the road east of the village ran south of the mountain where it became only a trail. Almost 700 feet high, Mount Barrigada would, it was hoped, give observation and control over the surrounding flat jungle plain over which the 307th was pushing on the left and the 305th on the right.

The 3d Battalion of the 307th passed through the village early on the morning of 3 August without meeting resistance. Just north of the settlement the advance was slowed down because of the dense undergrowth and scattered rifle fire. Two men were wounded when a burning Japanese ammunition dump exploded as they were passing by. An enemy sniper wounded five men before he could be found and killed in his camouflaged position. The Battalion commander, Lieutenant Colonel John W. Lovell, had to be evacuated.

The mission of the 2d Battalion of the 307th was to advance through Barrigada along the Finegayan Road to the same position which Company E had occupied the previous evening in its abortive attempt to strike the enemy's rear. When it was several hundred yards from Company Es position, three rounds of artillery came over. It looked suspiciously like a registration, so Lieutenant Colonel Learner, the Battalion Commander, telephoned to suspend artillery fire on his front. Just as the battalion arrived at Company E's position ten minutes later, a concentration landed along the trail. Several men were killed and wounded; Lieutenant Colonel Learner was wounded and evacuated. Major Thomas R. Mackin, the executive officer, assumed command. The 307th had now lost its regimental commander and each of its battalion commanders from wounds or illness. Shortly after mid-day the 2d and 3d Battalions of the 307th made a turning movement on the Finegayan Road for an attack on Mount Barrigada to the northeast. The assault troops advanced 200 yards behind artillery concentrations. Tanks led the attack and beat paths through the jungle growth. The frontages of the battalion were too broad for the jungle and units became separated from each other.

The enemy put up scattered resistance on the lower slope of the mountain, but this diminished to occasional sniper fire near the crest. The 3d Battalion reached the summit at 1500 but found itself out of contact with the 2d Battalion. There was a gap of 400 yards between Companies K and L. The 3d Battalion reorganized and sent out patrols to contact the 2d Battalion to its left. The mountain top was covered with dense jungle and offered no observation of surrounding terrain.

The 2d Battalion tried to maintain contact with the Marines on its left but had difficulty in doing so. A tank patrol from Company A of the 706th Tank Battalion was sent to establish contact. Three medium tanks with infantry riding on top moved north. The enemy had left a hastily erected road block which the tanks blew apart with their 75mm guns. Fifty yards beyond on the Finegayan Road, however, the leading tank struck a mine which blew off a track. Immediately Japanese guns opened fire from the brush. The tank crew managed to escape and returned on the other two tanks. Later the mediums returned and destroyed the tank to prevent the Japanese from converting it into a pillbox or making use of its gun.

East of Mount Barrigada the 1st Battalion of the 305th Infantry found that the road it was following became only a narrow trail. The scouts and leading squad of Company A were well into a clearing when they were fired on from their right rear. Company A lost several men killed and wounded in a few seconds. Captain Arthur G. Curtin and Lieutenant John Scullen, 3d Platoon Leader, were wounded as they tried to direct an attack against the unseen enemy. Staff Sergeant John Kane pushed through the brush and fell into a hole, squarely on two Japanese soldiers.

"Bring me a bayonet;" he yelled wildly. One Japanese tried to grab his leg; Kane kicked him in the face, jumped out of the hole, and opened up with his automatic rifle on the occupants. Just as he fired one of the Japanese exploded a grenade between his own face and the others, killing them both.

Staff Sergeant Benjamin Szafasz found an enemy soldier in a brush covered hole. He pitched in a white phosphorus grenade and ran. The Japanese promptly threw it out, but it struck a bush and exploded without harming either Sergeant Szafasz or the enemy soldier.

"Me no wanna die!" the latter wailed.

"Come on out then," the Sergeant yelled. But a hand grenade exploded in the hole: the frightened Japanese had decided to embarrass Sergeant Szafasz by killing himself.

By now Companies B and C of the 305th had become involved in a series of small actions throughout the area. These continued for some time as the troops, through the generous use of grenades and automatic rifle ammunition, finished off hidden enemy in the brush. Medium tanks helped to make trails so that troops could approach the enemy from the rear.

The 1st Battalion tied in for the night with the 2d on its right. Some progress had been made during the day, but the 305th was not yet abreast of Mount Barrigada.

PRESSING THE ADVANCE: 4 AUGUST

The 3d Battalion of the 307th completed its capture of Mount Barrigada on 4 August and, at 1300, pushed on to the northeast toward Yigo against little opposition. The 1st Battalion of the 307th relieved the 2d during the day. Medium tanks were used to break trail, but it was a heavy strain on their engines, which were not built to smash down trees hour after hour. At 1700 the assault battalions of the 307th dug in astride a trail a little over a half mile northwest of Mount Barrigada.

The 307th made contact with the Marines on the left during the day, but with unfortunate results. A section of tanks with infantry aboard started off toward the right flank of the 3d Division. Two Japanese roadblocks were successfully overcome and when they encountered a third the tanks were quick to open fire. Suddenly a man, waving his hands, came running up the trail. This was a Marine position. Somehow they had not heard of the arrangement for using colored grenades for friendly identification. Five men had been wounded.

The 1st Battalion was leading the advance of the 305th, with tanks preceding it, one on each side of the trail beating down the jungle growth and reconnoitering occasional clearings. Riflemen accompanied the tanks. Another tank fifty yards behind was in support.

At 1300 the head of the column halted at a bend in the trail. Lieutenant Colonel Landrum went forward and found Captain Frank E. Barron, commanding Company C, at the bend in the trail. Troops and tanks were congested there. Just then a member of Company C, forty feet in rear noticed a Japanese soldier lying in the jungle and shot him. The battalion commander remarked to Captain Barron, "This looks like an ambush." Then he saw an enemy soldier on the ground in a clearing a short distance away. Before the Japanese could raise his rifle, Lieutenant Colonel Landrum shot and killed him with his carbine.

"This is an ambush!" he exclaimed, moving back down the trail. The men were already hitting the ground as fire came in from the jungle on both sides. From the woods at the bend, where they enfiladed the trail, the Japanese opened fire. It was almost impossible to locate the enemy in the tangled vegetation although some were less than ten feet away.

Farther back other elements of Company C quickly deployed and crawled through the woods where they would be on equal terms with the enemy. The 2d Platoon circled to the left and came in on the enemy positions from the rear. The Japanese were not dug in and were quickly killed. A heavy and a light machine gun were captured at the bend of the trail. For so small an affair this skirmish was expensive. Company C lost four men killed and nine wounded, most of them at the bend. Captain Barron and a platoon leader were wounded. Company G of the 305th suffered casualties during the day in a wild hand-to-hand melee with Japanese hidden along its trail.

To the right of the 305th were the high cliffs along the extremely rugged east coast of Guam. The 77th Reconnaissance Troop had been given the mission of patrolling between the 305th Infantry and the sea. Its platoons were rotated in this mission. The terrain was more dangerous and difficult than the few scattered Japanese. Men came back from two days of patrolling exhausted, almost naked and with bleeding feet. The brush tore their clothes and the coral ripped leather to shreds.

It was about 1800 when the battalions of the 305th organized their night defensive positions. The regiment was well beyond Barrigada, but the weary troops knew little of their position; they wanted only a few hours of sleep which they hoped the night would permit. A member of the 2d Battalion wrote later:

Time marches on, and so do you. The rain continues to fall intermittently, only more so. Just before dark we reached a large clearing where well dig in for the night. Our places are assigned to us and I've drawn a lovely spot, about fifteen yards from the edge of the jungle. The first five inches of mud makes pretty tough digging but underneath there's a layer of coral and limestone rock. Frenzied hammering with the pick does nothing but wear down the pick and scatter white powder around the hole to make it stand out as though spotlighted.

ENTRANCE OF THE 306th INFANTRY: 5-6 AUGUST

From Mount Barrigada to the northern tip of Guam the island broadens out. This widening of the front required that additional organizations be placed in the line. Furthermore, the Division had made a wheeling movement to the right to capture Yigo. On 5 August the 306th Infantry was moved across the right and front of the 307th and given a zone of action on the left of the Division. After a day of rest the 307th side-slipped to the center, between the 306th on the left and the 305th on the right. Two days later, on 7 August, the 1st Provisional Marine Brigade was given a zone of action on the left of the 3d Marine Division.

This was the first opportunity the 306th had had to participate in the offensive operations. After its landing on 23 July it spent the following eight days defending the southern part of the southern beachhead. On 1 August it made the hard march across the island. During 2-4 August it moved up behind the leading regiments.

The movement of the 306th on 5 August to pinch out the 307th was a difficult one. It required several major changes in direction and involved the same difficulties the other organizations had met: dense jungles, poor or non-existent trails, and inaccurate maps. On reaching the Finegayan-Yigo Road at a point three miles southwest of Yigo, the 1st and 3d Battalions began to encounter small by-passed groups of the enemy.

Company A was hard hit in one such encounter. For two hours and a half it battled fifty Japanese who had attempted to stage an ambush on the road. For a time the company checked the enemy fire, but the Japanese filtered through the jungle and launched another attack behind heavy machine gun fire and a barrage of grenades. Sergeant Henry J. Drisch was killed by a grenade. For a time the mortar and headquarters sections were cut off from the rest of the company. The company was finally able to rout the Japanese at a cost of 3 killed and 7 wounded. Nineteen dead Japanese were counted.

The 1st Battalion of the 306th spent the night of 5 August fighting off infiltrators in heavy rain. In front of one machine gun position 12 enemy dead lay the next morning. Soon after moving out from near RJ 363, a tank ran over a mine and lost a track. A little farther up the trail the leading scout, Private Henry J. DeFilippo of Company B, came upon several Japanese. They were drying their shirts on trees. Private DeFilippo killed three of them and returned to report. Going forward again he came under heavy fire and was killed. Company B suffered six more casualties while waiting for machine guns, mortars and tanks to move forward through the thick vegetation. Thirty-eight Japanese were killed and others were scattered. The battalion continued north but the trail ended: the men made the last half mile by hacking their way through the jungle and breaking up coral so that vehicles could follow.

It fell to the 3d Battalion of the 306th to give clear-cut demonstration of how to use tanks and infantry to reduce a position. This battalion, commanded by Lieutenant Colonel Gordon T. Kimbrell, had developed, in conjunction with the 706th Tank Battalion, the Division's Standing Operating Procedure on tank-infantry co-ordination. The plan called for the attached tank platoon to advance with the support elements of the leading company: one just off the trail on one side, another echeloned twenty to thirty yards to the rear in the brush on the other side of the trail; the three remaining tanks of the platoon to follow about a hundred yards in rear. This formation was designed to enable the tanks to support one another if an anti-tank weapon was encountered; to keep the leading tanks out of the center of the trail; and to widen it for the foot troops. Infantrymen protected each tank from Japanese who might try to rush it with grenades or heavy charges. One moved in front, guiding it around holes and large stumps, and watching for mines. Fundamental in the plan was that foot soldiers should precede the tanks and not merely follow them into action.

This carefully planned teamwork brought excellent results on 6 August. On the Finegayan Road, two miles southwest of the village of Yigo, the leading scout of Company I observed the muzzle of a 47mm gun protruding from the brush about ten yards in front of him. Quietly he halted the column and reported back to Lieutenant William P. DeBrocke, his platoon leader. Lieutenant DeBrocke skillfully moved his platoon to within thirty yards of the enemy gun and a medium tank was brought up.

So well concealed was the enemy gun under its blue-green camouflage net that the first tank was almost abreast of it before seeing it. It was a Japanese tank. The enemy tank fired one shot which flattened a bogie wheel, and opened up with its machine gun. Fire also broke out from the brush on each side. Then the medium tank went into action. Its 75mm gun put two armor-piercing shots and one high explosive shell into the Japanese tank in rapid succession. It burst into flames and began to sputter and crackle. A quick rush of the infantry platoon accounted for the enemy around the tank. As the 3d Battalion S-3 later wrote of this action: "result — one Jap tank knocked out, eighteen enemy killed. Casualties to our troops — none. Time expended — ten minutes." Undoubtedly the Japanese expected to mow down a column of infantry and got the surprise of their lives.

ARMORED COUNTERATTACK: 6 AUGUST

The troops had been expecting a "Banzai" attack. Each night they prepared to receive an assault by a shouting, fanatical mass of Japanese, blindly rushing forward. No such attack ever was launched against the Division on Guam. It was believed that, because the jungle and poor Japanese communications hindered organization of such an attack, and because the enemy was being pushed so fast and so continuously he could not get set to launch a mass charge, attacks came in a different form — daring raids by one or two tanks and a handful of infantrymen. The 1st Battalion of the 305th Infantry received such an attack on 6 August.

The Japanese used tanks throughout the Guam campaign. By 5 August G-2 had identified the 9th Tank Regiment, of which the first and second companies were definitely present, as was a tank unit of the enemy 29th Division. By 4 August, 35 enemy tanks had been destroyed, 2 mediums and a tankette had been captured, 1 tankette had been knocked out, and 6 tanks had been listed as probably destroyed. This left the enemy a maximum of 19, though he could probably muster no more than 14 of those at one time. But 14 tanks were enough to offer a definite threat to the advancing troops.

Before daybreak on 6 August the men of Company A of the 305th who were guarding the northern sector of their battalion defensive area heard tanks and troops approaching from the north. The troops had been warned that friendly tanks were about and the approaching group was coming from the direction of the 2d Battalion; nevertheless, the sentinels watched carefully. The moon came out from under a cloud and disclosed two Japanese tanks, and a group of enemy soldiers mounting machine guns under a tree.

Company A immediately opened fire. A storm of bullets and grenades struck the Japanese. There was no response from the enemy soldiers, but the tanks moved off toward a sector to the right of Company A. A Japanese on top of the first tank yelled, "American tank — okay, American tank — okay!" but a stream of fire came from its turret. The men had not been able to dig deep foxholes that night because of the hard coral, and many of them left their positions in the face of the oncoming tanks.

As the enemy penetrated the position, antitank gunners shifted their weapons, but the tanks changed direction and moved out of the line of fire. Once inside the defenses they separated. One stopped and opened fire to the left, the other plunged on to the right.

The tank which turned to the right advanced toward the men so quickly that they hardly knew what was on them; terrified they ran before the blazing guns and then hit the ground. Throughout the area rifles and machine guns were turned on the tanks, but to no effect. One collided with a medium tank, backed off, crushed a jeep, and then sprayed the other vehicles in the area with machine gun fire.

The other tank rejoined it and together they charged toward the north of the position. The troops who had first sighted the Japanese had stuck to their positions after killing the soldiers. They had no defense from the immediate rear. As the tanks bore down on them, one man was hit in his foxhole by enemy or friendly fire; he staggered to his feet and fell. The other men huddled in their slit trenches and escaped harm as the tanks ground over them, although two had their rifles smashed.

As the tanks disappeared in the direction of the 2d Battalion, Private William D. Olsen took a last shot at the enemy soldier still clinging to the top of one. The man tumbled off and was found dead the next morning. Another soldier lay out in front and moaned all night in Japanese; suddenly he spoke quite plainly in English: "They'll come back, I'm too young to die." The men of Company A occasionally took shots at him and he too was dead in the morning.

The two tanks left a trail of devastation and casualties behind them. The killed numbered 16 and 32 had been wounded; many hit by friendly fire. An artillery forward observer party had been almost wiped out. Smashed and shot-up equipment littered the area. And the tanks had escaped, apparently unscathed.

The odyssey of the two Japanese tanks was not ended. They never reached the 2d Battalion defensive area because one of them broke down.

That morning the 2d Battalion received orders to countermarch and take another trail forward. The new orders brought the battalion back on the two Japanese tanks. The trail was so narrow that to reverse itself the battalion had to execute an "about face." This maneuver put Company E in the lead, with mortars and heavy machine guns from Company H attached. It was difficult to say which was more surprised when the 4-man point of Company E encountered a Japanese soldier on the trail just after moving out. The Japanese stood dumbfounded for a moment, and then shouted something to his mates; the point passed back a warning.

A vicious fire fight followed. The two enemy tanks were in defilade and their cannon and machine guns covered that part of the trail occupied by the troops for 200 yards. As the firing started, the leading men of Company E deployed to the right and left of the trail. Because of the slight rise and the dense undergrowth it was hard to locate the enemy. The Japanese fire played havoc with those men who remained on the trail. Shells burst against trees and sent fragments slashing through the woods and into the troops. Men fell with face, arm and back wounds. The cry went back for aid men and stretcher bearers.

Medium tanks slowly came up the trail, followed by more troops. As the leading tank came around a slight bend a shell burst against it. The tank stopped and the riflemen spread out on each side of it in the jungle.

Technical Sergeant James F. Walters of Company H had his heavy machine gun brought up and mounted close behind the tanks. The machine gunners were able to get off only a few bursts when a hail of fire descended on them. Walters heard one of his men yell, "I'm hit!" He turned to see Private Stanley S. Lauterstein, ammunition bearer, prop himself against a tree, blood streaming from a deep gash in his shoulder.

"You're okay, you chowhound!" Walters shouted at him. Lauterstein grinned and yelled, "Pass the damn ammunition up." He tried to move a box with his left hand.

Bullets cracked through the brush; tree bursts sent showers of steel on the men. Sergeant Walters turned to look at his comrades. There was a scream, "Goddamit, I'm hit!" from one as bullets smashed into his leg. Another was on his knees, blood streaming from his neck; "it looked like a broken wine bottle" to Walters. A shell exploded, mortally wounding two men. The machine gun crews were mostly casualties. The platoon leader was wounded. A courageous aid man, Private Howard N. Conwell, crawled from man to man and bandaged them. He was hit, and then Sergeant Walters too received a bullet in the leg. Riflemen began breaking under the heavy fire. The forward tank, afraid of being deserted, started to back out. In doing so it caused more confusion. The tank moved directly back and almost on top of a heavy machine gun. Sergeant Walters and Conwell, both wounded, managed to get it out of the way.

Captain Charles T. Hillman, 2d Battalion Executive Officer, came up the trail and started toward the enemy, but was hit by machine gun fire. Despite their wounds, Captain Hillman and Sergeant Walters, by exhorting the men to hold their places, were able to effect a partial reorganization.

It was no safer back along the trail. The enemy fire raked the whole length of it. Company H had mounted its mortars but one man almost immediately lost an arm, and another had a shoe blown off. A squad leader was killed by shell fragments. One mortar never got into operation because of the enemy fire and the lack of an opening in the vegetation overhead; another operated slightly over 100 yards in rear of the forward elements with good results. Private John H. Snyder was wounded by shell fragments, but not before he had lobbed mortar shells steadily on the enemy. The Japanese fire slackened and abruptly stopped. Rifle squads pushed out through the jungle on each side of the trail to approach the enemy from the rear. The fight ended as quickly as it had started. The troops found the two enemy tanks deserted. A husky Japanese in a new uniform lay near one; he was dead. Two others, killed by mortar fire, were just off the trail. The rest had fled.

They had exacted a good price. The 2d Battalion lost 15 men killed and 31 wounded seriously enough to be evacuated. Since vehicles had not been able to use the trail, evacuating the wounded was a laborious job. Some had to walk, some were carried for four hours on improvised stretchers, 8 men alternating on the job. The 2d Battalion moved east to a better position that day, but it got no nearer to Yigo.

The phase of the 77th Division's operations — the period of slow progress between Barrigada and Yigo marked by small but savage encounters in the jungle-ended on 6 August with the death of Colonel Douglas McNair, Chief of Staff of the Division. Colonel McNair was reconnoitering a site for the Division command post. Although many troops had passed by and others were still passing, a few Japanese stragglers were hiding in a hut on the edge of a clearing about 200 yards in from the road. Colonel McNair and his party were fired on as they started to investigate the hut. Thus fell one who had done much for the welfare of the division.

Chapter 11
The Final Push: Yigo and Santa Rosa

"INFANTRY regiments are in a position to continue the attack to the sea." This report made by the G-3 of the Division on the afternoon of 6 August, marked the opening of a new phase of the operation. The 77th on the right and the 3d Division and the 1st Provisional Brigade on the left were nearing the northern end of Guam. The enemy had his back to the sheer 500-foot cliffs which fringed the island shore. He could not withdraw any farther.

It was clear, however, that he could still offer desperate resistance in the jungle terrain. Intelligence reports indicated that at least 2,000 enemy troops were still effective, the bulk of them in the Yigo-Mount Santa Rosa area. Artillery observers, flying at tree-top level could see little activity, which indicated that he was well concealed and perhaps dug in. Mount Santa Rosa, an 800-foot hill mostly covered with grass and a few coconut groves, was a little less than two miles east of Yigo and a mile inland from the ocean. It constituted the last key terrain feature within the zone of action of the 77th Division.

The opportunity to destroy the remaining Japanese organized forces was, as General Bruce said later, "a Division Commander's dream." The conformation of the coast line was such that it was possible to bring enfilade naval fire on Mount Santa Rosa for several days and nights prior to an attack. Bombers were available at Saipan and could be concentrated intermittently on Mount Santa Rosa to soften it up. Not only was it possible to concentrate all of the artillery fire of the Division on Yigo, but this fire could be reinforced by the bulk of the Corps artillery. There were some open places near Yigo where chemical mortars as well as the division mortars could be concentrated. A battalion of tanks was available and the terrain was such that they could be employed en masse in the direct assault on Yigo. Furthermore, after capturing Yigo, there was an opportunity to wheel the division, capture Mount Santa Rosa and drive the enemy into the sea.

The plan for the attack closely conformed to the opportunities presented. Since the 3d of August the Navy, as requested by the Division Commander, had been shelling Santa Rosa day and night. Bombers from Saipan made several runs. Arrangements were made for the Division Artillery, reinforced by Corps artillery, and mortars to shell the village for twenty minutes before H-Hour. The 706th Tank Battalion would lead the attack of the 307th in the center. They were to advance through Yigo as soon as the artillery preparation lifted and were to be followed closely by the troops who would mop up the Japanese before they could recover from the tank blow. The 306th on the left would make a wide, enveloping movement north of Yigo and Mount Santa Rosa. The 305th on the right, acting as a pivot for the maneuver, would capture its objective on the southern slopes of Mount Santa Rosa. After Yigo fell, Mount Santa Rosa was to be captured and the enemy pushed to the sea.

THE ATTACK ON YIGO: 7 AUGUST

The three infantry regiments moved out early on the morning of 7 August. The 307th was in column of battalions with the 3d Battalion in the lead. Major John W. Lovell, who had returned from the hospital, was again in command. The battalion advanced in the center of the Division zone of action, along the Finegayan Road toward Yigo. The 305th advanced northeast toward the trails connecting Yigo and Mount Santa Rosa.

The 3d Battalion of the 307th made rapid progress and approached the village at 0900. Company I was in the lead and its commander, Captain William B. Cooper, saw two Japanese run across the road ahead. The jungle was dense and he sent the point up the road a short distance and put out scouts on each flank. He also brought forward heavy machine guns to "reconnoiter by fire."

The machine guns were no sooner in action than heavy fire was received from the front and flanks. The enemy fire was concentrated on the machine gun section and the crews scrambled for cover. Within a few minutes there were eleven casualties, most of them machine gunners. The men had to comb the woods foot by foot to hunt out the Japanese; some of the enemy were killed, others withdrew through the jungle.

Mopping up took so long that it was 1008 before the 3d Battalion could report that it was in position and ready to attack Yigo. Half an hour later the 307th received word from the Division Command Post that H-hour had been set at 1200. This meant that the artillery preparation would start at 1140. The forward elements of the 3d Battalion were 500 yards from RJ 415 in Yigo, around which the artillery fire would be concentrated.

At 1145 Lieutenant Colonel Charles W. Stokes, commanding the 706th Tank Battalion, received orders to report to the command post of the 307th Infantry, on the Finegayan Road. He had worked out the tank phase of the attack with General Bruce the previous evening. For the first time in the operation he was to employ a sizable group of his tanks as a unit.

Lieutenant Colonel Stokes did not yet know the hour of attack when he received orders to report to the command post of the 307th. On arriving he was informed by Lieutenant Colonel Manuel that H-hour was 1200 and that the prepared plan would be followed. It was now 1150 and the tanks were almost a mile to the rear. Hastily he radioed Captain Leonard H. Seegar of Company D to move out at once and execute the prepared plan.

The artillery preparation was devastating. Hundreds of 105mm shells rained down on the road junction and smashed buildings and installations. Concentrations were placed on the trails leading from the village to prevent escape. An artillery observer watched the trails leading from the village. An artillery observer watching from his plane saw enemy soldiers running in all directions from the terrific explosions. Some dashed directly into the fire of the waiting infantry. Others were caught along a trail running to the north.

"My God, this is slaughter!" the observer was heard to exclaim over his radio.

At 1200 the artillery preparation lifted but the tanks were not yet in a position to advance. They were still on the narrow road leading to Yigo. The 3d Battalion was expected to close on the artillery concentrations but its advance was delayed by the narrowness of the road and by enemy fire. The light tanks found it almost impossible to push through the columns of men and weapons-carriers on the road in order to take the lead. They could not travel off the road because of the jungle on each side.

Fifteen minutes after the artillery preparation lifted, the light tanks reached the head of the column of troops, 400 yards from RJ 415. They moved forward rapidly to make the breakthrough. Two hundred yards farther the woods opened up on the right. Through their vision slits they caught a glimpse of several machine guns manned by Japanese dug in along the right of the road. They overran them and roared on, echeloning to the right so that they could move abreast over the open ground which rose to a slight crest on that flank. The medium tanks followed along the road. Behind them the troops began to mop up dugouts and pillboxes by-passed by the fast moving tanks.

TANK AMBUSH

The light tanks swept to the right of the road. They were in a wedge formation. Captain Seegar commanded the advance from his tank at the right rear. As they pushed on there was an explosion on the left side of the tank directly in front of him. Captain Seegar radioed to Lieutenant Colonel Stokes: "There's a burst in front of me — could be a mine or AT gun. Call for the mediums."

Just before the medium tanks arrived more explosions sounded on the left. The tank crews could not locate the source of the fire because of the dense growth. Sergeant Joe Divin's tank was hit. He was in the turret and had been badly wounded in both legs. He could not move, blocking the escape of the remainder of the crew. The turret was off center and the driver and bow-gunner hatches could not be opened. Desperately Sergeant Divin tried to center the turret, but the mechanism had been damaged by gunfire. His strength ebbing from loss of blood, he put a tourniquet on his leg. With a supreme effort, he dragged himself out of the turret hatch onto the rear deck, leaving the way open for the crew to follow. The tank was now afire and was receiving machine gun fire from enemy positions fifty yards away. He lay in this exposed position and directed the escape of his crew. As they dashed for cover, he was killed by machine gun fire.

Another light tank was hit. Now the mediums were arriving. They came in driblets through the congestion on the road behind. One had thrown a track on the way up. When they reached the open area, they could tell that the light tanks were in trouble, but they could not see where the fire was coming from. Only when they advanced up the slight rise and began to receive fire themselves did they turn and pour fire back into the woods to the left rear.

The gasoline tank of one was hit and flames shot out and quickly enveloped it. The crew hastily climbed out just before the ammunition inside exploded. Another tank stalled under the heavy fire; the crew dashed for a shell hole. As more tanks came up they fired their cannons and moved on to the objective ahead.

Fifty yards behind the stricken tanks the foot troops struggled to push through the area the tanks had overrun. Japanese still fired from a pillbox which had been blasted by the medium tanks as they raced ahead. The troops put rifle and machine gun fire into it. They managed to land a grenade inside. The Japanese continued to fire from it. A flamethrower man maneuvered cautiously up and shot a searing flame through an opening. A lone enemy soldier staggered out and was riddled.

The enemy antitank gun in the jungle to the left which had knocked out several tanks was still firing. The foot troops were still mopping up on the right of the road. However, an effective flanking maneuver was developed on the left side of the road in the zone of the 3d Battalion of the 306th Infantry. When the 3d Battalion of the 307th pushed up the road, this Battalion moved through the jungle on its left. When Lieutenant Colonel Kimbrell, its commander, heard heavy firing on the right, he detached the 1st Platoon from Company K and personally led it through the jungle toward the Finegayan Road on his right. So intent was the enemy on blasting the targets in front of them that they were not aware of the platoon creeping up through the jungle on their rear. With a short rush the 1st Platoon was on them. They killed the Japanese with rifles, automatic rifles and bayonets. The 1st Platoon had no casualties during the brief struggle. Other elements of Company K moved up and attacked enemy positions along the edge of the jungle farther north. The Japanese position and tank trap, so cleverly concealed from the front but vulnerable from the rear, consisted of two tanks, one 47mm antitank gun, two 20mm guns, six light machine guns, and two heavy machine guns.

Across the road four tanks were still in flames. Riflemen were advancing on the right of the road toward the center of the ruined village. Several men rushed to one burning tank and extricated a wounded man. Despite exploding ammunition they were able to place him on a litter and have him evacuated. The troops were amazed at the devastation caused by the artillery; the settlement was swept clear of buildings.

The foot troops found the tanks waiting when at 1325 they reached the high ground northeast of Yigo. There was no sign of the enemy; he had been completely routed.

During the afternoon of 7 August the 307th moved into its objective area at the base of Mount Santa Rosa and organized for the night. The 3d Battalion of the 306th dug in half a mile north of the village. The 1st Battalion of that regiment, commanded by Lieutenant Colonel Joseph A. Remus, advanced on the left rear of the 3d Battalion during 7 August and late in the afternoon dug in west of Yigo. The 305th had spent the day moving slowly through the jungle toward Mount Santa Rosa and by nightfall was within striking distance. The 77th Division was in position to capture the mountain and drive to the sea.

SANTA ROSA AND BEYOND: 8 AUGUST

The enemy launched a tank attack against the position of the 3d Battalion, 306th Infantry that night. At dusk on 7 August and again at midnight, enemy patrols felt out the battalion's position which straddled a trail running north of Yigo. On the second occasion the troops held their fire until the patrol was within a few yards, then annihilated it.

Two hours later tanks were heard approaching from the north. The men lay low in their slit trenches. The leading tank appeared over a slight knoll and fired its cannon and machine gun. Another Japanese tank opened fire from a short distance behind. The machine gun fire passed over the men, but the high explosive shells struck trees overhead and showered fragments down on them. A platoon of enemy riflemen behind the tanks contributed to the heavy fire.

A "bazooka" and a flamethrower man were hit in quick succession when they attempted to use their weapons. Another soldier with a flamethrower moved up but bullets struck both him and his weapon. Some of the riflemen moved to the rear in the face of tank fire, but Privates Everett W. Hatch and Joseph P. Koeberle, manning a light machine gun, held their ground. They poured machine gun fire into its 6 x 10 inch aperture at close range. Tracers could be seen coming out the other side of the tank. They continued firing until the machine-gun barrel burned out and the tank stopped within five yards of them. There were no signs of life in the tank.

During the attack Lieutenant Keith Kenfield, commanding a rifle platoon, was wounded and evacuated. Technical Sergeant Charles E. Schafer assumed command and while directing the platoon was wounded in the neck by a 47mm shell fragment which completely paralyzed him. Although unable to move he could still talk. He ordered one of his men to hold him propped up in his foxhole so that he could see the action and direct the platoon. Sergeant Schafer skillfully commanded it, supported by one of his men, for over an hour. He was later evacuated but died aboard a hospital ship. He was posthumously awarded the Distinguished Service Cross for extraordinary heroism in action.

Finally "bazooka" rockets, and rifle grenades registered on the second tank and knocked it out; the third tank fled. Eighteen dead Japanese, including 3 officers, were found in the vicinity the next morning, but the battalion suffered 6 killed and 16 wounded.

The 3d Battalion reorganized in the morning and set out for Lulog, just north of Santa Rosa. From Lulog trails ran north and east to the sea. The 1st and 3d Battalions of the 306th were to cut off and destroy any Japanese attempting to flee to the north from Mount Santa Rosa.

The drive of the 3d Battalion to Lulog quickly developed into a massacre. The Japanese had taken shelter in huts along the trail. They had weapons and ammunition, but many showed little stomach for fighting. They simply waited in the huts to be killed; sometimes firing a few shots and then destroying themselves. In one building a new and unfired Japanese machine gun with plenty of ammunition was found.

All members of the Japanese armed forces had been completely indoctrinated with the propaganda that they and their family would be forever disgraced by surrender or capture, and that they could never again return to their homeland. As a result, when the Japanese found themselves in a hopeless situation they often either turned to suicide as a solution, usually with a hand grenade, or apathetically awaited death, which was not long in coming.

Over 100 Japanese were killed by the 306th Infantry. The advance took it well beyond Mount Santa Rosa and within 1,000 yards of the ocean. The 1st Battalion joined the 3d at Lulog at 1700.

The 307th had captured Mount Santa Rosa during the day. Thirty-five Japanese were killed approaching the mountain but no opposition was encountered on its steep slopes. Lieutenant Colonel Manuel reported with a considerable degree of elation that he and his observation post were on the summit. Santa Rosa afforded excellent observation of the island generally, although the jungle was so dense it was impossible to see small groups unless they moved into an occasional clearing. By that evening the entire

77th Division sector on Guam was occupied, except for a small portion of the left regimental zone on the north. Organized resistance in the Division's zone of advance was declared destroyed. However, this good news was not yet thoroughly disseminated when in the darkness a brisk but brief skirmish broke out between elements of the 306th and 307th Infantry regiments. Each group thought the other to be Japanese. Even tank guns fired in the few minutes before identities were established. Seven men were wounded.

MOPPING UP: 9-10 AUGUST

On the following day — 9 August — the Division began a vigorous mopping up program within its zone. The Marines had but a short distance to go before they could report all organized resistance ended. In all zones many small groups of Japanese had been by-passed. These remnants attempted to infiltrate into bivouac areas at night and even skirmished with the troops during the day. One artillery unit killed nearly fifty Japanese while, at the same time, firing a mission.

The Division made an effort to induce the remaining enemy stragglers to surrender by dropping leaflets on 9 August, but with no result. The 77th had taken ten prisoners through 8 August; one more was captured on 9 August, but that was all. This prisoner, a sailor, said he had been on Mount Barrigada with 1,000 other Japanese until the end of July and that he had decamped with three others before the Americans reached there. He had had no food for 5 days.

A mass hunt was ordered in a stretch of woods near the Division Command Post to clear out some prowling Japanese. The troops tried to beat through the woods in a long skirmish line. Soon the line broke up into small groups, which almost simultaneously lost contact and became disoriented. The jungle was infested with Japanese. As the men groped about they were picked off by the enemy. Rescue parties were sent to help evacuate the wounded, only to suffer casualties themselves. Some of the men fought their way out by firing into an area ahead, grenading it, moving forward and repeating the process. Lieutenant Harper of Barrigada fame was among the 7 killed. The Japanese, who were estimated as a company, lost 37 killed and fled during the night.

Before the Division reached Barrigada it had received information that the Japanese had an underground headquarters and radio station northwest of Yigo. Chamorros who had been forced to labor there told of two large concrete U-shaped tunnels opening into a hidden gully. Japanese documents mentioned a headquarters at Mataka Yama. However, in the fight at Yigo and the subsequent drive to Santa Rosa and the sea, the columns by-passed this area.

On 8 August Captain William Fuller, commanding the 77th Reconnaissance Troop, led a patrol northwest from Yigo to locate and reconnoiter the cave area. The patrol encountered and avoided ambushes at every turn for several hours, but could not reach the fortified gully. They reported many defended caves and well worn foot trails, on the heavily jungled ridges. It was clearly a task for a stronger force.

On 10 August the 1st Battalion of the 306th reconnoitered the area in force and located the gully about three-quarters of a mile northwest of Yigo. It was one hundred yards long, forty feet deep, and almost invisible in the jungle growth. The troops skirmished all day and sealed caves in the surrounding ridges, but could not get at the tunnels. The fighting was close and desperate. When a flamethrower man attempted to approach a cave, Japanese concealed in the thick undergrowth opened fire with rifles and machine guns. The enemy used mortars as well as small arms. When a man moved he drew fire. The 1st Battalion withdrew at dusk, having lost 8 men killed, and 17 wounded.

Rescuing and evacuating the wounded during this fight was an extremely difficult task. It was almost impossible to get a wounded man without being exposed to the same fire which he had encountered. Private Kenneth F. Dietz, a company aid man, saved the lives of many of his comrades that day by moving to their assistance in plain view of the enemy. He was wounded by a rifle bullet, but continued to render first aid to others and was evacuated only after they had been moved to safety.

The next day the same battalion launched a carefully prepared attack. The troops attacked behind tank fire and a mortar concentration. The tanks were unable to negotiate the steep sides of the depression but the infantry passed through, two companies abreast, and mopped up the Japanese who had survived the concentration. Few were still alive. The attack was made under the critical observation of a group of Marines on a hill a few hundred yards away, who broke into cheers as the foot soldiers quickly completed their job.

On one side of the depression, foliage had been blasted away revealing four cuts leading to tunnels with heavy concrete entrances. As the troops pulled away the brush, one man was hit by rifle fire from inside. Pole charges and white phosphorus grenades were thrown in the cave. Two Japanese soldiers armed with rifles ran out in rapid succession and were shot down. Just before the demolitions exploded the Japanese inside were heard singing a sort of chant. The chanting continued even after two series of demolitions exploded. Then four 400-pound charges of TNT were placed at the entrance to the tunnels. The tremendous blasts effectively sealed the caves.

Four days later when one of the tunnels was opened, the odor was so terrific that the men were forced to don gas masks. More than 60 bodies were piled up inside. The caves were large and elaborately constructed with four-foot concrete walls. A large, new transmitter was found. Other radio equipment might have been "Radio Guam." More than 300 Japanese were killed in the clean up of this by-passed stronghold.

On 10 August Colonel Stephen S. Hamilton returned from the hospital and resumed command of the 307th Infantry.

Radio Tokyo announced on 8 August that American troops were in possession of nine-tenths of Guam. On 10 August the Marines completed the occupation of their zones to the north tip of the island. At 1500 on 10 August General Bruce of the 77th received official notice from Headquarters, Southern Landing Force, that all organized resistance on Guam had ceased.

No time had been lost in capitalizing on the gains that had been made, and on final victory. The Island Commander, his headquarters, and part of the garrison forces had arrived with the assault convoys and had been established ashore and started to work even before the Final Beachhead Line was completely captured. Additional Seabee battalions arrived soon after with great quantities of heavy engineer equipment and materials. Apra Harbor was quickly developed so that vessels could land cargo on newly built quays. Orote Airfield was put into operation, existing roads were widened and surfaced, new roads cut through the hills, new buildings erected, and work on huge runways for the B-29's started.

When the troops of the Division returned to the west coast after the fighting a great deal of the landscape around Agat and Agafia was scarcely recognizable. The natives had returned to the villages and farms and were rebuilding their devastated homes.

Chapter 12
Camp McNair and Harmon Road

ALTHOUGH Guam had been declared secure on 10 August the L77th's job had not ended. Patrolling jungle areas and clearing caves of Japanese continued for several weeks. Hungry, sick and virtually defenseless, the Japanese showed remarkable tenacity. The 306th Infantry remained in the Yigo-Santa Rosa area for two weeks and added a large number of Japanese to its total killed. Just 10 minutes before the 3d Battalion left for its semi-permanent camp near Agat, several enemy soldiers were killed nearby.

On Guam the Division killed 2,741 Japanese and captured 36 prisoners. Final estimates of Japanese on the island were 18,500, about the same as the first pre-battle estimates. To accomplish this extermination the following ammunition was expended:

3,600,000 rounds of .30 caliber rifle
750,000 rounds of .30 caliber carbine
475,000 rounds of .45 caliber
46,000 hand grenades
24,716 rounds of artillery ammunition

The division lost 248 killed and 663 wounded. Eleven Japanese died for each American killed and 3 Japanese died for each American battle casualty.

By late August the entire Division, including attached troops, assembled in a large bivouac area on the hills east of Agat. It was named Camp McNair in honor of the former Chief of Staff. The battle-weary soldiers found little rest, comfort, or recreation there.

The Division had left a rear detachment, commanded by Major Warren Dodge, on Oahu. With it were many vehicles, heavy engineer equipment, tentage, extra clothing, and all the supplies and impedimenta needed for a semi-permanent camp. This detachment was not sent to Guam because the 77th was originally scheduled to be moved from Guam to Guadalcanal as soon as the battle ended. The rear echelon was sent first to Guadalcanal and then to New Caledonia where later plans had called for the Division to be rehabilitated. Months later it caught up with the troops on Leyte, Philippine Islands. The Division was not moved from Guam and it could not occupy areas needed for the base development, so it was parked in the hills.

Troops spread out over the ridges, pitched pup tents and built native type shacks of bamboo and palm. Almost everything had to be improvised. The rainy season was on and nothing was ever really dry. Clothing and equipment mildewed. Bedding on the ground — the cots were with the rear echelon — was often a soggy mass.

The carabao and cart road, variously known as Harmon Road or "Harmon Canal," wound uphill from Agat for three miles into the camp. The Engineers worked day and night on this route, but for several weeks it was a losing fight. One mud hole swallowed three Jap tanks with no noticeable effect. At one time only artillery tractors could negotiate the trail, later nothing but native carabao and pedestrians could pass. The men of the 132nd Engineer Battalion claimed to have had to extricate one carabao which bogged down in the road. This meant that all food and supplies for the Division were hand carried at least two miles uphill in mud and rain. Eventually the Engineers, with borrowed Seabee dump trucks and power shovels, laid a 5-foot-deep floating carpet of live coral atop the soggy Harmon Road and lo, there was a road for the Division's departure.

Gradually camp conditions improved somewhat although combat rations remained the staple food. The flies, rats, and mosquitoes decreased in number and consequently there was less diarrhea and dengue. Men gradually freed themselves and their clothing of the red soil of Guam.

Training was begun again. Patrolling exercises were over terrain still traversed by occasional Japanese stragglers, adding realism to the exercises. A rifle range was improvised.

The Division Artillery, now commanded by Colonel Royal L. Gervais, set to work to capitalize on the many valuable lessons of the campaign. Systematic analysis of the accumulated experiences of all resulted in an intensive training program which produced marked improvement in technique. Concurrently, training in patrolling and the ability of the artillerymen to defend their batteries and themselves was stressed. Training in adjusting fire from observation points well forward, where the limitations and effectiveness of shell burst on different types of terrain could be observed close to the burst was stressed. The Division artillery was perfected in all types of fire from swift and effective fire on targets of opportunity to TOT transfers, massed fire problems, and skillful manipulation of night defensive fires. Ammunition was not spared. The result was a high state of firing efficiency and skillful handling of infantry support requirements by forward observers, liaison officers and battalion commanders. By 25 October 1944 all battalions had reached the peak of physical and technical proficiency at the cost of but one casualty, and that from a tree burst. The artillery was now ready to go. On 31 October Colonel Ray L. Burnell joined and assumed command of the 77th Division Artillery.

Planning began again. The 77th Division was scheduled to be floating reserve for an invasion of Yap and Ulithi simultaneously with the assault on Palau. Iwo Jima was listed as an alternate target and the staff worked on that also. The Yap operation was cancelled but not before the Division had readied itself for loading and had actually moved supplies and some troops to the beach. Thereafter the 305th established a camp on Orote Peninsula and the 307th moved to an area above Asan.

Next the 77th was assigned a mission as land reserve for the October 20th invasion of Leyte, Philippine Islands. Again the plans were made and the preparation begun. Significantly, one of the plans drawn up by General Bruce was for an amphibious landing South of Ormoc on Leyte.

Late in October a squadron of transports arrived for the 77th. Simultaneously came orders to load commercially for a rest area on New Caledonia and to leave behind the ammunition, rations, maps and data prepared for the Leyte operation. The Division loaded out of Guam in 36 hours, from a harbor greatly lacking in facilities for such a large-scale embarkation, yet it left behind it immaculately policed camp areas.

Part III: The Liberation of Leyte

BRIEF: Arriving on the east coast of Leyte on Thanksgiving Day — 23 November 1944 — the 77th Division was first assigned various widely scattered tasks; then hastily assembled to break the stalemate in the Leyte operation by a landing on the west coast just south of Ormoc on 7 December.

The landing behind the Japanese lines was a complete surprise, and the subsequent capture of Ormoc and the Ormoc Valley campaign broke the Japanese resistance on the island. After landing at Deposito, the Division drove north and on 11 December captured Ormoc. Following a bitter fight at Cogon, the Division, with a two pronged, wide envelopment cut the main north and south road, captured the Valencia airfield and drove on to the Libungao road junction, just north of which contact was made with the 1st Cavalry Division on 21 December.

The Division then turned west with Palompon as its next objective. That town, however, was captured from the sea on Christmas Day by an LVT Task Force built around the 1st Battalion, 305th Infantry. The capture of Palompon officially closed the Leyte campaign, but the Palompon road remained yet to be cleared by the Division which killed fighting bands of Japanese in northeast Leyte until 5 February. It was then withdrawn to the east coast to prepare for the Kerama Retto-Ie Shima-Okinawa operations.

The 77th Division killed 19,459 Japanese on Leyte and took 124 prisoners at a cost of 425 killed and 1,549 wounded. The Ormoc landing and the campaign thereafter have been characterized by both friends and enemies as a divisional epic and the decisive factor in the Levte campaign, which in turn contributed materially to weakening the enemy strength on Luzon.

Chapter 13: No Rest for the Weary

THE SQUADRON of transports which sailed from Guam for New Caledonia on 3 November 1944 was filled with officers and men of the 77th Infantry Division, happy in anticipation of a restful voyage which would end at a peaceful island free of Japanese. All began to catch up on sleep, relax from the tensions of combat, and enjoy the good fresh food. Days and nights became increasingly warmer. The Equator was crossed and, on some of the transports appropriate initiation ceremonies were conducted making "hardshells" out of "polliwogs" and introducing them to Old King Neptune.

Then, on 11 November, four days out from New Caledonia, radio orders were received directing the convoy to turn northwest, and put in at Manus, in the Admiralty Islands. This apparent change in plan coupled with the news reports of the rather slow progress on Leyte stimulated speculation. The betting odds favored an immediate return of the Division to action. Manus was reached on 17 November and the large convoy dropped anchor in spacious Seeadler Harbor where it remained until the 19th. The troops watched the very black natives with their bleached, reddish hair maneuver tricky outrigger canoes among the ships of the squadron. Most of the men had an opportunity to spend part of a day on a recreation island where beer and bathing were available. Some of the officers visited the Navy Club and enjoyed brief but intense relaxation. On the 19th, the convoy departed from Manus for the east coast of Leyte, Philippine Islands.

During the remainder of the voyage, General Bruce and his staff worked on plans, and the few maps of Leyte which were at their disposal, in an effort to anticipate every feasible employment of the Division. The plans for participation in the Leyte operation which had been drawn up on Guam still seemed to meet almost every possible contingency.

Chapter 14: East Leyte: 23 November to 5 December

THE CONVOY bearing the Division arrived off Tarragona and Dulag, Leyte, in the early morning hours of 23 November and began unloading in a welcome rain at 0800. Japanese planes, which were usually active over Leyte Gulf, could not operate in the rains. Division Headquarters; Headquarters Company; Special Troops; Division Artillery; and the 305th and 306th Regimental Combat Teams, landed at Tarragona. The 307th Regimental Combat Team landed near Dulag with orders to move inland to La Paz.

Unloading cargo and equipment from the ships was difficult, as there were no piers. The vehicles of the Division were in only fair condition, and some had been left on Guam with the expectation that replacements would be received from the large supply base on New Caledonia.

It must be remembered that the east coast of Leyte had been captured by the Sixth Army before the 77th Division arrived. The Division was not expected to enter combat immediately but to a degree that is what occurred. The 307th Regimental Combat Team unloaded across the beaches at Dulag and moved inland to La Paz, where it was to protect the roads and passes leading to La Paz and the supply and airfield installations on eastern Leyte. All roads were almost impassable from the daily rains, and the attempts to improve them were inadequate and making little progress.

The mission assigned to the remainder of the Division was to establish beach defenses against counter landings along the east coast and carry on wide-spread patrolling of the area. In addition, a detail of 1,300 officers and men was furnished to handle cargo for a task force preparing to capture the island of Mindoro.

Patrol areas for the 305th and 307th Regimental Combat Teams included the east coast from a point below Tarragona north to Rizal. On 29 November, the 2d Battalion of the 305th moved to Baybay to relieve elements of the 7th Division in defense of that sector. The 77th Reconnaissance Troop established defensive posts at Catmon Hill to prevent enemy surprise attacks on the airfields at Dulag and Tacloban.

On 27 November the 306th Infantry, less its Antitank and Cannon companies, was attached to the 11th Airborne Division, which was relieving elements of the 7th Division near Burauen. The 1st Battalion was placed in XXIV Corps reserve, the 3d Battalion relieved the 17th Infantry of the 7th Division west of Guinarona, and the 2d Battalion went into regimental reserve near that village. Because of the almost impassable condition of the few existing roads, supply was extremely difficult. To make matters worse, the 3d Battalion, which was in contact with the enemy, was 2,000 yards west of the only road and that 2,000 yards was continuous rice paddies which were completely impassable for any type of vehicle. In addition, the 306th was virtually without artillery support because of the limited artillery available in an airborne division. The regiment had no more than arrived in position when the road to the 11th Airborne Division became permanently impassable.

Arrangements were made by Colonel Aubrey D. Smith with the 96th Division, which was nearby, for supply and evacuation through its channels. Then it was discovered that a battalion of field artillery, the 48th of the 7th Division, which had been left behind — literally stuck in the mud — could and would fire in direct support of the regiment. Native bearers were rounded up to hand-carry supplies across the 2,000 yards of rice paddies to the 3d Battalion. Tractors were borrowed from a Marine artillery organization to drag in supplies on sleds. The 306th Infantry found itself in a curious situation; its parent organization was the 77th Infantry Division; it was attached to the 11th Airborne Division; its supply and evacuation were by courtesy of the 96th Infantry Division; its fire support came from the 48th Field Artillery Battalion of the 7th Division; and it was using vehicles borrowed from a battalion of the United States Marine Corps.

On 30 November near Burauen, a large patrol from Company K, 306th Infantry, attacked a Japanese position 2£ miles west of Guinarona and killed twenty of the thirty defenders. Company I, which was moving southwest, captured one Japanese 900 yards from Guinarona. As it advanced through a coconut grove, it was fired on by automatic weapons and several men were hit. One squad of the 1st Platoon found itself within 50 yards of an enemy machine gun. Staff Sergeant John Lawrence, the squad leader, with one of his automatic riflemen attempted to rush the gun but both were instantly killed. The platoon leader, Lieutenant Clarence P. Dow, seeing that his platoon was suffering heavy casualties from this gun, attempted to destroy it. He, too, was killed, as was the company commander, Captain Robert L. Cummings, who had moved forward. Lieutenant Lemuel Goode, the company executive officer, seized an automatic rifle and advanced alone into the withering fire, firing from the hip. He silenced the enemy machine gun but was seriously wounded in the shoulder. At this time, a platoon of Japanese moved around the flank and attacked Company I from the rear. The company was quickly organized for all around defense by Lieutenant Sam Kurland and Staff Sergeant Carl G. Puryear. Company K made an aggressive attack around the flank of Company I and drove back the Japanese. Eighty-five of the enemy were killed. Both companies then withdrew to the battalion position. At 0900, 2 December, the 3d Battalion, with Company G attached, after an artillery preparation, attacked this stubbornly defended position once again. The artillery preparation killed or drove out almost all of the Japanese. The Battalion killed 3, counted 150 dead, captured several machine guns and a 70mm gun. Patrols continued 3,000 yards to the west, knocked out a cave, and killed 30 more of the enemy nearby.

This area consisted of finger ridges and deep ravines with almost perpendicular walls. The wounded had to be carried as far as two miles across the ridges and ravines. Not even a "jeep" could get across to the front.

The 2d Battalion, 307th Infantry, was ordered to protect a naval airfield being constructed on the southwest tip of the island of Samar, and departed in LCTs at 1500, 30 November. Company L of that regiment was sent from La Paz to defend the airfield at Dulag. The 1118th Engineer Group Headquarters had previously been attached to the XXIV Corps. The 132d Engineer Shore Battalion passed to the control of the 1140th Engineer Group for construction and maintenance of the Abuyog-Baybay Road. The 302d and 242d Engineer Shore Battalions remained with the Division, building bridges, maintaining roads, and assisting in moving the Division's supplies. Throughout the Leyte campaign, the engineers of the Division maintained a man-killing pace in an attempt to keep the roads and bridges from disappearing in the mire and swollen streams caused by the daily torrential downpours.

On the nights of 26 and 27 November, the Japanese sent four plane-loads of specially trained, specially equipped para troop raiders into the east coast area of Leyte. One of these planes crashlanded in the surf just south of the 77th's camp area, and another landed just north of the Division area.

The raiders got ashore and into the woods and though they did no damage, were the cause of considerable patrolling. Five Japs were subsequently killed in the Division area.

Warning orders were received late on the afternoon of 1 December alerting the Division for a shore-to-shore movement and assault landing on the west coast of Leyte in the Ormoc area. This operation was intended to disrupt Japanese resistance, prevent further reinforcement and break down enemy supply and communications. When the orders were received, the Division was dispersed from Baybay on the west coast to Tarragona on the east, and from Tacloban on the northeast coast to the mountains in the Burauen-Guinarona region. One battalion was on the island of Samar and 1,300 men were loading ships. Elements of the Division were under the control of the XXIV Corps, the 11th Airborne Division, and service organizations.

On 2 December, the assembling of the widely scattered organizations of the Division was begun. Grave transportation difficulties and long distances made this a complex problem. The 305th Infantry, less its 2d Battalion at Baybay, was at Tarragona and had little trouble in preparing for embarkation. The 2d and 3d Battalions of the 306th Infantry were in the mountains near Burauen and were yet to be released by the 11th Airborne Division. The 1st Battalion was released and prepared to move from the Tabirana River to a bivouac area near Tarragona.

The 307th Regimental Combat Team had the greatest problem in its move to a loading beach. Torrential tropical rains had reduced the La Paz-Rizal Road to a ribbon of mud, pocketed with deep holes through which trucks could move only with the assistance of bulldozers.

The patrolling responsibility of the Division ended 3 December. General and special staff officers were briefed on the forthcoming operation. The 2d Battalion, 305th Infantry, left Baybay and about half of it reached Tarragona by the end of the day. The 307th started its move from La Paz to the Rizal beaches, but all traffic was held up at Mayora because of the impassable road. The large detail of officers and men furnished by the 305th to load cargo for the postponed Mindoro operation returned to the regiment.

On 4 December, all organizations were assembling in embarkation areas on Tarragona and Rizal beaches. The 307th Combat Team found the road so bad that artillery howitzers had to be pulled through the mud by tanks and bulldozers; trucks had to be assisted by tractors. By nightfall about one third of the troops were on the beaches and most of the attached organizations, including tanks, antiaircraft weapons, chemical mortars, and light artillery had closed. The 232d Engineer Shore Battalion remained on the La Paz-Rizal Road assisting the 307th. The 305th completed its assembly and prepared for embarkation. The 2d Battalion of the 306th was released by the 11th Airborne Division and moved from Dulag to Tarragona. DUKWs and LVTs were the only vehicles capable of making the run between Tarragona and Dulag and were borrowed from the 7th Division and the XXIV Corps. The 3d Battalion, 306th still remained under the control of the 11th Airborne Division.

Assembly on the beaches continued through 5 December. It became apparent that all organizations would make it in time although the 306th and the 307th would have a close call. Loading of supplies began on the night of 5-6 December, but was slowed by air alerts.

The Navy did not control the waters or the air off the west coast of Leyte and the Division had been warned that the initial convoy would not remain off the landing beaches longer than two hours. This meant that all troops, equipment, and supplies for the first two days of the operation must be unloaded within two hours. Thus, everything must be mobile loaded. There was no reef and troops could be landed directly on the beach from landing boats and LCIs (Landing Craft, Infantry). It was, therefore, decided that all of the LVTs in the LSTs (Landing Ship, Tank) would be loaded, not with troops as was customary, but with supplies. No supplies, then, would have to be man-handled from vessels to small boats, and from small boats to the beach.

The Division could take only 269 vehicles of all types. This included LVTs, LVT(4)s (LVTs mounting 75mm guns), and self-propelled guns. Shipping allotted for the expedition included eight APDs (Assault Destroyer Transports), 25 LCIs (Landing Craft, Infantry), 10 LSMs (Landing Ship, Medium), and 4 LSTs. These vessels must carry all of the troops who could be taken, the vehicles, and supplies for two days.

The field order for the landing on 7 December was issued on 5 December. The Division was to land on the west coast between the Boad and the Bagonbon rivers and establish a beachhead. It would then turn north and drive to Ormoc. Sixth Army and XXIV Corps plans called for the 7th Division, then at Baybay on the west coast, to drive north; the 11th Airborne Division to push west over the mountains; and the X Corps, fighting south from Carigara Bay, to intensify its drive in order to make an early junction with the 77th. The 226th Field Artillery (155mm gun) Battalion, in position near Daro on the east side of the mountains was to support the landings.

Chapter 15: The End Run to Ormoc

LOADING was completed early on 6 December. The "tin can I fleet" of small vessels formed an array, impressive in numbers if not in size, and steamed south escorted by destroyers on the 225-mile overnight cruise around the southern tip of Leyte and up its west coast. The convoy of about 80 vessels included 26 LCIs, 12 LSMs and 4 LSTs, with an escort of 4 destroyers.

Each landing ship was crowded beyond its normal capacity. Soldiers sprawled, sat, and stood everywhere above and below decks. Everyone from General Bruce down was worried but trying not to show it. The mission of this force — and it included only seven battalions of infantry, one of artillery — was to sail boldly through Japanese dominated waters into an area where the enemy had air superiority, land within a few miles of the main Japanese port and base on Leyte, and attack!

Corporal Sam Blumenfeld, war correspondent for the Mid-Pacifcan wrote:

This is the night of December 6th. Only sailors are on deck. Some of us are lying, sitting, and standing around in the crews mess hall and passageway; others, more fortunate, are sleeping below on four-high bunks. The ship is crowded. Normally it carries 150 soldiers. There are more than 300 aboard on this trip. All but a handful of the troops are reconnaissance men. The handful is an eight-man team of QMs. An Ensign wants to know what the QMs are doing mixed up with the recon men. "We've got to eat, don't we?" says somebody. The Ensign turns to Sgt. Henry McLemore, Army Combat Correspondent, and says: "I've never seen a more unconcerned looking bunch of soldiers in my life." "These men have fought before," says the newspaper man who has made four landings. "They know if they stop to think what is coming its no good. Sure, they're scared. Everybody is scared. The Japs are scared too.

"But these guys have gotten over the hump every man has to climb when he first goes into action. That's when he imagines all the guns firing around him are aimed at him.

"Once he gets over that feeling he tries to keep himself from thinking about how scared he is." "That isn't easy," says the Ensign. "This is my first time in combat. I'm plenty scared!" "Who isn't?" asked several voices.

Somebody trying to sleep on a bench yells at us, "Why the hell don't you guys shut up!" There was a chorus of "Yeahs". Everybody shuts up and tries to sleep. McLemore and I go down into the radio room and listen to the usual broadcast from Radio Tokyo. "Wait till tomorrow," Henry says to the radio.

The convoy arrived off Deposito at 0545. The landing was delayed to take advantage of better light for the bombardment by destroyers of the beaches. It began at 0640. This included the 5-inch gun fire of four destroyers, and rockets from two LCI rocket boats; quite a contrast to the naval preparation on Guam. As the troops watched the bombardment the first Japanese planes appeared. The men looked eagerly at the shore. There were no foxholes on the ships.

P-40 air cover arrived over the convoy at 0700, after assault waves had crossed the line of departure. The first wave of the 77th Division hit the beach at 0707 on 7 December, and moved inland against very little opposition.

The beach area was extremely limited for such a rapid landing of so large a force, but detailed preliminary study of aerial photographs, and conferences with guerrillas and natives had shown that they afforded the greatest possibility for a successful surprise landing. The landing craft, including the LCMs, were able to beach within a few feet of the shore and the troops waded those few feet in water only knee deep. Division Headquarters, including the assistant division commander and General Staff Sections, were ashore at H plus 35 minutes. The entire force, including artillery and all supplies were ashore in two and one half hours.

The assault elements of the landing force lost little time in advancing to the initial beachhead line and by 0845 the 305th Infantry on the right reported its 1st and 3d Battalions on the objective.

The 307th Infantry, less two platoons of its cannon company, two M-10 destroyers and its 2d Battalion on Samar, but with the 1st Battalion, 306th Infantry, attached, landed on the left of the 305th, met a little resistance on its right but quickly reached its sector of the beachhead and captured the bridge over the Boad River.

The initial plan had been to hold the line of the beachhead pending the arrival of supplies and reinforcements on the D plus 2 convoy but, owing to the light resistance, the rapidity of the advance inland, and the desire to take full advantage of the situation before the enemy had a chance to regroup and counterattack, General Bruce aboard the flagship decided about 0745 to continue the attack to the north and extend the beachhead to the vicinity of Ipil. He issued orders for this attack. The 307th moved to the north toward Ipil, astride Highway 2. Initially, only slight resistance was encountered, but it increased somewhat as the troops advanced.

On landing, the 307th was dependent for supporting fires upon its own weapons and a platoon of 4.2 chemical mortars, although naval gun fire from a few destroyers was available for a short time. Soon, however, the 902d Field Artillery Battalion started its debarkation in those wonderful amphibious contraptions called DUKWs, each of which carried the howitzer, ammunition and personnel of one section. When the LST ramps were dropped, out streamed the DUKWs which swam ashore, lumbered up on the beach and to the battery positions where their precious cargo was unloaded. As immediate artillery support was essential and the front lines had not advanced far enough to permit more desirable positions, the battalion went into action near the center of the landing beaches. By 0920, it had registered and immediately began to fire on enemy infantry and machine guns.

The mission of the artillery was not an easy one. It was required to render support to the north and to the east where the action was taking place; then to the south and also to be ready to defend toward the sea in the event of a counter-landing. Company A, 776th Amphibious Tank Battalion took over the defense from the sea after the fighting moved inland and did yeoman service when Japanese planes strafed the shore line; but the lone 902d Field Artillery Battalion continued to meet its heavy responsibility until the 305th Field Artillery Battalion landed on 9 December. The 306th Field Artillery Battalion (155mm Howitzer), which was temporarily attached to the 7th Division, was available on call for support. The 226th Field Artillery Battalions "Long Toms," from positions east of the mountains at Daro were able to place fire in front of the Division during the day.

Resistance increased as the 307th advanced on toward Ipil. The Japanese used machine gun emplacements under native huts and these had to be mopped up house by house. Eighty-three of the enemy were killed and a prisoner was captured. Captured documents indicated that service elements of the Japanese 12th and 13th Regiments were occupying the area.

By 1600 the 307th had captured Ipil. A number of Japanese trucks were taken and these were immediately pressed into service. Considerable amounts of enemy supplies and ammunition were destroyed. At 1640, orders were issued to consolidate for the night, make contact with the 305th on the right, and prepare for counterattacks from the east. The beachhead now extended from Ipil on the north to the mouth of the Bagonbon River on the south. The 307th held the north and half of the east side of the beachhead.

As soon as the two regiments were in position, combat and reconnaissance patrols were sent out to obtain information on which to base the plan of attack for the next day. Three large patrols of platoon strength were sent to the south by the 305th. These, on their return, reported the destruction of three large enemy ration dumps.

The Division command post located initially near the landing beaches, moved across the Boad River at 1500 and was established in Deposito. The 7th Division was on the west coast of Leyte seven miles to the south and pushing north as rapidly as possible against stiffening resistance.

In anticipation of his drive to the north, General Bruce caused Ipil to be organized as the Division supply base. This would shorten supply lines for the attack toward Camp Downes. As General Bruce expressed it, he wanted to keep pulling in his tail behind him. Engineers reconnoitered the beaches and found them suitable to receive the LCMs of the D plus 2 convoy. The LVTs moved along the waters edge to Ipil and were unloaded. The Division Clearing Company organized a hospital in a church and a school house in Deposito during the early afternoon.

Enemy aircraft were active during the landings but most of their attacks were directed at the ships which hastily departed as soon as the Division had debarked. Five enemy planes were shot down by the air cover, the antiaircraft guns of the 7th AAA (AW) Battalion and the machine guns of the LVTs spread along the beaches. Only two air attacks were made on the beach, with no damage to installations; but the naval convoy lost four ships returning to the east side of the island. However, the Japanese lost to American air attack an entire convoy of ships carrying reinforcements bound for Ormoc.

With the shipping it was allotted, the Division had been able to transport and land the following organizations: A detachment from Division Headquarters and Headquarters Company; the 77th Reconnaissance Troop, plus a platoon of Filipino Guerrillas, detachments of the 77th Signal Company, 77th Quartermaster Company, 777th Ordnance Company and Headquarters and Headquarters Battery of Division Artillery; the 902d

Field Artillery Battalion; Company D of the 302d Engineer Battalion, with the 95th Portable Surgical Hospital attached; the 1118th Engineer Group Headquarters with the 233d Engineer Combat Battalion attached; one SBC Team; the 292d Joint Assault Signal Company; Battery D of the 7th AAA (AW) Battalion; Company A, 88th Chemical Mortar Battalion; the 92d Bomb Disposal Squad; the 6th Air Support Party; Company A, 706th Amphibian Tank Battalion; Company B, 536th Amphibious Tractor Battalion; the 305th Regimental Combat Team, less the 305th Field Artillery Battalion; the 307th Regimental Combat Team, less its 2d Battalion; and the 1st and 2d Battalions of the 306th Infantry.

The landing of a lone, unsupported division on the west coast of Leyte in the rear and within striking distance of all of the Japanese forces on that island, presented the Division Commander with a most difficult and unusual tactical problem. It is almost axiomatic that a division or larger force making an assault landing on a hostile shore must first capture and hold a final beachhead, more or less semi-circular in form, and about 10,000 yards in radius. Such a beachhead will prevent the enemy from placing light or medium artillery fire on the beaches where supplies and equipment are being unloaded, and where major supply dumps are being established.

With this doctrine fully in mind, General Bruce had two alternatives: (a) Establish a standard final beachhead to protect his supplies and await the arrival of the 7th Infantry Division, which was seven miles to the south and encountering stiffening resistance. To occupy a beachhead with a radius of 10,000 yards would tie down to a static defense all of the infantry of the Division, forfeit the enormous advantage of surprise the landing had gained, give the Japanese time to regroup for a coordinated attack; and make him a present of the initiative, (b) Discount the Japanese artillery, which was always poorly handled, count on promptly neutralizing it by the superb 77th Division artillery, and actually occupy a very limited beachhead to protect the beaches and dumps from small arms fire and infiltration, and thereby free at least two of his three infantry regiments for the drive on Ormoc and the capture of that town.

General Bruce, quite characteristically, promptly elected the second of the two alternatives, refusing to permit his entire division to be tied down to protecting beaches and dumps when he had such a unique opportunity to seize the initiative, create havoc in the enemy's rear, and bring the campaign on Leyte to a rapid conclusion.

Immediately after the Division had landed, the initial beachhead extended from the Boad River on the north, inland to the east and then back west to the mouth of the Bagonbon river on the south. Its maximum depth was about 1,500 yards. Almost before this initial beachhead had been gained, however, General Bruce ordered the 307th Infantry to advance on Ipil. As a result of the capture of that village, the beachhead became longer and flatter, extending from Ipil on the north to the mouth of the Bagonbon River on the south, with a depth of only about 1,000 yards; scarcely sufficient to keep long range machine gun fire off the beaches, had the enemy known how to employ long range machine gun fire.

Thereafter, until Ormoc was captured and elements of the 7th Infantry Division arrived, the Division beachhead was never more than 750 yards deep and crawled up the coast like a caterpillar pulling its tail behind it. Thus, only a minimum of troops was employed to occupy a static, defensive beachhead and the maximum number, two infantry regiments, were freed to carry an aggressive and strikingly successful fight to the enemy.

8 December. The Division had landed in an area occupied by service elements of enemy divisions operating to the east, north and south. It was estimated that it would take the Japanese a day or two to assemble troops to oppose the 77th and its move against Ormoc. Accordingly, General Bruce decided not to wait for the 7th Division to join him, but to attack rapidly to the north before the enemy had a chance to regroup.

This drive was launched by the 307th at 0800, supported by fire from the 902d Field Artillery Battalion, Company A of the 776th Amphibious Tank Battalion, and a platoon of 4.2 mortars of Company A, 88th Chemical Battalion. Increasing resistance was met between Ipil and Camp Downes. The terrain was very favorable to the Japanese. Finger ridges extended from the east to the road, and rice paddies bordered it on both sides. Self-propelled howitzers and guns were brought well forward and throughout the day delivered point blank fire on enemy positions.

Sergeant Bill Alcine, correspondent for Yank, reported:

When the Japs formed for a counterattack on the right flank of our lead elements, Colonel Stephen S. Hamilton, commanding officer of the 307th, called up a battery of 4.2 mortars. Then he sent his 1st Battalion through some sparse woods and up onto a ridge to cover his flank. About a quarter of a mile ahead, a road ran across flat cane-covered fields into another wooded rise. Japanese fire had come from there, and two M-10s moved out over the road that was built above the level of the fields like the top of a levee. A thin line of infantry spread out behind them and to their side. The M-20s blasted the wooded area and then the Colonels voice could be heard, hollering for the men to get moving into the woods. A young captain ran out in front and yelled, "Okay, dammit, let's go!"

The skirmish line moved forward. BAR fire cracked out from the line and the troops bobbed up and down in the waist high grass as answering fire came back at them. A short, skinny GI dashed out from a ditch and scooted across the road near the wooded ridge, his helmet joggling on his head. A burst of automatic fire crackled and bullets hit the road at his heels. He dived head-first into a ditch on the far side of the road.

Now the infantry pulled back as artillery blasted the wooded area. A sweating little GI passed lugging a harness full of mortar ammo and looking like one of the seven dwarfs that had been out all night. His fatigue jacket was black with sweat and he was mud up to his hip pockets. "Up and back, up and back, why the hell don't they make up their minds?" he muttered. Another GI slogged past, carrying the recoil mechanism of a 37mm gun. Somebody asked him how it was going. "Stinks," he said. He set down the piece, bummed a light, lit a cigarette and said: The guy who invented this weapon ought to get his butt kicked. Lugging this 72 pound piece of junk makes my ears ache."

He took off his helmet and ran the back of his hand across his face. "Why, I've carried that damn thing all over the States, lugged it all over the island of Guam and now I've got to carry the bastard all over the Philippines." He made a vague motion in the air with his hands, "If a tank ever does come at us, we might just as well wring our hands and scream as fire at it with this BB gun. We've taken it apart and set it up so many times, it's all wore out."

The clearing station, 500 yards behind the lines, was set in an acre of mud beside the road, there were small trees around, and occasional bursts of fire would bend the leaves and twigs overhead. There was the feel of rain in the air, and the small grove was a welter of bloody litters, blankets, A-packs, plasma, B-packs, dressings, bandages, S-packs and instruments.

A Jap truck with a couple of large white misshapen American stars painted on the sides, rolled up from the rear. They were Using the truck to evacuate the wounded; there were eight men going this trip, four walking and four stretcher cases.

As the truck pulled out, a company aid man was brought in suffering from battle fatigue. His denims were several sizes too large, making him look very tiny. His hands were shaking badly. "I feel okay" he kept saying. "I feel okay, but I can't stop trembling. What the hell is the matter with me?" He looked as though he were going to cry. The other medics tried to comfort him but it didn't do any good.

Then they brought in a GI who was in shock. He had a large dressing wrapped around his middle, with the pad in back of him slowly soaking up a pool of blood. He was a good-looking kid with white, even teeth, and he kept pulling up his knees until they almost touched his chin and then shoving them down and out with a small moan. They put his litter down and the medics went right to work, trying to give him plasma. While they tried to find the vein in his arms, he kept inching himself off the stretcher, pulling to get away from the pain. He raised up like a sleepwalker and turned to the doctor and said, "I'm okay, really I'm okay."

"Sure you are, fella," the doctor said, his hands busy with the blood soaked fatigues the man was still wearing. A medic cut them away. There was a hole in the man's back about the size of a quarter, not large but with a lot of blood around it. The doctor put a large dressing over the wound. While a medic tied it on, he shot a tube of morphine into the man's shoulder, the needle going in deep and the doctor's fingers gently working the drug out. The man slowly writhed again, pulling himself up and off the stretcher so that his forehead lay in the mud, his head hanging forward between the litter handles. A medic picked up his head and wiped the man's face carefully, then left a pad for it to lay on. A medic at the man's head suddenly said, "Doc, he's stopped breathing."

There was a quick change of positions and a heavy-set, grim-faced sergeant with huge, square hands began to give artificial respiration. Soon the man began to breathe again. "Keep it up," the doctor said. "Just enough to help him." The doctor asked for a cardiac injection; one of the medics brought the needle, and some coramine was shot into the man's chest. Then the doctor sat back on his ankles, his knees pressing into the mud beside the stretcher, the stethoscope at his ears, listening to the man's heart. Finally he sat back and said: "Well, his worries are over." The doctor looked very tired.

The sergeant who had been giving the artificial restoration stood up and walked away shaking his head. "That's the first one we've lost." he said, "the first one."

On the road beside the clearing station, the doughfeet still moved up. The day still felt hot and humid, the clouds hanging low and gray over the fields.

By the end of the day, the high ground about 1,000 yards south of Camp Downes had been reached. It afforded good observation and a position from which to launch a coordinated attack the next day. Camp Downes, formerly a small post of the Philippine Army, consisted of a number of wooden buildings on a commanding ridge. The road ran along the base of the ridge on the west.

The 305th Infantry, which had been protecting the south flank of the Division, withdrew northward to support the attack of the 307th and continued to protect the division from the south and southeast. The 1st Battalion of the 306th reverted to division control and went into position as division reserve just south of Ipil. The 2d Battalion of the 306th remained attached to the 307th Infantry. The service elements continued to operate the supply base in Ipil. The clearing station remained at Deposito and prepared a number of casualties for evacuation by water on 9 December, although occasional mortar and sniper fire still fell in the village. Major William Vaughan, Major Julian Fried and Captain David Kramer, surgeons, worked for fifty hours without relief and operated on 400 men.

Occasional air strikes were made by the Japanese during the day, and they had three planes shot down and one damaged. On each occasion heavy antiaircraft fire was delivered by the 40mm guns and .50 caliber weapons of the 7th AAA Battalion, the .50 caliber guns of the LVTs, and the truck-mounted .50 caliber machine guns of the infantry and the 233rd Engineers. During the first five days nine low-flying Japanese planes were shot down by ground fire.

9 December. The 307th launched its attack against Camp Downes at 0800. The enemy defenses had been strengthened during the night, and every foot of ground had to be forced through Japanese machine gun, mortar and rifle fire. The approaches were open and almost devoid of cover, and the enemy took every advantage of his small arms and artillery fires. At one time the 2d Battalion of the 306th Infantry was held up by intense fire from the crest of the ridge. It began to move forward again after Private George B. Kemple, of Company H, picked up a heavy machine gun and moved toward the enemy, firing it cradled in his arm. By dark, however, after extremely heavy fighting, the 307th had captured a foothold on the ridge, with its front lines across it at the north end of the

second building. During the day the 307th had knocked out two light machine guns, 11 heavy machine guns, two 40mm antiaircraft guns, and three 77mm field pieces. The men dubbed this fight the "Battle of Bloody Hill."

As the Division advanced north, it continued to pull up its tail. the 305th, behind it. At the end of the day that regiment was on the north bank of the Boad River and the Clearing Station at Deposito was well within small arms range from the south. The artillery and service troops had to provide their own close-in protection, as they had been trained to do, without benefit of infantry.

At about 0400, the D plus 2 Convoy arrived at Ipil bringing the remainder of the 306th Infantry and the 305th Field Artillery Battalion. The Division Clearing Station had brought many wounded to the beach to be loaded on one of the LSMs for evacuation to a hospital on the other side of the island. However, the Navy convoy commander, fearful of Japanese air attacks, refused to remain at the beach long enough to load all of the wounded and many had to be returned in the rain to the clearing station.

In order to maintain close contact with the front lines, the Division Commander ordered the displacement of his command post to a coconut grove on a hill immediately south of Camp Downes. The advance echelon moved forward at about 1000 and found itself in the middle of a fight between the 307th and the Japanese. It was under mortar and small arms fire on the road and later when it occupied the area. The remainder of the command post group arrived while the hill was still being mopped up.

At 1830 at the new command post, from which Ormoc was clearly visible, General Bruce issued orders for the attack on the town the next day. The plan of attack was to advance with two regiments abreast with a boundary between them extending from a point seven hundred yards northeast of the beach north of Camp Downes, to the Ormoc-Tambuco road. The 307th, on the left, was to make a frontal attack while the 306th, on the right, enveloped the enemy's northeast flank, maintained contact with the 305th and the 307th, and furnished one company at Deposito for close-in protection of the clearing station. The 305th Infantry initially was to remain in position defending the south and southeast of the Division. The 902d FA Battalion would support the 307th Infantry and the 305th FA Battalion the 306th Infantry.

10 December. Daylight of the 10th was heralded by the appearance of Japanese fighters and bombers. Every available antiaircraft weapon opened

fire. Lieutenant Reynolds, 305th Field Artillery Battalion pilot, and Lieutenant Burns, observer, were making an early air reconnaissance when the first of the planes appeared. To avoid them, they turned back and were caught in the heavy concentration of antiaircraft fire. Lieutenant Reynolds swooped low over the 902d Field Artillery Battalion area and while dodging in and out, the enemy dropped a bomb from directly above. It missed the plane but the ground explosion blew off part of the tail. By "sheer will power' Lieutenant Reynolds kept the plane in the air for the fifteen minutes required to reach the strip. Upon landing, Lieutenant Burns crawled out, looked at the dangling shreds of the planes tail and walked away muttering, "I thought there was something wrong." This same bomb landed almost directly on the fire direction center of the 902d Field Artillery Battalion, caused a number of casualties, but, for only ten minutes, disrupted the operation of the center.

An artillery preparation was fired on Ormoc and the defenses immediately south of it from 0920 to 0930 by two artillery battalions, infantry mortars, 4.2 mortars, self-propelled howitzers and guns, and the 77mm howitzers of Company A, 776th Amphibious Tank Battalion. In addition, rocket firing LCMs of the 2d Engineer Special Brigade moved in toward the Ormoc pier and sent showers of terrifying projectiles into the heart of the town. While the rockets were being launched, the crews of the LCMs traded machine gun fire with the Japanese defending the pier. The town became a blazing inferno of exploding shells and rockets, detonating ammunition and gasoline dumps, and blazing buildings. A heavy pall of black smoke hung over the area.

The approach of the two regiments was made under cover of this concentrated fire. A deep draw, extending east and west on the south of the town, was a serious obstacle. The enemy was dug in on both sides and had to be routed with grenades, mortars, bayonets and hip-shooting riflemen. The attack of the 307th was met by rifle and machine gun fire from dug-in positions under houses in the town. Mortars, machine guns and self-propelled weapons kept up a continuous barrage in front of the advancing troops.

At 1330 the leading elements of the 307th entered the town and fought steadily through it, house by house, in the face of enemy artillery, mortar, machine gun and rifle fire. By nightfall Ormoc had been cleared and the front lines were in its northern outskirts on the south bank of the Antilao

River. The 306th, on the right, made its envelopment and came abreast of the 307th at dusk.

Casualties, despite the fierce fighting, were extremely light, numbering only thirteen. Much credit for this must be given to the artillery, the 4.2 and infantry mortars, and the self-propelled howitzers and guns. The vigor and skill of the riflemen, however, were the deciding factors in the capture and clearing of Ormoc.

Throughout the day, the 305th Field Artillery Battalion, deprived of all infantry support on its east flank, was vigorously engaged in an aggressive defense of its position while at the same time giving effective support to the infantry in the battle for Ormoc. The Japanese had returned to occupy the commanding terrain 500 yards to the east of the Battalion's position along the main supply route of the Division. As the battery positions became untenable, it was necessary to call out all available personnel to clear the ridge. Cooks, drivers, mechanics, and clerks were deployed and advanced under the direct fire of the howitzers of Battery C which were turned to the flank and rear. Smoke shells and time-fire at minimum were used to screen and cover the movement of the advancing artillerymen. After a brief but hot fight with rifles and grenades, Captain Loomis, the Battalion Communication Officer who commanded the attacking troops, quickly drove off the enemy and established a defensive position on top of the ridge. From there, he was able to conduct artillery fire over groups of counterattacking Japanese until they were wiped out or dispersed.

At 1400, while Ormoc was still being mopped up in a house to house advance, the Division Commander in a note to the Commanding General, XXIV Corps, outlined his plans. The north boundary and artillery line of the 7th Division to be lifted to the Boad River, and a request was made that the Corps artillery line be lifted to run along the Antilao River, east through Aquiting, Paglascoon and Canale. To establish a defense in the Ormoc-Camp Downes area with elements of the 7th Division as soon as they arrived, and continue the advance of the 77th on Valencia. The troops moving north from Ormoc to Valencia to be supplied by heavily guarded convoys dispatched up Highway 2 past any isolated groups of the enemy. The Division to spend 11 December reconnoitering, reorganizing, moving supply dumps to forward areas, and establishing a hospital in Ormoc. The attack northward on Highway 2 to be resumed on 12 December with the 305th Infantry making the main effort. The 7th Division to come forward as soon as possible, take over the defense of the Camp Downes-Ormoc area, patrol to the north, east and south, and have one Battalion protect Ipil. One battery of the 306th Field Artillery Battalion to be moved by water to Ormoc and the remainder to come forward by road as soon as the 7th Division cleared the way.

Burning Japanese ammunition and gasoline dumps were still exploding and shooting their fire works skyward when General Bruce at 1645 sent the following message to the Commanding Generals of the 7th Infantry Division, the 11th Airborne Division, the XXIV Corps and the Sixth Army: "Have rolled two sevens in Ormoc. Come 7 and 11. Bruce."

Chapter 16: Cogon, Valencia, Tagbong River and Libungao Road Junction

A LIMITED attack to adjust positions on the north of the town was launched at 0930, 11 December, following a thirty-minute artillery preparation. Assault elements of the 306th and 307th attempted to cross the Antilao River, but were stopped by heavy small arms and machine gun fire from a Japanese position on the north bank at Cogon. This position astride Highway 2 was a slightly raised plateau, which covered the river banks on the south and rice paddies on the east and west flanks. It consisted of innumerable "spider holes" — individual emplacements roofed over with coconut logs or brush and dirt. The backbone of the defense was a reinforced concrete building which had been converted into a small fortress. Except for the building, undergrowth, high grass and clever camouflage made the firing positions almost impossible to detect at more than ten feet. As long as this area remained in Japanese hands, the use of the bridge and Highway 2 to the north was denied the Division, even though the strong point itself should be by-passed.

The 306th Infantry attacked north on the right of the 307th with its 1st Battalion on the left and the 3d Battalion on the right. The 1st Battalion was held up by the heavy resistance near the bridge across the Antilao River which even point-blank fire from self-propelled howitzers and guns, together with the fire of artillery and infantry weapons failed to knock out.

Company A, at the bridge, crossed the river at 1515 and penetrated about 100 yards into the Japanese position. Enemy light and heavy machine guns were emplaced in depth about every five yards, each with a very short field of fire. Only when the advancing infantry reached point-blank range would these guns open fire. Hip shooting and hand grenades eliminated some, but at too great a cost. The company was withdrawn to the south bank of the river at 1730.

The 3d Battalion of the 306th, on the right, made some progress against stiffening resistance. In addition, the battalion was also charged with maintaining a defense of the beachhead to its right rear. After advancing about 1,000 yards, a well organized enemy position was encountered. The Japanese were dug in on a steep ridge behind a deep ravine. This position was separated from that being attacked by the 1st Battalion by about 800 yards of rice paddies, but was a part of the same defensive organization.

Although able to bring only one company and a part of a second to bear on the position, the battalion commander called for an artillery preparation and attacked. Hostile reaction was immediate and intense and the riflemen advanced through heavy fire. A foothold was gained on the forward slope of the ridge but attempts to capture the crest were unsuccessful. The battalion was seriously handicapped because more than half of its personnel was echeloned to the right rear, manning a part of the outer defenses of the Division and could not participate. While the Battalion Commander, Lieutenant Colonel Gordon T. Kimbrell, was debating whether or not to stretch his thin lines a little more in order to release troops for the attack, the Japanese made up his mind for him. They threw a well organized counterattack against his right flank, followed in less than an hour by another against his center. After an hour of vicious close-in fighting, both counterattacks were beaten off. It was obvious, however, that further attempts against the ridge would leave the battalion in a very vulnerable position and so at 1600, orders were issued to withdraw the small group clinging to the forward slope of the hostile position and the battalion dug in for the night.

The 307th on the left met the same type of resistance. Its 1st and 3rd Battalions were abreast; the 1st on the right, with its right flank at the bridge, was unable to advance. The 3d Battalion moved through rice paddies to a position 800 yards northwest of the Cogon strongpoint.

At 1600 the 305th Infantry, with two battalions abreast, went into positions in the vicinity of the bridge between the 307th and the 306th, prepared to launch an attack astride the road the next day. The 306th shifted to the east to protect that flank.

The rear of the Division had been withdrawn to the north from Ipil and the remaining battalion of the 305th moved north to a position just short of Camp Downes, and continued to protect the Division's northward moving rear boundary. The 902d Field Artillery Battalion was in position among the Camp Downes buildings. Supply installations and the clearing station in Ipil were defended by the 2d Battalion of the 184th Infantry, 7th Division, which was attached to the 77th and joined at 1955 after a march from the south through no-man's land.

The 305th Field Artillery Battalion displaced forward during the day to positions on the northeastern edge of Ormoc. A sniper concealed in the midst of a battery position fired at an artilleryman and caused momentary consternation. Then a rabbit hunt commenced with about twenty indignant artillerymen blazing away into every pile of rubble until the offender was located and sent to join his ancestors. The position was made even more hazardous by the occasional mortar and artillery fire which came from the high ground to the northeast. The artillerymen were encouraged to accelerate the preparation of their individual defenses by the frequent whine of bullets and whistle of shell fragments. Registration on the Japanese positions along the river, however, was completed before darkness and defensive and harassing fires were continued throughout the night.

During the night of 11-12 December, organizations defending the water front and beaches — the 7th AAA (AW) Battalion, elements of the Amphibious Tractor Battalion, and the Tank Destroyer and Cannon Company weapons of the 307th Infantry — observed several enemy vessels moving into the bay, apparently with the intention of landing at Ormoc and on the beaches northwest of the town. The first vessel to be seen was a fifty-man barge approaching the Ormoc pier. By the time it came within range, all units had been alerted and the guns which bristled along the shore line were tracking the unsuspecting craft. Fire was withheld until it was fifty yards from the pier. Then the silent night was shattered by the point-blank roar of 40mm guns, .50 caliber machine guns, self-propelled howitzers and guns, and light and heavy machine guns, tracers from all of which converged on the barge. The first round of 40mm fire was a direct hit and the barge became an orange ball of flame. Some Japanese stood on the gunwales and screamed "Don't shoot," apparently in the belief that their forces still occupied the town. They were smothered by fire from all sides which literally blew the barge out of the water.

The light from the burning boat, augmented by 60mm illuminating shells, disclosed another Japanese landing vessel of the approximate size and type of an LST which, under cover of darkness, had beached northwest of Ormoc and was unloading troops and heavy equipment. Self-propelled howitzers and guns of the 307th Infantry, which were emplaced along the beach within 1,000 yards of the ship, opened fire while artillery forward observers of the 902d Field Artillery Battalion who were with the 307th, directed artillery fire on the landing point and inland. Excitement ran high as a terrific volume of fire was poured into the enemy ship. A gunner on an M-10 tank destroyer was heard shouting above the din: "Throw up another flare so I can hit the son-of-a-bitch again." The Japanese skipper attempted to retract his ship but had not withdrawn over fifty yards when it burst into flames and sank.

There were indications that another vessel had beached still farther to the west. The artillery shelled the area and at dawn a crippled ship was observed slowly making its escape far across the bay to the east. The shelling continued and before it got out of range its speed had been further reduced, its hull pierced, and clouds of black smoke were pouring from it. Planes later located and sank this vessel.

From prisoners who managed to escape and were later captured, it was confirmed that the Japanese had thought their own forces still held Ormoc, and that the two ships which had managed to reach the shore had unloaded about 150 men, eight amphibious tanks, and a quantity of ammunition; all were subsequently captured or destroyed. The amphibious tanks were the latest Japanese model and one was taken undamaged. The firing in Ormoc Bay during the night required the closest coordination as friendly vessels of a resupply convoy were also approaching. Communications between defensive areas, the 307th Infantry, Division Headquarters, and the incoming convoy worked perfectly and no damage was done to friendly vessels.

Before the smoke of battle had entirely cleared from the town of Ormoc, and while enemy snipers were still active in some sections of it, the establishment of supply dumps among the shattered buildings and warehouses was begun. Throughout the campaign, dumps were kept well forward, frequently within small arms range of the front lines in order to insure a constant flow of supplies to the rapidly advancing troops.

The supply difficulties in the Ormoc area were principally those of hoping that enough would arrive and of keeping what did arrive close to the troops. However, across the island at Tarragona, Lieutenant Colonel Henry O'Brien, Division Supply Officer, Lieutenant Colonel Allen T. Samuel, Jr., Division Quartermaster, Lieutenant Colonel Edward Hahn, Ordnance Officer, and Lieutenant Colonel William W. Stevens, Chemical Warfare Officer, and their assistants worked night and day to procure and transport supplies, to the Division. The task was next to impossible for many reasons. Supplies were slow in arriving at Leyte; weather and surf conditions hindered unloading; the 77th had been allowed to bring few trucks from Guam and those few were at Ormoc, so trucks had to be borrowed or begged at Tarragona; there were too few men to physically handle the supplies; Japanese planes constantly harassed shipping in Leyte Gulf and interfered with unloading and loading schedules; for days the only transportation to Ormoc was by ship but ships were scarce, frequently withdrawn after assignment to resupply missions, and ship captains reluctant to load to capacity; when the truck route across the island was opened by the 132nd Engineers it was a two-day, dangerous, Jap-infested journey and always subject to the whims of King Mud.

Somehow the task was accomplished. From Ormoc, and later Valencia, the list of needed items went by radio to Tarragona. All up and down the east coast, the 77th's scouts foraged personally and by telephone, finding, requisitioning, borrowing, and sometimes stealing supplies and the means by which to move the same. Men from the 706th Tank Battalion, and 292d Joint Assault Signal Company worked sometimes 36 hours at a stretch loading ships or trucks. Frequently they were assisted by convalescent infantrymen just back from the hospital, and anyone else who could be spared from his regular job. These men knew that the situation across the mountains was critical, that the 77th's actual existence depended on rounds of ammunition and cases of rations. So they worked till they dropped and somehow the supplies got through, never more than enough, never, in fact, as much as needed, but enough to get by. And the 77th got by.

12 December. After the bitter fighting of the 11th, the decision was made to take one more day to consolidate positions, reorganize, move up supplies and supporting artillery, and conduct aggressive patrolling to the front and flanks to gain further information of enemy dispositions, and approaches to and around them.

The 2d and 3d Battalions of the 305th remained between the 306th on the right and the 307th on the left, while the 1st Battalion of that regiment continued to protect the rear of the Division near Camp Downes. The 307th, still less its 2d Battalion, straightened its lines northwest of Ormoc. During the night Company F, reinforced, rejoined from Samar. The artillery battalions conducted harassing and interdiction fires on the enemy position across the Antilao River throughout the day and night.

General Bruce issued orders for the resumption of the attack at 0830 the next day, with the main effort on the left. The objectives were the road junction north of Cogon and continuation of the attack to the north. The 305th, in the center, was to attack astride Highway 2, making its main effort on the left of the road. The 306th was to protect the right of the 305th and echelon forward as the attack progressed. The 184th Infantry of the 7th Division was to relieve the 1st Battalion of the 305th and the 2d Battalion of the 306th in the rear of the Division so that those two battalions could rejoin their regiments.

After two self-propelled 75mm howitzers had been knocked out, a 105mm howitzer was moved into position on the south bank of the Antilao River directly opposite the Cogon strongpoint. A hundred rounds of direct fire was placed on the concrete building and the surrounding spider holes in an attempt to neutralize the position. In spite of heavy small arms fire against the howitzer, the crew was able to complete its mission and remove the piece from its exposed position without a single casualty.

13 December. The attack was launched at 1830 preceded by a thirty minute artillery preparation massed on the Cogon position. Participating in the preparation were the 902d Field Artillery Battalion, 305th Field Artillery Battalion, two batteries of the 304th Field Artillery Battalion, and one battery of the 306th Field Artillery Battalion (155mm howitzers) which were firing from positions only 200 yards in rear of the front lines. The attack was launched by the 305th with its 3d Battalion on the right of Highway 2 and the other two battalions on the left. Companies E and L were detached from their battalions and formed into a special attack unit under Colonel Paul L. Freeman, General Staff Corps, a War Department observer attached to the Division, for a direct assault on the block house once the north bank of the river was captured.

The 3d Battalion moved out in column of companies with Company I leading, followed by Company K. They moved up a deep draw which paralleled the river for a distance and then turned north. At 0925 the battalion, under cover of artillery and mortar concentrations, reached the ridge line north of the river bank, about 500 yards east of the concrete building. Company K moved up with one platoon on each flank of Company I to consolidate on top of the ridge. Just as the two platoons came abreast of Company I, the first of five counterattacks struck the battalion. All of the counterattacks which continued through the afternoon, were repulsed with heavy losses to the enemy, but the battalion also suffered severely.

The platoon of Company K on the left of the hill encountered a storm of fire which reduced it from 52 men to 11 in a matter of minutes. The platoon pulled back and the counterattack was finally stopped by mortar and machine gun fire. The platoon on the right started north and immediately ran into a counterattack. The initial fire knocked about a third of it out of action, and it withdrew over a small ridge. For the time being, the situation was a stalemate. The Japanese were on one side of a little knife ridge and the troops of the 3d Battalion on the other. Every time either would attempt to push forward, they met heavy fire as they reached the crest.

In the meantime, on the left, the 3d Platoon of Company K replaced the 1st. It tried crossing the front of the hill to help the 2d Platoon on the right and met another counterattack. The platoons of Company K were then pulled back and organized defenses for the night. Company I continued to hold the hill.

During the day the heat, humidity, uphill fighting, and the constant fever pitch of the men caused scores to keel over from heat exhaustion. They were evacuated to the aid station in a draw several hundred yards to the rear, splashed with cold water and laid in the shade. After resting awhile, they doggedly returned to the lines to continue the fight. Lieutenant Colonel Edward Chalgren, Jr., the battalion commander, said that the men were soaking wet from sweat all of the time. He spoke in the highest terms of their steadfast determination to keep fighting no matter what their condition.

At 1700, Captain Louis Hinson, commanding Company L, noticed a group of individuals on the west bank of the draw to the left of Company I. Knowing that no men from Company K were there, he asked the battalion commander for permission to place fire in the draw. Lieutenant Colonel Chalgren had sent a patrol to the draw some time earlier and withheld permission until he made sure the patrol had returned. Captain Hinson again called, this time with the positive statement, "Those are Japs in the draw, I can see them in the S-2 scope." Finally, certain that the patrol was clear, Lieutenant Colonel Chalgren permitted Company L to fire. Machine guns raked the draw from top to bottom. At first, Captain Hinson could not use the mortars because of the proximity of friendly troops, but as the Japanese fled up the draw the mortars opened fire. In addition, 37mm guns, one .50 caliber machine gun, two light and four heavy .30 caliber machine guns were used. The Japanese left 350 dead in the gully. The counterattack for which they had been forming never materialized. It was later determined that there had been an enemy reinforced battalion in front of the 3d Battalion, 305th Infantry, and that the counterattacks had been launched from the Japanese Command Post.

The position of this enemy battalion was originally discovered by a low-flying liaison pilot from the 305th Field Artillery Battalion. It consisted of a series of foxholes and emplacements on a plateau about 700 yards in front of the 3d Battalion. The position was completely hidden from ground observation. The air observer fired a number of battalion concentrations which destroyed its camouflage and disclosed its extent. Time fire was then adjusted on the enemy in the holes and trenches, and a series of concentrations were fired at irregular intervals over a thirty-six hour period. When the 3d Battalion finally captured this position, it reported that the artillery fire had torn to pieces hundreds of Japanese.

The 2d Battalion of the 305th crossed its line of departure at 0850. Company F was stopped almost at once by machine gun and rifle fire from the concrete building and the pillboxes to the west of it. Company G, on the right, was also stopped.

The 306th Infantry attacked on the right of the 305th and encountered no opposition. Three strong patrols were sent east to the vicinity of Dungnol but reported no enemy contact.

The 307th, on the left of the 305th, extended west along the Ormoc-Linao road to prevent enemy reinforcement and counterattacks from that direction. The villages of Punta and Linao were captured.

The artillery battalions, which were in position 200 to 300 yards in rear of the front lines, were able to fire by direct laying on many targets within a hundred yards of the infantry.

Orders for the next day were for the 305th to continue the attack, making its main effort on the left. The 307th to continue to protect the left flank and make a reconnaissance in force to Jalubon, and to determine the feasibility of a wide envelopment to capture Valencia from the west. The 306th to continue the protection of the right flank and reconnoiter Dunghol and Patag. The 306th and 307th were both assigned areas on the west of the Highway 2 to which they were to send patrols to determine enemy dispositions and to find routes and trails which could be used to move troops across country for an envelopment from the west. Guerrillas were to serve as guides.

14 December. The attack of the 305th Infantry was launched at 0830 with a local envelopment of the west flank of the Cogon strong point. The move was successful and by 1240 leading elements of the regiment had, on the west, passed beyond the concrete building and continued toward the road junction 1,000 yards to the north. In this attack by the 2d Battalion.

Company E made a frontal attack across the river by fire and movement, using grenades and bayonets to dig the enemy out of their spider-holes. This was the toughest kind of hand-to-hand fighting. Self-propelled howitzers and guns were brought forward to fire point-blank into the enemy spider-holes. The foot troops protecting these weapons were able to destroy the enemy in some of his deep holes by dropping grenades into each one. Armored bulldozers of the 302d Engineer Battalion drove straight into the position and buried many of the enemy crouching in their holes. Captain James E. Carruth of the 302d Engineer Battalion rode through the position in an armored bulldozer. As the blade cut off the tops of the spider-holes, he leaned out of the cab and killed the squatting occupants with his carbine. The crews of some self-propelled guns employed the unique method of dropping hand grenades through escape hatches into spider holes, as their vehicles passed over them.

The 1st Battalion of the 305th turned toward the east at 1225 and cut the rear of the Cogon position about fifty yards north of the concrete building. The 3d Battalion held the high ground east of the highway about 500 yards beyond the river. A small, isolated group of the enemy north of the blockhouse fought on until they were completely exterminated. The bitterest fighting the Division had yet encountered centered around the Cogon position. By the end of the day it, including the concrete building, had been reduced, most of its defenders annihilated and the road junction to the north captured.

Information gleaned from prisoners and captured documents disclosed that the 12th Regiment of the Japanese 26th Division had occupied the Cogon position, reinforced by an unknown number of men from service elements. Six hundred and thirty-three dead Japanese were counted immediately around the concrete building, and an unknown number had been buried by the bulldozers.

The 306th continued to protect the right flank. The patrols sent to Dunghol and Patag encountered no Japanese. Two patrols were sent to the west to reconnoiter routes for an envelopment of the Japanese west flank. Each consisted of one officer and six men. Lieutenants Buckner Creel and Milton Tepper led the patrols through the 307th lines just after daybreak. After crawling through the enemy positions confronting the 307th, they separated and moved north and east across the rice paddies toward Highway 2. After advancing a considerable distance, it became obvious to Lieutenant Creel that such a large patrol could be easily observed in the open rice paddies; he left his men concealed in an irrigation ditch under Staff Sergeant Michael Dean, and continued on alone. Both patrols traversed about five miles behind the enemy lines and Lieutenant Creel continued on alone for another two miles. As he neared his objective, he was seen from about 400 yards by five Japanese who were walking down Highway 2. Realizing that it was impossible to conceal himself he stood up, waved to them and boldly walked away. They mistook him for a Japanese, waved back, and continued on down the road. Both patrols returned late in the day and reported the proposed move feasible.

The scheme of maneuver for the 306th in the coming attack was to skirt the enemy positions west and north of Cogon and cut Highway 2 between Catayom and Dayhagan, ahead of the 305th. The 184th Infantry of the 7th Division relieved the 306th of its responsibility on the south flank and the regiment moved to Ormoc in preparation for the envelopment.

The 307th continued to protect the left throughout the day. Patrols were sent west and north to locate a route for a wide envelopment to capture Valencia and the air strip there. The reconnaissance in force sent west along the beach to Jalubon assumed the proportions of a "march to the sea." It consisted of two reinforced rifle companies, a dismounted Cannon Company, two self-propelled howitzers and two self-propelled tank destroyers. When, late in the afternoon this force returned, the coast line from Ormoc to Jalubon was dotted with fires and exploding Japanese ammunition dumps. It had destroyed six amphibious tanks, 7 landing barges, one 80-foot two-masted schooner, 50 tons of ammunition, 25 tons of miscellaneous supplies, four 40mm antiaircraft guns, four 20nim antiaircraft guns, one 77mm dual-purpose gun, several machine guns, a radio transmitter and generator, a coast artillery range finder, and it had burned about half the village of Linao to destroy enemy positions there.

15 December. The base for the operation and all supply dumps were now established in Ormoc and the dumps at Ipil were being closed out as rapidly as possible. A provisional force was organized and commanded by Brigadier General Edwin H. Randle, Assistant Division Commander of the 77th, for the defense of Ormoc so that the infantry of the Division could be freed for offensive operations. It consisted of the 184th Infantry of the 7th Division; elements of the 233d, 242d, and 302d Engineer Battalions; the 7th Antiaircraft Battalion; a Provisional Amphibious Tractor Battalion; Company A, 88th Chemical Weapons Battalion; Company A, 776th Amphibious Tank Battalion; and detachments of Division Special Troops.

During the night 14-15 December, the remainder of the 2d Battalion from Samar had landed at Ipil and re-joined the regiment at Linao. The reconnaissance patrol from the 307th, led by Lieutenant Earl Hodges, returned during the afternoon. It had reached San Jose west of Valencia and reported that the planned envelopment from the west was possible.

East of Highway 2 between Cogon and the road junction north of it, the enemy resisted stubbornly from dug-in positions. By the end of the day, the front line of the 305th had been straightened. During the night the 2d Battalion repulsed two counterattacks and killed twenty-eight of the enemy. Mopping up of determined small groups of the enemy in the Cogon area continued.

The 306th Infantry remained assembled in the vicinity of Ormoc and continued to prepare for the attack on the 16th. Patrols were sent to Catayom and Bai, and from Linao to the north of Mandang.

All of the Division artillery was consolidated in Ormoc, including the remainder of the 306th Field Artillery Battalion which had arrived overland from the south. It was placed in position 200 yards in rear of the front lines, under occasional sniper fire, prepared to support the Valencia attack on the following day.

16 December. The 305th Infantry continued its attack to the north at 0900 with the 1st Battalion on the left of Highway 2 and the 3d Battalion on the right. The 2d Battalion was in reserve. Resistance was sporadic but by local envelopment on the enemy west flank the regiment, by the end of the day, was 400 yards north of the Cogon road junction. Two battalions organized a position astride the highway and the reserve battalion dug in around the road junction.

The 307th started its wide envelopment to Valencia at 0730 in column of battalions with the 2d Battalion in the lead. Because the route crossed rice paddies and waist-deep rivers, no vehicles could accompany the regiment. All equipment, ammunition, and supplies were carried by hand. Native carriers were used to assist carrying parties. Soon after starting, scattered resistance was encountered but the movement was rapid under the circumstances. When San Jose was finally reached in the afternoon, about two platoons of Japanese were encountered in the edge of the village, but they were quickly eliminated. At 1600 San Jose had been captured and the regiment was digging in for the night. A distance of eight difficult miles had been covered and the regiment was on the flank of Valencia and its airfield, ready to attack on order. The few casualties were evacuated by artillery liaison planes.

The 306th moved out at 0900 and followed the rear of the 307th for a thousand yards west of Ormoc. At 1100, about 1,500 yards east of Liliam it swung north and advanced steadily during the day. Like that of the 307th, the march was a hard one. All equipment, ammunition, and supplies for a three-day operation had to be carried. Each man, in addition to his own pack, weapon, ammunition and rations, carried additional burdens. Machine guns, mortars, mortar ammunition, cases of hand grenades, boxes of extra radio batteries, litters, cases of blood plasma — all these items and many more were carried by hand. The route lay across five miles of rice paddies under a broiling tropical sun in a cloudless sky. On the rare stretches of relatively firm ground, the heavily laden men sank only ankle deep in the soft ground. But most of that five miles was through gooey, sticky mud which was usually knee deep and occasionally almost up to the waist. Now and then a man would hit a soft spot and sink to his shoulders; then it took the combined efforts of several to pull him out. That battle-weary, heavily burdened men could make the march and arrive at the objective with supplies and equipment intact and ready to fight if need be, was a tribute to their toughness and stamina. The 306th dug in 1,500 yards west of Cabulahan that night.

The artillery battalions were active through the day in support of the attack of the 305th Infantry, and were prepared to fire on call for the 306th or the 307th. They had been ordered to defend themselves and furnish their own close-in protection. This became necessary because all of the infantry was required elsewhere. It had been found before that artillery battalions were quite capable of protecting themselves.

Orders for the next day included air strikes on Valencia and the shelling of the road, town, and airfield by all artillery, including the 226th Field Artillery Battalion (155mm gun) firing from positions east of the mountains near Daro. The 305th Infantry was to attack north astride Highway 2. The 306th, from near Tipic, was to push on to Highway 2 well north of the 305th, attack to the north along the highway to beyond Cabulahan and, at the same time, attack south with one battalion to assist the advance of the 305th Infantry. The 307th Infantry was to be prepared to advance on Valencia on order.

Artillery planes were to reconnoiter road and bridge conditions along the highway so that an armored supply column could push through by-passed

Japanese resistance to the 306th and 307th Infantry Regiments. This column was to consist of five light tanks, self-propelled howitzers and guns, a company of engineers, a platoon of infantry, LVTs loaded with ammunition and supplies, and an artillery forward observer. The 302d Engineer Battalion was directed to keep well forward repairing the road and bridges, but to retire at night to the nearest infantry position.

Guerrillas of the 96th Infantry Regiment, Philippine Army, were to protect the left flank and keep the Pangsangahan River open from the bridge near Liloan to Catayom to permit LVTs to employ the river as an avenue over which casualties from the two forward regiments might be evacuated.

17 December. The famous double end run of the 77th Division was underway. The 306th and the 307th Infantry Regiments had broken loose from their base at Ormoc and headed into the unknown, while the 305th bucked the line up Highway 2. The former, with three days' rations and ammunition on the backs of their men were making a flanking movement which was cutting out big slices of enemy territory as far north as Valencia. The Division Commander was taking calculated risks. Supplying two infantry regiments depended upon the third driving through to open Highway 2 and effect a junction with them. But the enemy was disorganized and General Bruce was playing for big stakes, for if this bold move caused the immediate collapse of the enemy as far north as Valencia, it would result in saving many lives and much time.

The 305th launched its attack northward astride Highway 2 at 0930. Resistance was spotty and the attack progressed steadily until 1140 when it came to an abrupt halt south of Tambuco. The approach to the village was through coconut trees and high grass, sloping off on both sides to swamp and marsh land. A sharp skirmish ensued. The Japanese had dug in under the huts at the edge of the village, with a strong-point on the east flank. The self-propelled guns went in but made little progress due to lack of maneuver space. The resistance indicated about 200 Japanese, but their exact locations could not be seen until one was within ten feet of their positions. At 1530 a conference of infantry and artillery officers was held in a ruined building where rifle bullets kept nicking the timbers and from where enemy heads could be seen dodging behind coconut trees less than 200 yards away. It was decided to blast out the village with all available artillery and mortars, using sufficient white phosphorus to burn the shacks. On the left, the attack began to make progress. The leading units advanced close behind the self-propelled guns, blasting and spraying with grenades and automatic rifles all possible places of concealment. When the north edge of the town was reached, the attack met determined resistance again.

Time was slipping by. The objective for the day, the high ground at the junction of Highway 2 with the road to Dolores, just north of Tambuco, was still not in sight and the two artillery battalions had yet to be displaced into the defenses before dark. Every time Colonel Vincent J. Tanzola, the regimental commander, was asked about establishing his night defenses, he would reply, "Hell, we've only started this fight, just give me one more half hour." But the artillery had to have a little daylight in order to occupy its positions and register its defensive fires for the two regiments making the wide envelopment.

Off in the distance could be seen Lieutenant Colonel Elbert P. Turtle, commanding the 304th Field Artillery Battalion, with a pistol in his hand, wandering around by himself seeking suitable position areas for his batteries, while enemy bullets whistled about and mortar shells lobbed lazily through the air. As the advance slowly continued up ahead, batteries of the 902d and 304th Field Artillery Battalions alternately pulled into fields, which in some cases were not more than 100 yards behind a hot fire fight, but which they hoped would be within the regiment's defenses when the fight was over. Bullets spattered along the road and once in a while smacked into the sides of the amphibious truck companies' DUKWs which were hauling ammunition for the 902d, causing a temporary scarcity of Negro drivers until a big buck sergeant crawled out from behind a log, shook the woods with a roar and vented his spleen on the Japanese in general and his drivers in particular.

One officer of the 304th Field Artillery Battalion was wounded when a burning enemy ammunition dump exploded within fifty yards of the Battalion Command Post. The artillery sections and command post installations were repeatedly silhouetted by the gun flashes. Several batteries actually occupied a part of the defenses but all continued to fire missions in spite of their proximity to the enemy.

The 306th, from southwest of Tipic, resumed its attack northeast at 0730. As it approached Highway 2 from the west, the resistance became stronger; Japanese paratroopers recently arrived by air from Luzon were concealed in huts, but not dug in. There was a great deal of machine gun fire from these huts, but fire from the regiment's weapons rapidly eliminated resistance.

When it arrived within 400 yards of the highway, the 306th launched a coordinated attack. The approach was made in column of battalions, the 2d leading. The 2d Battalion made a three-pronged attack, a rifle company as each prong, to the right toward the road. This sucked the Japanese to the right and the 3d Battalion struck on the left to take Cabulahan by surprise. The 1st Battalion cleared out the Japanese between the other two. The regiment organized for the night with the 3d Battalion astride the highway facing north, the 2d Battalion astride it and facing south, and the 1st Battalion in the center. This made a long oval position along the road with the north end of it at the southern edge of Cabulahan.

Shortly after dark what sounded like a Japanese tank approached the position of the 2d Battalion, moving along Highway 2 from the south. As it reached the 2d Battalion, it was hit by a "bazooka" rocket but continued moving. Within the position it picked up speed and, mistaken for an LVT carrying supplies, the enemy vehicle passed through without being fired at. Lieutenant Colonel Kimbrell, commanding the 3d Battalion, called Company L and instructed the company commander to check his antitank defenses and make certain that the vehicle did not escape. A little later, the sound of a motor was heard approaching the company position. The men near the road were determined to get it and this time three "bazookas," one .50 caliber and two .30 caliber machine guns plus about ten automatic rifles were trained on the road as the motor was heard coming closer and closer. Throughout the regimental area all ears were turned toward the approaching vehicle and not another sound was heard. As it rounded a bend and reached the edge of Company L's position Technical Sergeant Jack T. Martin shouted, "Let him have it." The quiet was shattered by four simultaneous hits from the "bazookas" and steady streams of fire from the automatic weapons. The entire area was lighted as the vehicle burst into flames with a deafening roar. Investigation showed that it was not a tank but a truck load of Japanese soldiers. Not one escaped from the truck.

The regiment had had to carry its wounded with it as it advanced. It took eight men for each casualty; four litter bearers and four men to guard them. The Japanese always considered the wounded and litter bearers fair prey and the red cross flag and brassard were no protection.

General Bruce and Lieutenant Colonel Charles L. Davis, S-3 of the Division Artillery, flew in a liaison plane during the early morning to San Jose to coordinate air strikes and the artillery fires of Corps and Division artillery in softening up Valencia preparatory to the attack of the 307th

Infantry. Because of the large number of enemy troops reported in the Valencia area by guerrillas, it was planned to blast that region with air bombardment and heavy artillery fires prior to the attack. Commencing in the morning the 155mm guns of the 226th Field Artillery Battalion at Daro placed heavy fire on the village and the vicinity of the air strip. This fire continued until called off at about 1230 to permit an air strike on the village from 1240 to 1330, which was highly effective. Then the "Long Toms" and division medium artillery opened fire again. Artillery observers reported 2,000 of the enemy fleeing to the east.

At 1415, the 307th Infantry attacked in wedge formation astride the San Jose-Valencia road. The 2d Battalion was leading with the 3d echeloned to its right rear and the 1st to its left rear. The Japanese resisted strongly as the regiment left San Jose and approached the air strip. Some of the enemy troops were paratroopers who were in excellent physical condition and well equipped. At 1640 leading elements of the regiment were within a thousand yards of Valencia and on the southwest corner of the air strip, where preparations were made to remain for the night.

Patrols of the 77th Reconnaissance Troop operating on the right of the Division encountered an estimated 200 of the enemy near Dunghol and Patag and were forced to withdraw and join the 305th near Dolores. The platoon of the Reconnaissance Troop on the left of the 307th continued its aggressive reconnaissance to the west and north and protected the flank of the regiment.

Liaison planes of Division artillery did outstanding work during this day, not only in directing artillery fires but also in evacuating casualties from the 306th and 307th Infantry regiments. As soon as Highway 2 was cut near Cabulahan by the 306th, artillery planes landed on the road and evacuated the seriously wounded.

The Division Command Post at the southern entrance to Ormoc received about eighty rounds of enemy 70mm artillery and 81mm mortar shells between 1800 and 1900. One man in the Division Artillery Command Post was killed but no one else received a scratch and the only installation damaged was the General's latrine (unoccupied). The enemy guns were located near Dayhagan and silenced ten minutes after the observers found them.

18 December. The 305th Infantry resumed its attack north astride Highway 2 to join the 306th. Resistance was relatively light and by 1410, leading elements were in Dayhagan. Catayom was captured.

At 0830, the 307th resumed its attack on Valencia and the adjacent air strip, using the same formation it had employed the previous day. Again the Japanese defense stiffened but by 0905 the airfield and the village were captured and patrols were sent out to make contact with the 306th Infantry on Highway 2. Contact was gained by 1100. In addition to killing 369 Japanese in the final drive on Valencia, the regiment captured three steam rollers, two tractors and a motorcycle. Several Japanese trucks had been destroyed by the heavy artillery preparations.

The 306th astride the road near Cabulahan attacked north at 0830 with its 1st and 3d Battalions to join the 307th, while the 2d Battalion attacked south to make contact with the 305th. Concerning the fighting during these two days Colonel Smith pointed out later, "The enemy put up a stout fight during the afternoon of the 17th, and for about an hour on the 18th; then his resistance collapsed and we really had a field day. As we moved into Cabulahan proper, the resistance broke and two companies killed over 1,000 enemy in one day. Sixty sabers were found along the road that day." By evening, physical contact had been made with the 307th Infantry, and leading elements of the 305th were met between Dayhagan and Huaton.

Supplying the 306th and the 307th had been of serious concern to all. They had been attacking across country and away from roads for two days. From the 305th Infantry, native carriers brought supplies across country to both regiments, but this was slow and inadequate. Accordingly, as soon as the 305th and 306th made contact on Highway 2, the armored supply column which had been organized and waiting for that purpose, was pushed forward through remaining by-passed pockets of the enemy and succeeded in bringing supplies to both regiments.

The Reconnaissance Troop sent patrols from Valencia to the bridge where the Libungao-Palompon road crossed the Tagbong River to reconnoiter and report on the possibility of sending a regiment across country to that point.

The Division Commander requested authority to continue the vigorous drive in order to make contact with the X Corps which was moving down from the south, and to start a column west along the Palompon road.

19 December. The plan of attack on this day was for the 305th Infantry to move north to Valencia and relieve the 307th of the defense of that area. The 307th to attack north from Valencia astride Highway 2 and capture the Libungao road junction. The 306th to attack across country from

Cabulahan northwest to capture the crossing of the Libungao-Palompon road over the Tagbong River.

The 305th moved up the highway at 0800, relieved the 307th and by 1400 had organized positions defending the airfield, Valencia, and the Division Command Post which, during the day, moved to that place.

The 306th started across country from Valencia at 1100. Again its advance was over terrain impassable for vehicles, so once again all supplies and equipment for a three-day operation were carried by hand and on the backs of the men. The march was hard, but uneventful, until a point some 800 yards south of the Palompon road was reached about 1500. Here the leading battalions, the 1st and 3d, encountered resistance. After a preparation by the artillery and regimental weapons they attacked. The Japanese opposition was, as usual, bitter and fanatical, but the regiment advanced steadily and by 1800 its leading platoons reached the Palompon road. The 306th dug in covering the road and four Japanese trucks which attempted to use it during the night were destroyed.

The 307th Infantry moved north from Valencia along Highway 2 at 0900. It soon became evident that the Japanese had organized the defense of the road in depth with positions on the ridges flanking it. Machine guns had clear fields of fire on the advancing troops and Japanese light artillery was employed for direct fire. By 1700 the leading elements of the regiment had reached Libungao after an advance of three miles from Valencia. At this point, the 2d Battalion was stopped by a defensive position on the high ground north of the Naghalan River. The enemy skillfully employed his machine guns and mortars and placed effective fire in the 2d Battalion zone. Although all supporting weapons were used the position was not broken during the afternoon. Time did not permit the employment of either the 1st or 3d Battalions prior to darkness. During the day, 221 Japanese had been killed, bringing the regimental total for the campaign to 1,419.

The two artillery battalions which had been left in position near Ormoc were ordered to Valencia but were delayed by the many weak or broken bridges along the highway. The 302d Engineers worked day and night building and strengthening bridges over which the artillery and other heavy equipment could be moved. The men worked at night with lights, although bands of the enemy were still roaming the area. Guerrillas guarded all bridges between Ormoc and Valencia.

Orders were issued for rapid attacks to capture the crossing over the Tagbong River and the Libungao road junction. An armored column was organized and held in readiness to drive west along the Palompon road as soon as the Libungao road junction and the river crossing were captured. This force consisted of the 1st Battalion of the 305th Infantry; self-propelled weapons of the 305th and 306th Infantry Regiments; Battery A, 305th Field Artillery Battalion; a platoon of the 302d Engineer Battalion, with bulldozers; detachments of the 306th Field Artillery Battalion with five tractors; a detachment of the 718th Amphibious Tractor Battalion with fifty LVTs; a detachment from Company A, 302d Medical Battalion with ambulances; air liaison and artillery forward observer parties; a guerrilla patrol; an armored car, and a platoon of light tanks.

Information received from guerrillas concerning the bridges between the road junction and Palompon was favorable. They believed it would be possible to send heavy equipment over them. They further gave assurance that they would be able to arrange with the natives to place coconut logs or heavy timbers at bridge sites and that bridges could be seized by the guerrillas whenever it was desired. In order to verify this information, however, an engineer reconnaissance patrol was organized to operate behind Jap lines and survey the bridges.

20 December. The 306th Infantry, with orders to capture both the bridge at the Tagbong River 800 yards to the northwest, and the junction of Highway 2 and the Palompon road 800 yards to the east, divided its forces. The 1st Battalion was told off to capture the bridge while the 3d Battalion received the road junction assignment. The 2d Battalion, in reserve, protected the regimental command post and Company B of the 302d Medical Battalion. Company B had carried the wounded from the previous days' fighting as there was no way to evacuate casualties until the road junction was captured. Captain Richard H. Saunders of Company B, 302d Medical Battalion, spent the entire night of the 19-20 operating on the wounded by the light of a flashlight concealed under a poncho, while artillery concentrations continued to fall near the aid station.

At 0830, following a ten-minute artillery preparation, the 1st Battalion attacked through a small village on the southeast bank of the Tagbong River against heavy opposition from the high ground on the north and west of the bridge. Company C gained the far side of the river several hundred yards south of the bridge, but was held up by fire from the road. Company B cleared out the village and held the near end of the bridge. Company A in its first attempt to cross the river north of the bridge, got one squad of eight men to the west bank but all were killed or wounded and the company could not force a crossing. At 1500, the situation had reached a stalemate and Company C was withdrawn.

The 3d Battalion of the 306th attacked to the east at 0830 to capture the road junction. The attack was preceded by a ten-minute artillery preparation. Progress was slow and costly but by 1500, Company K was on the objective. Enemy fire plus fire from the 307th Infantry, which was advancing from the south, forced the company to withdraw slightly. On Division order the entire 3d Battalion was withdrawn 300 yards to permit the 307th unrestricted fire to its front. The 306th less its 1st Battalion then dug in for the night on the Palompon road 300 yards from the road junction.

Preceded by a heavy artillery preparation, the 307th Infantry attacked at 0830 with its 2d Battalion leading. The 3d and 1st Battalions were echeloned to the right and left rear. The enemy positions were the strongest the regiment had encountered since the fight at Camp Downes. Infantry of the Japanese 1st Division and of the 5th Regiment of the 8th Division were identified in the zone of action of the 307th. These divisions were classed among the best of the Japanese Army. It was estimated that on this day, the enemy opposing the 307th numbered 2,000 well equipped men with machine guns, mortars, and some artillery. During the day two counterattacks of about 200 Japanese each were launched against Companies G and E in true "banzai" style, supported by mortars and machine guns. These were repelled and the attackers totally exterminated. A number of other small counterattacks met the same fate. During the advance more than thirty enemy trucks were captured and many were immediately put to use by the regiment. Large ammunition and supply dumps were captured. The regiment advanced 2,000 yards during the day and killed 1,497 Japanese, but was still being bitterly opposed by a stubborn enemy as the advance was halted for the day 1,000 yards short of the road junction.

The 305th Infantry remained during the day covering Valencia and the Valencia airfield, and kept the provisional armored column in readiness for an immediate move to the west toward Palompon.

In a continued effort to hold the initiative at all costs and to prevent the enemy from stopping the Division steam roller drive, the Division Commander issued orders to prepare for a pursuit on 21 December by direct pressure along Highway 2, and an encircling movement to Palompon. The 306th Infantry was to capture the Libungao road junction, advance north to meet the 1st Cavalry Division of the X Corps, and on order be prepared to support the armored column with one battalion. The 307th was to establish a defensive position at the road junction and support the 306th in its attack to the north. The 305th was to have one additional battalion prepared to follow the armored column in trucks and its remaining battalion also prepared to support that force on order.

During the night 20-21 December, artillery ammunition in sufficient quantity having at long last arrived, the most intensive intermittent artillery bombardment of the Division's action on Leyte was fired. One half of a unit of fire was expended.

21 December. Enemy activity at the river about 0400 led the 1st Battalion, 306th Infantry to suspect that the enemy was preparing to counterattack. The surmise was justified, for at 0403, the Japanese dropped a mortar and artillery concentration on the battalion which killed two officers and four enlisted men, and wounded seven others. At 0500, the fire lifted and about 500 of the enemy launched an attack from the west and south. Thirty-seven of the enemy penetrated the position before they were killed. The counterattack then swung to the south but artillery fire broke it up. The Japanese followed their usual form, yelling "Banzai," screaming wildly, and cursing in garbled English. This stupid procedure, as always, failed to frighten the troops into headlong flight or hypnotize them into torpid insensibility, but rather it helped to locate the attack, orient all weapons against it, and always ended in the extermination of almost the entire howling mob of fanatics. From very early childhood, Japanese boys had been indoctrinated with the belief that their greatest happiness would be to die for their Emperor. Though not so intended, "banzai" attacks were almost always a sure way to attain that glorious end. Often "banzai" attackers found that generous draughts of sake fortified their devotion.

In the morning, 400 dead Japanese were counted around the position, but the battalion was very short of ammunition; it had expended more than half a unit of fire during the night. There remained only two boxes of ammunition for each machine gun, and a total of only 17 rounds of 81mm and 15 rounds of 60mm mortar ammunition.

At 0800 the Battalion Commander, Major Claude D. Barton, received orders to continue the attack. It was to be launched at 1000, preceded by a ten-minute artillery preparation fired by six batteries. Company E was attached to the battalion and joined, bringing with it all the ammunition the rest of the regiment could possibly spare. The scheme of maneuver was for two companies to attack abreast, Company B on the right and Company E on the left, crossing the river south of the bridge. Major Barton requested permission to delay the attack so that the ammunition which Company E had brought might be distributed. The attack was set for 1250, with the artillery preparation starting at 1240.

Following the preparation, the battalion jumped off; Company C crossed the river, swung through the native village and covered the high ground to the north. Company E was held up by fire at the road but Company B crossed the river and captured the high ground to the northwest.

At 1330, orders were received to push on to the Pagsangahan River. Company commanders were palled to the Battalion Command Post at the bridge to receive orders. The attack was to be made astride the road, Company E on the right, Company C on the left, Company A echeloned to the left rear of Company C. Company B, on the high ground to the north of the road, was to turn down the ridge line toward the road and place itself in rear of Company E.

Somehow the orders to Company B were misconstrued and that unit withdrew from the hill to the river, leaving behind a covering force of about one platoon. The Japanese selected that moment to counterattack, and the remainder of Company B was driven off the hill. This prevented the attack to the west.

The mistake cost the battalion a day and a half of fighting. Major Barton decided that the battalion must retake the high ground before any further advance would be possible. At 1600, Company A attacked, moved across the river and assaulted the lower slopes and nose of the hill. The attack was successful and the company destroyed about two thirds of the defenders. It was then withdrawn for the night across the river.

One of the most heroic acts of the campaign occurred during the attack of Company A. When a rifle platoon supporting a light tank hesitated in its advance, Private George Benjamin, radio operator for the company, voluntarily and with utter disregard for personal safety ran across bullet-whipped terrain to the tank, waving and shouting to the men of the platoon to follow. Carrying his bulky radio and armed with only a pistol, he fearlessly penetrated intense machine gun and rifle fire to the enemy position, where he killed one of the enemy in a foxhole and moved on to annihilate the crew of the light machine gun. Heedless of the terrific fire now concentrated on him, he continued to lead the assault until he fell mortally wounded. After being evacuated to an aid station, his first thought was still of the battalions advance. Overcoming great pain, he called for the Battalion Operations Officer to report the location of enemy weapons and valuable tactical information he had secured in his heroic charge. For his unwavering and unswerving devotion to the task at hand, and aggressive leadership, Private Benjamin was posthumously awarded the Congressional Medal of Honor.

The 2d and 3d Battalions, 306th Infantry, continued their attacks toward the Libungao road junction at 0800, and captured it soon afterwards.

The 307th, attacking north astride Highway 2, resumed its advance at 0600 with the 1st and 3d Battalions abreast, the 3d Battalion on the right. The 1st Battalion was halted 300 yards short of the road junction and contact was made with the 306th at 0745.

During the fight for the road junction, the 304th Field Artillery Battalion was in direct support of the 306th Infantry, and the 902d Field Artillery Battalion of the 307th Infantry. As the two regiments converged from right angles, artillery support became more and more difficult. The coordination of fire of the two artillery battalions was accomplished by the observers with one regiment assisting by radio the adjustments of the observers of the other. In spite of the narrowness of field of fire, the results attained were excellent. The situation was even further complicated by the approach of the 1st Cavalry Division from the north.

The 3d Battalion of the 306th turned north at the road junction to make contact with the 1st Cavalry Division and ran into a strong defense. The road junction lay on low ground in the midst of rice paddies. Three hundred yards to the north, the Japanese had dug in on a ridge from which they swept the area with small arms and mortar fire. At 0900 General Randle, who was coordinating the action at the road junction, directed Colonel Hamilton to commit his 2d Battalion on the east of Highway 2 and attack north on the right of and in conjunction with the 3d Battalion of the 306th. The 2d Battalion of the 307th was under the command of Colonel Smith during the attack. Both battalions battled furiously to advance. The 2d Battalion of the 307th, commanded by Lieutenant Colonel Joseph B. Coolidge, had a little cover from a series of low finger-ridges, but the 3d Battalion of the 306th, commanded by Major George T. Larkin, was forced to attack across exposed rice paddies. Company I, in the lead, received heavy casualties. All platoons of Company I were greatly depleted. In one light machine gun squad, most of the men had been killed or wounded and Private Harold T. Bevis was carrying the gun and ammunition and firing the weapon unassisted. By 1200, little progress had been made by either battalion. At 1210, the 2d Battalion of the 306th, less Company E, was ordered to envelop the northwest flank of the enemy position with one company. Company G was selected to make the attack down a small ridge leading to the enemy's flank. The attack was successful in that it removed pressure from the two assault battalions. The Japanese were fighting for their last supply route, the Palompon road, and were defending with fanatic savagery. While both the 306th and the 307th had troops at the road junction, machine gun fire was still falling around it.

It was essential that the enemy be driven back so that the road junction could be used by supply vehicles and ambulances which were waiting, a short distance to the south, to make the turn onto the Palompon road as soon as the junction was reasonably safe. The 306th had been without re-supply of any sort, except for air drops of plasma and bandages from artillery planes, for two days. More pressing even was the need for evacuation. Company B, 302d Medical Battalion, now had over a hundred casualties in its care, some of whom had been wounded two days previously.

In addition to the machine-gun fire being placed near the road junction by the Japanese astride Highway 2 to the north, an additional obstacle to evacuation was a partly destroyed bridge over a small stream some thirty yards to the south. A detachment from the 302d Engineer Battalion moved to the bridge with fighting in progress a mere 300 yards to their front and, coolly ignoring mortar shells which fell in the water around them and occasional bursts of machine gun fire, repaired the bridge. The quarter ton ambulances of Companies B and C, 302d Medical Battalion, then ran the gantlet of fire at the road junction and began evacuating the wounded.

The engineers worked rapidly to strengthen the bridge and at 1430 self-propelled howitzers and guns and light tanks were able to cross. These weapons joined the two assault battalions and with their assistance at 1500 a coordinated attack overran the Japanese positions. The advance continued to the north against greatly weakened resistance. Colonel Smith was able to release the 2d Battalion of the 307th and about 1730 it rejoined its own regiment after having crossed the river which was the boundary between the 77th Infantry Division and the 1st Cavalry Division. By 1630, the 3d Battalion, 306th made contact with the leading elements of the 1st Cavalry Division 1,000 yards south of Kananga. This joined organizations of the X and XXIV Corps and opened the road from Ormoc to Pinamopoan and Carigara.

Chapter 17: The Road to Palompon

AN AERIAL reconnaissance of the Palompon road and bridges on 22 December, and a report from the engineer sergeant operating with a guerrilla patrol made it apparent that it would not be possible to send a fast armored column over that route. Some of the bridges had been destroyed and others were not strong enough to support heavy vehicles. Because of their numbers it would take too long to repair and reinforce the forty-four bridges between Libungao and Palompon.

The mission of the 1st Battalion of the 305th Infantry, around which the armored column had been built, was changed. Palompon was the only port yet remaining available to Japanese forces on Leyte. Speed was essential in capturing it and breaking organized resistance on the island, other operations in the Philippines could then be launched. General Bruce decided to alter his original conception and send a special task force from Ormoc to Palompon by water. This would establish a beachhead at that place from which attacks to the east could be launched to join with the troops advancing from the west. The Commanding General of XXIV Corps was requested to arrange for PT boats to support this bold move.

The amphibious force was to consist of the 1st Battalion, 305th Infantry; one provisional company of amphibious tractors; Company A, 776th Amphibious Tank Battalion; one platoon, Company D, 706th Tank Battalion; three self-propelled howitzers from the Cannon Company, 305th Infantry; the 2d Platoon, Company A, 302d Engineer Battalion; detachments from Company A, 302d Medical Battalion: the 292d Joint Assault Signal Company; the 305th Field Artillery Battalion; the 306th Field Artillery Battalion; and Battery A, 531st Field Artillery (gun) Battalion.

Details of the former plan were changed to require the 306th Infantry, with the 1st Battalion, 307th attached, to protect the road junction and the bridges aver the Tagbong and Pagsangahan rivers.

The 307th Infantry was to protect Valencia while the 305th, less its 1st Battalion and detachments, as a light striking force was to advance west on the Palompon road. Artillery battalions would be prepared to echelon forward to positions from which they could pound Matagob on the night of 22-23 December and Palompon on the night of 23-24 December.

The 1st Battalion of the 306th attacked at 0800 on 22 December, following a ten-minute artillery preparation. Self-propelled howitzers, a light tank, and infantry mortars closely supported the attack against the high ground which had caused so much trouble the two previous days. By 0815 the objective was completely captured: most of the defenders had withdrawn during the night.

The 2d Battalion, 305th Infantry was moved by truck from Valencia to the Tagbong River where it detrucked at 1030 and advanced astride the road, passing through the 1st Battalion, 306th. The trucks returned at once to Valencia, stopping en route to entruck a battalion of the 307th Infantry. After discharging it at Valencia they picked up the 3d Battalion, 305th and carried it forward to join the 2d Battalion. On their return the trucks brought another battalion of the 307th to Valencia. The 1st Battalion, 305th, remained in the vicinity of Valencia and developed plans for the landing at Palompon. The 305th Infantry proceeded west along the Palompon road to a point approximately 2,000 yards southwest of Humaybunay where it dug in for the night.

The 1st Battalion of the 306th covered the Tagbong and Pagsangahan river crossings, while the remainder of the regiment, with the 1st Battalion, 307th attached, covered the Libungao road junction, with the 3d Battalion at the bridge south of Kananga.

The 307th Infantry, less its 1st Battalion, relieved the 305th in the defense of Valencia and the airfield there. Company F moved to San Jose to protect Battery A of the 531st FA (155mm gun) Battalion.

The 302d Engineers reinforced by the 232d Engineer Battalion continued "the battle of the bridges" along the Palompon road immediately behind the advancing infantry. The men worked day and night, usually without infantry protection, reinforcing the bridges to carry 2¾-ton trucks, later to carry the heavier self-propelled weapons and tanks. Bailey bridges had been promised by 20 December. They were to have been put over the rivers for immediate use and the engineers would then construct wooden bridges. When the latter were completed the Bailey bridges would be removed for use elsewhere. The patented bridges failed to arrive, however, which materially slowed the progress of bridge construction. The engineers also made minor repairs on the Valencia airfield to permit the landing of C-47's for the evacuation of the wounded to the east side of Leyte.

23 December. From guerrillas, natives, and patrols it was learned that a large group of the enemy, estimated as a battalion, was in position at Matagob (Dipi). The 305th would encounter this position before the end of the day and, accordingly, an air strike was made at 0955 and fighters bombed and made forty-two strafing runs on the town. Fires were started, ammunition dumps were blown up, and considerable damage was done, but the pilots were unable to observe the effect upon the enemy.

The 305th, less its 1st Battalion, resumed its attack west along the road at 0800 with the 2d Battalion leading. The troops found the positions at Matagob but the enemy had withdrawn and the regiment stopped for the night 500 yards west of the town. Meanwhile the 1st Battalion moved to Ormoc in preparation for its unique movement to Palompon. The 306th and 307th continued their defensive missions.

The military police of the Division came in for their share of frontline action, particularly during this phase of the campaign. They followed closely behind the 305th Infantry and accompanied the engineer bridge construction crews to regulate traffic and keep the extremely narrow Palompon road free of congestion. In the performance of these usually routine duties, they frequently engaged in small skirmishes with Japanese stragglers and killed several.

24 December. The 305th Infantry in its position 500 yards west of Matagob was attacked at 0245 by an estimated 200 Japanese troops. The attack was beaten off. One hundred of the enemy were left dead around the position and the 305th suffered not a single casualty. The regiment continued westward at 1000. Resistance throughout the day was light, but progress was slow because of the difficult foothills over which the road now rose. The enemy defended in small groups from dug-in positions, each of which had to be cleared out. Some 70mm artillery fire was received but it was effectively countered by 81mm mortar fire and by the fire of the 4.2 mortars of a platoon of Company A, 88th Chemical Weapons Battalion. Gun crews were destroyed and the guns captured. Colonel Tanzola and his headquarters in the school house in Matagob spent most of Christmas Eve dodging Japanese artillery shells. For over an hour the enemy seemed to be zeroing in on the headquarters, some shells landing right in the command post. The men held a tight grip on mother earth and prayed until it was over. An artillery forward observer finally spotted the guns and adjusted the 105s and 155s on them. After several volleys all was quiet and no further casualties were suffered.

It had been planned to move artillery to Matagob to support the Palompon landing, but though the engineers worked frantically, the weak bridges prevented the passage of the guns and the landing could be supported from the east only by Battery A of the 531st Field Artillery (gun) Battalion at San Jose. Late in the afternoon a 90-foot bridge collapsed under the weight of an artillery prime mover and a 155mm howitzer and these valuable pieces of equipment dropped into 24 feet of water. The engineers worked all night and most of the next day under sniper and machine gun fire to bring from Tagbong River a Bailey bridge to replace the broken span. An ingenious soldier rigged a diving mask from an old gas mask, some hose and an air pump and went down to put cables around the sunken but irreplaceable equipment. These were raised and the 777th Ordnance Company soon had them in action once more.

Arrangements were made to provide air support on ground alert, prepared to strike the landing beaches at Palompon on call. Protection for the long water movement was to be provided by Navy PT boats operating from their base at Ormoc, but this protection would be available only until dawn. Communication between the Amphibious force and supporting air and artillery was by SCR 193 radio mounted in an armored car, M-8, to the Division Command Post at Valencia and thence to air or artillery.

At 2000 the amphibious force, transported in LVTs of the 718th and 536th Amphibious Tractor Battalions, and LCMs operated by the 2d Engineer Special Brigade, departed from Ormoc for the long night passage to Palompon. The voyage was made without incident as far as enemy action was concerned, although three LVTs sank en route because of mechanical failure. The ten-hour ride for a distance of 44 miles in the small landing craft which were only intended to transport troops a few thousand yards, was long and tedious. This unique operation was the longest tactical movement by LVTs yet recorded.

During the day the 1st Battalion of the 307th rejoined its regiment at Valencia. The 306th remained on its assigned mission and during the day killed 65 of the enemy without suffering any casualties.

25 December. Christmas Day notwithstanding, the 2d and 3d Battalions of the 305th attacked to the west along the Palompon road at 0800; the 3d Battalion passed through the 2d and took the lead. The terrain was rugged and enemy resistance stubborn. The attack was made even more difficult because reinforcement of the bridges was not yet completed and medium tanks and heavy self-propelled weapons could not be brought forward. At

1115, one and a half miles west of Matagob, the attack was stopped by small arms, mortar, and artillery fire from positions in the hills northwest of the road. The 2d Battalion attempted to flank the position from the south, but was unsuccessful and withdrew for a try at the enemy north flank. The Japanese were attacked continuously but the battalions could make little headway. The 3d withdrew to permit artillery fire on the enemy, but the 2d remained on his north flank.

The Japanese Christmas present to the 305th Combat Team was another direct fire attack from a 75mm gun emplaced in a draw about 1,000 yards south of Matagob. The first round was a close over, barely missing the school house then occupied by the regimental command post and the fire direction center of the 305th Field Artillery Battalion. The next round was also an over, but even closer. The flash of the second round was seen by an artillery observer who called the 1st Section of Battery B into action and pointed out the location. Before the third round could be fired the section had turned its piece and was pouring fire on the Japanese gun. No more fire was received. Reconnaissance the following day disclosed the bodies of several Japanese cannoneers, the remnants of a small artillery ammunition dump, and portions of the 75mm gun. Continuing aggressive patrolling by the artillery battalion prevented any further enemy artillery activity from that flank.

The 1st Battalion, 305th Infantry, reinforced, completed its amphibious movement to Palompon with no casualties to personnel. After preparatory fires by the 155mm guns of the 531st Field Artillery Battalion near San Jose, and from mortar boats of the 2d Engineer Special Brigade, the troops made a successful landing just north of Palompon near Buaya. A column was dispatched to the north to clear the road and prevent enemy counterattack from that direction, while the remainder of the force struck rapidly through the village of Look to Palompon, which was captured at 1206. The successful landing denied to the enemy his last available port for reinforcing or evacuating troops, and assured the complete destruction of all remaining enemy resistance on the island of Leyte.

A message from General Bruce to the Commanding Generals of XXIV Corps, Sixth Army and the Commander in Chief of the South-West Pacific, read, "The 77th Division's Christmas contribution to the Leyte campaign is the capture of Palompon, the last main port of the enemy. We are all grateful to the Almighty on this birthday of the Son and the Season of the Feast of Lights."

This day General MacArthur declared organized resistance on Leyte destroyed. What remained to be done was mopping up of scattered pockets of the enemy throughout the Ormoc-Palompon corridor. This was to be no easy job. Private GI Doughboy's comment on General MacArthurs announcement was, "Well, maybe it will help bolster morale at home." The doughboy of the 77th didn't need his morale boosted, he was doing all right.

26 December. Every man in the Division had a turkey dinner. It had been decided that for several reasons it would be better to eat Christmas Dinner on the same day the folks at home were enjoying theirs. Leyte was one day ahead of the United States on the calendar; and besides, the 25th had been a busy day.

The 3d Battalion of the 305th sent strong patrols to locate and reconnoiter the enemy position and guns one and a half miles northwest of Matagob, and direct artillery fire on them. At 1130 self-propelled howitzers advanced along the road in front of the 3d Battalion and fired point-blank into an estimated enemy battalion entrenched along the high ground to the right of the road. Company K had killed about 100 Japanese there the day before.

The self-propelled howitzers fired on Japanese occupying buildings in a small village to the left of the road before retiring. At 1300 a patrol from Company I, moving wide around the left flank, circled back to the road and burned all of the huts in two small villages to prevent the enemy from re-occupying them before the battalion attacked the next day. A soldier of the 305th Cannon Company described one incident:

Lieutenant Fasso had gone ahead of the front line in Corporal Palermo's M-8. The Japs in shacks on both sides of the road opened up with everything they had. The Lieutenant ordered fire on the shacks. He got up above the turret with his field glasses to survey the results of the fire. Suddenly he exclaimed, "Dammit, I'm hit!" Blood was rushing from his mouth from a wound above the chin; he calmly gave Corporal Palermo charge of the M-8 with final orders, and was removed to an aid station. A few minutes later, Major Fife — Regimental S-3 — jumped on a tank to get a view of the area. He was wounded in the head by a snipers bullet. The M-8 took Major Fife back to Matagob, and returned with Lieutenant Wayne Hogancamp, who left the CP to take charge of the M-8s.

The 1st Battalion of the 305th continued its occupation of the area round Look and Palompon and sent patrols to the north and east. Six Japanese were killed during the day near Look, but these were obviously stragglers who had become lost trying to reach the coast.

The 306th and the 307th continued in occupation of their assigned areas and did extensive patrolling. The latter killed 27 Japanese during the day.

27 December. Company E, part of Companies F and H, and detachments of attached units were selected from the 2d Battalion, 305th, moved to Ormoc by truck and then to Palompon by water to reinforce the 1st Battalion in its attack to the north and east.

The 3d Battalion of the 305th launched a dawn attack, wide around the left flank of the Japanese position covering the road. Enemy machine gun and artillery fire from the right flank slowed the advance over the mountainous terrain. Friendly mortar and artillery fire knocked out two machine guns which greatly assisted the battalion in capturing its objective. The attacking force knocked out two 70mm field pieces, killed 160 Japanese and the remainder fled to the hills. The engineers had repaired and strengthened all bridges up to the 305th.

With George Washington and the Hessians at Trenton in mind, that night the 2d and 3d Battalions burned camp fires, sang songs, shouted boisterously and generally tried to give the impression of celebrating the Christmas season with strong drink, of which there was none; not even a captured bottle of sake. The idea behind this strange conduct was to encourage the Japanese to "Banzai," as the easiest known method of killing off large numbers without much effort. The enemy failed to fall in with the idea but the apparent celebration at the regimental command post attracted several curious enemy patrols which were, in the main, annihilated.

At 0100 an emergency call from friendly planes which had fled from the island of Mindoro at the threat of a Japanese task force, was picked up by the 6th Support Aircraft Party at the Division Command Post. The planes were running short of fuel and were prevented by bad weather from crossing the mountains to Tacloban. They needed a landing place quickly. The support aircraft party and G-3 alerted the 307th and within very few minutes the landing field was surrounded by "jeeps" and lighted by their headlights. Six planes, including two P-40s, two P-47s, one P-51, and one B-25 landed safely.

28 December. At 0730 the 3d Battalion, 305th, attacked astride the highway with light tanks and self-propelled howitzers to capture the highest ground between it and Palompon, 1,000 yards to the west. After advancing 300 yards the troops encountered machine-gun fire from a hill to

the front. Mortar fire quickly silenced the gun and the advance continued. A self-propelled howitzer knocked out an enemy field piece on the hill. After an artillery concentration and a heavy fire fight the 3d Battalion captured the hill. There were 350 dead Japanese on it. From that point on the advance of the 305th was down grade.

At 0800 Company C of the 1st Battalion moved east from Look and encountered scattered enemy patrols. By evening it had advanced to Tenilian where it dug in for the night. The company had captured a Japanese truck and killed 17 of the enemy.

The 306th remained in position covering the bridges and the road junction and sent combat patrols in all directions. These patrols killed 49 of the enemy. Patrols of the 307th, in the Valencia area, made no Japanese contact. One, which penetrated south and west of San Jose, found eight native women who had been raped and bayoneted by Japanese soldiers. One, still living, was evacuated to the Division Clearing Station.

The 77th Reconnaissance Troop sent two platoons, accompanied by artillery observers, to Hot Springs to evacuate 3,500 natives who were reported being held there. Scattered groups of the enemy were encountered along the route; the patrol placed artillery fire on one group of about 150 on a high ridge overlooking Hot Springs. The patrols killed 26 Japanese in brief skirmishing, rescued the natives and evacuated them to Valencia.

This procession of several thousand grateful but disorganized and destitute Filipinos made a great impression on all who watched it stream through the Division area at dusk. They were of all ages; men, women, children and babies; wearing all sorts of costumes, or none at all. Many were sick and all were loaded down with battered household possessions: some were riding carabao, others were mounted on scrawny cows or ponies. But mostly they walked. As far down the road as one could see they kept coming, smiling but desperately tired and emaciated. They were being shunted along by PCAU (Philippine Civil Affairs Unit).

Throughout the campaign, Lieutenant Colonel Albert E. Hallett, Division Judge Advocate and Civil Affairs Officer, and his PCAU units worked day and night to feed, clothe and care for the refugees. There were 152,000 natives whose homes were in the Division area; 79,000 in Ormoc alone. As fast as the Division captured a region these people came streaming down out of the mountains to their destroyed villages and towns. Handling and caring for them was an almost impossible job for so small a unit. When the Japanese first captured the island the natives fled to the hills and mountains and there raised what little food they could. When the Americans landed the Japanese fled to the hills and the Filipinos returned to the lowlands.

Lieutenant Colonel Hallett and his Civil Affairs Unit also coordinated the employing of native labor. Most of the Division dead were buried by native details employed by the Quartermaster. The villagers took great pride in their work in the cemeteries and they pledged themselves, when the Division finally departed, to tend them and keep the graves forever beautiful.

29 December. At 0800 the elements of the 2d Battalion of the 305th Infantry which had been sent by water to reinforce the 1st Battalion at Palompon, passed through Company C at Tenilian and advanced northeast astride the Palompon-Libungao road to make contact with the 3d Battalion, 305th, driving along the same road from the other direction. The 2d Battalion advanced 3,000 yards, captured a Japanese field piece, and killed 40 of the enemy found in shacks along the route. Company I, supported by two light tanks, attacked west at 0800 after a ten-minute artillery preparation. It advanced rapidly to Cambutoy through groups of disorganized Japanese.

Artillery battalions were active in support of the 305th during the day. One concentration killed approximately 140 Japanese and destroyed one 75mm gun. The enemy losses for the day totaled 479 killed and 1 prisoner. One American was wounded.

30 December. The 3rd Battalion, 305th, again launched its attack to the west at 0800. Large groups of the enemy were observed fleeing before the rapidly advancing troops, and were shelled by artillery and mortars. At 1300 the leading tank of the battalion rounded a bend in the road and ran into point-blank fire from six 70mm field pieces emplaced 200 yards to the west. The tank was destroyed. The foot troops flanked the positions, self-propelled howitzers moved up for a gun duel, and the artillery took the enemy under fire. All of the guns were knocked out and 206 Japanese were killed.

Elements of the 2d Battalion of the 305th which had reinforced Lieutenant Colonel Landrum's task force at Palompon advanced northeast and reached to within 4,000 yards of the 3d Battalion. During the day they killed 32 Japanese. The 1st Battalion continued patrolling around Palompon, while Company C made an amphibious landing and a reconnaissance in force at Abijao farther north. The landing was met by Japanese mortar and small arms fire, but the resistance was overcome and the town was burned to prevent its reoccupation. The company then continued north along the coast to Jordan without encountering any more of the enemy. It succeeded in establishing radio contact with a patrol of the 1st Cavalry Division in the vicinity of Villaba.

The 306th and 307th Infantry Regiments continued patrolling in their areas and conducted a reconnaissance to the north, preparatory to relieving the X Corps of patrolling responsibility in that sector.

31 December. The 3d Battalion of the 305th attacked to the southwest at 0720 with L Company astride the road. At the same time the elements of the 2d Battalion moved out to the northeast. Radio communication between the two converging forces coordinated artillery concentrations on the Japanese between them. The concentrations were especially effective and killed many Japanese who were being compressed between the two closing organizations. Contact between them was established at 1215.

With the junction of the troops of the 305th from the east and the west, the Libungao-Palompon road was opened for traffic over its entire length. Those of the enemy who had managed to get out from between the two columns fled north into the hills. During the two days when the gap was being closed, 1,232 Japanese were killed by the infantry and artillery.

The 2d Battalion of the 307th discovered four Japanese tunnels 800 yards west of Valencia which contained 800 drums of aviation gasoline, five hundred 500-pound bombs, and one hundred bomb fuzes. This added to the work of Captain George C. Sarauw and his 92d Bomb Disposal Squad. Those men, quiet heroes of a profession where mistakes are made only once in a lifetime, were veterans of Makin, Tarawa, Kwajalein, Roi and Guam. They supervised Filipino work gangs in the collection of hundreds of tons of Japanese ammunition and explosives which had been captured by the Division, and skillfully deactivated mines and booby traps. Then they destroyed these hundreds of tons of Japanese munitions in 200-ton lots at well advertised, but not well attended daily "blowings".

1 January. The 305th Infantry consolidated in a bivouac at Look and confined its tactical activities during the day to local patrolling. An emergency resupply of ammunition was sent by LVT to elements of the 1st Cavalry Division at Villaba, where they had become engaged in a heavy fire fight.

The Division had been ordered to effect the relief of X Corps units to the north as soon as possible, and organizations of the 306th started moving to occupy areas around Calubian. The 2d Battalion closed into a defensive area at Pinamopoan prepared to complete its move to Calubian by water the next day.

2 January. Company C of the 305th, reinforced by a platoon of heavy piachine guns, a platoon of LVTs, a section of 81mm mortars, and an artillery forward observer party, made an amphibious landing at Villaba. It killed 10 Japanese out of sixty encountered. The 1st Cavalry Division units which had been patrolling near Villaba were relieved of their responsibility for that area.

The 1st Battalion, 306th, occupied a position midway between Kananga and Linoy on Highway 2 to patrol an area taken over from X Corps. The 2d Battalion moved from Pinamopoan to Calubian by water. The regimental command post opened at Linoy, and the 3d Battalion and special units prepared to move there the next day.

Company I of the 306th was in the vicinity of Matagob where it had reinforced the 305th. The Company, with self-propelled howitzers and light tanks attached, attacked a position held by a company of Japanese 800 yards southwest of Matagob. A patrol from the 306th Field Artillery Battalion had located the position earlier in the day. A brisk fight ensued, but after an artillery concentration had been placed on the position, the enemy withdrew to the north. Fifty-two Japanese were Killed and four tons of rations and three ammunition dumps were destroyed.

The 307th Infantry began its reassignment of areas. The 1st Battalion moved to the vicinity of Libungao where it relieved the 306th.

3 January. Division operations during the day consisted of patrolling and movement of organizations to new areas. The 2d Battalion of the 306th completed its movement to Calubian and the 3d Battalion, the remainder of the regimental command post, and special units closed on Linoy and Kananga, joining the 1st Battalion.

4 January. The 1st Battalion, 305th, less Company C, remained in Look while Company C occupied Villaba. The 2d Battalion, with Battery B of the 305th Field Artillery Battalion attached, moved to Villaba to establish a base from which patrols would cover the surrounding region.

From the 306th six long distance patrols were sent out. Three followed the Punta River to the Catalotolham River, and one to the Hatabsgan River. Three additional patrols were sent to Pina and two to Kananga. Twelve enemy were killed during the day and 24 more were found dead. Four Japanese artillery pieces were destroyed.

The 307th continued the defense of Libungao and Valencia. It sent out a number of patrols which killed 16 of the enemy and brought artillery fire to bear on another group estimated to be a platoon. One battalion also conducted a reconnaissance for the defense of Ormoc preparatory to relieving elements of the 7th Infantry Division there for an operation in the Camotes Sea.

5 January. The 305th sent strong patrols from Villaba south to Baliti and a mechanized patrol along the Palompon road: other patrols moved north from San Miguanal to Cabas, and south from Palompon to Rizal.

A resupply truck convoy of the 305th was shelled by Japanese mortars along the Palompon road but no damage was done. About one mile southwest of Matagob a convoy encountered 23 more Japanese, killed 3 of them and the remainder fled to the south. The 306th sent out nine strong patrols to Calubian, Bulsu, Santa Cruz, and the Artusan and Calubian rivers. One patrol found 25 dead Japanese.

The 1st Battalion of the 307th moved to Ormoc to establish close-in defenses. Its patrols covered the area as far northeast as Hot Springs where 50 of the enemy were killed.

6 January. Patrols of the 305th operating around Villaba found evidences of recent enemy activity, but few live Japanese. Natives claimed that about 800 were scattered in the area three miles northeast of Abijao. The two other regiments continued patrolling but few Japanese were found.

7 January. Patrolling continued to mark the Division's activities. A motorized patrol on the Palompon road was the only one to make contact with the enemy. It received a little rifle fire which was quickly stopped.

The 306th sent patrols from Calubian to Babian Point, Tuktuk, and San Isidro gaining no contacts. Other patrols operated west of Kananga, north of Humaybunay, and near Tangubay. Twenty Japanese were discovered digging in near the latter place and were shelled. The 307th sector was quiet and only 2 Japanese were killed.

8 January. The 305th sent patrols from its 1st Battalion to Himarco, where 6 of the enemy were killed. A patrol consisting of one reinforced company went from Villaba to the Sangabon River, Baliti and an asphalt mine nearby, and killed 19 Japanese with small arms and mortar and 25 with artillery fire. A reinforced platoon sent from Villaba to Sanlagon killed 3 Japanese. Patrols from the 3d Battalion to Santiago and Balunasan killed 4 in a small unnamed village.

Patrols of the 306th in the San Isidro area captured a prisoner but made no other contacts. Patrols from Linoy to Agayan killed 3 Japanese, and patrols west of Highway 2 reported no Japanese in that area.

Guerrillas attached to the 307th killed 9 of the enemy during the night at the Libungao road junction and reported observing about thirty others in that area during the day. Patrols from Libungao to Catotocan sighted fifty Japanese and killed 7. An overnight patrol returned from Hot Springs, killing 12 of the enemy en route.

9 January. Company C of the 305th, moving by LVT to San Pedro, and by trail to Tabinian and Rizal, encountered no enemy. A patrol from Company D moving from Sabang, Tagbubingan to Lomoken ran into twelve Japanese, killed 7 and took one prisoner. Only about half of this group of the enemy was armed.

A patrol of the 306th annihilated, with machine guns and mortars, a group of 50 of the enemy near Humaybunay.

A guerrilla outpost on the Palompon road near the Tagbong river was fired on during the night and a telephone line was cut near the Libungao road junction. Patrols of the 307th located 150-200 Japanese 2.000 yards northwest of Valencia and placed artillery fire on them. The patrol later found 53 of the enemy dead on the position and observed the remainder fleeing west. Another patrol near Aquiting saw fifty Japanese and killed 32 of them.

The movement of heavy equipment of the Division which was no longer needed was started back to eastern Leyte. The Division's totals for the day were 190 killed, 7 prisoners of war, and no casualties.

10 January. Patrols of the 305th made several enemy contacts near Villaba and killed 41 in the area. Many reports indicated that the enemy, by groups and individuals, was attempting to reach the northwest coast to flee from the island. Scattered groups, killed while trying to cross the mountains from the east to the west, carried overlays with orders for them to be on the coast south of Palompon by 11 February for evacuation. Several thousand Japanese managed to collect in the western mountains, but constant patrolling kept them contained there in an ever-narrowing pocket.

The 2d Battalion, 306th, was relieved of responsibility for the Calubian area by the 1st Battalion, 96th Infantry, of the Philippine Army, and moved to Tacloban on order of the XXIV Corps to work as a port detail.

Patrols of the 307th, operating on Highway 2, killed 21 of the enemy. An overnight patrol returning from Hot Springs killed 33 Japanese near Hangakitanon. Another patrol northwest of San Jose saw a number of small groups of the enemy, about 150 in all, moving west along the Pagsangahan River. Five were killed near Bao but the remainder escaped. The 777th Ordnance Company and the Military Police platoon, bivouacked near the Division Command Post at Valencia, killed 9 Japanese and took one prisoner during the day.

11 January. The 305th Infantry intensified its patrolling. An enemy defensive position was located about 1.000 yards northeast of Taburan, consisting of four machine guns and a considerable number of riflemen. Ten of the enemy were killed. The 3d Battalion encountered several small groups of Japanese, 15-20 in number, throughout the day. The 2d killed 18 at Guinarunan. Motorized patrols along the Palompon road made no contacts. Artillery observers operating with the 305th Infantry saw one group of 75 and another of 50 of the enemy near Butnga. They placed artillery fire on both groups. Patrols returning from Halas reported killing 83 of the enemy in that vicinity and 17 at Canbutoy.

The 306th Infantry continued patrolling in its area but found only one Japanese.

A patrol from the 2d Battalion of the 307th operating southwest of Valencia encountered a group of approximately 75 of the enemy 500 yards south of San Jose. Eleven were killed and the others attempted to withdraw to the east. They were pursued by the patrols and 38 more were killed before the remainder managed to escape. A patrol from the 3d Battalion operating near Colisao saw 25 of the enemy on the west side of the Pagsangahan River. The patrol fired on them but was unable to pursue owing to the flooded condition of the river. This patrol succeeded in killing 10 of the enemy. Another patrol operating northwest of Valencia killed 10 Japanese, of which 3 were officers. An overnight patrol returning from Hot Springs reported killing 28 of the enemy and capturing 5 prisoners of war. The 1st Battalion remained in defense of Ormoc.

12 January. Enemy activity increased in the Villaba area. During the night, enemy patrols carrying satchel and pole charges attempted to enter the Villaba defenses. LVTs operating between Villaba and Palompon were fired on from the shore by enemy mortars. Patrols of the 2d Battalion, 305th, north and east of Pinarut, killed 25 of the enemy. During the day the 1st Battalion killed 150 Japanese and took up defensive positions for the

night two and one half miles north of San Miguel. The 2d Battalion proceeded to Tibur and killed 25 of the enemy south of Baliti during the day. The 3d Battalion knocked out one enemy machine gun and recaptured a U. S. heavy machine gun.

Patrols of the 1st and 3d Battalions, 306th, operating in the Agahang area made no contacts but found 2 dead Japanese.

The 307th killed 5 of the enemy near Valencia during the night. A two-day patrol returning from Hot Springs reported killing 24 in that area. A patrol from Kananga to Bagatoon made no contacts. Another killed 6 of the enemy in a warehouse area north of Valencia.

13 January. Company A of the 305th landed at Tuburan coordinated with an attack by Company G which moved from Villaba north to Abijao. The town was captured after light resistance. The 3d Battalion, attacking north toward Butnga, met groups of poorly equipped Japanese and killed 125 with artillery and rifle fire. Returning along a creek bed it killed 21 more east of Abijao.

The 306th made no contacts during the day and, less the 2d and 3d Battalions, started preparations for a shuttle move to an assembly area near Siguinon, en route to Tarragona on the east coast of Leyte.

The 307th killed 3 Japanese near Valencia during the night. Patrols sent west of Valencia and north of Humaybunay made no contacts. An overnight patrol to Macalpe killed 8 of the enemy in Hilbunaway.

Local security patrols of the 306th Field Artillery Battalion killed 2 Japanese in a shack 1,000 yards south of Valencia, and guerrillas killed 4 near Aquiting and 6 near Vale.

Company A, 305th, attacking high ground inland from Abijao, ran into a strong position and asked for help. Company B moved wide around the right flank but encountered another strong position 500 yards inland from the one confronting Company A. Both companies, unable to establish contact, withdrew under cover of darkness due to a shortage of supplies. The two companies killed approximately 140 Japanese during the day.

15 January. The enemy positions which had withstood the pressure of the 1st Battalion of the 305th the day before were again attacked, this time with success, and 123 Japanese were killed. The battalion then returned to Look. At 0430 a strong force of the enemy attacked the 2d Battalion at Villaba with artillery and mortar fire. At 1230 a charge by the enemy was beaten off. More than 265 Japanese dead were piled up in front of the 2d

Battalion's outer defenses. At 1400 Companies B and K arrived to reinforce the position.

Because the enemy was showing a marked increase in activity on the west coast and in the hills along the Palompon road, the 306th Field Artillery Battalion was moved to Matagob. From there it was able to reinforce the fires of the 305th Field Artillery Battalion around Villaba. Battery C went into position on the western edge of the village with a clear field of fire up the valley. Shortly before noon natives called attention to Japanese on the hills. An enemy column was seen crossing one ridge and disappearing behind another. The battalion quickly swung into action at 1,500 yards range. The first round landed on top of the ridge, scattering debris and Japanese in all directions. The next were placed slightly short and into the gully where at least 75 enemy soldiers had already gone. The artillerymen, searching the hills with their glasses, found that many of the native huts were occupied by the enemy. They fired on them and for the next two hours had a field day.

Late in the afternoon a truck column carrying supplies from Valencia to Palompon was ambushed at a bend in the road 3,000 yards northeast of Tipolo. This trap was cleverly prepared and caught the convoy between two bridges, with high ground on the north side of the road and a precipitous slope on the south. The escorting tank and truck load of troops were permitted to cross the west bridge when it was destroyed and the Japanese opened fire. As the tail of the column closed, the bridge behind it was also destroyed. The Japanese had two machine guns near the head of the column which enfiladed the ditches as well as the road, and another covering the rear half of the column. From the high bank north of the road they threw grenades into the trucks. The column was caught completely by surprise and those men who were not hit immediately slipped off the road into the gully. Lieutenant Colonel Morgan of the PCAU unit left his jeep, ran back along the column to a command car and while telling the driver to abandon his vehicle was killed by machine gun fire. The driver elected to remain with his car and was uninjured. The intense fire from the ambush lasted about three minutes and then stopped completely. The men gradually assembled, collected the dead and wounded, repaired the bridge in rear and started back. Half way to Matagob they were met by a patrol coming to their assistance. The patrol continued on to the scene of the ambush where it found that the Japanese had returned and set fire to the vehicles. Eight trucks containing mail, post exchange supplies and ammunition were damaged. Six .50 caliber machine guns were gone. The enemy had not been able to completely destroy the trucks and all but three were towed away and repaired the next day. No explanation could be found for the sudden departure of the ambush force. The Regimental Headquarters and special units of the 306th moved by truck to Tarragona. Company I arrived in Matagob to protect the 306th Field Artillery Battalion and clear the Palompon road.

Patrols from the 307th, operating from the Tagbong River to Kananga and Paglocsoon, killed seven Japanese. An enemy fighter plane attacked an LVT evacuating casualties from Abijao to Palompon at 1025 and further wounded several men.

16 January. The 305th Infantry was again attacked at dawn and 133 of the enemy were killed by artillery, mortar and small arms fire. The 3d Battalion of the 306th moved to Matagob to thoroughly comb the hills along the Palompon road. Company I, advancing west from Matagob, worked through the ambush area but met only scattered resistance. The remainder of the battalion moved out at 1000 and killed 55 of the enemy in the hills during the day.

Patrols of the 307th were sent to Matagob and to Valencia without enemy contact. Others west and south of Valencia and near Aquiting found several groups of Japanese and placed artillery fire on them. Three enemy soldiers attempting to move through the Valencia area during the night were killed.

An enemy plane tried to strafe Palompon at 1905 but was driven off by antiaircraft fire. The plane turned west and strafed four LVTs which were bringing casualties from Villaba. One bomb was dropped near the amphibious vehicles but no damage was done.

17 January. The 2d Battalion, 305th, sent patrols 1,000 yards in all directions from Villaba and the bag for the day was 17 Japanese. One large motorized patrol was sent from Look to San Miguel and Rizal. Several bands of the enemy were encountered and 22 Japanese were killed. An enemy barge loaded with ammunition was destroyed on the beach near Baliti.

In the 306th sector, the 1st Battalion remained at Kananga and the 3d, still mopping up in the Matagob area, killed 22 Japanese and captured a heavy machine gun.

The 307th killed three or the enemy around Valencia during the night and three more near Libungao.

18 January. A reinforced company of the 305th encountered a strong force of the enemy near Nambu. In the resulting fight 32 of the enemy were killed and one captured. Two reinforced companies of the 306th from the 3d Battalion moved out from the Matagob area at 0730 to clear an area along the road 4,000 yards to the northwest. Company K met approximately two platoons of the enemy and placed artillery fire on them with undetermined results.

The 307th area was quiet and only 8 Japanese were killed during the day.

One battery of the 304th Field Artillery Battalion moved from Kananga to Matagob, bringing the total to two batteries of the battalion at that place. The third battery remained at Kananga.

19 January. The Japanese at Villaba had sustained heavy casualties during the past week and their activities decreased. Company C of the 305th moved inland from Sabang, found three dead Japanese and destroyed a field piece. A reinforced company of the 2d Battalion encountered a large group of the enemy at Silad and along the road from that place to Pinarut. The Emperor lost 23 of his soldiers.

The 306th had a quiet night and at 0730 the 3d Battalion at Matagob moved out to attack an enemy position located the previous day in the hills to the northwest. By 1005 this position had been overrun and mopped up. The 1st Battalion left Kananga at 0730 and closed in Tarragona on the east coast at 1900. This battalion was to be employed with other troops of the Division as an unloading detail for the 38th Division at Tisson.

20 January. A heavy patrol from the 2d Battalion of the 305th encountering a number of strong Japanese positions along the road from Silad to Pinarut, killed approximately 100 of the enemy in fierce fighting.

The 3d Battalion of the 306th added another 164 enemy dead to the total counted the day before in the area they had already mopped up. In a recount the 306th soldiers, who had lost two killed and nine wounded in the battle, found that the enemy warriors had died in hastily-constructed squad and platoon positions.

21 January. Word was received from natives in the area of Baliti that the Japanese, who were known to have strong positions there, were receiving supplies and evacuating personnel on a two-masted sailing vessel that was making nightly trips from somewhere in the Camotes Sea. Plans were made to send a reinforced company to this sector.

Only scattered groups of the enemy were encountered by Division troops patrolling.

22 January. Inasmuch as the company from the 2d Battalion, 305th received only scattered rifle fire near Baliti at 1100, an artillery concentration was placed on a hill 1,000 yards southeast of the town with unknown results.

A radio direction finder unit operating in the 305th sector located enemy stations at Agobob and Butncja, with a possible station at Hugasan. Artillery fire was placed on these locations.

23 January. In the 305th patrolling action around Villaba and Baliti, a company of the 2d Battalion was shelled by enemv artillery 800 yards north of Villaba. Counter-battery fire silenced the Japanese guns after 33 rounds had fallen. North and east of Silad the company encountered very strong enemy positions defended by at least four machine guns, automatic rifles, mortars and small arms. Bitter day-long fighting failed to reduce the position.

24 January. Preparations were made for a final mopping up in the hills east of Abijao and along the west coast by the 305th and 307th Regiments as soon as elements of the latter could be relieved from responsibility at Valencia and Ormoc.

25 January. The 1st Battalion of the 305th moved to Villaba to join the 2d Battalion with which unit it was to initiate the attack to the south while the 3d Battalion moved north from Look to enclose the enemy in a narrow corridor. The 307th was then to drive west toward the coast, penetrate the enemy positions and annihilate the defenders.

Patrolling action by the 305th from Look to San Miguel netted about 40 enemy killed.

26 January. Several units readied themselves for the coming attacks. The 3d Battalion, 306th was to sweep along Highway 2 from Pinamopoan to Valencia on a front of 1,500 yards. The 2d Battalion, 307th moved from Valencia to Casa, for the attack west to the coast. The 902d Field Artillery less Battery B, moved to Matagob to support the attack.

27 January. The 1st and 2d Battalions of the 305th, from the trail between Villaba to Silad, advanced north and east at 0800. Although the plan was for them to move south and pocket the enemy in the valley of the Pagsangahan River, they first had to move northeast to Otin and capture a high ridge which paralleled the coast and on which the Japanese had dug in.

The 1st Battalion cleared the area between Villaba and Silad along the coastal plain and killed 10 of the enemy. It remained overnight in the foothills 1,000 yards east of Silad, while the 2d Battalion remained near Villaba.

The 3d Battalion was moved by water to Taburan and the town was occupied at 0943. This place was about half way up the coast between Tinabilan and Abinao. The battalion advanced inland and made its first contact with the enemy about 400 yards east of the town. This was a small group and was quickly brushed aside. At 1600 it came under heavy fire from .50-caliber machine guns, rifles and mortars and stopped for the night.

The 2d Battalion, 307th, launched its attack from Casa to the west at 0800. Early in the day resistance was slight, but as it came within 1,000 yards of Agobob it increased and artillery fire fell among the troops. The battalion remained overnight about midway between Casa and Agobob. Because of the extreme ruggedness of the terrain, which made visibility poor and communications practically impossible, artillery planes were used to supply the battalion with emergency ammunition, rations and medical supplies. The 1st and 3d Battalions of the regiment remained at Valencia, the 1st Battalion prepared to move to Casa on order.

The 3d Battalion, 306th, continued its sweep south along Highway 2, made only a few contacts and killed 4 of the enemy at Linoy, 4 at Kananga, and 8 at Libungao.

Enemy casualties during the day were 127 killed and 1 prisoner of war. The Division suffered 4 killed and 19 wounded.

28 January. The 1st Battalion of the 305th resumed its attack against increasing resistance northeast of Silad. By the end of the day it had cleared the area from Silad to Otin and was on the ridge ready to move south. The 2d Battalion moved south to Baliti, and the 3d continued north from Taburan toward Abijao.

The 2d Battalion, 307th, resumed its advance to the west at 0800. Enemy resistance, consisting of numerous small dug-in positions along the ridge lines perpendicular to the line of advance, was difficult to overcome because of the rugged nature of the terrain. The enemy was very skillful in covering all avenues of approach with automatic fire. The hills were covered with high grass, in which the enemy was concealed.

The advance command post of the 307th, and the 1st Battalion, moved from Valencia to Casa. The 3d Battalion remained in Valencia and surrounded a group of about 150 of the enemy just west of the airstrip. This group consisted of about half of the headquarters of the Japanese 26th

Division which in fleeing west across Leyte had blundered into the defenses around the 77th Division Command Post. During the night the group had suffered about 20 casualties and had turned north just beyond the airstrip. They were pocketed between the airstrip defenses on one side and several patrols from the 307th on the other.

While this enemy group was thus boxed in, the 304th Field Artillery Battalion placed heavy concentrations of time fire over the area. After the concentrations lifted the artillery liaison planes lived up to their nickname of "B-77s" by dive-bombing and grenading the cornered Japanese. This technique consisted of dropping rifle grenades out of the cabin of the plane onto the enemy. The "bombers" killed a number of them in this manner. When the area was mopped up more than 40 Japanese officers' swords were found among the 70 dead.

The enemy lost 301 killed and 1 prisoner of war during the day. The Division suffered no losses.

29 January. The 1st Battalion, 305th, drove south from Otin through scattered groups of the enemy and cleared the area from Baliti, Silad, and Gunaguyan to Toag. The 3d Battalion attacked and captured Abijao from the sea. Company L, moving inland from Hubasan, took the high ground overlooking the entire area and established a battalion command post on it.

The 1st and 2d Battalions of the 307th continued the attack to the west and patrols from both battalions were sent to Sulpa and Agobob. The 2d Battalion sent a strong reconnaissance force northwest from Butnga along a ridge line. It encountered a strongpoint defended by a Japanese company. The patrol withdrew and artillery fire was placed on the position.

The platoons of the 77th Reconnaissance Troop swept the area from Valencia to Hot Springs in a final drive to clear that region. They found no evidence of Japanese activity.

30 January. The 1st Battalion of the 305th continued its advance toward San Vicente and at 1515 encountered a strongpoint defended by riflemen, machine guns, and mortars. It was overrun after a brief skirmish and the battalion reached its objective. The 3d Battalion patrolled to Baliti and Silad where 37 Japanese were killed. The battalion command post established the previous day observed 100 of the enemy in a draw east of Abijao moving to the southwest in two groups. They were taken under fire by the artillery. Visual contact was established with the 307th moving from the east.

The 307th had resumed its attack at 0800 with the 2d Battalion leading. During the morning it encountered an enemy reinforced company about 1,000 yards west of Agobob. By 1300 the battalion had overrun the position, killed 150 Japanese, and captured 3 machine guns and 2 mortars. It dug in for the night 900 yards farther west.

On this date the 1st Battalion, 164th Infantry, of the Americal Division, accompanied by the 245th Field Artillery Battalion, relieved the 3d Battalion, 306th, and the 304th Field Artillery Battalion of the defense of Valencia. The 3d Battalion entrucked for Tarragona.

As the advance echelon of Division Headquarters; Special Troops; Headquarters, Ordnance, Quartermaster, and Signal Companies; the Engineer Battalion; the Medical Battalion; and Division Artillery Headquarters started for Tarragona at 0800, the CIC Detachment 300 yards south of the command post observed about 100 of the enemy moving through a creek bed. Assisted by guerrillas, the detachment started a fight and killed 31 Japanese before the remainder escaped.

During the day 417 Japanese soldiers were killed and 1 was captured. The Division lost 7 killed and 33 wounded.

31 January. The 1st Battalion of the 305th, moving to join the drive of the 307th from the east, found a well organized position west of Bugabuga. The enemy was entrenched and had machine guns, mortars, and small arms. With artillery and mortar support the battalion overran the position and stopped for the night just east of it.

The attack of the 307th met considerable resistance during the day, particularly in front of the 2d Battalion which was on the right. By nightfall it had reached a point 1,000 yards south of Sulpa.

A truck convoy of the 305th Infantry was attacked on the Palompon road near Cambutoy. One truck was overturned and a native was injured, but the convoy got through safely.

Enemy losses for the day were 217 killed and 1 prisoner of war. The Division suffered 7 killed and 3 wounded.

1 February. During the night Company L of the 305th was attacked but the enemy was beaten off by artillery and machine gun fire. The Japanese also attacked machine gun positions of the 3d Battalion at 2400 and at 0400 but were driven off, leaving 30 dead.

By the end of the day the 305th and 307th had joined and the former returned to Villaba and started to move to Palompon. In the final mopping up of the Bugabuga area the 305th killed 150 Japanese and a sweep to Baliti netted 57 more. All of these were stragglers.

The 307th drove through the final enemy resistance and by the end of the day the 2d Battalion, reinforced by Company C, had advanced through Butnga to Abijao and killed 45 of the enemy en route.

Thus the coordinated drive of the two regiments had liquidated a large pocket of the enemy and cleared the west coast of serious resistance. The work of the Division was finished and its organizations, tired and ragged, were relieved by a part of the Americal Division.

The period from 2 January to 2 February was, for the 305th Field Artillery Battalion and Battery A of the 306th, an artilleryman's dream. Positions were established in coconut groves between Palompon and Look, and an airstrip was built on one of the main streets in the center of Palompon. With the aid of willing native crews, who erected huts for a fee of $2.00 each, all personnel moved into bamboo and palm thatched quarters.

The 305th Field Artillery Battalion, operating from the airstrip, maintained a schedule of four flights daily, each lasting about two hours. All artillery officers participated as observers, and Lieutenants Dowdy and Hamlen shared the piloting tasks. Most were independent search missions and during the month it was rare when a flight did not yield at least one good target. Enemy personnel in groups of 10 to 100 were the usual targets. When no personnel could be seen from the air a few trial rounds near some of the innumerable native huts would usually start a movement of the enemy toward wooded draws or near-by clumps of trees. Supply dumps, ammunition dumps, radio stations, and command posts were plentiful throughout the area and made the period a field day for the "Red Legs." It was evident that the Japanese had been ordered not to fire at the small liaison planes for fear of giving away their positions. Fortunately for the planes the enemy obeyed the order to the letter and the pilots would frequently get close enough to see the expressions — usually of consternation — on the faces of individuals.

All this, with native house boys, laundry service, sailing, fishing, cock fights and pleasant tropical dalliance made this month the most enjoyable period of warfare encountered by the artillerymen in the Pacific. Unfortunately, the doughboys had tougher work under much less pleasant circumstances.

2-5 February. The organizations of the Division consolidated at Palompon and Ipil preparatory to moving back to Tarragona on the east coast. Local security patrols were sent out each day by the 305th and 307th but contacts were infrequent and only 16 Japanese were killed.

On 3 February Company L of the 164th Infantry arrived at Palompon to relieve the 305th of the defense of the area. The 1st Battalion of the 164th remained at Valencia.

At 1200 on 5 February the X Corps assumed responsibility for the sector of the 77th Infantry Division in northwest Leyte. The Division discontinued all patrolling and concentrated on moving to Tarragona. By 9 February all organizations had closed in that staging area.

It was the stated intention of the Japanese High Command to make the Leyte Campaign the decisive one for the Philippine Islands. This has since been confirmed by General Yamashita, the Tiger of Malaya, in a statement made in Manila after the surrender. To that end reinforcements were poured in without stint. The surprise landing of the 77th Infantry Division behind the lines just south of Ormoc, and its slashing, relentless drive to the north and west broke the stalemate. General Yamashita confessed that the landing of the Division and its subsequent operation was the decisive factor in the Leyte campaign.

Between 7 December 1944 and 5 February 1945 the 77th Infantry Division captured Ormoc, Valencia with its airfield, and Palompon. It cleared 42.5 miles of main supply roads, killed 19,456 Japanese soldiers, took 124 prisoners, and captured and destroyed vast quantities of ammunition and supplies of all kinds.

The Division suffered 543 killed and 1,469 wounded. For every American soldier killed 36 Japanese died. For every American battle casualty the Japanese lost 10 men killed. It is believed that these ratios are the most favorable attained by any American division in any major campaign in the Pacific War.

The entire operation, including such daring conceptions as the original landing, the shifting beachhead, the wide envelopment of Valencia, and the 44-mile amphibious tractor invasion of Palompon was characterized by a War Department observer as, "A Divisional Epic."

Part IV: Kerama Retto

BRIEF: While still engaged in mopping up northwest Leyte the 77th Division was ordered to prepare for landings in the Kerama Retto, a group of small rocky islands less than 20 miles west of Okinawa. These islands were to be seized for a protected anchorage and seaplane base which would subsequently be used by the U. S. Navy during the assault on Okinawa.

After hurried preparations and rehearsals the Division sailed for the Ryukyus and arrived off Kerama Retto at dawn on 26 March, 1945. The landings were a complete surprise to the Japs who had equipped the island group as a hideout for suicide boats but had not prepared it for defense.

With a smoothness born of practice and experience five battalion landing teams hit five separate islands almost simultaneously. Resistance was sporadic and occasionally bitter but not effective. Geruma, Hokaji, and Yakabi were captured quickly. On Aka and Zamami fighting continued to the 27th.

On 27 and 28 March landings were made on other islands. On Tokashiki hundreds of civilian suicides were found but the fighting was negligible during the two-day search of this mountainous island.

The 77th remained in the Retto despite increasing Jap air attacks. On 31 March the four low, sandy islands called Keise Shima, just off Naha Harbor, were seized and two battalions of 155mm guns were emplaced thereon to support Tenth Army's landings on Okinawa the next day.

At a cost of 78 killed and 177 wounded, the 77th made 15 assault landings, killed 530 Japs, captured 121, and seized a well protected anchorage and seaplane base for the American assault forces. There was an additional dividend. More than 350 Jap suicide boats and their fanatical pilots were destroyed or captured in their hidden base without once having an opportunity to cause damage. Inasmuch as the enemy plans called for these craft to sortie against U. S. transport shipping off Okinawa, our surprise landings undoubtedly prevented subsequent damage to the American fleet.

Chapter 18: Getting Ready for the Next One

THE DIVISION was still killing Japs along Palompon Road and near Villaba on Leyte when it was alerted for the Okinawa operation. On 11 January 1945, just a few days following the warning orders for the forthcoming operation, a planning group consisting of Brigadier General Edwin H. Randle, Assistant Division Commander, Lieutenant Colonel F. Clay Bridgewater, Assistant Chief of Staff, G-2, Lieutenant Colonel Frank D. Miller, Assistant Chief of Staff, G-3, and Major Earl P. Schlotterbeck, TQM, left for Oahu, where it prepared the preliminary plans for the 77ths part in the Ryukyus operation. Early in February, this group returned to the Division for the more detailed and final planning. During their absence, General Bruce had been kept advised by radio as to the trend of planning and was himself making plans to dovetail into the large scale operation.

Meanwhile, the fighting men of the 77th continued to ply their trade and found sufficient enemy west of Ormoc Valley to maintain business at a high level of activity.

The task of preparation was great and the time until target date was short! The Division could not be completely relieved from battle by the Americal Division until 5 February. It was scheduled to start loading on 5 March, to conduct rehearsals prior to 22 March and to be on the target by daylight of 26 March. As the General and Special Staff officers studied the schedule, it became apparent that it was a schedule just adequate for a fresh Division to iron out the many tactical and logistical problems that accompany an amphibious assault and subsequent campaigns. The 77th, however had just finished a 2 1/2 months' campaign and faced the additional necessity of refitting, rehabilitating, and replacement. The Division had arrived on Leyte with about 55 percent of its organic transportation, and the months of traveling over the rough tropical roads had not improved the vehicles. Weapons of all calibers had taken a beating, and had to be checked and renewed or replaced. The men had to be reclothed, and issued new equipment adapted for the Okinawa operation. New weapons and vehicles authorized on new tables of equipment had to be picked up and the men trained in their use. These items included the new M-18 Tank Destroyers, the amphibious personnel carriers called weasels, the ultra-secret

Snooperscopes and Sniperscopes, and the new models of Medium Tanks mounting flamethrowers and 105mm cannon.

These problems were not unusual but had to be accomplished in less than a month. Most of the items of supply were to be found on the island of Leyte, but certain articles had to be "sweated out" from Pearl Harbor and the States.

The Division came out of the Leyte campaign considerably understrength and the replacements arrived too late to permit field training on Leyte. Actually not yet enough replacements arrived to bring it up to strength, and it left for the Kerama Retto with 900 enlisted men short. The officer strength, however, was on the line after 117 field commissions from the ranks had gone through. Many of these became official en route to Kerama. Furthermore, the veterans were tired.

These were merely added difficulties. The planning and the work were speeded up. From the time of the initial warning of the landing in the Keramas, the divisional and regimental staffs kept up a continual schedule of detailed planning. Map studies and interpretation of aerial photos by the intelligence agencies of the Division, corps, army, and the naval task group were constantly amplified. Later intelligence data were inserted into the blanks left on the first studies and new estimates of enemy strength, units, supplies, and defenses were prepared and distributed. The final estimates of enemy strength in the Kerama Retto prior to the invasion were placed at between 2,500 to 3,000. Suspicious items picked up on the aerial photos, a series of tracks and long objects in caves were estimated to be amphibious tanks of some sort. Actually these were suicide boats, of which hundreds were found on the islands.

In all, twelve separate plans for possible employment of the Division throughout the Nansei Shoto were prepared. In addition to the planning for the Kerama Retto, the Division had to be prepared for any one of several possibilities as Tenth Army reserve. Plans were ready for employment in the Keramas, Keise Shima, Tonaki Jima, Ie Shima, the islands guarding the Eastern approaches to Chimu Wan and Nakagusuku Wan, and landings on the east and west coasts of Okinawa.

The Division's Preferred Plan for the capture of the Keramas involved battalion landings on Yakabi, Zamami, Aka, Kuba, Gemma, and Hokaji Islands on 26 March. These were to be followed, on order, by landings on Amuro and Tokashiki. Protection was to be furnished Naval Underwater Demolition Teams when they prepared passages through the reefs of Keise

Shima between 27 to 31 March. Garrison troops were to be established on Zamami to protect the radio intelligence and air warning services, weather detachments, and the small boat pool there. The final mission was to land two battalions of 155mm guns in Keise Shima on 31 March to support the main landings on Okinawa beaches.

Supply agencies tackled a large task. Hundreds of tons of supplies, mostly from island dumps on Leyte, were marshalled on the Tarragona embarkation beaches for loading. Several palm-log piers were constructed by the Division on the beaches, but these were battered to pieces by the waves and the heavy landing craft and could not be used. Therefore, all loading had to be done by small craft moving from the shore to the ships. To further complicate matters, a high surf rose for some days. Small craft broached in the surf and larger ships such as LSTs and LSMs could seldom get close enough to the beach to allow vehicular loading. The close time schedule, however, necessitated the use of all types of craft in all types of conditions.

Assault shipping, including 58 transports of various types, was combat loaded throughout and carried three units of fire for all weapons, fifteen days' rations for all personnel, and necessary miscellaneous supplies for the initial assault phases. Each fighting team was so loaded as to be able to move on any independent mission that the situation might dictate.

All this spelled headaches for the planners, but backaches for the troops. The soldiers were constantly on the run. They lived in a fast moving whirl of loading details, camp building, camp wrecking, shots, drawing new equipment, water-proofing vehicles, pulling guns out of mud, and stowing gear on ships. In between work details, the rumor merchants speculated on the next target. There were really only two probabilities: Formosa and Okinawa. Soldier-readers of Time and Newsweek were betting on Okinawa.

All major elements of the Division were embarked, prepared to engage in rehearsals, prior to 9 March, the first day of the rehearsal phase. Although some of the small attached units, such as the Photo Interpretation and Signal Photo Teams, and some shipping allocated to the transport group had not arrived, provisions were made for their loading by leaving shore party and TQM elements on the beach when the attack group departed for rehearsal. During this rehearsal, one transport loaded with one Battalion Landing Team ran aground, necessitating the transfer of all personnel and equipment to newly assigned shipping.

By 21 March, all elements of the Division and attached units were loaded and ready for what was ahead. The LSTs had already sailed north.

Chapter 19: Five Assault Landings on L-6 Day

WHILE still on Leyte the people briefed on the operation began to get "that lonely feeling," for the Division was scheduled to invade the Ryukyus six days before the main invasion force would appear. The 77th was to land on a group of small islands within 350 air miles of Kyushu. Intelligence reports brought out that there would be at least 35 operational Jap airfields within fighter range of the Kerama Retto and at that time the Jap Navy had not come out for its last fight with an American Task Force. It was not a reassuring picture.

For the movement to the objective area, shipping allocated to the Division was separated into two convoys according to the speed of the vessels. In general, LSTs and LSMs were organized into a tractor flotilla. Transports and large cargo vessels were organized into a transport group. The tractor flotilla with its own screen of warships departed from Leyte 20 March, while the transport group left 22 March.

While en route, each ship conducted training schedules. Military and physical training, orientation, and routine shipboard instructions on abandon ship, fire and general quarters were among the subjects for instruction. Operational plans were discussed completely, and each man was thoroughly briefed in his part in the operation. Maps, aerial photographs, and terrain models were utilized in this orientation.

The troops learned that all of the islands of the Kerama Retto were small, but very rugged. The islands were to be approached through reefs, sprinkled with slender, sharp, and treacherous coral heads that could and would rip the bottoms out of boats, and upset amtracks.

The beaches of the islands were narrow, and led directly into the steep slopes of the mountainous terrain.

The largest island of the group was Tokashiki, measuring 10,000 yards long and 3,000 yards wide. Throughout its entire length and breadth, it was a mass of serrated ridges and high rocky hills. At north and south ends and in the middle of the island were hill masses topped by peaks over 200 meters high (640 feet). Between these high ranges were connecting ridges that stayed along the 100-meter line. There were two main towns on the island, Tokashiki, the larger, and Aware. A reef fringed the entire island

and there were three coastal indentations that served as anchorages. There were no roads and only a few steep, narrow trails that could not be traversed by vehicles.

Zamami, the next largest of the group of islands was approximately 5,500 yards in length by 4,000 yards at the widest part. Ridge lines followed the longitudinal axis of the island, with the peaks reaching an average of 150 meters in height. Beach areas on the southern shores were 200 to 300 yards wide and in scattered areas there were valleys flanked by sharp ridges leading in from the beaches. There were two fairly deep coves on the island that could be taken for harbors. As on Tokashiki, the ridges were wooded with scrub and tall grasses.

Aka Shima 5,400 by 3,000 yards at its extreme dimensions, was next in line of size in the Keramas. Shaped like a sting ray, it was covered by a pyramiding succession of ridges dominated by two peaks. Reefs surrounded the island, and the beaches for the most part were narrow and rose abruptly to the hill mass.

Hokaji and Geruma Shima were linked longitudinally by an encircling reef that followed the contours of the two land masses. Both were hilly. Hokaji, 1,800 by 800 yards, contained a hill mass roughly 80 meters high that covered the length of the island. Geruma Shima, 1,500 by 1,500 yards, held one main hill mass that gradually rose to 154 meters. The hills were wooded, and the natives had terraced and tilled the lower slopes. Both islands were mainly agricultural.

Amuro Shima, although approximately 2,000 yards long by 800 yards wide, had little to offer in the way of hills. The southern end of the island contained one ridge that rose to a height of 99 meters. The northern half of the island was barely above sea level, with three small knolls rising about 30 to 40 meters.

Kuba Shima was 2,000 yards long by 900 wide, and entirely mountainous, the slopes rising abruptly from the beaches. The hills were precipitous running to well over 200 meters with one peak on the southern coast rising 270 meters above sea level. Generally within 200 yards of the beach the ridges rose to the 160 meter contour line. The hills were very rough and covered with brush and trees.

The last island of any dimension of the group was Yakabi, a rough and steep hill mass to the water's edge, measuring 1,500 by 1,200 yards. It had practically no beaches, but the buildings of a large copper mine hung to its slopes above the most passable landing.

An anchorage was formed by Tokashiki on the east and Zamami, Aka, Geruma, and Hokaji on the west. Amuro lay roughly in the center of the anchorage. The naval berthing space was roughly 12,000 yards long by 6,000 wide. Except for the Nase-Iwa rocks in the center and the Hiraso-Iwa rock off Amuro, the anchorage was deep and excellent for any type ship. The northern and southern mouths to the sheltered waters could be protected by submarine nets.

In addition to tactical information, the men were told of the peoples of the islands, of their habits, customs, government, history, geography, climate and other pertinent data. Booklets on the Nansei Shoto were distributed.

No particular events, other than numerous general quarters caused by suspected submarines (which usually turned out to be fish) and Jap planes believed to be scouting, occurred during the voyage. There were no enemy attacks en route.

Early in the morning of 26 March, both the tractor flotilla and the transport group arrived in the vicinity of the Kerama Retto, prepared to launch the invasion forces. Prior to the hour set for the initial landings, reports of beaches and obstacles were received from the Underwater Demolition Teams. Their reconnaissance indicated beaches on Kuba and Yakabi unfavorable for landing boats.

General Bruce, aboard the Mount McKinley, upon receiving this last available information, issued the go ahead for the preferred plan but delayed the time of landings on Kuba and Yakabi until LVTs (landing tractors) which could crawl over the difficult fringing reefs would be released from use on Aka and Gemma. The invasion of Japan's inner ring of defenses was launched. This was the first landing on actual Jap Homeland. American landings prior to 26 March had been on Jap mandated islands and colonies. It was believed that surprise would be obtained because the Japs did not expect a landing in the Keramas. This was subsequently borne out by captured documents and prisoners. Several gun emplacements were found on Tokashiki and one on Gemma, but the Japs departed when the naval and air bombardments ripped the landing areas.

The Kerama Retto was used by the Japs as an operating base for Special Sea Raiding (suicide boats) units, which patrolled the waters of the southwest coast of Okinawa and were to attack Allied assault shipping which the Japs expected would lie east of Tokashiki. These suicide boats, small speedy craft, powered by gasoline engines, had two depth charges tied together on a launching rack on the stern of the boat. It was planned to run these boats alongside a large ship and trip the charges overboard. The depth charges had about a five second delay which probably would not be enough to allow the small boat to escape. Volunteers, known as Special Shipping Officer Candidates were promised a posthumous promotion to 2d Lieutenant after one mission.

To install and operate this base, approximately 2,335 Jap troops had been brought to the islands. As the need for combat troops on Okinawa became acute, shortly before the invasion, the main strength of the base battalions in the Retto was sent to Okinawa. This movement apparently started in January and was completed by 17 February. Each unit as it withdrew left a skeleton force to maintain the base. On 17 February the departing base units were replaced with Korean laborers who had been employed unloading ships arriving in Naha. Thus there were left in the Retto the 1st, 2nd and 3rd Sea Raiding Squadrons with a Table of Organization strength of 310, the equivalent of one company from each of the 1st, 2nd, 3rd Sea Raiding Battalions with a strength of 750, and the 103rd Korean Labor Company of 700, a total of 1,760 men. However, just prior to our landings, many of these troops went to Okinawa. Tokashiki was almost completely evacuated by both soldiers and civilians by 24 March. There is no evidence of the exact number of troops which left the area at this time but it was believed by G-2 that base units departed leaving only the Sea Raiding Squadrons of 300, the Korean laborers numbering about 600, and almost 100 base troops. These were spread through the Retto as follows: Zamami 400; Aka 300; Gemma 75; and Tokashiki 200, a total of 975. These units left a mass of order of battle documents that were very helpful in determining what and how many of the enemy troops were on the main island.

On the morning of 26 March the islands to be assaulted were worked over by naval aircraft and naval gunfire. Two cruisers, 4 destroyers and 42 gunboats participated. The first landings were made on Zamami, Aka, Hokaji, and Gemma. Later in the day Yakabi was seized. The Gemma assault by the 1st Battalion Landing Team, 306th Infantry, was made at 0825 over a smooth sea. The landing on the narrow beach was unopposed except by long range rifle fire. In three hours the island was occupied after one short fight during which time about 25 Japs were killed. The island was declared captured at 1130, when a flag given the battalion commander,

Major Claude D. Barton, by Lieutenant John H. Judge, captain of LST 829, was raised, from the hilltop overlooking the small town.

Meanwhile BLT No. 2, 306th Infantry had landed on the beaches of the adjoining island of Hokaji at 0920. The landing was unopposed and combat patrols which fanned out to scour the island encountered no opposition. At 1130 the Battalion Commander, Major William D. Cavness, declared the island captured and raised an American flag carefully brought along for just this occasion. This flag and that of the 1st Battalion were the first raised on the Japanese homeland.

Two light artillery units, the 304th and 305th Field Artillery Battalions, were landed in DUKWs on Gemma and emplaced for support of landings the next day on Tokashiki. The landings of these two battalions in DUKWs proved to be particularly difficult. The sea wall and walls within the town of Gemma were of stone and several feet thick, preventing passage through the town. Steep cliffs and embankments prevented encirclement of the town by land. As the 304th Field Artillery Battalion occupied the town the only available gun positions for the 305th Field Artillery Battalion were on the inland side of the town, and it became necessary to find other landing beaches that would give access to the east side of the island. The approach to the East between Geruma and Hokaji was effectively blocked by sharp coral heads and deep pot holes. All DUKWs of the 305th Field Artillery were forced to completely encircle Hokaji to get to the east beach of Geruma. Once there, the jagged coral ledge proved an obstacle, and, once clear of the coral, the steep, soft, sandy beach presented additional difficulties. The loaded DUKWs immediately sank into the sand up to their hubs. Every vehicle had to be winched or towed across the 25-yard strip of beach. The muddy terraced rice fields on the other side of the beach were traversed with comparative ease. The 304th Field Artillery Battalion had to blast a path through the sea wall and bulldoze the rubble in the town to provide a position for its guns. In spite of the many obstacles, both battalions were able to occupy positions and register by early afternoon.

The troops on Geruma were the first to witness the horrors of mass civilian suicides. In caves, valleys and hillsides the tortured and mangled bodies of women and children were found. Children of all ages were strangled by their mothers who, in turn, killed themselves or were killed by others. Some were shot by the retreating Jap soldiers. Some formed groups in which each person was simultaneously strangled by another. Survivors whose bloody bodies or partially severed necks demonstrated the mute horror of their experiences, were carried by our troops to aid stations where they were promptly treated. Medical treatment and supply of food by the troops soon brought a definite emotional reaction. In the POW pen for men the one lone Jap soldier was ignominiously ostracized by all the civilians.

The 3rd Battalion of the 305th assaulted Aka Shima at 0904 on 26 March. Mortar and rifle fire fell among the assault waves of landing craft, but no damage occurred. Initial resistance was light. Aka Town was quickly captured, and the battalion moved rapidly inland. The advance was contested by only scattered rifle fire during the early part of the afternoon. An organized position in the center of the island was encountered during the afternoon but was reduced by mortar and rifle fire. Twenty-four Japs died in this set of caves and fortified foxholes. An LMG and several more caves and pillboxes were wiped out in the vicinity by night when the battalion took up defensive positions.

On the 27th, after a quiet night, the battalion conducted extensive patrolling throughout the island, captured quantities of supplies and weapons, and isolated a relatively strong position held by 75 Japs supported by automatic weapons and mortars on the northeastern shore of the island. An air strike was called and 4.2 and 81mm mortars laid a barrage on the caves and pillboxes. For over an hour the navy planes flew over the mountain, dove into the enemy-held hollow and bombed and strafed. Then a company of infantry attacked the position, forcing the enemy to withdraw to the brush. The pursuit had to be foregone due to impending nightfall and the battalion stopped.

For the next two days intensive patrolling was instituted. No further organized enemy stands were uncovered and the island was cleared of stragglers and small groups without much trouble. The battalion withdrew and reembarked on 29 March.

The first waves of BLT No. 1 of the 305th Infantry hit the Zamami Beach at 0900, March 26th, encountering only light opposition. A sea wall 15 feet from the waters edge caused immediate debarkation from amtracks and movement by foot into the depths of the island.

Sporadic mortar and small arms fire was received on the beach, but soon died as the troops moved inland toward Zamami Town just in the rear of the beach. On the approach of the battalion an estimated Jap Company reinforced by 300 Korean laborers, fled from the town into the hills. The town was secured at 1200 and forward elements advanced into the high ground against mortar and rifle fire. The advance into the hill mass continued throughout the afternoon against light opposition and by nightfall approximately one-third of the island had been captured. In the later part of the afternoon resistance stiffened.

During the night the Japs launched nine separate Banzai attacks against Company C and an attached section of Company D. These attacks by approximately 100 Japs armed with sabers, rifles and pistols and supported by mortar and automatic weapons, were all repulsed. In all more than 113 Japs were killed during the night. The fighting was marked by intense hand-to-hand combat, and one machine gun position changed hands five times. Of the 17 Company D men, seven were killed and nine wounded. The following description of this night fighting was written by Corporal James Goble, correspondent for Yank:

The battalion chased the Japs through Zamami Town, already flattened by pre-invasion bombardment, into the terraced hills beyond. And now the men of Companies C and D waited in the underbrush for dawn.

The wind frequently rustled the limbs of bushes, and the men peered into the darkness trying to determine if the noise was made by Japs. "This is a helluva place for a perimeter," grunted Pfc. Bob B. Merrill to another man in his foxhole, Pvt. Frank C. Woolstrum. They could barely see each other. "I got a feeling it wont be long until something happens," answered Woolstrum. The crackling underbrush and the blackness had everyone on edge. They could neither hear nor see any advancing Jap. There were only about 200 Jap soldiers on the island. However, there were about 300 Korean laborers, all of them armed and in Jap uniforms. So far there hadn't been a single Jap counterattack or Banzai charge. Now was the time for one, and the underbrush was the place — provided the Japs could find it. They did. The rustling became louder. Woolstrum looked down a shallow gully and saw man-sized shadows moving forward only 15 yards away. He opened fire with a carbine. Then other Japs broke out of the underbrush and charged the foxholes. Some yelled "Banzai." One screamed, "Look out American bastards, were coming after you."

The men in the foxholes had no chance to use the machine guns about them. The Japs were too close. The Americans opened fire with carbines, as had Woolstrum, and with rifles and pistols. There were about 120 Japs but in the foxholes on the outer edge there were only 14 Americans. Behind them, however, were more men, but those on the tip would have to bear the brunt of the attack.

One Jap jumped into the foxhole occupied by Merrill and Woolstrum. The Jap slashed at Merrill with a saber. Merrill grabbed a foxhole shovel and began beating and slashing the Jap with it. The Jap didn't live very long.

Then another Jap jumped into the foxhole. He, too, swung at Merrill with a saber. The flat of the blade caught Merrill in the face and stunned him. Woolstrum held his fire. He couldn't tell which man was which. The Jap climbed out of the foxhole. Merrill staggered after him, but fell on his face before he could take many steps. The Jap didn't get far either. Pfc. Leon Blackwell in another foxhole got him with one shot.

In still another foxhole, Sgt. Joseph Woolwich saw Merrill but couldn't tell who he was. Woolwich swung his .45 around and called "Who's there?" Merrill knew what was coming. "No, no, no" he screamed. Then realizing that any Jap could yell the same words he cried, "It's Merrill, an American." Woolwich held his fire and Merrill got the hell out of sight.

In other foxholes men were fighting the Japs in hand-to-hand combat. The Japs used sabers and pistols, their favorite weapons for a banzai attack.

Pfc. Woodrow H. Montgomery was one of the few men who got a machine gun into operation. It accounted for several Japs. In the same hole with him, Sgt. Hurley Gilley got two Japs with a pistol. He got one of them as the Jap started to slash at Pvt. Robert E. Lacey with a saber. Gilley who had seen action on Guam and Leyte, described the charge, after it was over as "the worst fighting I was ever in."

T/Sgt. Theodore S. Rycharski was one of the men farther back from the perimeter's tip. Next morning he and six other enlisted men were to be commissioned 2nd Lts. for outstanding duty on Leyte, but Rycharski had no time to think about that. Jap after Jap ran toward him. One by one they fell, hit by bullets from Rycharski's carbine.

Then as suddenly as they had charged, the Japs retreated into the underbrush. They didn't stay there, however. They made eight more attacks before dawn. On five occasions the Americans were forced back, but the lost ground always was regained. Next morning the bodies of 60 dead Japs were found around the outpost. Our losses were only a fraction of that number.

At 0900 on March 27th the battalion resumed the attack to the north against negligible resistance. Ama Village was quickly secured and the northeast peninsula cleared. It became apparent that the Japs had destroyed themselves in the night's banzais and that there was no organized resistance left in the eastern half of the island, so the 1st Battalion was withdrawn to bivouac near Zamami for the night. The battalion was to continue the mop up next day. Meanwhile the 2nd Battalion of the 305th, destined for the garrison force, commenced landing and occupied positions near the beach for the night.

After a quiet night, the 1st Battalion sent company-sized patrols to cover the northern and eastern sections of the island but found nothing. The 2nd Battalion, assigned the patrolling and securing of the southern and western portions of the island, sent platoon patrols into these areas. Small groups of Japs were found and killed, and one organized position, on a low hill at the end of the island, was located. This was probed and reconnoitered on the 28th for an assault on the 29th.

The 1st Battalion was withdrawn the 29th of March and the island turned over to the 2nd Battalion. This unit commanded by Lieutenant Colonel James Doyle (the king of Zamami) destroyed the Jap position scouted the previous day and instituted widespread patrolling to wipe out scattered groups of the enemy. The position destroyed consisted of caves and entrenchments, which were blasted by amphibious tanks. Satchel charges tossed in the holes and caves by the infantry and engineers finished the resistance. Except for a few stragglers, Zamami was secure. The garrison which included a DUKW platoon from the 77th Quartermaster Company, Battery D, 7th AAA Battalion, and other units of the Military Government personnel, proceeded to develop it as a temporary base.

At 1341 on the 26th, the 2nd Battalion of the 307th landed on Yakabi Shima against little opposition. The island was overrun and declared captured at 1600. A few Japs were killed and small quantities of enemy material captured. With each battalion that landed went, of course, their less publicized teammates, the engineers, artillery forward observers and liaison parties, medics, and signal corps men necessary to smooth functioning of the teams. As an innovation required by the "shotgun" nature of the landings, each battalion was accompanied by a small detachment of intelligence specialists whose sole job was to collect at once and get back to the Division flagship any information which might affect the Tenth Army Landings on Okinawa.

Chapter 20: Later Landings

TOKASHIKI, the largest of the group of islands, was invaded by the 1st and 2nd Battalions of the 306th Infantry on 27 March at 0920 and 0908 respectively. Opposition on both beaches was slight. The 1st Battalion landed on the west center of the island with the mission of driving north. The 2nd Battalion landed further to the south with the mission of driving north, parallel to the 1st Battalion. The fire of the 304th and 305th Field Artillery Battalions from Geruma was adjusted by 77th Division "cub" planes flying from their own "poor man's aircraft carrier," an LST equipped with a Brodie device. The planes took off from and landed on a hook which ran on a cable suspended between two booms. It looked like something by Rube Goldberg and according to Major J. C. Kriegsman, Division Air Officer, landing was similar to threading a needle, but it worked. The "B-77s" were up when needed.

Both landings were preceded by air, naval gunfire, and artillery preparations. The rugged terrain made initial progress slow, but by nightfall the two battalions were abreast across the island ready for the next day's attack. The 3rd Battalion, initially in reserve, landed on the south beach during the day and cleared the southern tip of the island. Two battalions, the 1st and the 2nd, continued the attack on 28 March at 0800 against little resistance. The extremely rugged terrain made progress slow, but Tokashiki Town was seized without a fight and the bay area on the west captured against slight fire.

The 1st Battalion, on the left, advanced to within 1,500 yards of the north coast against scattered resistance which was quickly eliminated. The 3rd Battalion patrolled the south end of the island but found no enemy.

Late in the evening the 1st Battalion, camped about 1,500 yards from the north end of the island in very rugged hills, began to hear explosions and what seemed to be the screaming of a mass of women and children. The sounds continued all night. In the morning the advancing infantrymen found a pretty little valley that was horribly littered with dead and dying civilians of all ages. Children had been killed or terribly wounded, whole families had committed suicide by grenades and strangling, and others had committed hara-kiri with knives. It was a scene of awful sacrifice of lives by innocent people deluded by the military into thinking that suicide would be better than falling into the hands of the Americans who would "ravish the women and children and torture the rest." Approximately 250 civilians had taken their own lives. The rest were taken down to Tokashiki Town and given food and medical care. While the medics were carrying some of the wounded down the steep trails to an aid station, a Jap machine gun opened up on the litter parties. No one was wounded, but time had to be taken out to wipe out the Jap soldier who was trying to kill the medics aiding his own people.

The remainder of Tokashiki was captured on 29 March. Patrols and mopping up parties cleared the island of Jap stragglers. The 2nd and 3rd Battalions were withdrawn and reembarked in the afternoon. The 1st Battalion remained until 31 March patrolling neighboring islands and bringing in civilians. No enemy contacts were made during this period. To a platoon of Company B, 302nd Engineers, fell the task of burying 160 "suicides."

It is typical of modern war that the radio correspondents went along. On Tokashiki Captain Paul R. Leach, 1st Information and Historical Service, and Jack Hooley, Blue Network, handpacked a wire recording device to the top of a ridge overlooking Tokashiki Town and recorded a play by play, boom by boom account of the attack on the town. A few hours later this transcription went over the airwaves to the radios in American homes.

Company B of the 305th RCT moved from Zamami to Amuro Shima on 27 March at 1300, found no enemy and returned to Zamami.

It had been planned to land a battalion on rocky Kuba Shima, but General Bruce, economizing on men and materials, sent only Company G, 307th Infantry there on 27 March at 1103. There was no opposition.

Nests of suicide boats were found hidden in caves on Aka, Geruma, Zamami and Tokashiki. None was used. It was typical of the Japanese that having laboriously completed a boat base and laid careful plans against an American invasion of Okinawa, they did not react to an unexpected American landing in the Kerama. They had no plan to attack American shipping here and no local authority to act without a plan. So, according to Lieutenant Someya, a prisoner, they either burned or abandoned their boats which "had not lived up to expectations."

Sometime after Geruma was declared secure, an artillery observer discovered an extensive nest of suicide boats concealed in a hidden cove on the North side. The installations, although well camouflaged, were considerable and as there were indications of occupancy he returned without further investigation. A reconnaissance patrol was then sent out to determine the extent of the enemy activity. In many of the boat caves were the bodies of the crews, who, when they discovered they were trapped and their boats useless, committed suicide by shooting themselves. However, in one of these groups of caves some of the Japs were more enterprising. A carefully constructed manually operated trap was prepared by some of the enemy survivors. So, on the 29th of March, when a reconnaissance patrol from the artillery approached the entrance of one of the caves, the bomb-loaded boat was detonated by someone hiding in the caves. This explosion killed Lieutenant Colonel Leever, Captain Nelson, First Sergeant Oden, and Technical Sergeant Marino, and wounded two officers and four enlisted men. Other patrols located Jap army warehouses well stocked with food, underground garrisons, a high powered radio station and a large machine shop used for the repair and maintenance of the suicide boats. Sixty boats in all were located of which fifteen were destroyed by the artillery and the remainder by the engineers.

Major Charlie F. Talbot assumed command of the 305th Field Artillery Battalion following Lieutenant Colonel Leever's death.

The 2nd Battalion of the 306th landed on Keise Shima on 31 March at 0755, but no enemy was found. The four small closely grouped islands making up Keise were then ready for the 155mm guns which were to support the main Okinawa landing the next day. The 531st and 532nd Field Artillery gun battalions and a platoon from Battery B, 7th AAA Battalion, were landed from LSTs and LSMs that day, emplaced and were ready for action by nightfall.

In all, combat elements of the division made 15 separate and distinct landings involving five ship to shore movements by LVTs, two by DUKWs, three by LCVPs with subsequent transfer to LVTs, and five shore to shore movements by LVTs. All landings were smoothly carried out. This was mainly possible due to practice landings while on Leyte and through close coordination among the infantry and tank teams.

Enemy air activity was heavy during the stay in Kerama Retto. During the six-day stay seventeen enemy planes were shot down by combat air patrols and AA fire. There were 21 alerts. However, no damage to Division elements resulted. The casualty figures for the Jap garrison in the Keramas consisted of 530 killed, 121 prisoners of war, and the rounding up of 1,195 civilians. Our casualties were 78 killed or dead of wounds and 177 wounded.

Thousands of tons of enemy material were captured and either destroyed or turned over to the military government agents for Jap civilian use. In addition, a great potential menace to Allied shipping was removed when 359 "suicide boats" were captured or destroyed.

In this natural "Pearl Harbor of the Western Pacific," the U. S. Navy was given a base from which to operate, protected from undersea and surface raiders and from the air by a ring of antiaircraft weapons on land and on the ships themselves. From this base was to come the initial flow of supplies to the beaches of Okinawa. From Kerama the very vital seaplanes shuttled to Guam, and patrolled the China Sea. This strategic group of islands, almost abandoned by the Japs, gave the American forces an initial base for operations against Okinawa.

The following message came on 31 March to the Commanding General 77th Division:

"My congratulations on the speedy and effective manner in which you accomplished assigned tasks in Kerama Retto. The present readiness of the 77th Division to go again is characteristic of its spirit and comes up to the expectations I have learned to have for that fighting organization. Signed NIMITZ."

Part V: Ie Shima: Important Little Island

BRIEF: Ie Shima, a flat-topped, two-by-five mile island which is dominated by one rocky peak, lies less than three miles west of central Okinawa. On its plateau the Japs had constructed a good, three-strip airfield. The 77th Division which was then floating around dodging Jap suicide planes was ordered to assault Ie Shima on the 16th of April.

The Commanding General of the 77th decided to attack Ie Shima from the western end where the Japanese defenders considered landings to be impracticable. The Division Artillery, less the 304th Field Artillery Battalion, was landed and emplaced on Minna Shima, an undefended sandbar about 6,500 yards southeast of Ie, on 15 April,

The 305th Infantry and the 306th Combat Team struck Ie from the southwest on the morning of 16 April. Initial resistance was light and more than half of the island was quickly overrun. But the island was found to be heavily mined and resistance increased as troops neared the town and the mountain.

Two battalions of the 307th Infantry landed south of Ie Town on the morning of the 17th. A bitter and prolonged battle developed as our forces tried to enter the town. The enemy in thoroughly prepared positions and reinforced by hundreds of fighting civilians fought for every building and every rock. Counterattacks were frequent and suicidal in nature.

During the period 17 through 21 April the Division slowly forged a ring of men and weapons around the town and the mountain. Then they inched forward through the rubble. It was costly, desperate work. Finally the 306th took Iegusugu Yama, and the 305th and 307th cleaned out the town.

When, on 25 and 26 April the bulk of the Division moved to Okinawa, 4,794 Japs had been killed and 149 prisoners taken on Ie. The 77ths losses were 239 killed, 897 wounded, and 19 missing. Among the killed was Ernie Pyle, well known war correspondent.

Although overshadowed by the larger campaign on Okinawa, Ie Shima was an important battle in its own right. The airfield captured here was quickly developed into a huge B-29 Bomber base from which American planes blasted Japan and swept the China Sea.

Chapter 21: Dodging a Divine Wind

FOLLOWING the mop-up of the Kerama Retto, 26-31 March, the Division was reboated. On 2 April the convoy, less the Division flagship, put to sea. The three Navy Transport divisions carrying the 77th moved 350 miles out to sea to escape Japanese air activity, and stayed there until 14 April. During the few days before the Division left for sea, it had not been definitely decided whether the 77th would be sent to Ie Shima, and it was not until 14 April that the small unit commanders were informed of the final attack order.

While moving away from the Kerama Retto on 2 April, the convoy was attacked by a flight of eight Japanese "Kamikaze" suicide aircraft. At 1645, the enemy attacked, and before the ships' gunners had time to get off more than a few rounds, five ships had been hit. The radar operator on the flagship, the U.S.S. Chilton, had located a plane but could not confirm it as an enemy because an American plane on the tail of the Jap was sending out recognition signals.

The first Japanese plane was hit while directly above the U.S.S. Goodhue, flagship of the 307th Infantry, and leading ship in the right column. The plane fell on the after deck, cutting a cable which dropped a heavy cargo boom to the deck and killed three men. Flaming gasoline spread over the deck. Four soldiers were killed and 34 wounded.

The U.S.S. Chilton was leading the center column. The Japanese plane being chased by an American Hellcat came in diagonally over the starboard stern. While trying to crash dive he sheared off the port radio antenna and hit the water and exploded just off the port side, throwing debris over the ship. A Jap machine gun and one of the pilot's legs lodged on the forward deck. The wristband manufacturing industry benefited from the pieces of aluminum scattered over the ship. Damage to the ship was superficial and there were no casualties.

Two minutes after the attack on the Chilton a Japanese plane crashed into the superstructure of the U.S.S. Henrico, the lead ship of the left column. Its two bombs hit first and exploded in the superstructure, immediately followed by the plane which entered the Captain's cabin. The Commodore of the Transport Division, the Captain of the ship, the Regimental

Commander of the 305th Infantry, Colonel Vincent J. Tanzola, the Regimental Executive Officer, Lieutenant Colonel Lyman O. Williams, the S-3, Major Robert Brink, and the S-l, Captain E. H. Rennick, were killed. The S-2, Captain Hugh S. Fitch and the S-4, Major Winthrop Rockefeller and other officers were injured. Several enlisted men vital to the operation of the headquarters were killed or wounded and virtually all of the regimental records were lost.

A plane hit by a shell from the Chilton attempted to crash into the U.S.S. Telfair but only raked the port bow with its wing and then exploded in the water. Nevertheless one Army man was killed and four were wounded. At the same time a suicide plane struck one of the escort vessels, wrecked the superstructure and caused a serious fire.

Private First Class Max Drucker, Company M, 306th Infantry was given credit for saving the U.S.S. La Grange from damage. Drucker was on deck near a 20mm antiaircraft gun when the surprise attack began. One of the Kamikaze planes approached the La Grange in a steep glide. Drucker leaped to the gun, got into action and directed an accurate stream of fire at the Jap. His was the only gun engaging the enemy. About 200 yards from the ship the Jap veered suddenly and fell into the sea. The U.S.S. Montrose was also credited with destroying two Jap planes in this attack. One transport, the U.S.S. Wyandotte, which had stayed in the Kerama anchorage, was also hit that day, but with no 77th Division casualties. The 77th's total casualties for the disastrous evening were 22 killed, 76 wounded and 10 missing.

The Henrico returned to the Kerama anchorage for emergency repairs and the army personnel aboard were transferred to the U.S.S. Sarasota, which became the regimental flagship. The Division quickly transferred officers to the weakened regiment. Lieutenant Colonel J. B. Coolidge assumed command of the 305th and a new regimental staff went to work.

While the troops of the 77th aboard transports swung in leisurely but wary circles several hundred miles southeast of Okinawa, the Division Headquarters remained aboard the U.S.S. Mount McKinley anchored in Kerama Retto. In the intervals between frequent air alerts General Bruce and the staff kept in close touch with the progress of fighting on Okinawa. The future employment of the Division was uncertain and hinged upon the advances on Okinawa. However, it became more and more apparent that the Division's next target would be Ie Shima.

The island of Ie Shima, lying off the northwest coast of Okinawa, constituted a massive, permanent "aircraft carrier" at the doorstep of Japan proper.

This five by two-and-a-half-mile island had a level plateau which covered almost the entire top of the island, but was broken at the eastern central part of the island by the 587-foot mountain of Iegusugu. The Japanese had established an airbase on the plateau with three strips, each over 5,500 feet long.

When alerted for the "Iceberg" operation on Leyte, the Division had prepared three plans for the capture of Ie Shima, should the 77th be assigned that mission. The regiments had made corresponding plans for such an operation, and during the Division's two-week stay at sea, the units studied the plans and what intelligence information there was available, just in case Ie was to be the next stop.

There had been no ground reconnaissance of Ie prior to W day, and very little information had been obtained from prisoners in the Kerama Retto or on Okinawa. Accordingly, the emphasis in prior intelligence was placed on intensive photo interpretation and map studies. Estimates of the enemy garrison on Ie Shima ranged from zero to 5,000. Studies of aerial photographs, and interrogation of prisoners, had almost convinced higher headquarters that the island had been evacuated by the enemy. Frequent reconnaissance flights failed to show any evidence of enemy troops, other than slight activity near one of the airfields.

Even though the evidence pointed to evacuation of the island Gen. Bruce and his staff looked on these reports with suspicion, for similar conditions on Leyte had proved that the Japs are masters of camouflage and deception. It was believed that at least 2,500 Japanese occupied Ie Shima. Therefore, the General successfully objected to an Army proposal that the 77th land two companies in daylight to reconnoiter the island.

Field Order No. 26 was completed on 12 April. The Commanding General had used a rule of "landing where they ain't" on Guam and Leyte to good effect, and he utilized this rule in planning for Ie Shima. The poorer beaches on the south and southwest coasts, Green T-1 and Red T-1 and T-2, were selected for the landings. Those charged with the unloading of supplies objected to this because of the rough fringing reefs which prohibited small boat or LVT landings for all but four hours during high tide. Certainly unloading of supplies would constitute a problem. The plan was, however, to carry only what was immediately necessary over the reefs, and to unload the bulk of the supplies over the good beaches, Red T-3 and T-4, after they had been secured by attack from the west.

According to the plan the 306th RCT was to land on W day at S hour on Beach Green T-1, advance diagonally across the island toward the east with two battalions abreast, secure the airfields and reduce Iegusugu mountain with the assistance of the 305th.

The 305th RCT, less the 2nd battalion garrisoning Zamami Shima was to land on W day at S hour over beaches Red T-1 and T-2, with battalions abreast. Its mission was to swing to the east, secure beach Red T-4, capture Ie Town, and assist RCT 306 in the reduction of Iegusugu Yama. The 307th RCT was to be prepared to embark assault elements of BLTs 2 and 3 in LVTs, with two companies of the 708th Amphibious Tank Battalion, and land them on beaches Blue T-2 and T-3 on the southeastern end of the island. The mission was to advance north, aid in the reduction of the pinnacle of Iegusugu, and secure the eastern end of the island.

In order to provide artillery support for the assault the 305th, 902nd, and 306th Field Artillery Battalions and a portion of Division Artillery Headquarters under Col. Royal L. Gervais were to be landed on Minna Shima on W-1 day. Minna was a tiny island lying 6,500 yards to the southeast of Ie. The 304th Field Artillery Battalion was to be landed on Ie on W day.

As soon as higher headquarters decided that the Ie operation was to be conducted when tide conditions permitted, and 16 April was named as V day, Naval Underwater Demolition Teams reconnoitered the reefs, surf, obstacles and beaches. These daring scouts provided accurate information that was very helpful in arranging time tables and landing routes.

The enemy obviously wanted the Division to think that the good beaches on the island were poorly defended, while the poor beaches were heavily defended. Reconnaissance parties from the UDTs roamed the approaches to the good beaches at will without drawing fire, and one enterprising enlisted man managed to stroll unconcernedly along the shore. From the poorer beaches however the UDTs received rifle fire.

The 77th Division Headquarters transferred from the U.S.S. Mount McKinley to the U.S.S. Panamint on 11 April.

The field orders for the operation were issued 14 April, 1945. There was a last minute rush to deliver orders, to orient commanders and troops, and issue the latest intelligence data, because the Division convoy did not return to anchorage until two days before the attack was launched. This, however, did not disrupt the plans or the landings.

The employment of the third regiment, the 307th, remained in doubt due to the lack of adequate information as to what enemy was on the island, and because this regiment was being held in readiness for a feint landing on southern Okinawa as part of the Tenth Army plan. Actually the plan was carried out with only one change. The 307th less one battalion landed on beaches Red T-3 and T-4 on 17 April, and assaulted Ie Town and the mountain in conjunction with the 305th RCT.

On 15 April the ships carrying the 305th, 306th and 902nd Field Artillery Battalions sailed to the south end of Minna Shima and in the early morning disgorged the DUKWs and LCMs carrying the howitzers and crews. The island had been seized without difficulty a day earlier by a Marine Reconnaissance Battalion temporarily attached to the Division.

Now the bulldozers went in first. A way had to be cut through the 25 foot sand dunes which fringed the island into the horseshoe-shaped, ten-acre central lowland. The battalions could take up only one position, the howitzers had to go side by side around the lowland. Only four hours of high tide were available for the landing of the artillery and three days' supplies but this proved sufficient. Unloading of ammunition from LSTs continued throughout the day. The few Okinawa civilians on the island used their shovels and hoes to help dig the gun positions. Their clean, undamaged houses served for command posts and fire direction centers.

The Division Artillery Command Post and the attendant wire and radio nets were installed and by evening the artillery was ready to support the Ie Shima landings.

Chapter 22: Assault Through the Back Door

SHORTLY before dawn on 16 April, the Division convoy, plus units of the 5th Fleet, including two battleships, two heavy cruisers, two light cruisers, seven destroyers, 24 mortar boats and six gunboats arrived off Ie Shima. These ships blanketed the island with projectiles ranging from 16-inch shells to 20mm bullets. The ammunition expenditures included: 335 rounds of 14" or 16"; 1,000 rounds of 8" or 12"; 5,173 rounds of 5", and 1,200 rounds of 4.2" mortar. In addition there were countless thousands of 40mm, 20mm, and .50 caliber rounds fired by support craft and guide boats preceding the LVTs. The Navy Air arm took its turn with bombs and strafing. The mountain disappeared from view in a cloud of smoke and dust as it was frequently to do for several days. After the landings the artillery on Minna Shima maintained a screen of fire in front of the assaulting troops.

There was no confusion in the amphibious landings because all of the units had reboated on the same craft that had landed them on the Kerama Retto. Landings were an old story to the troops, and the debarkation of the LVTs from LSTs went smoothly. At 0650 the tractors began leaving the ships and by 0650 the first waves were in the assembly areas.

The 715th and 773rd Amphibious Tractor Battalions were employed in moving troops to the beaches. Landings were made without incident and the seven waves of the 305th RCTs two battalions and the eight waves of the 306th's two leading battalions were all ashore by 0835. One tractor was disabled by a mine on Green Beach.

The 3rd Battalion of the 306th, in reserve, was loaded on a transport and could not be embarked directly into LVTs. The troops were first loaded into LCVPs (boats) and taken to the line of departure where transfer was made to LVTs. By 1100 this battalion had been landed on Beach Green T-1.

The 304th FA Battalion, the only one to land on Ie Shima, went ashore in DUKWs over Beach Red T-2 and by 1420 was in position, firing in direct support of the 306th RCT.

The 1st Battalion, 305th Infantry, on hitting Beach Red T-2 at 0800, moved inland with Company A on the left and C on the right. The landing was unopposed and the initial advance north and inland 400 yards was slowed only slightly by machine gun fire from a position to the northeast. The landing zone was roughly in the center of the southern shore of the island. Upon reaching a road which ran along the high ground 400 yards north of the beach, the battalion swung east. From this point east into the village, the enemy had prepared extensive mine fields, which, though hurriedly laid and crudely camouflaged, slowed the movement of all vehicles. The passage of tanks and self-propelled guns was extremely restricted.

The troops reached the first phase line, the coastal road, at 0940, and attacked east parallel to the coast on order at 1250. The move east was made with Company B on the right and C on the left. The advance was slow against machine-gun fire from the western outskirts of Ie Town and rifle fire from all along the route of advance. The battalion held for the night 800 yards west of the town. During the day 65 Japanese were flushed from small positions and killed. Two officers and six enlisted men of the battalion were killed and 19 enlisted men wounded.

The 3rd Battalion, 305th Infantry, landed on Beach Red T-1 at 0759 and was all ashore by 0828. Company K on the right and L on the left advanced parallel to and to the left of the 1st Battalion to the phase line, then swung northeast and east. Company L swung into line, its left flank passing just south of the easternmost airstrip, and headed for Ie Town 1,500 yards ahead. Company I, in reserve established contact with the 2nd Battalion, 306th on the airstrip at 0910. The battalion crossed the phase line where the lines came abreast of those of the 1st Battalion at 1230. The advance east and slightly north was made through a heavily mined area, and the reserve company was kept busy marking mines for the engineers.

The advance during the afternoon was limited to 300 yards. The enemy was dug in along the outskirts of the town in coral-rock emplacements and had to be ferreted out one by one by close-in infantry and engineer team work. Armor and self-propelled weapons were of little use because of the mines. By nightfall, advance elements of the battalion had reached a north-south road 1,200 yards west of the town, and they held there for the night. One officer and 15 enlisted men were wounded and three enlisted men killed during the day.

Thus the 305th Regiment had landed two battalions abreast, moved north (inland) then pivoted on the 1st Battalion near the beach and swung the line so that it ran north and south, perpendicular to the beach. During the night the enemy in front of the regiment tried counterattacks. In the 1st Battalion sector small groups of the enemy contacted the line at various points, trying for a gap or weak spot, but were repeatedly driven off, and 47 were killed. An estimated company of Japanese attacked the 3rd Battalion from three directions starting at 2000 16 April. The enemy tried his usual tactics of punching repeatedly at the line trying to find a gap, but failed in this and lost 152 men in the attempt. These Japs carried rifles, sharpened bamboo stakes, bags of grenades, and mortar shells in wooden boxes fuzed as satchel charges. Many of the attackers blew themselves up, their intentions being to take as many Americans as they could with them in the explosion. One American had his arm broken by the flying leg of one of these Japs.

The 306th Infantry landed with the 1st and 2nd Battalions abreast on Beach Green T-1 at 0800. Both immediately moved inland in a northeasterly direction, up the gently rising ground and arrived on the airfields southwestern tip. This rapid advance of the 306th Infantry was made against scattered, light, ground opposition, but drew mortar, AT, and long range machine-gun fire from the mountain, Iegusugu Yama. The leading battalions crossed numerous mine fields and captured the airfield. Fortunately these Japanese mine fields, which made extensive use of the aerial bombs buried nose down, were poorly camouflaged and easily avoided.

The 1st Battalion, 306th Infantry on the left held for the night 1,000 yards short of the northern beaches and about 500 yards northwest of the pinnacle of Iegusugu Yama. The 2nd Battalion, 306th Infantry had its lines running parallel to and about 350 yards west of the mountain slopes.

The 3rd Battalion of the 306th Infantry landed behind the first two at 1015, and echeloned to the left rear. The unit swept around the western and northwestern end of the island mopping up small groups of Japs in coastal and inland caves and entrenchments. The advance was marked by many small but hot fire fights and at the end of the day this battalion had advanced to the northern coast midway between the two airstrips. The battalion lines were in the shape of a figure seven, with the top bar pointing to the north coast. The shaft of the figure ran north and south near the end of the X-shaped airfields.

The advance of the 306th had been so rapid that a gap existed between it and the 305th. The gap ran roughly north and south about 1,300 yards southwest of the mountain. Company K of the 306th was put in position on three Jap-constructed bunkers in the center of the island about 500 yards east of the center of the eastern airfield. This unit was to cover the gap by fire until the 306th came abreast.

Division Headquarters remained throughout the operation aboard the U.S.S. Panamint where superior communications permitted more efficient coordination of ground, air and naval activities. However, early on the day of the landings Brigadier General E. H. Randle, Assistant Division Commander, took ashore an Advance Command Post Group which included his aide, Lt. Robert Fowler, an Assistant G-3, Major Marshall O. Becker, an Assistant G-2, Lt. Harvey N. Daniels, and several enlisted specialists. This group set up operations with the Command Post of the 305th Infantry. Although General Bruce and staff officers were ashore daily the control of the ground fighting was left to General Randle.

On the 17th the 1st Battalion, 305th Infantry, with its right flank on the bluff overlooking Red Beach T-3, attacked east at 0800 with Company A on the left and B on the right. After a 200-yard advance toward Ie Town, a machine gun in a pillbox in an open field opened up and tied the left flank down. A flanking move by a squad of Company B men knocked out the position at 1020. Scattered rifle fire was encountered throughout the day. At 1300 troops from the 307th RCT passed through the battalion and took up the attack. The battalion reverted to regimental reserve and held for the night near the beach of Kabira.

The 3rd Battalion attacked east at 0818 toward Ie Town and by 0930 had seized a bulge of high, level ground that pointed toward the beach. This was about 80Q yards short of the town. During the fire fight for the ground, Lieutenant Colonel Edward Chalgren, Jr., the battalion commander, was wounded and evacuated. Captain Louis C. Hinson, executive officer, assumed command. A nest of machine guns in front of Company K, on the right, held up the movement until a platoon from Company I, aided by several tanks, blasted the position. Company L, on the left, was not having much trouble other than with scattered fire. By 1245 forward elements of the two companies had reached the outskirts of Ie Town. Company I, in reserve, was assigned the fob of marking the hundreds of mines in the area and blowing caves left by the leading troops. A few small groups of Japs had been by-passed by Company K, and Company I cleaned these out. At 1500 the 2nd Battalion of the 307th passed through the 3rd Battalion, 305th Infantry and attacked east of the town proper. The 3rd Battalion held for the night on the western outskirts of the town. A patrol from Company I was dispatched late in the day to check the progress of the 2nd Battalion, 307th, which was fighting in the town. The patrol found the 307th, looked around, and on the way back was jumped by a small group of Japs. The patrol fought its way out safely.

During the night of 17-18 April, the Japanese made numerous determined but futile efforts to infiltrate the 3rd Battalion positions, particularly through Company I. In the morning 44 dead Japs were found in the front lines. Many of these had come through the lines from the left rear, evidently from by-passed positions.

The 306th Regiment was ordered to hold its lines static on 17 April until the 305th could get abreast. Company K supported the advance of the 305th by fire until its fire was masked, then returned to its battalion. The 1st and 3rd Battalions patrolled the north and northwest coasts, sealing caves and blowing Jap supply dumps. The enemy in the regimental sector appeared to have his left flank anchored along the southwest corner of the base of the mountain, and his position extended generally northeast for 800 yards.

Despite the light resistance on 16 April the 2nd and 3rd Battalions of the 307th were landed under fire on Red Beaches T-3 and T-4, respectively, at 1150 on 17 April and began to move inland to take over the fight from the 305th. These beaches remained under intermittent mortar and machine-gun fire all day. The 2nd Battalion was on the left and passed through the 1st Battalion of the 305th into the outskirts of the town, where a heavy house to house fight ensued. The Japs had an organized line in the village, including wire entanglements and mines. An attempt was made to bring up two M-18 (self-propelled guns), but these were halted by the heavily-mined roads and the debris-filled streets of the town, which was also swept by Jap machinegun fire. Late in the afternoon the battalion received orders to close the gap between it and the 3rd Battalion on the right. To do this, it had to move about 300 yards to the right, and even then the contact was visual. This gap was covered by fire. The left flank of the battalion was now on the edge of the village, instead of in the middle as it had been earlier in the day. The line ran toward Beach Red T-4 and passed just under the western slopes of Government House Hill which jutted out toward the southern beach from the plateau at the base of the mountain. The 3rd Battalion, 307th Infantry moved inland from the landing beaches, swung to the east, and advanced about 1,000 yards along the gently rising ground. By nightfall the lines ran from the lower slopes of Government House Hill to the beach, at Kabira. Heavy fire hit this battalion from the three-story concrete Government House, on its commanding ridge. This was the strongest Japanese position on the south side of the mountain and in the town. Enemy minefields were widespread and mortar fire was particularly heavy. The battalion dispositions placed Company K on the right flank at the beach, I in the center, and L on the left, about 400 yards inland.

The Division plan for 18 April called for a continuation of the attack by the 307th supported by the 305th, on the southern side of the mountain and in the town of Ie, while the 306th pivoted on its right flank to swing around the north and northeast side of the pinnacle. This was the age-old, but still workable, plan to forge a ring of steel around the enemy position, then squeeze.

At 0830 on the 18th the 1st Battalion, 305th Infantry, received a warning order for an attack along the right flank of the 307th with the mission of protecting the Divisions main forces from the southeast. At 1120 the battalion moved to a position near the south coast, 700 yards west of Hamachi-Hama, covering a zone from the right flank of the 3rd Battalion, 307th, to the beach. Contact with the left flank of the 307th was established at 1500, and the battalion came under 307th control. At 1530 the battalion attacked to the north with Company A on the left and B on the right. The unit moved approximately 1,000 yards against little resistance. When the battalion reached the road running east from Ie just beyond Agarli-Ue, the advance stopped and the men withdrew to the starting point for the night.

On the morning of the 18th, the 3rd Battalion commander, Captain Louis C. Hinson, his OP party, and the company commanders, walked 500 yards into Ie Town, up and down several streets looking for the 2nd Battalion of the 307th which was the unit they had seen on the road the previous night. The group found no friendly unit, and returned to the battalion command post. Two radio men sent out after the party, walked through the town to the little lake at the base of the mountain and returned without drawing a shot. The amazing thing about this was the fact that the town was full of Japs, as this battalion found later.

The 3rd Battalion of the 305th was told to attack east through Ie Town as the contact unit between the flanking regiments of the 306th and 307th.

The attack, over the 800-vard front necessary to maintain contact, lumped off behind an artillery preparation at 1130. A determined house-to-house fight ensued, and each street became a chase line. The Taos fought from mutually supporting pillboxes and from under the rubble of the blasted town. The attacking companies, L and I, could not be given much aid by artillery, due to the proximity of friendly troops, and self-propelled weapons and tanks could not negotiate the mine-strewn, debris-blocked streets. Enemy machine-gun and mortar fire was particularly heavy, and snipers were everywhere.

The 1st and 3rd Battalions of the 306th jumped off at 0750 in the first move to swing the regimental lines around the northern base of Iegusugu mountain. The 1st Battalion worked northeast from positions at the western side of the mountain to the northern side, while the 3rd Battalion swung in from the north coast to the northeastern side of the mountain, slightly behind the 1st Battalion and to its left. The 2nd Battalion held its position just north of the town on the west side of the mountain, about 500 yards from its base. By noon the regiment had a curving line around the west and north end of the mountain. The northern curve was about 500 yards from the base. The remainder of the day was spent patrolling and mopping up some 75 caves and rock emplacements near the north coast.

The 307th Infantry was visited by Japanese in the early morning of the 18th. At 0230 a strong counterattack, supported by mortar fire, was launched against the 3rd Battalion. The battalion line ran roughly north and south with Company K on the right, Company I in the center, and Company L on the left flank, facing the nose of "Government House Hill." The enemy fire was extremely heavy, and the company command post on the bluff overlooking Beach Red T-4 was pinned down. Five infiltrating Japs came through the CP with satchel charges strapped to their backs, evidently looking for tanks and amtracks. All five were killed after a short but very hot fight. Several of the enemy satchel charges exploded, wounding six Americans. One officer, Captain N. W. Lamb, artillery liaison officer, was buried in his foxhole by the explosion of one of the satchel charges. The Jap who threw the charge at the captain missed, then threw a grenade which landed right on top of the officer, who by this time however was protected by two feet of dirt. The grenade did no damage. The officer had a headnet which helped keep the dirt away from his face, and by-working an arm out of the earth had a chance to breathe. He was dug out in the morning by his section sergeant, who was sure he had been killed.

The two battalions of the 307th resumed the attack after daylight, swinging to the right, so that at the end of the day the lines were parallel to the beach and facing the mountain. The front lines were near the base of the Government House Hill and extended about 500 yards on either side of it. Although neither battalion moved any great distance, the fighting was fierce. The Japanese, who were well entrenched in the caves and pillboxes, had to be eliminated in very close fighting by infantrymen and engineer demolition teams.

Now the Division squeeze play was beginning to take a definite shape. The 306th was spread around the northwest and northern side of the mountain, the 307th was at the southern slopes and the 305th was on the southwestern approaches in the town of Ie.

The 77th Infantry Division lost a real friend, Ernie Pyle on 18 April 1945 when he was killed on Ie Shima. He went ashore at the request of the doughboys even though he had been ill aboard ship. He landed in the afternoon of 17 April, stayed at the 305th Infantry OP, and went to the command post of the 305th Infantry about 1700 to spend the night. He was enthusiastically received during his hours ashore and was frequently asked for his autograph, which he smilingly provided. Although his visit was brief, he did much to raise the morale of the men on the island.

Early on the morning of 18 April 1945 Ernie Pyle left the command post of the 305th Infantry in the company of the regimental commander, Lieutenant Colonel Joseph B. Coolidge, for a trip by jeep to visit his beloved doughboys in the front lines. As they approached the outskirts of Ie Town the jeep was fired on by a Japanese machine gun hidden in the terraced coral slopes along the side of the road. The first burst missed and both jumped into the ditch alongside the road.

The fire ceased and after a few minutes both men raised their heads cautiously above the level of the road in an effort to locate the enemy. Immediately a second burst from the concealed gun whined around them and they both dropped. Lieutenant Colonel Coolidge, uninjured, looked at Ernie Pyle and discovered that the burst had caught him full in the temple just below the rim of his helmet, killing him instantly. Lieutenant Colonel Coolidge crawled along the ditch to get help in the removal of Ernie Pyle's body. Tanks called up to knock out the hidden enemy were unable to reach him because of the terrain, and it was only after three hours of intense infantry patrol action that the gun and the Jap who manned it were destroyed.

Upon receiving word of Ernie Pyle's death, the Division Commander sent the following message to the Commanding General, Tenth Army: "Regretfully report Ernie Pyle, who has so materially aided in building morale of foot troops, was killed instantly by surprise Jap machine-gun fire while beside regimental commander of foot troops, 77th Infantry Division, Lieutenant Colonel Coolidge, on the outskirts of Ie Shima town about 1015 today." John Hooley of the Blue Network also paid him tribute in a radio broadcast direct to the United States.

Ernie Pyle's body was carried to the 77th Infantry Division cemetery and buried with deep sorrow and reverence beside the bodies of the doughboys he knew and loved and who died with him in the capture of Ie Shima. His body was lowered into the grave in a casket constructed by soldiers of the Division from the material salvaged from packing cases. The burial service was led by Chaplain Nathaniel Saucier of the 305th Infantry. Sorrowing soldiers erected a crude marker over the spot where Ernie Pyle fell, as tribute to the esteem in which they held him. "On this spot the 77th Infantry Division lost a buddy, Ernie Pyle, 18 April 1945."

This first marker was soon replaced with an attractive sign painted by engineer units who were working on the beaches nearby. This sign was later replaced with a suitable permanent concrete marker designed by the 302nd Engineer Combat Battalion of the 77th Division. The marker, which was made by the 1118th Engineer Combat Group, attached to the Division in support of the landing on Ie Shima, is in the form of a truncated pyramid five feet high and three feet wide at the base, mounted on a terraced coral base. Two brass plaques adorn the face of the monument; one a carefully tooled replica of the Statue of Liberty, insignia of the 77th Division, and the other a plaque bearing in raised brass letters the inscription which appeared on the earlier signs.

The 77th Infantry Division lost a buddy on 18 April 1945, but the loss was not the Division's alone, for the "little man" was deeply mourned by every soldier in the army and by all those at home who were brought closer to their loved ones in the service by the stories that Ernie Pyle wrote.

Chapter 23: Iegusugu Yama

ON THE 19th, the 1st Battalion, 305th Infantry, under control of the 307th was assigned the mission of attacking northwest between the 2nd and 3rd Battalions of the 307th and taking the high nose and hill which was 300 yards east, on line with, and slightly overlooking Government House Hill. The attack started at 1350.

The 1st Battalion, 305th, with Company A on the left and Company C on the right, fought through heavy enemy fire from the high ground and at 1430 reached the objective.

As soon as the battalion had taken the hill, a hail of Jap mortar and machine-gun fire fell on the position. The unit suffered heavy casualties. The battalion commander asked General Randle by radiophone for permission to withdraw, and as the troops could not stay atop the hill the General authorized a slight withdrawal to the reverse slope. Whereupon the battalion withdrew to its previous night's positions, some 800 yards back, near the beach, where the men had holes already dug and gun positions chosen.

The 3rd Battalion of the 305th attacked into Ie Town at 0900 after a half hour artillery preparation. Company I was on the right, L on the left, and one platoon of Company A acted as contact unit between the battalion left flank and the 2nd Battalion of the 306th. The troops ran into the same heavy fire as the day before from machine guns and riflemen in pillboxes and under the concrete rubble of the town. The streets were full of mines which the engineers could not remove because of the machine gun and rifle fire covering the avenues of approach for tanks and self-propelled guns.

The progress or the attack was slow and costly. As the primary mission of the battalion was to maintain contact with the units to the right and left, the battalion commander had to extend the line into parallel zones of advance, with each platoon taking a street. Contact between squads was difficult in the maze of rubble and fields of fire ranged from 10 to 20 feet. Because of the width of the battalion front, and the channelized fighting, the unit could not concentrate any appreciable force against any one position, and without the use of artillery or armor, the movement was very slow. After a day of driving slowly into the town, the battalion withdrew to the outskirts again for the night. Due to the wreckage and the very short fields of fire, a night defense inside was all but impossible.

Positions of the three battalions of the 306th Regiment remained static during the day except for small moves to straighten the lines around the north side of the mountain. During the period the 1st Battalion searched out and took under fire Jap pillboxes and caves which could be seen on and at the base of the mountain. Preparations were made for a coordinated attack the next day.

No place on Ie was safe. The Japs seemed to come out of the ground. At 190515 about 30 by-passed Japanese sneaked into the bivouac area of the 304th Field Artillery Battalion near Red Beach Two. A confused, bitter fight occurred as the enemy, armed with knives, grenades, satchel charges, spears and clubs, attempted to kill the artillerymen sleeping in foxholes. Two of the raiders assaulted Lieutenant Colonel Elbert P. Tuttle with clubs and grenades, but he fought them off. After a few wild minutes, the artillerymen killed 28 Japs and captured 3 machine guns, but 11 Americans were injured.

The 307th Infantry made the main effort of the Division for the day, with the mission of taking and securing the town and advancing toward the base of the mountain. At 0900, following a 30-minute artillery preparation, the 2nd and 3rd Battalions attacked with the 3rd on the right.

The 2nd Battalion, with the mission of taking Government House Hill, jumped off with Companies F and G abreast, E in reserve. The attack moved forward slowly, under heavy fire, up the slopes toward the Government House on top of the hill. A frontal attack proved impractical because of the enemy's long fields of fire, so the two companies were swung to the left into the village, and worked out onto the nose of the ridge and into the building late in the afternoon. The 1st Battalion, 305th, occupied a hill about 300 yards to the right, but withdrew without notifying the 307th.

Just after the 2nd Battalion had reached the Government Building, the troops received heavy fire from the hill formerly occupied by the 1st Battalion, 305th. This fire struck them from the right flank and rear and forced the unit off the top of the hill onto the west slopes. The fighting around the building wavered back and forth all afternoon, and the building changed hands twice.

These men ran low on ammunition, and an amtrack started up the hill from the beach with a resupply. The vehicle got almost to the top of the hill, within 100 yards of the troops, when a group of Japs ran out of a small draw and threw a 25-pound satchel charge onto the load. The charge failed to explode, but the drivers got out of there fast.

As the position was untenable, the commander of the 2nd Battalion, 307th Infantry, received permission to withdraw. The right flank stayed about 40 yards from the base of the slope, and the left flank swung back about 250 yards along a northwest-southeast line. During the day this battalion lost six officers killed or wounded.

The 3rd Battalion of the 307th was more successful. It advanced against moderate resistance and by dusk reached the northern outskirts of Ie Town on the southeast side of the mountain.

The Division's ring of steel was slowly closing around the mountain of Iegusugu and all was ready for the last phase of the island fight, the reduction of the Jap stronghold on the mountain and its slopes, and in the town of Ie. Within the ring of infantry were the tanks, M-18s and M-8 self-propelled guns, which though restricted in movement, could add their weight to the blasting.

On the morning of the 19th those elements of the 307th Infantry not committed on Ie Shima conducted a demonstration landing off the southeast coast of Okinawa as part of a Tenth Army plan. Colonel Hamilton put his troops into landing craft but returned them to their ships at 1030 without touching shore.

On the morning of the 20th, the Division tried a ruse on the enemy with the preparatory artillery fires. At 0850, a heavy ten-minute preparation was placed on the mountain. At 0900, the fire lifted and the infantry poured on machine gun and mortar fire, but did not attack. Ten minutes later, the artillery barrage dropped on the mountain again, this time at a greatly increased rate. The fire lasted for 15 minutes, after which the infantry jumped off. It was hoped that during the lull the Japs would come out of their holes and be caught by the second concentration.

The 1st Battalion, 305th, now commanded by Major Eugene Cook, attached to the 307th, attacked north toward the mountain at 0915, moved through heavy fire, and succeeded in re-occupying the hill overlooking the Government House from the east. The troops, Company B on the right and Company A on the left, dug in at 1140 and remained there for the rest of the day and night. The Japs resisted this advance with everything they had, mortars, machine guns, rifles, grenades, and satchel charges.

The 3rd Battalion, 305th, under the command of Captain Hinson, resumed its attack east through the town following the artillery concentration. The bitter house-to-house fighting of the previous two days continued. They advanced a block at a time with streets used as phase lines. It was necessary to maintain close coordination with the 307th on the right and the 306th on the left for the employment of artillery and mortar fire. At 1505 Company K on the left flank attacked northeast to straighten the battalion line. The troops drove to within 300 yards of the base of the mountain before retiring to the outskirts of the town for the night.

The 1st Battalion of the 306th with Company B of the 302nd Engineers and Company D, 706th Tank Battalion attached, moved forward at 0730 to an LD along a road running parallel to the beach and approximately 600 yards from the northern base of the mountain. This battalion jumped off in the attack at 0915 as the assault element of the regiment; the 2nd Battalion maintaining contact on the right, and the 3rd Battalion protecting the regimental flank to the left rear of the 1st Battalion.

A deep tank ditch lay in front of the battalion about 300 yards south of the LD. Heavy enemy fire came from this position, from a string of mutually supporting pillboxes and reinforced caves on the lower slopes of the mountain, and from the peak. The enemy used the "Benning Solution" of crossed, grazing machine gun fires protecting their positions at the base of the hill, and it was through this that the right assault element, Company B, moved. The movement was slow and very costly, and though the company moved to within 200 yards of the base of the hill by 1355, it was so badly shot up that Company C was passed through to continue the attack. In this four-hour fight Company B lost its commanding officer and 26 men dead or wounded. Company A, however, suffered less.

During this advance Company B was able to cross an extensive antipersonnel mine field because of the efforts of Sergeant Harold F. Murray. Sergeant Murray cleared paths through the field by crawling forward under heavy fire and exploding the individual mines with accurate bursts of fire from his sub-machine gun.

At 1430 a coordinated attack to capture the mountain, jumped off. The attack was preceded by a preparation by the 304th Field Artillery Battalion and was supported by tanks and self-propelled howitzers of the regiment's Cannon Company. The main effort was made by Company C, the fresh company which had just been passed through Company B.

Captain Joseph A. (Kat) Katalinas, C Company Commander, crouched in a shell hole beside an artillery forward observer as the preparatory fires fell. As the last rounds dropped he removed his ever present big black cigar and asked the artilleryman, "Is that it?"

The artilleryman replied that it was.

"OK," said Katalinas, replacing his cigar and scrambling to his feet, "watch our smoke." Company C crossed the 200 yards of open, fire-swept grain fields that separated them from the mountain with a spirit that could not be denied. In a matter of minutes they were on the mountain engaged in the dirty, dangerous business of digging the Japs out with bayonets, grenades, flamethrowers and satchel charges. Before dusk they had secured the northern slopes of the mountain to within a few feet of the top where a sheer cliff stopped them. Just to be sure that everyone realized that this battalion now owned the heights, one enterprising soldier threw a smoke grenade over the top.

A definite factor in the success of the attack was the superior performance of a platoon of M-8 self-propelled howitzers from the regimental Cannon Company. Technical Sergeant La Verne E. Northrup, the platoon sergeant, managed to get his guns into position by personally leading them, on foot and under heavy fire, to a favorable location.

Commenting on this attack, a War Department observer stated: "It was the most remarkable thing I have ever seen. The attack looked like a Fort Benning demonstration. Why, I saw troops go through enemy mortar concentrations and machine gun fire that should have pinned them down. But instead they poured across that field and took the mountain against really tough opposition without even slowing down." The Battalion received a citation for this attack.

Captain Katalinas was wounded twice during the assault but refused to relinquish his command until he had completed his mission and reorganized his company on the objective. For his services he received the Distinguished Service Cross. His citation, in part, reads, "The extraordinary heroism and superb leadership displayed in this action by Captain Katalinas inspired his company and the remainder of the battalion to follow him in the assault and accomplish the capture of the objective in the minimum time against overwhelming odds."

On the 1st Battalion's right the 3d Battalion was protecting the 1st Battalion's flank during the attack. As the 1st moved toward the mountain the 3rd's commander, Major Marion G. Williams, decided that the best way to accomplish his mission was to attack also. So what had originally been scheduled as a one battalion assault developed into a two battalion attack. On its right the 3rd kept pace with the 2nd Battalion's advance, but its left company, Company I, ran into a series of concrete tombs converted into pillboxes. Company I assaulted these tombs under cover of direct fire from supporting tanks and destroyed them with flamethrowers and satchel charges. During this assault Sergeant David D. Shenloogian of Company I spotted a well emplaced machine gun which had inflicted several casualties and was holding up the advance. A tank was ordered up but could not locate the target, and opened fire on the wrong cave. Efforts to communicate with the tank were meeting no success until Sgt. Shenloogian decided to take matters into his own hands. Completely disregarding the hail of fire that had the company stopped, he calmly walked to the tank, pounded on its side until the tank commander unbuttoned a hatch, directed the fire at the proper cave and strolled back to his position. The tank silenced the enemy gun and the company resumed the attack. The battalion command group that day killed 24 Japs, captured 2 and took 25 civilians from six caves by-passed by the assault companies.

The 2nd Battalion made a pivoting maneuver during this attack to keep contact with the 1st and at 1530 sent Company G onto the northwestern slopes of the mountain to clean out caves and pillboxes. By nightfall the 306th controlled all of the mountain north of an eastwest line drawn through the peak. The regiment killed more than 700 Japanese during the day.

The 2nd Battalion, 307th Infantry which had received mortar fire and numerous unsuccessful Jap attempts to infiltrate around the two open flanks during the night 19-20 April, moved out at 0915 on the 20th supported by a company of medium tanks, and took the plateau around Government House after a bitter fight which lasted the better part of the day. As both flanks remained open, a platoon of M-8s covered the left by fire and a platoon of M-18s the right in the same manner. By the end of the day the building had been occupied, machine guns mounted on the second floor covered the front toward the mountain and the companies occupied the ground north of the building to a shallow draw that led up to the slopes of the mountain.

The hill to the east, which had caused so much trouble the day before, was held by the 1st Battalion of the 305th. This made the Government House Hill position tenable. The assault companies had been severely weakened by losses so a squad of engineers was added to Company E on the right and another squad of engineers was assigned to Company G on the left. This proved a wise precaution because the Japs started probing the lines just after dark, making thrusts all along the lines, looking for the weakest spot.

The 3rd Battalion, 307th Infantry, which had held for the night, 19-20 April on the eastern outskirts of Ie Town, made an about face and swung south and west into the village with Company I on the right, Company L in the center, and K on the left. The companies moved from house to house through the town. The position for the night consisted of a line running from a point about 100 yards northeast of the hill overlooking Government House, northeast to the eastern side of the village.

The 305th, 306th, and 902nd Field Artillery Battalions on Minna Shima continued their support of the assaults, frequently firing within 50 yards of friendly troops. During the final phase of the battle it became necessary to place fires at a range of 10,000 yards in an ever diminishing rectangle surrounded by friendly troops. This was successfully accomplished only because of careful coordination, excellent radio communications and the exceptional accuracy of the artillerymen.

Minna Shima was bothered only once by Japanese. A small group including women and children escaped from Ie Shima in a small boat and reached Minna. As they landed they were challenged by an outpost of the 902nd Field Artillery. One of the Japanese soldiers in the party promptly exploded several hand grenades and killed himself and the other passengers.

On 20 April at about 0745 twenty to thirty rounds of 155mm artillery landed on Minna Shima killing two enlisted men, wounding two officers and several enlisted men, damaging a howitzer and several trucks. Immediate study of the shell furrows and fuze lot numbers indicated that the fire came from American weapons. A cease fire message and directions for the location of the offending unit were given to the pilot of a "cub" plane, Lieutenant Reynolds, who found a U. S. Marine Gun Battalion on Okinawa and delivered his message before it arrived by radio; a mistake had been made in firing data for support of a Marine attack on the Motobu Peninsula.

The 21st of April marked the final all out fight by the Japs, the capture of the mountain peak, and the start of the final mop-up of the island.

One of the deciding factors of the final breaking of Jap resistance on the southern side of the mountain and in Ie Town was the action of the 2nd Battalion of the 307th in smashing an all out enemy counterattack early the morning of the 21st. All night long small groups of the enemy had probed the battalion line drawn around the plateau on which stood Government House. This line was weak even though the flanks had been reinforced by the engineers.

The Japs evidently decided that Company G on the left, on the edge of the plateau and extending into the town, had the weakest position and at 0430 attacked in force. The enemy approached in three columns, one driving in from the north, another from the northwest, and a third from the west out of the town. Supported by the heaviest mortar barrage yet seen on the island, the Japs plowed into the left flank. The right platoon of the company held fast, but the left unit was pushed back into the battalion command post just under the rim of the hill on the west side. Three tanks in the command post opened fire and all available personnel, including CP clerks, cooks, drivers, engineers, and the battalion commander and staff, formed a line around the crest of the hill and managed to stop the attack after an hour of vicious fighting. Many of the Japs got within 15 yards of the CP center before being shot down. Each American in the position had a box of grenades, and after a hard skirmish in the CP the group drove the Japanese back and retook the position from which the Company G platoon had been driven.

At dawn the fight ended. Most of the attackers had been killed within our lines. In the Company G area there were 280 dead Japs. Fifty-two more were found in front of Company E on the right and 32 were killed in front of Company F in the center. The Japs had made this a fight to the finish, and were determined to die in the attempt. Many of them blew themselves up with satchel charges, trying to get among the Americans before detonating the charge. Several Americans were injured in this way, some by flying Jap bodies. There was a high percentage of officers and noncoms among the attackers, and eight women were found dead among them. One woman was armed with a saber, and the rest with spears. The enemy had attacked in force through their own mortar barrage, seeming to be oblivious of the fact that their ranks were being decimated by the deadly hail of fragments.

This night attack practically ended opposition in the vicinity of Government House Hill, but it had been costly for the Americans.

Company G was almost wiped out during the night. Company H also suffered. It lost 6 of its 8 machine guns and had only 19 men left of its two machine-gun platoons. The 2nd Battalion, 307th, probably suffered most during the entire fight on Ie Shima. It lost eight officers killed and 12 wounded, more than half of the battalion complement. Company F started the six-day fight with 153 men and ended up with 45, counting the cooks and drivers. Company H had 49 men left. Company G had 36, and Company E had 57.

At the close of the fighting on the 20th the 3rd Battalion of the 305th Infantry was facing east in the western edge of the town. General Randle directed Colonel Hamilton, Commander of the 307th Infantry, to withdraw his 3rd Battalion, under Lieutenant Colonel Lovell, at daylight from his extreme right to a position from which it would attack almost due north. However, it was necessary for the 3rd Battalion of the 305th to advance about 300 yards before Lovell could launch his attack. This advance took until noon, at which time the 307th laid down a preparation with 81mm mortars and heavy machine guns. Artillery could not be employed because American troops were too close.

The attack by the 307th was a beautifully coordinated affair. Plenty of 81mm mortar ammunition had been assembled and the full fire power of the regiment was employed in the preparation and to support the attack. The 3rd Battalion with this support quickly reached the base of the mountain. The attack this day was like a prize fight. We hit the enemy first with the 3rd Battalion of the 305th attacking from the west and then as soon as it reached its objective the 307th laid down its terrific preparation and struck in from the south. The slopes were mopped up and the 1st Battalion, 305th reverted to its regiment at 1520. At the end of the day the 3rd Battalion, 307th was resting across the southern slopes of the mountain, and the 2nd Battalion was in position at Government House.

The northern half of the mountain, in the 306th sector, had been partially cleaned out the day before. Mopping up continued throughout the day. Early in the morning a patrol of men with mountain climbing experience led by Captain Stephen K. Smith, regimental S-2, scaled the 50-foot cliff which had barred the way to the peak the day before. Although sniped at by the Japs, the patrol clambered up the sheer wall and at 1025 one man flew the American flag from his hands at the highest part of the mountain. The men at the base of the hill tried to bring up a flagpole, but the rifle fire by this time was so intense that the project had to be abandoned. The patrol descended the mountain over the slope to escape the fire. In addition to Captain Smith, the patrol included Staff Sergeant Paul E. Szypka, Private First Class William McDonald, Sergeant Vernon Fuquay, Private First Class Joseph M. Cotter, and Private First Class Joseph Giepo.

The 3rd Battalion, 306th, attacked on the regimental left flank at 210830 to clean out a series of emplacements and entrenchments which lay at the base of the mountain on the east side, between the village and the lower slopes. Company K sent a platoon-strength patrol into the east central sector of the town. This platoon ran into a large group of the enemy and killed 4 of them. The rest of the company followed the platoon and killed 31 more. The company tried to contact the 1st Battalion of the 305th in the town farther to the west and south, but was unable to do so.

Finally, with the 307th driving toward them, the 3rd Battalion cleaned out the pillboxes and emplacements under houses in the eastern part of the town, and contact was established at 1600.

The 1st and 2nd Battalion of the 306th mopped up the north and northwest slopes of the peak during the morning. The 2nd Battalion ran into severe machine gun and mortar fire with Company G taking the brunt of the fire. At 1400 Company E attacked in conjunction with the 3rd Battalion, 305th, to push onto the southwest slopes and reduce hostile positions on a level stretch of ground at the base of the mountain. The proximity of other division troops made artillery fire and most tank fire impossible and the assault of the caves and pillboxes was made, with small arms, grenades and demolitions. The spirit of the attacking infantry was reflected in the actions of Staff Sergeant Joseph A. Ziomek, who spotted a Jap machine gun which was holding his squad up. Ordering his men into position to give him some covering fire, Ziomek made a one man assault, killing three enemy and knocking the machine gun out. During this fighting the company commander, Captain Eberhard Klostermann was killed.

At 1445 Company E was tied down temporarily, but two tanks were brought up, and by carefully sighting in their fire, silenced the enemy weapons in a large fortified cave about halfway up the hill. The battalion overran the peak and by 1720 the fight was over. The 2nd Battalion met the 3rd of the 305th at the lake at the southwest corner of the mountain. Approximately 900 Japs were killed in the 306th sector during the day.

Many Japanese civilians fought to the end with these Jap soldiers. Most of them were armed with grenades, though some had rifles and satchel charges. There were quite a few women, some dressed in Jap uniforms, among these civilians.

The 1st Battalion of the 305th worked through Ie Town from the southwest, attacked through the remnants of the defenders at 1230 and was pinched out at 1345 after a 500 yard gain.

The 3rd Battalion of the 305th, on the western edge of the village above the 1st Battalion, received a small counterattack from two enemy platoons early in the morning, but by 0830 the attackers were wiped out. Thirty Japs were killed, two light machine guns were captured, and one knee mortar destroyed. At 0830 on 21 April, the battalion attacked east into the village with the two-fold mission of seizing and holding a north-south line running from the lake at the southwest corner of the mountain to a point in the center of the village about 300 yards south of the lake, and guiding the 3rd Battalion, 307th, into contact with the 2nd Battalion, 306th. By 1130 the assault troops were on the assigned line. Company L destroyed 12 Jap emplacements in the three hour fight. Company K on the right did not have much trouble. Flamethrowers, bazookas, and pole charges were the main weapons used during the morning's advance because mines in the streets prohibited the employment of self-propelled weapons.

At 1250 the 3rd Battalion of the 307th attacked north and northeast across the front of the 3rd Battalion, 305th, and Company K of that unit rolled back with the attacking unit and guided it into contact with Company E of the 306th on the western slopes of the mountain.

During 21 April, from early in the morning until dark, every battalion on the island fought the last of the fanatical Jap defenders, and by the end of the day the enemy had been reduced from a well organized fighting force to a few scattered groups of completely disorganized and beaten soldiers. The island was declared captured at 1730, April 21st, after a fight that, according to observers, paralleled that for Mount Suribachi on Iwo Jima.

The infantry did not do the job alone. It took teamwork all the way. Units which were seldom mentioned in the news releases were working day and night side-by-side with the riflemen. The 706th Tank Battalion used 60 medium tanks in the assault, and lost five by enemy action. The 776th Amphibious Tank Battalion went in shooting with the first waves and accompanied the infantry inland, losing four amtracks to Jap mines and fire. Observers and radiomen of the 292d Joint Assault Signal Company brought in the ever-ready naval gunfire and air support. At the beaches the 1118th Engineer Group, composed of the 132nd, 233rd and 242nd

Engineer Battalions worked day and night, often under fire, to bring in the supplies and material, and also served as litter bearers. Captain G. C. Sarauw and his 92nd Bomb Disposal Squad, veterans of the whole Pacific War, cleared away Jap bombs and mines and died at their job. The 7th AAA Battalion guarded against enemy planes. The medics, the supply men, the Nisei interpreters, and all the rest of the specialists had a part in it.

At noon of 21 April orders had been issued for the mopping up phase on Ie Shima. The 307th Infantry was assigned the eastern end of the island and the 306th Infantry was assigned the zone west of the mountain and south to the road which parallels the beach about 700 yards inland. The area south of that road extending to the west end of the island was assigned to the 305th Infantry.

Mopping up on the southeastern end of the island had actually started the previous day when this mission had been assigned to the 77th Reconnaissance Troop. The troop had landed on 19 April and had occupied positions initially near the 305th Infantry CP. From this area it operated local patrols investigating caves and bringing in civilians. These patrols encountered scattered groups of the enemy and killed several snipers. At 1430 on 20 April the Reconnaissance Troop was ordered to move to an assembly area near Kabira and was attached to the 307th Infantry. Upon arrival at the area the troop received enemy mortar fire coming from a cave northeast of its position. A patrol went out with an M-18 self-propelled gun, killed the crew of the mortar, and sealed the cave. At 0900 on 21 April the troop began its mission of clearing the southeastern end of the island, with three medium tanks attached for the purpose. At 1240, about halfway between Kabira and the end of the island, it engaged in a brisk fire fight with a group of about fifty of the enemy. The fight lasted two and one-half hours and resulted in forty-two enemy dead and two machine guns captured. Near the southeast tip of the island the troop found a submarine cable in serviceable condition which connected Ie Shima and Okinawa. On the following day the Reconnaissance Troop continued mopping up in the assigned zone, destroyed five pillboxes and sealed eight caves.

On the 22nd of April, both the 1st and 3rd Battalions, 307th, spent the day in assembly areas, cleaning equipment, destroying enemy material and installations and burying Jap dead. Civilians streamed into the area and were sent to the beach and turned over to military government personnel.

Special engineer-infantry squads destroyed booby-trapped mines throughout the area.

All battalions of the 306th spent the day mopping up caves and supply dumps in the northeastern quarter of the island. The 1st Battalion cleaned up Iegusugu Yama, buried enemy dead and blew up caves. The 2nd Battalion found and marked.an extensive antipersonnel minefield on the western outskirts of Ie Town, and this was blown up by engineers aided by infantrymen.

The 307th regiment mopped up the southeast quarter of the island during the day, destroying isolated pockets of Japs in caves and pillboxes along the shore cliffs.

During the period 23 to 27 April, mopping up continued all over the island. A few Japs were found and either taken prisoner or killed. Hundreds of civilians were "talked" out of caves and turned over to military government agencies. On 23 April the 305th Infantry (less 2nd Battalion on Zamami) and the 3rd Battalion went into bivouac on the east coast as garrison troops.

The 307th Infantry left the island on 25 April, and the 306th followed the next day. By evening of the 27th, only the garrison force of the 305th remained on Ie Shima.

During the six days of fighting and six days of mopping up on Ie Shima, the 77th Division killed 4,794 Japs and took 140 prisoners, a total of 4,934. Of these about half were members of identified Jap military organizations, the remainder belonged to unidentified units, labor groups and armed civilian organizations. The Japs must be credited with superior camouflage discipline. They kept nearly 6,000 soldiers and civilians so well hidden for weeks prior to the landings that air observers and photo interpreters came to believe the island practically uninhabited.

Subsequent study brought to light the extent of the Jap preparations. Ie Shima had been provided with sufficient positions, emplacements, pillboxes, caves, trenches, and holes to have been occupied by two regimental combat teams. These defenses were well distributed over the entire island. Immense effort had been expended in the construction of antitank barriers, including ditches, mines and rows of boulders. However, the defense actually employed was apparently predicated on the assumption that the Americans would assault the better southeastern beaches. Therefore, the defending forces were concentrated in the Iegusugu

Yama-Ie Town positions which commanded those beaches, but the western 60% of the island was merely outposted and mined heavily.

The airfield had been abandoned early in February when the runways were ditched and blasted and the whole area sown with mines. The mines included bombs rigged variously as pressure detonating or controlled charges, wood, metal and terracotta antitank and anti-personnel charges, and fougasse mines made from gasoline filled drums.

Within the sector chosen for the actual defense, the town and mountain, the terrain and structures were fully exploited. Each house and tomb was made a pillbox; each ridge and reverse slope was honeycombed with trenches, tunnels and emplacements; and each hedgerow was utilized for hidden rifle pits, machine gun and mortar emplacements. The numerous natural caves were augmented with tunnels and holes dug into the limestone rock. Some caves were three stories deep and had numerous outlets for firing positions on each level. Mortars were emplaced in holes 20 or more feet deep. The various positions were made mutually supporting and in many cases were connected by subterranean tunnels. Some cave mouths were fitted with sliding steel doors.

The 302nd Engineers alone destroyed 559 caves and pillboxes, removed 2,156 large mines and many smaller ones and destroyed 405 fifty-five gallon drums of gasoline rigged with detonators. The 1118th Engineer Group and the infantry regiments conducted additional demolitions work.

The Japs not only defended to the death, house to house, cave to cave, pillbox by pillbox, and yard by yard, but also employed three strong offensive measures — vicious, repeated counterattacks ranging from platoon to reinforced company strength; hidden detachments which allowed our troops to pass and then came out to harass them; and many night suicide infiltration groups.

A wide variety of weapons was used, and all of them were used well. Speaking of a Jap mortar crew which rushed out of a cave and set up its mortars to assist a counterattack against our forces on Government House Hill, a rifle company commander said. "I've never seen anybody get into action as fast as they did. They had those mortars mounted and were dropping shells on us almost before we knew what they were doing!"

In addition to the mines previously mentioned and the usual pistols, rifles, grenades, machine guns, and mortars, the Japs had a few 13mm and 20mm antiaircraft dual purpose guns, 47mm antitank guns, and 75mm guns. A new fire grenade about five inches high which looked like an ordinary tin can was used frequently. The night raiding and suicide parties carried pole charges and satchel charges with which they blew themselves up near or in the American positions. Other suicide parties carried only crude spears and grenades.

It is estimated that more than 1,500 of the civilians were armed and supplied with Japanese Army uniforms. These actively and fanatically resisted the attack of our forces and participated in the suicide counterattacks and night infiltrations. Numerous instances were reported by infantry units of finding in front of night defensive positions armed civilians, including women, who had been killed the previous night. In the great majority of cases the difference in the fighting of civilians and soldiers could not be told. Soldiers were found in civilian clothes and civilians in army uniforms. Other civilians, some of them unarmed, accompanied the Jap soldiers, carried grenades and satchel charges for them and were killed with them.

If morale is measured in terms of the willingness of troops to fight, with or without arms, and despite a hopeless situation, an inch by inch, cave by cave fight to the death, then the morale of the Japanese on Ie Shima was excellent. They defended well, utilizing what they had to the limit. That they lost Ie Shima can be attributed to a combination of factors: surprise, the Americans' great advantage in weapons and equipment, the well coordinated sea-air-ground attack, the flexibility and mobility of American tactics, and the superior fighting ability of the American Infantry.

It appears doubtful whether the 77th Infantry Division will ever receive, in the eyes of the public, credit due it for the capture of Ie Shima. Communiques described the resistance as "moderate," and even other Army and Marine units engaged on nearby Okinawa considered it an insignificant show which should take a day or two at the most.

Actually the capture of Ie Shima represented the bitterest fight this Division had been in up to that time, including the landing at Ormoc on Leyte and the subsequent advance up the Ormoc corridor. Other campaigns had been longer and had resulted in larger numbers of enemy dead, but none had been so desperately contested as was this one.

The casualties sustained by the Division in the capture of Ie Shima closely approximate those for the entire Guam campaign. In twenty-two days of action on Guam, the Division suffered 265 KIA, 876 WIA, and 2 MIA. During the six days of intense fighting in Ie Shima casualties were 217 KIA, 821 WIA and 9 MIA. Casualties caused by enemy air activity while the Division was afloat from 1 April to 15 April were 22 KIA, 76 WIA, and 10 MIA. These might logically be included in the total for Ie Shima, which would bring it up to 239 KIA, 897 WIA and 19 MIA. This represents a total figure for the battle casualties on Ie Shima of 1,155, as opposed to 1,143 for Guam. Judging from these figures and from the value of the land area gained, it appears that Ie Shima was more than a sideshow. Rather, Ie Shima takes its place with Kwajalein and Iwo Jima as one of the little islands vital to U. S. success in the Pacific War.

Part VI: Okinawa: Final Blow to Dai Nippon

BRIEF: The 77th Infantry Division's participation in the battle of Okinawa called for the utmost of effort, fortitude and endurance from all personnel. They were tired when they entered the line on the 29th of April, just three days after the conclusion of the Ie Shima battle. They took over positions just north of the "escarpment" near Urasoe Mura, north of Shima, from the even more weary men of the 96th Division.

Between the 29th of April and the 5th of May, the 307th Combat Team took the "escarpment," which was a bitter battle, and mopped up, which was even more bitter. This was a war of scaling ladders, cargo nets, satchel charges, grenades and flaming gasoline.

The Japs threw a counteroffensive on the 4th-6th of May, the brunt of which was caught and stopped by the 306th Combat Team on the left of the 307th. Then the Japs, still strong, went on the defensive.

For almost a month the 77th slowly pushed south. The Japs were thoroughly prepared with an underground defense in depth. They had ample weapons and ammunition. The terrain was difficult and confusing. The weather and mud favored the defense of this area just north of Shuri, which was the core of the enemy hold on Okinawa. Somehow, with the regiments taking towns in costly, slow but skillful attacks, the job was done. It took 32 days to advance about 3,500 yards on approximately a 1,000-yard front. En route, 14,000 Japs were killed. But Shuri fell and the remaining enemy gathered farther south.

The 305th Combat Team had the last try at the enemy. Attached to the 96th Division on 18-22 June, it executed several skillfully coordinated local attacks to clear the Yuza "escarpment" and Hills 79 and 85, the last organized resistance on Okinawa.

Fighting on Okinawa cost the 77th 837 killed, missing, or dead of wounds, and 3,076 wounded. But the Division assessed the Japs a fee of 16,127 killed and 58 prisoners in return, or 18 Japs killed for each American dead or missing.

Even as the island was declared secure on the 26th of June, the 77th loaded for a move to the Philippines to stage there for the next operation.

Chapter 24: The Escarpment

THREE DAYS after the finish of the mop-up in Ie Shima, the 77th Division was in line on Okinawa. This was the 29th of April and the weary 77th had been ordered to replace the more weary 96th Division pushing south down the backbone of the island.

The movement to Okinawa had been accomplished in less than three days, mainly by LSTs. The trip was short, and there had been no time for any shipboard orientation other than limited time for planning. However, something had been done in anticipation. Although the Division had been given primary missions of cleaning up the Kerama Retto and Ie Shima, it also made plans for possible employment on the main island of Okinawa. These plans had been formed while the 77th was in the staging area on Leyte, and had been amplified as the Division finished the Kerama Retto and Ie Shima. Hundreds of aerial photographs had been interpreted, terrain studies made, and estimates of enemy strength and order of battle summaries made available to all troops. The G-3 section had, in addition to its regular plans for commitment, made a careful and continuous study of the situation on Okinawa. As a result, when the warning order came for the participation on the main island, the limited time available was devoted to a final reconnaissance and study of the positions to be occupied on the battle line. The G-4 group had a workable plan ready when the time came. A traffic circulation plan was established for the movement of cargo and personnel from the beaches to the designated assembly areas. Supply distribution points were established close to the front lines. Cargo had been diverted to Okinawa as early as the 19th of April.

The actual warning order for the commitment of the Division on Okinawa had been received while the Ie fight was in progress. Quartering parties and reconnaissance elements under Brigadier General Ray L. Burnell had landed on Okinawa on the 20th of April. They selected beach areas, supply routes and a rear area bivouac. The 77th was to once again become part of XXIV Corps, which also included the 7th and 96th Infantry Divisions.

When, on the morning of the 27th of April, General Bruce and his staff landed on Okinawa, they went directly to XXIV Corps CP and from there, forward to the 96th Division CP at Futema to make arrangements for the relief. By the time the General arrived at his own rear area command post, the 307th Combat Team was already moving south to initiate that relief. It was temporarily attached to the 96th Division.

The 77th assumed responsibility for the central zone of the Okinawa front on the 30th of April. Division Headquarters was established in defilade in a deep gully near Ginowan. The 307th was on the right, the 306th on the left. The 305th was scattered, the Headquarters and 1st Battalion on Ie Shima, the 2nd Battalion on Zamami, and the 3rd Battalion in reserve on Okinawa. All units were understrength and tired.

The Japs, hurt, but strong and determined, still held the trans-island ridge line on which the 96th and 27th Divisions had expended themselves.

On the Division's right (west) front stood the "escarpment," a long, high, rocky ridge running west through the 27th Division and Marine sectors to the sea. It dominated the terrain to the north for miles, and from its concrete, steel and rock observation posts, the enemy could see the landing beaches, the complete island roadnet leading south, and all movements of troops over the low rolling terrain to the north. The approach to the north side of the escarpment was across an open valley half a mile wide. A series of gradual slopes led up to the main escarpment ridge, which reared above these slopes for 300 yards at a 45 degree angle. The plateau top of this barrier was protected by a sheer cliff which varied from 30 to 70 feet in height. At the eastern end of the escarpment were a series of sharp rock pinnacles dominating the top of the ridge. The elevation at this point was between 480 and 500 feet.

Running to the east of the escarpment was a second, smaller and lower ridge line which turned to the south and led to Shuri Town. This ridge line made the right leg of a horseshoe-shaped ridge series which confronted the Division. The two prongs of the horseshoe faced the Division with a large open valley in the center between the prongs. Highway 5, which was the central route south, ran from the right rear of the Division zone in a long curve through this central valley and over the ridges at the base of the horseshoe to Shuri.

On the 30th of April, the 307th on the right occupied the approaches to the escarpment. In the center and left, the 306th extended from the ridge next to the escarpment east across open, rolling ground to the western outskirts of the town of Kochi, which was in the 7th Division sector. In front of the left flank of the 306th stood the series of ridges and hills that made up the left leg of the huge horseshoe.

The fight for these ridges was to cost the Division heavy casualties. Each ridge was strongly defended and supported by fire from other ridges. Our troops were to try again and again to take the key points, succeeding only after desperate fighting. From the survivors of these fights came some of the most amazing stories of bravery, determination and devotion to duty of the war in the Pacific.

The 307th Infantry Regiment, attached to the 96th Division, moved into assembly areas behind the 381st Infantry of the 96th Division on 28 April. Commanders went forward to reconnoiter the routes of approach and the front line positions. The 1st and 3rd Battalions of the 307th were to move forward abreast the 1st on the left, in the relief of the 381st the next day. The 2nd Battalion was to remain in reserve initially.

The relief began at 0630 on 29 April and was completed by 1020. The approach was made under small arms fire but there were no casualties. The 1st Battalion, on the left, ran its lines from the pinnacle rocks on the left (east) end of the escarpment right about 500 yards. Company C was placed on the left front at the southeast corner of the escarpment, but facing west. The 3rd Battalion ran from that point to a gap between it and the 27th Division on the right, a distance of about 400 yards.

The 1st Battalion lines were under the lip of the escarpment on its northern edge. A sheer cliff here gave the men some protection against fire coming from the front and flanks. The line was about 50 yards horizontally from the plateau and about 40 feet below it on a vertical plane. The Regiment's 3rd Battalion, to the right, was in a similar position.

The men of Companies A and B started climbing up the cliff, using ropes and ladders to gain the top. Reaching the top of the cliff, they could look over onto the plateau and see across it; but Japanese hidden in folds in the ground and in mutually supporting pillboxes and fire trenches made such observation a dangerous thing. Hand-grenade battles ensued, and both sides took casualties. A cluster of small, cleverly camouflaged, concrete and steel pillboxes on this plateau made movement in the open inadvisable and usually fatal. A great deal of knee-mortar fire came from the reverse slope. In addition, artillery, antitank and heavy mortar projectiles landed from Jap positions farther south. As dark fell, Japs sneaked out of cracks in the limestone ridge and sniped at the Americans with rifles and hand grenades.

The 3rd Battalion on the right tried sending Companies K and L across the top of the escarpment, but they were forced back by a storm of fire that came from the defenses on the reverse slope and pillboxes on the plateau. These two companies held the north lip of the plateau for the night. Company I was in reserve at the base of the ridge.

On April 30th, Company B blew the top of a pillbox on top of the escarpment. This was one of three pillboxes in line. Under mortar fire called for by the company, one man carried a heavy satchel charge along the hp of the cliff until opposite the right one of the three positions, then crawled out on top of the ridge under heavy fire and tossed the charge onto the box. The blast blew in the top and grenades accounted for the enemy inside.

It was very difficult to keep the 307th fighting men supplied with sufficient quantities of food, water, and ammunition. All supplies had to be hand-carried under fire from the base of the ridge to the top, about 350 yards at a 30 degree angle. Likewise, evacuation of casualties was difficult.

The struggle of the men to get up the cliff to the top of the escarpment was facilitated the next day by the use of four 50-foot ladders and five cargo nets, which were carried up the steep slope during the night. No progress forward had been made during the day, and the two companies held for the night at the north edge of the plateau.

On 30 April, Companies K and L tried again to get across the escarpment, but the terrible rain of fire from the reverse slope prevented any forward move.

By 0630, 7 May, the ladders, cargo nets and a special trough for piping gasoline across the escarpment to burn out a huge cave on the reverse slope had been assembled in the 1st Battalion CP. The ladders were erected on the east end of the ridge at the tall pinnacle of rock. A Company A unit had been trying to get onto these pinnacles for two days, but fire had prevented it. The ladders made it possible for the men to gain the top of the ridge. Men went up one at a time. The first man to reach the top made a mistake of standing up and was killed instantly. Another followed and he was likewise killed.

Finally, after several attempts, an assault squad was assembled on top under cover of the scattered rocks. One man stood up and was hit in the leg. The squad leader, followed by four men, started to move on to the plateau, and all hell broke lose. Mortar shells of all sizes hailed down, machine gun fire swept the area and Japanese riflemen fired as fast as they could load. In a matter of seconds, all four men were out of action, two of them dead and the other two seriously wounded.

After these wounded men were evacuated, another group tried, and this time was successful in getting on the cliff edge of the plateau and moving to the right to contact a squad from Company B which had climbed the cargo nets farther to the west on the ridge and had moved to the east along the escarpment. This made the 1st Battalion lines solid along the eastern edge of the escarpment, but the men had a 40-foot cliff at their backs and only a few yards of cover among the rocks on the plateau edge.

Company B had its 1st and 2nd platoons on the edge of the plateau, in the middle right of its battalion line. Company A had one platoon around the pinnacle rocks on the very end of the escarpment, one platoon around the battalion observation post to the left of the escarpment on the lesser ridge, and one platoon extending around to the left front in the gap between Companies A and C.

Just before dark, the Company A platoon pulled out of the pinnacle positions to the base of the cliff, leaving the Company B platoons holding the cliff edge.

At midnight the enemy counterattacked at the pinnacle rocks and got into the Company B area. The men on the edge of the ridge were cut off on the left and received flanking fire from that direction. Knee mortars and hand grenades were rained down, and it became impossible to hold the position. Men groped through the dark to ropes and slipped down to the base of the 40-foot cliff. Some fell or jumped over the edge. A handful of Company B men reached the Company A area, and several were wounded by their own troops as they moved down the ladders.

Fighting continued in the darkness. Men at the base of the cliff threw hand grenades at the Japs on the top, but had to be careful that the grenades went over the lip in order to escape being wounded by their own explosives. The Japanese tossed down grenades and knee mortar shells and the fighting became very confused. The attacking enemy were finally driven back to their reverse slope positions by very accurate fire from the 60mm mortars of Company B.

The 3rd Battalion on 1 May pulled out of position on the right of the 1st Battalion and moved west around through the 27th Division lines, over a saddle in the Urasoe Mura Ridge into the village of Awacha behind the escarpment. Companies K and L abreast moved through the north section of the town, L on the right (south) in the village, and K on the lower slopes of the escarpment. The units attacked east, parallel to the escarpment, toward a large Japanese barracks standing on a level section of the slope. Fire from the top of the cliff was heavy and these companies dug in at the north and west edges of the level on which the barracks stood. These barracks were not defended, but the companies had more cover in the area just below.

The 2nd Battalion of the regiment was moved up from reserve and placed abreast of the 3rd Battalion on the south slope of the escarpment. All three companies were committed in the move, Company G to the right rear in the village, and Companies F and E moving to the left (east) parallel to the ridge and to the right of the 3rd Battalion. Company G stayed in the southern edge of Awacha, unable to move south because of heavy Jap fire from the right flank. Companies E and F advanced 300 yards along the base of the ridge and past the Japanese barracks. Fire from a nest of small hills to the south and from the escarpment proper made it necessary to pull these two companies back 150 yards onto a ridge that ran out from the barracks. About noon a Jap mortar shell detonated the battalion ammunition dump at Awacha, killed five men and disrupted the supply lines for several hours.

This was fighting in which commanding oflBcers shared the fighting and the dangers with their men. The citation for the Bronze Oak Leaf Cluster awarded in lieu of a second Silver Star to Colonel Stephen S. Hamilton, Commander of the 307th, for his actions on May 1st read in part as follows:

"Colonel Hamilton moved across open terrain under intense enemy artillery, mortar, and machine gun fire to a forward observation post on the front lines near the west flank of the enemy position, from which he personally directed the attack of the Second and Third Battalions, 307th Infantry, in an envelopment from the right. This observation post was exposed to enemy observation and was under intense enemy fire throughout the attack. Disregarding his personal safety, Colonel Hamilton moved along the front, reconnoitering the terrain and situation, encouraging officers and men, formulating decisions and issuing orders concerning the employment of his own and supporting troops to influence the action."

At dawn on May 2nd, Company B which had managed to stay on top of the cliff throughout the night's fighting was pulled off, and 4.2 chemical mortars located 800 yards to the rear dropped a concentration on the ridge top. Mortars of the battalion also registered and dropped more than 200 shells on the plateau.

Throughout the day, the 1st Battalion mopped up. Six caves which connected with a central shaft dug down through the top of the escarpment were sealed. Tanks on the valley floor behind the battalions, and to the left on Highway 5, aided the troops in blasting fortified positions with direct fire from 75mm guns and 105mm howitzers. One cave mouth was blown open and 6 phosphorus shells slammed into the hole. The troops noticed that a little of the white smoke drifted out of this cave. Within fifteen minutes, observers saw the white smoke filtering from more than 30 concealed openings in the ridge. This showed to some extent the maze of inter-connected positions in the escarpment.

Companies A and B consolidated the north edge of the plateau, and several patrols got across the top and looked down the south side of the escarpment at the caves and pillboxes there. One patrol sneaked to the edge and killed six enemy on an open emplacement below the south rim of the plateau. On returning, the men of the patrol organized a "killing group" of eight men. The group, spread out in a skirmish line, contained two BAR men on each flank, two riflemen, and two men loaded with satchel charges and grenades. The team slipped back to the south lip of the cliff, volleyed their grenades and satchel charges, emptied the magazines of the BARs, and then "ran like hell" back to their positions. The Japs didn't like this tactic, and rained knee mortar shells and grenades onto the plateau from their positions on the reverse slope.

The 1st Battalion did not clean out enough of the enemy on the south side of the escarpment to make it safe to occupy that area, so the lines remained on the north edge of the plateau for the night.

On the right, in front of the escarpment, the 3rd Battalion began its mop-up of the Japanese on the south slopes of the ridge. Companies K and L stayed in position around the Jap barracks, while Company I, to the left rear, began to move east on the escarpment slopes. Caves and pillboxes were blown throughout the day, but the going was slow and the company did not come abreast of the other two. One cave was found to be three stories deep. A satchel charge thrown in the mouth of the cave tore out the floor, disclosing another level. Two more charges tore out yet another floor. An additional two charges and 25 gallons of gasoline finished the job.

The 2nd Battalion, farther to the right, pushed out ahead of the Japanese barracks about 150 yards and stopped on a small ridge which fingered out to the south from the cliff. This unit thereby thrust a wedge into the reverse slope of the escarpment. Company F was the point. Company G remained in Awacha.

On May 3rd, the 1st Battalion made some headway in clearing the escarpment and started on the reverse slope. The center of the battalion line, in front of Company B, was cleaned out in a terrible hand grenade battle. The men were throwing grenades as fast as they could carry them from the human supply chain at the base of the north cliff. The top of the escarpment was swept clear, and the grenading continued to the reverse slope.

The enemy replied in kind and added hundreds of mortar shells. Our men could not obtain an advantage in any way. Officers of the battalion said later that the men would come back to the northern side of the ridge weeping and swearing they would not go back into the fight. "Yet in five minutes time, those men would be back here tossing grenades as fast as they could pull the pins," one platoon leader explained.

The focal point of the Japanese defense on the south slope of the escarpment in front of the 1st Battalion, was a huge cave which extended back into the ridge for some distance. From this ran numerous shafts and tunnels that opened farther along the slopes. One shaft which ran for 60 yards along the slope was almost impossible to close. The roof covering the tunnel was too light to block the shaft when blown, and charge after charge of TNT was exploded in it, just uncovering more of the position. One shaft down into the ridge contained a makeshift elevator and a number of levels. It is believed that this shaft was at least 100 feet deep and that it housed a hospital, dormitories, ammunition and food storage vaults, and water reservoirs. However, no one ventured to investigate and this shaft was closed by a large blast.

The 2nd Battalion, on 3 May, was pulled back from the regimental right flank and sent through the 306th on the left to relieve Company C in Maeda at the eastern and southern foot of the ridge, abreast of forward elements of the 1st Battalion, 306th.

In the 307th's 3rd Battalion sector on the south side of the escarpment near the Japanese barracks, Company I was still moving slowly along the slope, blowing caves and mopping up small groups of Japanese. This company had not yet pushed abreast of Companies K and L around the barracks.

The stage was now set for the mopping up of the southern slopes of the escarpment. The 3rd Battalion was on the slope at its southwestern end; the 2nd Battalion was at its eastern end; and the 1st Battalion was on the ridge top, ready to go over the cliff and clean out the many caves and tunnels that were holding up the advance of the two flanking battalions.

After a night under enemy artillery fire from the Chinen Peninsula to the east, and from positions south of Shuri, the regiment jumped off at 0800 on May 4th. The 1st Battalion spent the morning cleaning up the plateau on the top of the escarpment and bringing up cases of grenades, satchel charges and gasoline. These were carried to the base of the cliff at the north side of the ridge, raised to the top in cargo nets or on ropes, and carried up ladders.

The men of Companies A and C, which had replaced Company B, lined up on the southern edge of the ridge top, each with a box of grenades. At noon the two companies started a grenade barrage, each man throwing grenades as fast as he could pull the pins. After twenty minutes of this, there was shouted "go," and the two companies poured onto the reverse slope, blowing holes, caves, pillboxes and shaft openings. A confusion of explosions marked the fighting. Several of the huge caves were too strong for the 25-pound explosive charges and resisted these blasts. A double charge was dropped into one such hole, and arms, legs and bodies were blasted 20 feet into the air along with fragments of a machine gun and a field piece. A charge was thrown into the next cave on the face of the cliff, and two Japanese were blown from a hole on top of the cliff. By 1630, however, most of the reverse slopes close to the ridge top had been cleared, and the 1st and 2nd Battalions were in contact.

The 2nd Battalion, which had replaced Company C the day before on the eastern end of the escarpment in Maeda at the base of the reverse slope, ran into a heretofore undetected Jap strongpoint on the ridge just below the pinnacle rocks, less than 75 yards southwest of the battalion observation post. Tanks, firing back into the hill below the 1st Battalion, blasted the Japanese position, and the infantry, advancing under this fire, was able to wipe out the dazed enemy. There had been one heavy explosion while the tanks were working the position over, and it is believed that one shell hit an ammunition dump in one of the caves. This explosion helped take the fight out of the Japanese in the area.

As the strongpoint was knocked out, the battalion pivoted. Companies E and F worked along the south slope of the escarpment, up toward the 1st Battalion, mopping up the top of the slope. This battalion now had contact with the other two of the regiment, the 1st above them, and the 3rd to the west on the slope. The 3rd Battalion had a field day at dawn. Companies K and L were still spread around the Japanese barracks waiting for Company I to come abreast along the slope from the rear. Early in the morning, a Jap counterattack hit the left flank of Company L from the slopes of the escarpment. One machine gunner on the left flank of the company was in a hole that overlooked a shallow draw leading to the barracks hill. He heard two Japanese approaching just at dawn. He opened up and cut them down just as they started a rush for his hole. This was the signal for about a company of enemy to charge the position, dropping smoke as they came. The smoke was blown away and the gunner saw "hundreds of the little vermin" coming up in front of his gun. He opened up and his grazing fire mowed down more than fifty of the enemy and dissipated the attack. Mortars also took a heavy toll among the attackers. Company I came abreast of the barracks during the afternoon, having blown more than 75 of the large caves and pillboxes in the last three days.

Late in the day, a man of the 1st Battalion working around the mouth of one of the large caves on the south slope of the position was wounded and fell in the very mouth of the cave. Private first class Desmond T. Doss, a medic attached to Company B during the day, though his own unit was resting, calmly walked to the wounded man in the mouth of the cave, and in the face of almost certain death, administered first aid, then carried the wounded man through fire to safety.

Doss had distinguished himself throughout the escarpment light, and time after time had remained alone on the top of the plateau after the infantrymen had been driven off, administering to the wounded and lowering them down to the base of the cliff on ropes. Doss's uniform, by the 4th of May, was so crusted with blood, that his platoon leader finally ordered him back and "promoted" a new uniform for him. This man, a Seventh Day Adventist, would not touch a gun and had become famous in the Division for his insistence on not working Saturday, the Adventist Sabbath, but restricting himself to reading his Bible. One Saturday during the escarpment fight, Doss who was the only remaining medic in Company B, was needed to go up on the cliff to help with any casualties that might be suffered in a proposed attack. Doss overheard the Company commander talking about his problem of not wanting to ask Doss to break the Sabbath. Doss turned to the officer and said, "Sir, I will go with you, but you will have to wait a while, while I read my Bible." Doss read his Book for 15 minutes, then raised his head, smiled and said, "I am ready if you are."

The company went up on the cliff, and after a bloody fight, was driven off with heavy casualties. When the men had reassembled at the base of the cliff, Doss was not present. Twenty minutes later, the men were amazed to see Doss wave from the cliff top. Signalling that he was going to lower the wounded on ropes, mountain style. Though ordered down, the medic stayed and lowered approximately 50 wounded men to the base of the 35-foot cliff. This was just one instance of the mans devotion to duty, for which he later received the Congressional Medal of Honor. He was finally wounded almost at the end of the Okinawa campaign.

On May 5th, the bulk of the enemy strongpoints left on the south slope of the escarpment were cleaned out by the regiment. Company C lost its three remaining officers during the day in the bitter close-in fighting that marked the destruction of these positions. The First Sergeant of the Company took over and braved heavy rifle fire to walk out on the open slope to direct the fire of three tanks on a very heavily defended position that was holding up the advance of the 3rd Battalion to the west. This action was instrumental in the reduction of a position, which at the end of the day contained 350 dead Japanese.

The 2nd Battalion advanced 300 yards west along the south slopes of the hill, cleaning out caves and small positions. The area was full of enemy, and every fold in the ground was organized and well defended with small mortars and machine guns. The fighting in this sector was as tough as any on the whole ridge. The gains were measured in yards, and the going very slow.

The 3rd Battalion, early in the day, moved Company I into the gap between Company K and the 1st Battalion which was above it and to the east. Company I moved out from the barracks building, crossed a deep draw, and worked south from the high ground through the western edge of the unnamed village. They advanced about 400 yards south before being held up by heavy fire from a line of ridges in front of the 306th on the left.

This move by Company I had closed the ring of men around the Jap positions on the slopes south of the escarpment, and it became only a matter of time before the remaining Japs would be completely wiped out. There was no route of withdrawal left open for them.

The next day, 6 May, marked the end of the fight. The 1st Battalion cleaned out the last of the huge caves to its front. The 2nd Battalion spent the morning mopping up, and moved to rest camp in the afternoon. In the battle, all of the battalions had taken heavy casualties. For example, Company G had 37 men left out of 60; Company F had 27 out of 70; and Company E had 22 out of 70.

The 3rd Battalion was now headed south in the valley made by the escarpment on the north and the ridge to the east, which was the right leg of the horseshoe of ridges to the Division front.

Late in the evening of May 5th, the enemy to the south of the escarpment launched a counterattack on Company L. This company was in poor shape to withstand any type of attack. Eight riflemen, seven machine gunners, and eight mortarmen — a total of 23 men — made up the fighting strength of the company. In answer to a call for reinforcements, the regiment sent a group of 20 men from Cannon Company to Company L's position. These men, armed with carbines, were split into two groups, eight staying with the company and twelve going to a high knoll on the right, 100 yards away, to cover the open area on the company right flank. Marines to the right rear of the company sent down a section of machine guns, one light and one heavy, with twelve men, to join the Cannon Company group on the knoll.

At 0230 on May 6th, one of the men on the forward slope of the company position reported hearing Japanese coming up a trail below the Cannon Company group's position, between them and the main position. This was an enemy company. The attackers split; one group attacked the knoll and the other came across the open ground toward the main Company position. The Marine squad position on the right side of the knoll was overrun and the heavy machine gun there was turned on the American troops.

A machine gun on the right of the company sector started firing across the front of the knoll and moved its fire back across the open ground into the side of the position. Americans still on the knoll fired down on the Japs to their front flanks. The attackers tried to fight through the lines but failed, and then attempted to withdraw through the gap between the two positions. The machine guns mowed them down, and the enemy beat a hasty and disorganized retreat.

To the front of the 3rd Battalion was a line of small brown hills running off from the ridge in the 306th zone. The battalion advanced 800 yards during the day and reached this objective. This put the battalion on a salient protruding in front of the Division line and the Marine lines to the right. This salient received heavy mortar and machine gun fire from the Japanese in front of the Marine sector.

The battalion suffered heavy casualties among its officers during the day. Lieutenant Colonel Lovell, Battalion Commander, the commander of Company M, and several enlisted men were wounded. The battalion executive, Captain Gregory, the Mortar Platoon leader, a Marine liaison officer and radio operator were killed when two heavy mortar shells landed in the Observation Post. Major Ernest Dameron, Regimental S-3, was sent forward to take command of the battalion.

In this week-long action, the right anchor of the Japanese line of defense running around Shuri, the escarpment ridge, which commanded all the approaches from the north, was taken. In the period for 29 April until 5 May, the 307th Regiment lost four officers and eighty-three enlisted men killed, 17 officers and 396 enlisted men wounded, three enlisted men missing, and two officers and 110 enlisted men non-battle casualties. The regiment had been far from T/O strength when it entered the line. Rifle companies on their return from the escarpment fight could muster only a handful of riflemen.

Thus the Division had cleared the way for its move toward Shuri. There remained on the right flank a series of parallel ridges running west from the main ridge pointing toward Shuri Town. On the Division left, another large ridge mass waited for the 306th which was cleaning out the hills west of the town of Kochi, leading to the main ridge.

While the escarpment fighting went on, the troops of the 77th became accustomed to life on Okinawa. They became intimately acquainted with the terrain of red soil, rice paddies and corn fields between pine-covered limestone ridges somehow reminiscent of South Carolina. They took careful looks at the walled farmsteads, the buildings with heavy tile roofs and upswept eaves, and the elaborate womb-shaped hillside tombs. Occasionally they saw the solid, stolid Okinawan-civilians at work near Military Government camps. And they worked night and day improving roads and bringing up huge quantities of supplies.

There were occupational hazards even for troops in the rear. Enemy artillery dusted off roads and crossroads at dusk and dawn. More dangerous were the air raids, not because of the Jap planes, which were after U. S. shipping and airfields, but by reason of the hail of U. S. flak which pattered down indiscriminately during the raids. Newcomers to

Okinawa would stand (briefly) to watch the magnificent fireworks, but veterans ran for a covered hole at the first alarm.

Small parties of enemy operated behind the lines and occasionally caused considerable trouble. On the night of 2 May an infiltration party attempted to blow an ammunition dump in the field train bivouac of the 306th Infantry. T/4 Mervin Bennett, T/5 William A. Magill and T/5 Michael Skillaci discovered the enemy. The darkness and presence of other friendly troops made promiscuous fire dangerous, so Magill crawled to a near-by truck and turned on its lights, illuminating the scene. The three soldiers then engaged the enemy raiding party. In several minutes of fast and furious fighting, they succeeded in preventing the enemy from placing explosive charges in the ammunition dump. A rifle shot struck one of the satchel charges carried by the enemy, and in the resultant explosion, Skillaci was killed and Magill wounded. Although their normal place of duty was well behind the front lines, the three soldiers gave an inspiring demonstration of courage and ability, and prevented the destruction of hundreds of thousands of rounds of vital ammunition.

The escarpment battle was one main factor in the smashing of the Japanese outguard in front of Shuri ridge. Another important battle was the 306th Infantry's repulse of a three-day, all-out enemy counterattack through the main valley. This attack, if it had proved successful would have delayed the Tenth Army advance to the south by weeks, if not by months.

Chapter 25: The Japs Strike Back

DURING the latter part of April, the Japanese still had their Shuri Line and its escarpment bastion under control, but American attacks on the flanks had begun to endanger the major defenses of Okinawa.

The 96th Division had pushed through the middle of the enemy outposts and had started the assault on the Japanese left flank strongpoint, the escarpment. The enemy apparently knew that a counterattack was imperative, but also realized that he should bide his time and let his positions on commanding ground take the force of the American attack until such time as the attacking forces would be weakened and battle weary.

The Japanese waited just a little too long. A relatively fresh Division, the 77th, replaced the weary 96th and launched an attack that smashed the left outpost bastion of the Shuri Line. The enemy, however, apparently thought that in a perfectly coordinated attack along the entire front, the Americans could be driven off the ground they had taken.

With this in mind, the enemy perfected his plan for a counter-offensive. This was to include a main attack through the valley and ridges just north of Shuri, in the 77th Division sector, an attack in the 7th Division sector, and several audacious, amphibious stabs at rear areas on both coasts.

The Japanese had carried on continuous scouting and infiltration and had learned the American deployment pattern through which they must thrust; Their intelligence of American forward positions was good. They succeeded in determining our strong and weak points and the exact location of the gaps in our lines. The Japanese also succeeded in hiding their attack preparations. Our failure to capture any prisoners on the days immediately preceding the counterattack assisted the enemy to obtain advantage of partial surprise. The fighting in the 77th's zone was of such nature that the taking of prisoners was neither easy, nor from the line soldier's viewpoint, desirable. As of May 6th, 3,500 Japanese had been killed and no prisoners taken. It became necessary for Division Headquarters to order the taking of prisoners for intelligence purposes.

The 306th Infantry Regiment, which occupied the center and left of the Division zone, had replaced the 383rd Infantry of the 96th Division on

April 30th. The line ran along the small ridge to the east of the escarpment, crossed Highway 5, where it turned south around the foot of the right leg of the horseshoe of ridges to its front, and spread in an arc to the left across the open valley, onto the left ridge, thence back to the outskirts of Kochi.

The 1st Battalion was in the valley southeast of the escarpment, with its right flank on the eastern edge of Maeda at the southeastern base of the escarpment ridge and its center and left flank running up and over the ridge line that ran to the south into Shuri. The 2nd Battalion ran from the foot of this ridge onto the westernmost of two hills which lay in the curve of Highway 5. A gap existed between the 2nd and 3rd Battalions. The gap was in the open valley.

The 3rd Battalion position formed a U, with the rounded end of the U pointing south at the base of the ridge line on the left. The right flank lay 200 yards from Highway 5 in the valley. The line ran southeast to a point at the base of the ridge flanking the valley's left, thence back along the ridge base to the point where a trail entered the village of Kochi.

Although an overlay will give the indication that the Division was on line with its two flanking units, from a terrain standpoint the Division actually had thrust a salient well out to the front of the XXIV Corps line. This was necessary for defense, but it exposed the troops to fire from both flanks.

Japanese artillery fire at this time, the first days of May, was particularly intense and accurate. Every night the enemy would concentrate from 2,000 to 3,000 rounds on the front lines and the regimental CP areas just to the rear in the valley which ran east from behind the escarpment.

Our troops took a beating, but they held on grimly. At the end of the first week in the lines, the infantrymen were eating K and C rations, and were a ragged, dirty and haggard bunch. This did not mean their discipline was gone or their spirits low. They just didn't have the chance to get clean; they had to stay in their holes because any movement attracted artillery, mortar and small arms fire.

The enemy counterattack was set for the morning of 4 May. The enemy plan, captured on the 4th, read as follows:

24th Division plan of Attack, dated 1, May 1945. I Plan. The Division as the backbone of the army (32nd) offensive will annihilate the main force of the enemy XXIV Corps. With this objective, begin the attack at X-day. After speedy break-through of the enemy's first lines, annihilate the enemy with continuous day and night attacks. With the main force advance to the Atsuta-Atanya Line. A portion of the force will advance to Kishaba. It is expected that May 4th will be X-day. II Essential directions. (1) Until X-day, hold the present defensive positions firmly, destroy the enemy to the front and learn the enemy situation. At this time, in order to facilitate the offensive on the Maeda-Kochi front line it is necessary to stop the enemy's penetration and at the same time disrupt the enemy preparations for attack east of that area and ensure freedom of movement for the coming attack.

(2) On X-l-day after sundown, start moving. Complete attack preparations before 0300 of X-day.

(3) At daybreak on X-day, the first line infantry will begin the attack and at Y-hour, attack the enemy line at Kuhazu, Onaga, and the southeast side of Maeda. Try to advance to the rear of enemy infantry fire support weapons by sunrise. Make use of smoke during later phases. Y-hour is temporarily set at 0500.

(4) After daybreak, cut the enemy lines from Onaga to Hill 155 and from northeast of Maeda to Hill 141.6 (Jap Map 1:10,000) with the principal support of Infantry Guns. Break through and proceed respectively to: Hill 155.2; Minami Uebaru; Hill 141.6 and south of the Kaniku Line.

(5) The Kochi front will in the beginning cover the attack of the breakthrough units. When the breakthrough units advance to the line west of Ushikundsbaru, to the north of Tanabaru, tanks and infantry will cooperate, annihilating the enemy as they advance to the sector east of Tanabaru.

(6) When the first line of the main force of the Division advances to the northeast of Tanabaru, antitank trenches will be constructed in that area and preparations made for enemy counterattacks. At the same time, with a part of the force, secure important communication facilities in the vicinity of Kitauebara, and approximately 1 Km. west of Kitauebam. Then, prepare for a breakthrough and at the same time send out penetration units. Attack important targets south of the Fudema east-west Line. Then, annihilate the enemy day and night continuously as you advance toward the Atsuta-Atanya Line. After sundown on X-day, units must control (organize) their attack.

This order committed the better part of an almost fresh, well trained Jap division (the 24th) on the 77th Division front, with one regiment directly in the area, and battalions to move through our flanks. The attack plan showed good knowledge of our weak points: the hilly area to the front of Maeda at the base of the escarpment; along Highway 5 in the gap between the 1st and 3rd Battalions of the 306th, along the ridge line on the 306th left flank; and the gap existing between the 77th and 7th Divisions.

The terrain favored the enemy attack. His routes of advance to the Line of Departure were for the most part covered, and the small units on the right and in the center were able to creep, without detection, up draws to within 100 yards. Weather also favored the attack, for the nights were very dark and windy, and sounds did not carry well. The rains had not yet begun in earnest, and the ground was in good condition for the use of tanks.

The Japanese small unit commanders followed orders, and their attacks were well timed and coordinated. The original orders were modified somewhat after the first days attack, to concentrate all attacks into one blow in the 77th Division left sector.

A prelude to the main attack occurred early in the morning of May 2nd, when the 1st Battalion of the 306th, in front of Maeda, and the 3rd Battalion on the division left were hit by estimated companies of Japanese infantry.

Just before the dawn, the enemy infiltrated through a small draw running diagonally through Company A's front. About 84 of the enemy crept through the draw into the area before being discovered. The draw had not been occupied, but was booby-trapped and covered by fire.

The fight began abruptly. Company As men fired rapidly, but the Japanese dropped smoke in the low ground and the riflemen could not see their targets. The penetration was made good, and one machine gun on the company right flank had to shift its fire behind the front lines, through the Command Post.

Unable to see the Japs because of the smoke, the infantrymen jumped out of their holes and advanced into the smoked area, the draw in which the Command Post was located. One clerk in the Command Post killed six of the enemy with his pistol, by leaning out of his hole on the bank and firing into the overrun position.

As the sim came up, the men of the company found that the Japanese were still in the shallow draw in a ditch about two feet deep. The Americans started a mop-up that was very successful. The Command Post area was quickly cleaned out and the enemy withdrew to the south. Every time an enemy soldier would raise up in the trench to shoot or throw a grenade, he exposed himself to our troops on the higher ground, and usually got a bullet for his audacity.

In the two-hour fight, all 84 of the attackers were killed. The enemy had been well equipped, carrying eight knee mortars and four light machine guns, and were loaded with satchel and shaped charges and grenades. Their uniforms were new and each soldier wore camouflage netting over his body.

Company B, to the right front of Company A, also had a slight attack, but there was no penetration and 50 of the enemy were killed.

This draw through which the attackers came was 300 yards long, and the Japanese soldiers had crawled all the way. Earlier in the evening trip flares in the mouth of the draw were exploded, but no enemy were seen. This move by the enemy was evidently an attempt at the first objective of the large plan, the prevention of forward movement by our troops, particularly in the Maeda sector.

In the 3rd Battalion area, Company K, near Highway 5 in the open valley, and Company L, spread back along the main ridge on the division left, were hit at 020230 by an undetermined number of enemy who moved from the southern end of the ridge and Ishimmi Valley. The attack struck between Company K's left and Company L's right, along the side of the ridge, and a grenade battle ensued. After a two-hour fight, the Japs faded back into their holes around Chocolate Drop, Wart Hill, and Hills 140 and 150.

With the exception of these attempts on the two flanks, enemy activity during the first four days of May was negligible. The Japanese scouted our lines and at the same time carried out the first instructions in their counterattack plan, the prevention of forward moves by American forces.

Jap artillery fire during this period was unusually heavy. These shells were of all calibers from 37mm through 75, 105, 150 to include the 320-mm mortar rounds. Two thousand to three thousand rounds fell in the regimental areas each night. At 2200 on 3 May, the enemy artillery dropped an extremely heavy concentration along the whole division front. The 306th area received 2,000 rounds in less than an hour. Again at 0430, 4 May, another 2,000 rounds fell in the front lines and 1,500

more in rear areas. Colonel Stephen S. Hamilton, Commanding Officer of the 307th, whose Command Post to the rear of the 306th lines had been plastered in the concentration, said that "except for that terrible barrage on the Champagne front in 1918, when the Germans tried to wipe out the French forces, last night was the worst shelling I have ever experienced."

In the early hours of 4 May, the enemy launched his counterattack to penetrate the 306th positions and push the Division back. The first attempt at a breakthrough failed entirely, and the Japs lost the better part of two battalions.

In the zone of the 1st Battalion, 306th Infantry, an estimated battalion of Japanese hit the two front line companies. Company B was on the right on a series of small hills just south of the road running southwest out of Maeda, and Company C was on the left, extending from the base of the ridge, left over its crest. The attack, which struck the whole battalion front at one time, was aimed at three weak points, a gap between Companies B and C, another gap between platoons on the left of Company B, and in the gap between the 1st and 2nd Battalions on the eastern side of the ridge.

The Japs first appeared out of their own barrage at a barbed wire barricade on level ground to the front of the gap between the two companies. The attackers dropped their packs and crossed the wire in a bayonet assault. An A Company platoon on a small knoll in the center of the gap had excellent fields of fire across the hills in front of the two company positions, and its machine guns and automatic rifles were instrumental in splitting the attacking forces into two streams.

The attack on Company B was more successful, and a platoon holding a small hill on the company left was driven off with 11 of the 18 men in the platoon casualties. The penetration stopped there, however, and the position was retaken later in the morning. The fighting in the sector was bitter and was marked by a number of heavy grenade battles and bayonet charges.

During this action, Sergeant John A. Smith, manning a machine gun alone, was causing great damage to one assaulting force. Two enemy squads assaulted his position, one frontally and one from the rear. Disregarding the hail of fire, Sergeant Smith stayed at his gun and killed the attackers in the frontal assault. Realizing that there was no time to turn his gun around, he grabbed an automatic rifle, jumped from his hole and attacked the group which was attempting to destroy his position from the rear. He killed five of these and the remainder fled. Although painfully wounded, Sergeant Smith returned to his position and manned his machine gun throughout the remainder of the counterattack.

Company C on the left, covering the eastern slopes of the ridge line by fire, was not rushed, but the enemy infiltrated into the rocky folds of the ridges and carried on a grenade battle. The Japanese on the ridge tried to get at the light machine guns which covered the open valley to the left front, but were unsuccessful.

By 0730 the attack had been stopped and the enemy was trying to withdraw into the main draw in front of the battalion positions. They used smoke to cover their withdrawal, but our men, following them back, killed most of them. There was one pocket of the enemy that could not be driven out of the rocks on the ridge to the front of Company C. Two tanks were sent out along Highway 5 shortly before noon, and wiped out this pocket. The 1st Battalion killed 255 Japanese and lost only 9 dead and 30 wounded in the three-hour fight.

The attack against the 3rd Battalion, 306th, consisted of a series of platoon-sized attempts at infiltration. The first attack hit the right of Company I at the ridge top at 0320. The effort was concentrated against a light machine gun position on the extreme right flank of the company. The enemy crawled up the ridge to within twenty yards of the position and assaulted. Private first class Charles Shiver, one of the riflemen protecting the guns, received a bayonet wound in the left shoulder, but all of the enemy were killed or forced to withdraw. Sergeant Harold F. McGarty, light machine gun section leader, was largely responsible for the successful defense of the position. He not only destroyed many of the enemy himself, but reorganized the position, redistributed ammunition, and prepared his men for another attack which was made about an hour later. Half an hour later, a similar attack was made against the left of Company I on the eastern base of the ridge, in the gap between the 77th and the 7th Divisions. The Japanese platoon had infiltrated through a narrow draw up to the company left front. Riflemen on both sides of the draw held their fire until the enemy group was well bunched up, then opened fire with M1s and BARs and kept firing until the last enemy had stopped kicking.

A third attack was made in Company Is right, at the top and western side of the ridge. The Japanese moved out from several hills farther south (150 and 140), and filtered through the rocky ground to the company lines. A bayonet and grenade fight started and lasted from 0415 until daylight, about an hour later. Knee mortar fire was particularly heavy during the fight.

At dawn, the enemy on the exposed slopes of the ridge began running back to their former positions. They made their withdrawal attempts in groups of five and six through artillery fire called down by Company I.

This fire, mixed with that of machine guns and mortars, accounted for more than 100 of the dead during the morning.

There were, however, still some Japanese on the slopes of the ridge 40 yards to the front of Company I. Troops in the Company L area could see them digging in in front of Company I, and noted one group setting up a radio. Company I men were given the target designation and destroyed the radio with grenades. A six-man patrol from Company I, led by Staff Sergeant Karl G. Purgeon, moved out over the top of the ridge, surprised 30 of the enemy in a trench and wiped them out. In the mopping up around Company I's positions, nine enemy machine guns were found deserted or knocked out.

Several small attacks hit Company L, which was spread along the western slope of the ridge, about 0400. There were no penetrations effected, and in the two-hour fight 40 enlisted Japs and five of their officers were killed. During the day, our men had a series of rifle matches, seeing who could knock off the most Japs as they retreated from in front of Company I.

Company K's left flank, in the valley, was hit by two platoons of the enemy at 0400. A hand grenade fight lasted until daylight. Tanks had been heard at about 0300. At dawn, two enemy tanks were seen about two hundred yards from the company's position, both firing their 47mm guns and machine guns. Private first class James E. Poore took a bazooka and crawled forward of the front lines until he was within a hundred yards of the tanks. He succeeded in destroying one with several rounds and then started back to his position for more ammunition. While going back, he was wounded in the shoulder by a shell fragment. Nevertheless he obtained more ammunition and went back to his firing position. He scored a hit and disabled the second tank. The tank crews were killed by BAR fire as they tried to escape.

The 2nd Battalion, 306th, did not get into the fight during the night. At noon, Company G was attached to the 3rd Battalion and its platoons distributed among the companies.

The Japanese failed miserably in their first attack, which had been aimed at shattering our defensive pattern. The enemy 32nd Regiment had sent in two fresh, newly equipped battalions only to have both of them cut to pieces. The enemy had little better luck the night of the 4th and 5th of May, when he made a penetration in the gap between the 2nd and 3rd Battalions of the 306th. The attack this time was limited to the eastern slopes of the ridge marking the western boundary of the large valley, along Highway 5.

Company C, spread over the top of the ridge and down its eastern slope, had the gap between the 1st and 3rd Battalions, in the open valley in front of the 2nd Battalion, covered by fire from the ridge, and physically by a group of 20 men and an officer near Highway 5 at the base of the ridge.

At 0100, Company C outposts heard a party of Japanese go past on the other side of the highway, and at 0330 another body of enemy passed, accompanied by four tanks. This unit turned off the road and hit the left of Company C. The Japs set up one heavy machine gun but had another gun blown to pieces by a mortar shell. They dropped a knee mortar concentration on the slopes of the ridge but did not attempt to push through the positions. The 20-man outpost called for previously registered 81mm mortar fire, which dropped in among the attackers, who tried to get to a new position, and in so doing exposed themselves to machine gun fire. At dawn, the Japanese used smoke to cover their withdrawal, leaving 248 dead, two heavy and three light machine guns, and five knee mortars. Of the 20-man outpost near the road, seven men and the officer were wounded. They had taken the brunt of the attack and had held their position to prevent a penetration. Most of the fight had been at short range, but there was no hand-to-hand combat.

Five men of the 3rd Battalion Intelligence Section had volunteered to remain overnight in an observation post atop a hill which lay directly behind the gap between the 1st and 3rd Battalions. The men, under the command of Private first class Richard H. Hammond, were attempting to locate Japanese artillery pieces by observing the flashes. At about 0400, one of the observers saw a column of Japs moving down a road which ran along the side of the hill below the observation post. Hammond quickly notified the battalion commander that a force, which he estimated to be a reinforced company, had infiltrated through the lines and was heading, unopposed, for the area occupied by the Battalion Command Post. He then ordered his men to open fire on the enemy. As soon as the observers opened fire, the enemy deployed and turned to attack the small group. The observers were dug in at the base of a rock wall which jutted out over them and provided some overhead cover. As the first wave of enemy came up the hill, they were stopped by a steady stream of accurate fire from M-1 rifles, pistols and one M-3 submachine gun. The enemy quickly reorganized and swept up the hill again, screaming and shrieking, firing and throwing grenades as they advanced. Private first class Joseph C. Zanfini was killed instantly by a bullet which struck him in the head. His comrades met this new attack with hand grenades and fire, and stopped the enemy within five yards of their position. All the observers were wounded by this time, as bullets which struck the rock at their backs ricocheted into their emplacement and exploding grenades had covered them with fragments. At this time, Hammond sent one more message to the battalion commander over his SCR 300 and stated that the OP was surrounded by the enemy. A few minutes later, an enemy grenade destroyed the radio.

The Japanese had, by this time, climbed up on the rock which projected over the observers position and were dropping grenades into the emplacement from directly overhead. The observers threw the grenades out as they dropped into their position, but, when he was unable to grab one of them in time, Private first class John P. Kenny placed both his legs over it and took the full force of the explosion. One of his legs was blown to shreds and the other was badly torn. Private first class Raymond L. Higginbotham jumped from the position during a lull in the fighting, and firing a pistol in each hand, succeeded in driving the enemy off the overhanging rock. The enemy made repeated fanatical assaults against the position but were stopped before they reached it.

Throughout this fight, Hammond directed his men and encouraged them to continue fighting, although all were badly wounded. Private first class Dale Dunmire, who was less seriously wounded than the others, assisted him in giving first aid to his comrades. At daylight, a patrol from the 2nd Battalion mopped up the enemy who remained on the hill. Over one hundred Japanese were killed on this position, and many of them were within a few feet of the emplacement occupied by Hammond and his men. The stand made by this small group against repeated attacks by an overwhelmingly superior force will live forever in the minds of their comrades. All but Zanfini survived and were evacuated early in the morning.

This attack also struck Company E, 306th Infantry, which was located on a piece of dominating terrain directly in the path of the attack. The initial assault was made around 0300 and was successfully repulsed. The enemy re-formed and attacked again. This time a penetration of the company position was made. In the terrible confusion of night fighting, the company battled indomitably, refusing to give ground to the numerically superior enemy. The battle lasted till dawn when the Japs, beaten, attempted to withdraw. Company E followed the enemy with local attacks and artillery concentrations, completely annihilating the Japanese force. Daylight disclosed a scene of carnage on the Company E position almost impossible to describe. The entire company area was covered with enemy dead — stacked three and four deep in places. The company's losses were miraculously light, but over 400 dead Japanese were counted in and around the area. During this attack, Staff Sergeant William Matson of Company H distinguished himself by ignoring the terrific volume of small arms and grenade fire and moving to the top of the ridge. From this point, he directed devastating mortar fire on the enemy.

The second party of Japanese to come down Highway 5 got through to the east of the OP hill and filtered into the valley to the rear. One Japanese officer was killed in the 3rd Battalion CP.

One platoon of Company G, attached to the 3rd Battalion, had been placed in a gap to the left (east) of Highway 5, along a trail leading to Kochi. At dawn, this unit, constituted as a patrol, began to clear the rear area by sweeping from the Observation Post hill. The four survivors of the OP party were rescued by this patrol. As a Company F group was already mopping up this hill, the Company G patrol continued down Highway 5 and killed several infiltrators who had dug in along the bank under the highway.

The patrol then swung east in the valley behind the front lines, mopped up a group of 23 Japanese who had started to reactivate a disabled 75mm dual purpose gun, got nine more snipers who were dug in along the south slopes of the valley, and then swung back to the battalion lines. The unit killed a total of 41 Japanese.

A Company F platoon strength patrol, carrying six Browning Automatic Rifles and a quantity of grenades, mopped up the OP hill from the left rear and killed 76 enemy. There were no casualties in this patrol.

Mopping up in the valley and in the gaps continued all day. The dead Japanese all wore new equipment and many carried documents showing plans for the attack. This clean-up netted three new machine guns, 32 rifles and 5,000 rounds of various types of ammunition, including several hundred rounds for the 75mm gun the enemy had attempted to get into action during the night.

In the floor of the main valley to the front, Company K had resisted for two hours a two-platoon night attack. At daylight the Japanese dug positions in ditches about 15 yards in front of the company. Tanks which were called cleaned out the ditches by killing 80 of the enemy and capturing 10 machine guns and 10 mortars.

This second attempt by the enemy to penetrate the Division lines had, for them, been disastrous. Very few of the attackers ever got back to their lines. The day's score by 1600, 5 May, came to over 800 enemy dead, making a total of almost 2,000 for the two days of fighting, which represented about three-fourths the strength of the 32nd Regiment, 24th Division.

One right flank element of the Jap 24th Division succeeded in reaching its objective. Early on the morning of 5 May, the 7th Division's 17th Infantry, in reserve east of Tanabaru, discovered Japanese combat groups and machine gunners astride the 17th's supply road just on the boundary between the 7th and 77th Divisions. These enemy belonged to the 1st Battalion, 32nd Jap Regiment, and they had seized a high, table-topped ridge at Tanabaru, from which they could harass the rear areas of the 7th Division.

Both American Divisions acted promptly to isolate and exterminate the break-through unit. The 7th Division sent infantrymen of the 17th and later of the 32nd Infantry against the Jap-held hill from the east and south. The 77th committed its entire reserve, the 77th Reconnaissance Troop, which blockaded the Japanese on the northwest and west and prevented their escape. In a well fought two-day action the combined forces killed about 435 Japanese at Tanabaru. Some remnants tried to escape south toward their own lines on the night of 6 and 7 May. This group moved into the valley behind the 306th Infantry and encountered trouble there.

As these enemy passed behind the 3rd Battalion CP, the Company M mortar platoon heard them and opened fire. The Japanese, led by scouts with red flashlights, veered away from the mortar platoon and ran into the battalion CP. Again the column turned, this time back the way it had come, but was trapped. A stream bed in the floor of the valley was used for the retreat, but it was heavily booby-trapped. The combination of heavy mortar concentrations, rifle and machine gun fire from the booby traps in the stream bed, resulted in the annihilation of the Jap unit.

On 6 May, the 1st Battalion of the 306th launched an attack, in conjunction with the 3rd Battalion of the 305th (attached to the 307th), to straighten the Division line on the right. The objective was the first of a series of small ridges running out into the Maeda Valley from the main ridge which pointed toward Shuri. Companies B and C jumped off at 1100, and by 1300 had moved about 150 yards to the south onto the objective.

This short jump was made through broken terrain, and the fighting remnants of the Japanese attack forces of the previous days made movement slow and costly. This 150-yard move cost the battalion five killed and nine wounded. The riflemen killed 57 of the enemy.

There occurred during this attack an example of the heroism and devotion to duty that causes the infantryman to have such high regard for his foxhole buddy, the combat medic. Private first class Charles E. Menther, an aid man from the Regimental Medical Detachment, was accompanying a group of riflemen who were acting as security for a tank. One of the men near the tank was hit and Menther went forward to help him. On the way up, Menther was hit, painfully, but he continued toward the wounded rifleman and began to dress his injuries. A Jap carrying a satchel charge ran out of a near-by cave and attempted to hurl his explosive at the tank. The Jap was killed but his satchel charge, ignited, fell to the ground only a few yards from Menther. Instantly, the aid man threw himself between his patient and the explosive in order to shield the wounded man with his own body. The explosion stunned Menther but left his patient unharmed. Menther finished dressing the man's injuries, then, despite his wounds, went forward to assist another rifleman who had been hit.

The battalion was ready to move forward again at 1330, but conditions on the right did not warrant it. The 3rd Battalion of the 305th had been stopped in its attack by a storm of fire from in front of the Marines.

Throughout the rest of the Division sector, troops mopped up what was left of the Japanese attackers. A period of heavy rains which began this day rendered the roads almost impassable.

The 1st Battalion of the 306th launched another attack the morning of 7 May to gain the highest of the series of parallel ridges, running west from the main ridge. The attack jumped off at 0730, with Company A passing through B and C and moving south over the broken terrain. At 0815 the company had reached the half-way point, the middle of three ridges which lay in succession to the front.

The reverse slopes of all these ridges and small hills along the route of advance were a maze of caves and fortified tombs, and these had to be destroyed one by one as the unit advanced. Tanks were brought up along a small road that ran south around the noses of the ridges, and were used to aid the infantry in reducing the fortified positions. The objective was the main ridge which was about 75 yards north of a road brandling out from Highway 5 leading to the northwest of Dakeshi.

This terrain commanded the entire valley which lay in the center of the Division sector. From this position, an observer could see the main ridge and its outcropping hills on the Division's left, including Chocolate Drop and Hill 10, the Ishimmi ridge line at the base of the Shuri ridge, and the open tableland to the right front at the outskirts of Shuri Town.

After a 10-minute artillery preparation, Company A jumped off with three platoons abreast, reached the ridge and prepared to defend it at 0935. The advance had been supported by fire from Company C, which had spread over the ridge 300 yards to the rear. The eastern side of the ridge, facing the open valley, was also covered by fire by Company C and part of Company E.

For the next week, the 1st Battalion, 306th, was to hold this ridge and its roots, which branched out to the west. During that time, approximately 100 caves were blown in that sector.

By 8 May, it was evident that the Japanese counteroffensive had failed completely. The amphibious forces which had tried to land behind the Americans on both coasts had been wiped out and the main attack through the center had not broken our positions.

This offensive had been well planned and well coordinated. It was wrecked on the alertness, fighting ability and superior fire power of all the American units. Almost 5,000 Japs died on Okinawa during that two-day attack. As a result the enemy, still numerous, still determined, was on the defensive with all his major combat units committed to battle.

Chapter 26: Breaking of the Shuri Line

DURING the days of the Japanese counterattack on the Division center and left, the right flank had mopped up the escarpment and had started south through the rough, rolling terrain toward a line of hills which dominated the approaches to Shuri.

The 307th, by 6 May, had cleaned up most of the escarpment and its 3rd Battalion had jumped off in the valley to the south of the Urasoe Mura ridge toward a line of small brown hills 800 yards to the front. The 3rd Battalion of the 305th, moving up from reserve, replaced the 2nd Battalion of the 307th and joined the 3rd Battalion of that regiment in the drive south the next day, which left the 305th in control of the sector.

The 307th moved back for a short rest. The Division had established a rest camp in a rear area near Chibana where battalions exhausted from fighting could clean up, assimilate replacements and just rest. This camp was much appreciated by the weary infantrymen.

"Plenty of quiet, that's what I like," is the way one dough put it. "The rest camp has plenty of quiet. That's one of its big advantages."

One wounded infantryman said, "The chow back here is damned good, and there's no shells whining over your head."

In addition, the resting men got a chance to catch up on their letter writing — to let the folks at home know that everything was OK. They had a chance to work on their equipment which was usually in bad shape after combat. In the big theatre tent they saw a movie to get their minds off thoughts of war. Those who wished to read found a library of books and magazines.

Nearby was another quiet camp for the Division's convalescent, lightly wounded, and the battle fatigue cases. Somehow, principally through the efforts of such volunteer "promoters" as Major Chester Huff, Division Dental Surgeon, these camps had fresh food on the menu, and fresh food was not officially provided for Army installations or even for hospitals on Okinawa.

By 7 May, the Division lines had been straightened along the front. On the right flank, the 1st Battalion of the 305th relieved the 3rd Battalion, 307th Infantry at 1700, and tied in with the Marines on a small ridge 300 yards southwest of the Japanese barracks, which lay at the base of the escarpment. The 3rd Battalion, 305th, was on the left, moving through an E-shaped series of ridges in conjunction with the 1st Battalion of the 306th.

The 1st Battalion, 306th, had jumped off early in the day and advanced to its objective, the end of the ridge, running parallel to Highway 5. The 3rd Battalion, 305th, was to the right rear of the 1st Battalion, 306th, and was held up by fire coming from clusters of fortified caves on the slopes of the E-shaped series of ridges the 1st Battalion, 306th, had passed to the left of during the day. The battalion held for the night at the top of the first of the three ridges.

On the Division left, the 2nd and 3rd Battalions of the 306th had completed mopping up the remnants of the Jap counterattack and were waiting for the order to start an attack along the ridge bounding the Division left flank. Due to the fact that the 7th Division had not yet come abreast of the 77th on the left, and the ridge occupied by the 1st Battalion had not been completely cleaned out as yet, the regimental attack was held up.

On 8 May, the Division action was restricted to battalions of the 305th on the right flank. The 3rd Battalion, which had been held up the day before by fire, spent the day jockeying for position. The two front line companies, L on the left and K on the right, carried on a grenade fight with the Japs over the south slope of the middle ridge. Company I moved from its reserve position onto a small hill to the left rear of the battalion to clean up a nest of enemy by-passed the day before.

The 1st Battalion, 305th, on the extreme right flank of the Division next to the Marines, had moved into line the day before. Company C, in reserve, moved to the left behind the 3rd Battalion to mop up scattered groups of Japs. Companies A and B were spread along two ridges 300 yards southeast of the Jap barracks, with a draw between them. They could not move forward because of extremely heavy fire coming from the right in front of the Marines. The Marines were having their own troubles with a large pocket of Japanese who just would not be flushed from a deep draw.

The 77th was ready and willing to move forward but could not because of the situation to both flanks. The adjacent units were not keeping abreast, and flanking fire from in front of them raised havoc with our troops. Although on this day came the momentous V-E Day proclamation, there was little or no celebration throughout the Division area. Minds were weary of the fight still going on. Bodies were still dodging the bullets of a fanatical Japanese enemy. As Staff Sergeant Harold T. Roche, an infantryman, expressed it: "The men over there are entitled to a binge but we over here aren't enthused about V-E Day. The news did not really hit home. The battlefield of Okinawa is our home and we are still living in hell." Said Technical Sergeant Americo Gazzero, another infantryman: "I am happy for the soldiers in Europe and also because we will now get the relief and supplies we need. But the people at home should not forget that there is a very bitter war on over here."

On 9 May, the 3rd Battalion of the 305th was ordered to continue its push through the line of hills to its front and get on line with the 1st Battalion, 306th to the left front. Japanese infiltrators had tried a penetration in the small gap between K and L Companies during the night, and 63 had been killed for their trouble.

Company I, which had moved to the left rear of the battalion the day before to clean up a by-passed hill, moved forward early in the morning and advanced to the northeast base of the ridge which Companies K and L were striving to take. This was the middle one of the E-shaped series. There, Company I was held up by heavy fire from the front and right front.

Company K then pulled out of its position to the right rear of Company I, pulled back and to the left into the sector of the 1st Battalion, 306th and came to the left and abreast of Company I to put the battalion on line and in contact with the unit to the left front. The battalion lines ran around the base of a deep draw between the middle and top ridges of the E-shaped series.

To the right of the 3rd Battalion, Company C moved into a draw between Companies A and B and out in the right front along a trail that ran southwest from the edge of Maeda to a main road marking the Division right boundary. The object of the move was to gain a position on the right of the 3rd Battalion to aid that unit in its attack to the south. Two things happened to foil this maneuver. The 3rd Battalion didn't take the nose of the ridge to its front, and Company C was exposed to heavy fire from there and from in front of the Marines and could not advance farther to the right front.

Company C held its position in the low ground until 1600, when it was apparent that the 3rd Battalion was not going to move forward, then returned to positions in rear of Companies A and B.

Meanwhile, the 306th (using artillery, tanks and M-18s to blast Jap strongpoints) carried on a long-range fight against fortified positions on the

Ishimmi and Shuri ridges. This regiment was ready to attack whenever the situation on the flanks eased somewhat.

The May 10th attack of the 305th bogged down. The 3rd Battalion, with its three companies on the line, tried to go through the deep draw to its front, but was held up by strong Japanese positions in the draw and from the ridge to the front. Fire was also enfilading the valley from the right in front of the Marines. Most of the day was spent cleaning out caves and pillboxes in the draw.

In the 1st Battalion sector it became necessary to move to the east to take over the left rear of the 3rd Battalion area, as that unit was to advance. Company B, which had taken a position in the 3rd Battalion zone on the north slope of the first ridge of the series, moved farther to the left, taking one platoon of Company A to hold their former positions on the western edge of the ridge.

An attack order for the regiment on the 11th of May put the thrust in front of the 1st Battalion. This sector included the ends of the middle and top bars of the E-shaped cluster of ridges.

In the attack, the two battalions pulled a cross-buck play, the 1st Battalion attacking to the left across the front of the 3rd Battalion, and the 3rd Battalion moving to the right to take over the territory through which the 1st Battalion had moved.

The 1st Battalion attacked across the forward (southern) slopes of the middle ridge, through the draw, and onto the base of the objective, the top of the E-shaped series. The advance had been made through mortar, machine gun, and rifle fire from concealed and fortified positions on either side of the draw on the slopes of the two hills. The infantryman-engineer demolition teams came into their own on this day's fighting, blowing cave after cave, pillbox after pillbox, as the two companies advanced a yard at a time.

The 3rd Battalion moved to the right through the draw onto the slopes behind the 1st Battalion, cleaning up the positions by-passed in the advance.

This cross-buck by the battalions of the 305th put them on the north side of the ridge to the right of the 1st Battalion, 306th, commanded by Capt. Louis C. Hinson, which held the nose of the main ridge to the left, and part of the 305th objective. The next move was to cross over the ridge, the top bar of the E-shaped series, consolidate with the 306th unit, and then prepare to clean out the open area to the right front, near the boundary.

The 2nd Battalion of the 307th was moved to the right rear of the 305th to plug the gap between it and the Marines. The battalion dug in on the western noses of two ridges that covered the gap. The line ran from the western end of the middle ridge of the E-shaped series, northwest across a draw onto a long hill that lay in the curve of a road which ran west and then south from the western outskirts of Maeda.

A large pocket of Japanese in a ravine 200 yards south of Awacha, in the Marine sector, lay to the right of the 2nd Battalion, 307th. The area was full of concealed rifle and machine gun positions. The battalion, in moving into the position in the morning, had to seal seven caves and kill 30 Japs to make the place safe. While digging in the battalion command post on the north slope of the middle of the three hills occupied by the troops, a message center man dug into a cave that had previously been sealed. A Jap popped up in the hole and threw a satchel charge at the man, but missed. White phosphorus grenades were thrown into the cave and smoke came out of four different openings in the hill. The hill slope had been practically hollowed out by the caves and shafts dug by the Japanese. The entrances were sealed and flamethrowers were used in two of the larger openings. A number of small explosions were heard during the afternoon. It was decided that the Japanese were committing suicide inside the sealed positions. A fire also started inside the hill, and exploding ammunition rocked the position periodically throughout the night.

The Division left flank assault toward Shuri ridge also started on 11 May, with the 3rd Battalion of the 306th launching an attack toward Hill 140 and the Chocolate Drop. The battalion was spread across the main ridge on the Division left, with Company K at the base of the ridge extending out into the main valley floor, and Company L astride the fop of the ridge. Company I was to the left rear of Company L, on the northeastern slopes of the ridge.

Company K had as its objective the Chocolate Drop and the saddle which ran to the left (east) from it to Hill 140. The battalion jumped off at 0700 after a heavy artillery preparation. After an advance of approximately 200 yards, the attack stalled. A rain of mortar and artillery fire fell among the advancing troops. In addition, the Japanese had fields of crossed machine-gun fire which converged in front (north) of the Chocolate Drop from positions on Hill 166 and from Ishimmi Valley.

Company L attacked along the ridge top, but was stopped by a round knob called Wart Hill. This position covered both sides of the ridge and the valley. Trenches around its base, and pillboxes and reinforced foxholes on the top and reverse slopes, made advances very costly. Company I was brought up from the rear and committed to the left of Company L on the Division boundary in an effort to flank Wart Hill. The company immediately ran into trouble on the exposed eastern slopes of the ridge. A number of enemy emplacements on Hill 140 covered the slope, and one platoon, more in the open than the others on the lower eastern slopes of the ridge, sustained 11 casualties in the first few minutes of the advance.

This attempt failed, and the company shifted its attack higher on the ridge to try the base of Wart Hill. Although several attacks were launched on this position, the company could make no progress against an estimated company of Japs on the hill. All support weapons of the regiment, including tanks, M8s, M18s, mortars, artillery, and the 1st and 2nd Battalion heavy weapons fired in support of the attacking battalion, but to no avail.

The positions of three companies, K in the valley 300 yards short of Chocolate Drop, and L and I on the ridge at the base of Wart Hill, were untenable, and the lines were pulled back to the previous night's positions. The battalion suffered 17 killed, 62 wounded, and 4 non-battle casualties during the day.

The 2nd Battalion was pulled out of its positions west of Highway 5 and shifted to the left, to the rear of the 3rd Battalion.

The 305th attack on 12 May was to be another cross-buck, with the 1st Battalion at the base of the objective ridge (the top one of the E-shaped series) attacking west and south across the top and reverse slopes, mopping up. Then the 3rd Battalion was to move to the left of the 1st toward a hill mass farther to the south. That was not the way it worked out, however.

Company A launched its attack at 0800, and in 50 minutes had moved 100 yards along the north slopes of the objective against some opposition. Company B launched its attack at the same time and moved past As left farther onto the top of the ridge. This company reached the south side of the ridge, looking down into a draw which ran to the right from in front of the 1st Battalion, 306th.

The situation at 1000, with A and B Companies well established on the top and eastern base of the objective, made it advisable for the 3rd

Battalion to move down the draw behind the objective, cross the right front of the 1st Battalion, and take the remainder of the ridge.

Company K jumped off at 1000, moved through the draw and occupied a small hill which came from the northwest to bisect the mouth of the draw. Company I passed through K out to the left, and moved onto the objective. Upon reaching the top of the ridge, Company I spread to the left in front of the 1st Battalion. The southwestern end and top of the objective had been taken in the cross-buck tactics during the day.

The 2nd Battalion, 307th, closing the gap between the 305th and the Marines to the right rear, moved abreast of the 3rd Battalion, 305th during the day's advance. Company F and part of E moved through open ground to the immediate right (west) of the finger ridges the 305th had been fighting for, mopping up as they went.

The battalion objective was the nose of the ridge to the right front, on the road leading south into Dakeshi. This formed a barrier to the valley which ran along the ends of the E-shaped series of ridges in the 305th sector. Company F, on the right in the advance, moved onto the nose and surprised a group of 30 Japanese who were eating and watching the fight in the 305th zone. The enemy was wiped out, and 6 machine guns captured. The nose of the hill was quickly cleaned out before the enemy could gather his wits. Two huge caves were closed. One cave, when its main entrance was blown shut by a heavy charge, disgorged mortars, machine guns, and very dazed Japanese from three other openings. The other cave had two enemy 2 ½-ton trucks parked end to end inside. The position was organized for the night. The 1st Battalion of the 306th to the left of the 305th, had aided the attack by fire and local patrols along the objective ridge.

On the Division left the 2nd and 3rd Battalions of the 306th held their positions and assisted the attack of the 96th Division on the left toward Hill 150. One platoon of Company G, accompanied by a platoon of medium tanks, was sent onto the eastern slopes of the ridge line on the Division boundary to secure the flanks of the friendly unit. The team ran into heavy artillery and mortar fire, but had some protection in a nest of small knolls in the boundary valley. The infantrymen stayed close to the tanks, directing fire on enemy positions on Hills 140 and 150, and prevented any enemy assaults on the vehicles. At 1630 the platoon and the tanks returned to our lines.

On 13 May the 1st Battalion, 305th, moved off the ridge they had taken the day before, went through the draw to the front, and onto a smaller ridge to the south, which ran southwest toward the Marine sector. At 1045 contact was established with the 7th Regiment, 1st Marine Division, on the western nose of the ridge. At 1400 Company A, supported by tanks, started across the top of the ridge and down its gently sloping sides in the direction of Dakeshi, but was ordered to stop 600 yards short of the town.

Company C moved behind Company A in the draw at the western end of the nose that company was on, with the mission of mopping up the many caves and pillboxes in that area. Heavy fire from the right front hit the company as it came from behind the hill, and further advance was difficult. Company B held positions on the end of the hill behind Company A.

The 3rd Battalion, 305th moved from behind the 1st Battalion and along the top of the main ridge to a point where Highway 5 came up from the valley floor to join a trail which ran along a ridge, and spread on to a hill just forward of a road running to the west. This put the battalion on the high ground overlooking the northern approaches to Shuri. This position overlooked the first of a string of small fingers running out from the lesser ridge of Highway 5 into Shuri.

The 2nd Battalion of the 307th, on the Division right flank, spent the day sealing caves on the position it had taken the evening before.

On the Division left, the 2nd and 3rd Battalions, 306th launched an attack for Hills 140 and Chocolate Drop. Following a half-hour artillery preparation, the 2nd Battalion jumped off at 0730 and moved south along the western side of the main ridge with the two-fold objective of taking both Hill 140 and Chocolate Drop. The plan was to attack in column. Company F was to keep straight on and take Chocolate Drop, and Company E swing out of column to the left and take the nose of the main ridge, then Hill 140. The first part of the plan worked and Company E got to the Chocolate Drop fifteen minutes after the jump-off. The assault had been made through heavy enemy mortar and machine gun fire. The company spread around the north base of the hill, but was unable to move farther. A storm of mortar, antitank and artillery fire drove the company back after a three-hour stay. The Weapons Platoon was almost completely wiped out in the concentration. Rifle squads and platoons were so badly decimated by the heavy enemy fire that they were unable to operate. Staff Sergeant Henry C. Einig, a rifle squad leader in Company F, started the attack with seven men. On the way to the Chocolate Drop, five of the seven were wounded. The squad leader continued forward with Corporal Karl E. Posson and killed four Japanese soldiers who were firing a light machine gun. They destroyed the gun, and started to advance again, but both were wounded by an enemy mortar shell, Posson fatally. Einig was able to crawl back to the other wounded men in his squad and directed their evacuation before he was carried to the aid station. Staff Sergeant James Gormley and Private first class George Moe, also of Company F, reached the top of Chocolate Drop. Moe killed ten Japs from his position, but had to withdraw when he was wounded. The company moved back 300 yards to some cover offered by a fold of ground in the valley floor.

The following extract from a news release written by W. H. Lawrence for the New York Times concerned the tank-infantry efforts of Company F:

The story of a tank whose crew included T/5 J. Baris, illustrates vividly the intensity of the action fought here. It moved into battle at 9 a.m., accompanied by a Browning Automatic Rifle team of three men and four riflemen. As this combination moved forward, well concealed Japanese snipers shot again and again at the infantrymen, who were on foot. The tank directed its 75mm gun at enemy pillboxes and caves, and its 30 and 50 caliber machine guns sprayed the hillsides for the unseen foe.

Three times this tank went out to fire its 75mm shells and machine gun bullets. Three times the armed infantrymen walked with it, both to shoot at snipers and to protect the tank against satchel charges of explosives that the Japanese try to plant under the treads of our armor. On the first mission forward, an infantryman fell, badly wounded as a result of Japanese artillery fire. One of the crew members climbed from the tank and loaded the wounded man on the tank top, just behind the turret. As the tank went back toward our lines, Japanese snipers hit the wounded infantryman once more.

On its second mission the tank got in an exposed position well beyond its infantry support to send its heavy gunfire in the reverse slope of Chocolate Drop Hill, from which the enemy was pumping artillery and mortar fire. But shell-fire from other ridges was directed at the tank and it had to withdraw — firing all the way.

Its ammunition was exhausted, and, as it rolled back toward our lines once again accompanied by foot-soldiers, one of them was cut down by a Japanese bullet. He was fatally wounded, but the men in the tank did not know it. They stopped, and Pfc. Fred J. Gleich climbed through the escape hatch, picked up the wounded man and dragged him in.

Again it was loaded with ammunition, and again it went out to fire all its ammunition. Around it, other infantrymen were falling in the face of intense artillery and small arms fire.

For the day, this tank and the others that fought beside it, and the infantrymen who tried to move along with them, could count no tangible gain in yards won. To be sure, they had probably killed lots of Japanese. Undoubtedly they had knocked out a few more pillboxes and smashed in the mouths of caves from which Japanese weapons operated. But our men had fallen too, and our armor had taken a terrific beating.

This is war on Okinawa.

Company E swung out of column and headed for the side of Wart Hill, which was close to the end of the main ridge. The attack was stopped at the base by heavy fire from the vicinity of the Chocolate Drop, the saddle to its left, Hill 140, and from Hill 166. After feeling out the Wart all afternoon, the company dug in at its base at 1600.

Company G, initially in reserve, moved up to the rear of Wart Hill at 1430. The unit started an assault over the top and right side of the position, but was held back by the same type of concentrated fire power which held up the rest of the battalion during the day. A deep trench on the south and west sides of Wart Hill was the focal point of resistance, and both Companies E and G tried to get at the enemy in it. A wall just below the hill prevented tanks from coming up to its rear from the valley to the right. Part of the ditch was burned out by one flame-throwing tank that got into range, and the Japanese in it moved out. As the tanks withdrew, the men of Companies G and E started around the west side of the hill and met the Japanese troops coming back into the ditch from the other side. A fire fight ensued, but the match was a draw and no gains were made.

The battalion lines ran across the north slope of Wart Hill and curved around to the left rear on the eastern slopes of the main ridge. The right flank extended into the valley floor.

The 3rd Battalion supported the attack of the 2nd by fire. Company K advanced behind the attack of E and F by infiltration and got onto a small ridge in the main valley 200 yards right and slightly to the rear of Chocolate Drop. The company stayed there until the 2nd Battalion units on the left withdrew, then pulled back under heavy fire and tied in with the right of the 2nd Battalion. In the withdrawal, which was aided by tanks, the riflemen said they passed so close to Chocolate Drop that they could hear a Jap radio in operation on top of it.

The attacks by the 1st and 3rd Battalions of the 305th on 13 May had given that regiment the high ground at the south end of the main ridge and its fingers on the Division right front. This ground overlooked a rolling plain to the front, and the Ishimmi ridge and valley to the left front. Bisecting this open ground was a narrow ridge leading directly into the town of Shuri. Highway 5 ran along the ridge.

A series of short fingers jutted out from there into the plain on the right, all of them well defended by the enemy. Each finger, which ran perpendicular to Highway 5, was a maze of fortified caves, pillboxes and rifle positions. Cuts in the ridge tops, through which the highway ran, were also well defended.

The next job of the regiment was to advance in short jumps along this series of ridges into Shuri Town. It would be very advantageous to the Division left front elements, fighting for the Chocolate Drop, Hill 140, and the Ishimmi Ridge, to have the Highway 5 ridge under control, for it overlooked the Ishimmi Valley.

As it was, a heavy volume of American support fire originated from the 305th positions. Tanks and self-propelled guns, established in hull defilade in saddles along the main Highway 5 ridge, sent thousands of rounds daily into enemy strongpoints to the front and left front. Mortars and machine guns from the 1st Battalion, 306th, which held the eastern and southern end of the ridge along with the 305th, also lent their support.

Artillery forward observers all along the front were carrying on a constant "sniping" at Jap positions. As the periodic, normal and called barrages fell on the Shuri and Ishimmi ridgeline, observers would see enemy positions appear where before there had been nothing but rock and vegetation. The blast of the explosions would blow camouflage off hidden positions. Time after time, observers saw Japanese run out of an exposed position in an effort to re-establish the camouflage. Usually a prompt artillery concentration knocked out that position before its defenders had a chance to restore the camouflage.

Front line commanders sang the praises of many forward observers for their services in knocking out enemy positions hiding the vicious 47mm antitank guns, 75mm dual purpose cannon, mortar batteries, and heavy artillery. Every time a hidden position was destroyed, the infantry gained a little ground.

Throughout the Okinawa campaign the infantry called frequently for artillery, naval gunfire and, to a lesser extent, for air support. Air strikes were difficult to control in the confused terrain and close fighting. But the heavy guns slowly battered all surface installations, such as Shuri Castle, into rubble, and nothing discouraged Jap night attacks as well as artillery fire. The front line commanders became acquainted with and fond of T. O. T. fire (Time on Target), wherein the projectiles of numerous guns landed simultaneously and without warning to the enemy. On one occasion, 21 battalions (252 guns) fired a T. O. T. on a target 400 yards square, and fired for several minutes. [Rifleman's note: There were, nevertheless, some live, fighting Japanese on the target, after the shooting. The nature of the terrain frequently required high angle fire, less effective than low angle. Furthermore, the much publicized V-T (Hellfire) fuse proved of little value in this type of jumbled terrain.]

Late in the afternoon of 13 May, Lieutenant Colonel James E. Landrum, commander of the 1st Battalion of the 305th, was wounded and evacuated. Captain Frank E. Barron assumed command of the battalion. At the same time, Lieutenant Colonel Joseph B. Coolidge, regimental commander, was ordered to duty at XXIV Corps Headquarters. Lieutenant Colonel Gordon T. Kimbrell, executive officer, assumed command, and Lieutenant Colonel Frank Miller became executive officer of the 305th. At Division Headquarters, Lieutenant Colonel F. Clay Bridgewater became Chief of Staff, replacing Colonel Oliver Trechter.

On May 14th, Company A, 305th, started to mop up the valley into which it had moved late the day before. This position, in the draws which skirted the series of ridges the battalions had just passed over, 400 yards northeast of Dakeshi, was "lousy" with caves and fortified positions. The 1st Battalion was ordered to hold up the advance until it had completely cleaned up the area. This task was a hard one and was complicated by enemy fire coming from a ridge to the right front, on the boundary between the Division and the Marines. By 1500, eight caves had been sealed, 43 Japanese killed, and a collection of documents sent back to Division Headquarters. The 3rd Battalion also spent the day clearing the area of caves. The draws which had been passed through in the previous three days were given a final cleaning in conjunction with the mopping-up operations. The battalions also set up OPs all along the front to help supporting weapons locate as many enemy positions as possible. Company K moved forward at 0915, destroyed 11 ammunition carts at the junction of Highway

5 and the road which led northwest, and straightened out the battalion lines.

The 2nd Battalion of the 307th, which had been protecting the right rear of the 305th, was withdrawn during the day in preparation for an attack through the 306th left the next day.

The 2nd and 3rd Battalions of the 306th were in a bad way. The casualties had been extremely high during the three days' fighting for the Chocolate Drop, Wart Hill, and Hill 140, and it became necessary to regroup the regiment into one composite battalion. Each battalion scraped all the remaining riflemen together to make a composite company. This composite force was place under the command of Lieutenant Colonel Marion G. Williams, 3rd Battalion Commander. It attacked at 0830, with the objective of capturing Hill 140 and Chocolate Drop.

The 1st Battalion company, 150 men, moved from its positions along the eastern side of Highway 5 ridge, across the open valley under heavy mortar fire, toward Green Hill, a knob in the saddle to the left of the Chocolate Drop. The trip across the valley was made safely, and the first step was Wart Hill, 200 yards behind the objective. The company then moved forward onto the objective and ran into extremely heavy fire from the left and right front and the left rear. The assault platoon, led by tanks, was cut down to half strength in a matter of minutes. The platoon leader and platoon sergeant were wounded, and one squad leader was killed. The platoon reached the top of the knoll and a line of trenches on the forward slope. The terrible cross fire across the saddle made it impossible for the platoon to stay there, and it pulled back 75 yards into a nest of rocks near Wart Hill.

Tanks supported the company in the attack, and as the hulls came into sight over the saddle, enemy antitank fire knocked out nine. Men advancing behind the tanks were mowed down by a hail of mortar shells. The reserve platoon of the company aided in cleaning out Wart Hill during the day. Company casualties were nine killed and 23 wounded.

During the night of May 13th-14th, Company G on Wart Hill was attacked by the Japs who occupied the trench at the south side of the hill. The attack was so fierce, and the grenading by the enemy so heavy, that our men were driven out of their holes. Afraid to use rifles for fear of hitting their own buddies, the men took their entrenching shovels and bayonets and waded into the attackers. The riflemen moved back to their own holes, which had been occupied by 11 or 12 Japs and killed the enemy with shovels. Two large holes on the crest of the ridge, occupied by eight of the company men, were the center of the fighting. During the brief but fierce fight, 31 Japanese were killed.

When three companies of the 2nd Battalion were consolidated into one, the contributions were as follows: Company F, 13 riflemen; Company G, 42 men; and Company E, 24 men — a total of 79.

The 3rd Battalion company joined the 1st Battalion unit in the drive forward against the Chocolate Drop. The company got onto the base and right side of the hill and stayed there until late afternoon, when they were driven off by intense fire from the left front and right flank. The Japanese on the top of the "Drop" dropped grenades into the company's lap all day, and our men could do very little about it because of the grazing fire coming across the sides of the hill from the front and flanks.

The 2nd Battalion company was initially moved back to the base of the main ridge and into the valley between the 77th and 96th Divisions. Their objective was Hill 140, which formed the right bank of a deep cut forward of the valley, into which the company had moved. The company moved forward until opposite Wart Hill, then was stopped by mortar and machine gun fire from Hill 140, in our zone, and Hill 150 in the 96th's zone. One platoon moved up on the slopes of Wart Hill and cleaned out a few Jap riflemen. This company stayed in position 200 yards short of Hill 140 with its right platoon holding the "Wart" and its other two platoons extending down the sides of the ridge into the valley. A band of infiltrating Japanese tried to re-occupy the trench on the south side of Wart Hill, but were wiped out in a grenade fight.

The 306th was relieved by the 307th in the morning of 15 May. During the period from the end of the Japanese counterattack on 6 May until noon the 15th, the regiment suffered 79 killed, 379 wounded, 13 missing, and 93 non-battle casualties. These losses were among front line infantrymen.

Though the cost had been high, the regiment had pushed through a strong defense in depth along the ridge on the Division left, and prepared the way for the final attack on the dominant terrain features of Chocolate Drop, Wart, Green, and Flattop (140) Hills. This fighting had consisted of hundreds of grenade and bayonet actions, continuous small unit assaults on fortified positions, and a constant barrage of fire from every available weapon.

The 307th Regiment attacked through the 306th at 0900, 15 May, following an all-night artillery preparation on the Shuri and Ishimmi defenses. The battalions moved out in column, the 3rd leading. The scheme of maneuver included a simultaneous attack on Hill 140 on the left and Chocolate Drop on the right. Companies K and I were in the assault. Company I had as its objective the Chocolate Drop and Green Hill to its left in the saddle leading to Flattop (Hill 140).

By 1030, Company I had reached its objective, with one platoon on the base of the "Drop" and another on the small knoll to the left of the saddle. The same crossed machine gun fires from left and right held the company close to the base of the hill, preventing any mass assault on any side of the objective.

Company K had little trouble in its advance until it got to the base of Hill 140. Fire from the objective and from Hill 150, across the way in the 96th zone, slowed movement but an assault was made up the slopes. The troops in this charge up the hill utilized grenades, satchel charges and flamethrowers, and were supported by tanks firing at the top and left side of the hill. The attack stopped on the north slope of the hill just under the crest. A grenade battle around the top continued all afternoon. The company stayed there for the night.

The 2nd Battalion had attacked to the right of the 3rd, moving slowly through the open valley onto a little ridge that ran to the right and 200 yards forward of Chocolate Drop. Company E was on the right at the foot of the ridge 200 yards forward and 400 to the right of Chocolate Drop. Company G was astride a road that ran through a cut in the ridge with a line of telephone poles running through the company center. Company E was several hundred yards to the rear, in reserve.

The 307th succeeded in reaching the objective, and was prepared to take it. This would cover the Ishimmi Valley and dominate all approaches to the main Shuri ridge, both on the 77th and 96th Division fronts.

On the Division right, along Highway 5, the 305th slowly spread west over the dominating terrain covering the open ground to the front. The 1st Battalion cleaned out a draw on the regimental right 500 yards northwest of Highway 5 and was ordered to finish the job and then advance by fire and movement to a series of small hills to its front. At 0910, following an intense artillery, 4.2, 81 and 60mm mortar barrage, Companies A and C, supported by tanks, attacked southwest from the draw across open country toward a ridge on the Division right boundary. The advance was parallel to a road which ran to the south in a long curve into Shuri Town. By 1030, Company A advanced along the top of the ridge line, and by noon reached a position on the road about 400 yards due east of Dakeshi. After a quick reorganization, the company moved onto a nose of high ground which jutted out from the right.

Company C, meanwhile, moved along the low ground to the left of Company A, mopping up the many caves and dug-in tanks that littered the area. Satchel charges and flamethrowers were used very effectively. With the gradual elimination of the enemy fire points along the ridge on the right, Company B was able to leave its position on the main ridge to the rear and move onto a small knob 30 yards to the left rear of Company A.

Late in the day, heavy mortar fire began falling in the Company area. In order to better hold the battalion line for the night, the unit pulled back 200 yards on line with the other two companies. This gave the battalion control of the rolling valley to the left and the approaches to Shuri on the front. They were also able to assist by fire the 1st Marine Division units to the right.

The 3rd Battalion jumped off at 0900, following a heavy artillery preparation along the Highway 5 ridge to the front. This artillery preparation included fire from 8-inch guns of Corps Artillery, and 105-mm howitzers of the Division. Company L spread out on the forward slopes of the high ground which ran to the right, along the road which branched west from the highway, and mopped up to the point where it established contact with the 1st Battalion. Companies I and L moved out parallel and 300 yards west of Highway 5 toward a series of knolls and small ridges that ran out to the front. Enemy resistance was stiffening as the companies moved across the open ground toward the first small rise. Each of these small ridges was pock-marked with innumerable caves and fire trenches, and the reverse slope cave positions housed many knee mortar positions. The first of the series of knolls was taken and mopped up. This was a little Y-shaped piece of ground. The attack was not continued because of the lateness of the hour and the heavy mortar fire which started coming in from the Shuri ridges.

On 16 May, the 305th slowed down the activity on its right flank and put the emphasis on the left, along Highway 5. The 1st Battalion zone, on the right rear near the Division boundary, was exposed and heavily blanketed by fire from in front of the Marines, who were held up on a line even with that of the 305th. This battalion was to continue mopping up small pockets of resistance in draws and along the base of the ridge line on the right, and at the same time support the advance of the 3rd Battalion with every available weapon. Company A moved onto a small knoll in the center of the open plain 300 yards east of the Dakeshi road junction and closed a number of caves and trenches on its north slope. The south slope of the position was exposed to heavy fire of all types from the south, and both flanks and the approaches to the knoll were covered by mortar fire. By 1600 the demolition teams formed within the battalion had destroyed 30 caves in this area.

Following a five-minute artillery, mortar and machine gun preparation, Companies I and K, supported by flamethrowing tanks moved out at 0810 toward the broken ground to their front.

At 1300, Company L attacked to the left of the two companies and, with tank support, took the south leg of a loop-shaped ridge, mopped it up and went 75 yards farther west to occupy the shaft of the hook. This last position was a little too hot for comfort, and as the men did not have enough daylight left to allow a complete mop-up, the company withdrew to the hill it had taken earlier.

Although the advance of the companies during the day had been hotly contested, the unit commanders reported that the Japanese seemed confused and disorganized, permitting our forces to advance with a minimum of casualties. The three companies killed 387 Japanese, captured four light machine guns and three heavy machine guns, and sealed 45 caves during the day.

On the Division left, the 307th had its troubles with Chocolate Drop and Hill 140. Company I, 100 yards north of the base of the "Drop," repelled two small counterattacks during the night. The attackers came from a huge cave on the south side of the hill. In this fight, eight enemy were killed. All of them had been armed with knee mortars. The company had pulled off the hill late the day before, after one platoon had suffered heavy casualties. Five men in a ditch on the right side of the hill had been cut off and stayed there during the night, thinking the company was still with them. Two of them were killed, a third wounded, and two remaining escaped from the trap in the morning when the company again advanced to the base of the hill. The wounded man was rescued a short time later.

A new platoon replaced the one that had been mauled the day before, and kept a continual probing around the sides of the hill in an effort to get at the Japs on the top and reverse slope. Heavy fire restricted maneuver and the unit did not have much success. One Jap position to the right about a hundred yards, which had been bothering the troops on the hill, was eliminated by 60mm mortar fire during the afternoon. The platoon refused its right flank late in the day to tie in with the 2nd Battalion, but the platoon to the left, on the saddle leading to Hill 140, stayed in place.

Company K attacked Hill 140 at 0800 and one platoon got on its flat top almost immediately. This platoon was driven back to the north crest of the hill by a heavy mortar concentration coming from Hill 166 (Tom Hill) to the front. Three different assaults were made by the platoon during the morning, all ending the same way. At 1615 the whole company assaulted the hill from the front and right side. The troops got on top again and were digging in under smoke and an artillery screen, when a storm of mortar and artillery fire landed on the position. There did not seem to be any adjusting by the enemy, the concentration broke all at once, and at just the right place.

The company got off the exposed top of the hill and dug in just below the top of the north slope. In the platoons that had made the morning's assaults on the hill, only one officer was left. He had been wounded but had kept on and was an inspiration to his men, leading every attack. His platoon sergeant called him a "wild man, but a man to trust in a pinch."

The 2nd Battalion, along a ridge to the right of Chocolate Drop, tried all day to push farther to the right toward Ishimmi, but was held up by heavy fire of all types from all along the front. Dorothy Hill, which lay across the Ishimmi Valley from the 2nd Battalion, was a particular nuisance. From caves and tunnels along its sides and top came mortar, machine gun, and antitank fire. The whole reverse slope of Dorothy position was later found to consist of tier upon tier of fortified caves and shafts which ran through the hill.

During the early morning hours of the 17th of May, the Division made the first night attack of the Okinawa campaign, the first by any unit of the Tenth Army and one of the first in the whole Pacific area. Both regiments on the Division front launched pre-dawn attacks, and both were successful.

The 3rd Battalion of the 305th jumped off at 0415, with L Company leading. The company moved parallel to the highway onto the north of a U-shaped ridge lying with the base of the U on the highway. At 0505 they moved to the south arm of the ridge, 75 yards farther forward. Company K moved to the right of L and into a little wooded knoll 100 yards forward.

The advance had been made without alarming the Japs and it was not until shortly after dawn that the enemy woke up to the fact that he had been tricked by the Americans, who, according to Jap manuals, "never attack at night" Many small enemy positions had been by-passed in the darkness, and Company I followed up the attack to take care of these positions. Late in the morning Company K was pulled off the wooded knoll and brought to the right of Company L for better defense.

This attack had been made on a shoestring. Company L had as its attacking force seven riflemen and 14 men of the Ammunition and Pioneer platoon, including drivers and cooks. Company I was in a little better shape — it had about 20 riflemen.

Armor was extremely helpful during the day, not only in burning out pockets of the enemy with flamethrowers and blasting caves with 75mm guns, but carrying supplies and evacuating wounded.

The 1st Battalion initially supported the advance of the 3rd by fire, then sent Company A 200 yards forward to a small ridge at the Dakeshi road junction. Company C moved up to the right of Company A. Company B moved to the left of the two, parallel to the advance of Company K, and occupied a knoll near the base of the hill mass (110.5) which covered the actual entrance to Shuri Town. One platoon, close to Company K, ran into heavy machine gun and mortar fire and was forced to take cover in a cave. Company C tried to flank the enemy position, believed to be a company on the slopes of the hill mass to the front, but was unsuccessful. One particularly well hidden machine gun was holding the Company B platoon in the cave. At 1300 the platoon attempted to get back to the company under cover of smoke, but this was unsuccessful. Finally, behind a smoke screen laid by 4.2 mortars and covering fire from both battalions, the unit made it back to a safe position. The battalion dug in for the night along the ridge and road east of Dakeshi.

The predawn attack of the 2nd Battalion, 307th, toward Ishimmi Ridge was too successful. It resulted in the advance of Company E, 307th Infantry, into a situation similar to that of the "Lost Battalion" of World War I. The story of Company E, 307th, as told by 2nd Lieutenant Robert F. Meiser, the 2nd platoon leader, follows:

At 1730, on May 16th, Company E's commanding officer, Lt. Theodore S. Bell, called a meeting of his platoon leaders. The plan of action for the following day was that Company E might be put in action along with Companies F and G, who were already on the line. By 1830 the platoon leaders had passed this information on to the platoons, whose members immediately began preparation to move out. At 1830 the commanding officer called for his platoon leaders to accompany him to the battalion

Observation Post. There, high atop a rocky pinnacle, Company E was given the order to make a surprise night attack on distant Ishimmi ridge. In the hazy dusk of late evening, the objective was only faintly visible and only a few minutes were available for the distant reconnaissance before dark. We returned to the CP where, in the dark, plans and details for the attack were given.

The plan was to advance, single file, 450 yards beyond the escarpment east and south to the Line of Departure, which was Company F's position. From there our objective was 800 yards to the southwest on Ishimmi Ridge, which was the very core of the Shuri defense line. The order of march would be the 2nd platoon, weapons, 3rd, and 1st. In addition, a section of heavy machine guns from Company H were to be attached, plus a reinforced rifle platoon from Company C.

The men were told all the known details of the attack. They were instructed to load and lock their weapons, fix bayonets, and use them if enemy were encountered in the advance. Canteens were filled, extra ammunition issued, and all made ready in the darkness by 2200.

At 0215, May 17th, the company was awakened and in pitch darkness prepared to move out. Everyone was very confident, no apprehension being displayed by anyone. Preparations to leave were accomplished with a minimum of confusion in spite of the darkness, and the column started moving forward at 0300 sharp. The route was through a deep cut in the left edge of the escarpment, down its forward slope, and thence southeast by way of the wide open valley to the Line of Departure. The company moved slowly due to the ruggedness of the terrain and the inability to see any distance. Water-filled shell holes had to be avoided and several ditches detoured. Flare shells were going up regularly but everyone hit the ground in that instant before each flare burst.

By 0350 the head of the column had reached Company F's position and the squads began forming in line, each in a close skirmish formation. The platoon from Company C joined us there and took up a formation to the right center. All was in readiness, each platoon leader and each squad leader had been given his specific instructions. Meanwhile Lieutenant Bell and I were having difficulty in definitely locating our objective. We were now down in the valley, at a new angle, and still about 800 yards from our goal. By close observation in the dim light of the distant flares, we were finally able to locate the target. Our guide was three or four limbless trees on the two highest points of Ishimmi Ridge and those were only faintly visible in the clearest of flarelight.

Promptly at 0415 the company left the Line of Departure. Guiding was rather difficult as we had to skirt a number of small rocky knolls and keep in the ravines and depressions to lessen our chances of being discovered. Fear of being discovered by the enemy was our greatest worry, as we could have easily been ambushed in this land which was physically occupied and thoroughly controlled by Japs.

Flares caused numerous delays but we were never caught moving, which might have proved our undoing. On the way up, no attack was made on us, but the sound of battle was all around. Rifle and machine-gun fire was heard continually and the whine of heavy artillery shells was incessant.

Dawn began to break as we came upon our objective. About 50 yards from it, the 3rd platoon echeloned to the left of the 2nd and nearly on line, forming the left front and flank. The 2nd continued straight forward to occupy the center and foremost position, while the platoon from Company C held the right front and flank. Our rear was protected by a well formed semicircle of the 1st platoon.

We now found that the 125 yard part of the objective we were able to occupy was a very prominent, table top ridge. It was quite flat and made up of rock and coral where digging was very difficult, and some places impossible. The forward edge of the ridge was only slightly curved, with the center being foremost. The 1500 yard long valley running parallel to our front was extremely deep and steep and on the opposite side was commanded by a higher hill than the one we were on.

The top center of the Ishimmi Ridge was very narrow, being only about seven or eight yards wide, and then fanning out to either flank in a leaf-like pattern. Directly to the rear of the narrow section of the ridge was a pocket, 20 yards in diameter, in which the company Command Post was located, and this, ultimately, was the location of the company's final stand. To our right rear, 250 yards away, were two grassy mounds of earth, each about 30 feet higher than our position and affording perfect observation into it. Likewise, to the center rear was a finger ridge extension which afforded the enemy an excellent Observation Post as well as machine-gun positions.

At 0505 we were on our objective, and as daylight was coming we hastened to dig in. The enemy on the ridge was completely surprised and was not aware of our presence for nearly 20 minutes. While initially caught napping, they soon made up for lost time and all hell broke loose at 0530.

Mortar fire, heavy and light, began falling on our area in such fury and volume that one would believe the place had been zeroed in for just such an eventuality. Machine-gun and rifle-fire began pouring in from all directions and within a short time even enemy artillery began shelling us.

As daylight came, we finally realized that we were in a spot and that the enemy controlled the position from every direction, including the rear. The platoon on the left was receiving murderous fire, especially from both flanks and the high Shuri ridge across the valley to our front. Foxholes were only partly completed and to raise one's head meant death on that fire-swept plateau. Mortar shells very often dropped directly in the foxhole, usually taking at least one man's life or badly wounding several. The same action was taking place on the right flank as that area was almost identical to the one on the left.

In the rear, the 1st Platoon was faring no better and was taking a terrific pounding from all types of fire. However, they maintained continuous and effective fire on the enemy, especially to the right and left rear, greatly reducing his advantages there. Our light mortars were in this area and though only partially dug in, the mortar crews fired as long as the mortars were serviceable. By 1000 the first day, enemy action had knocked out all but one of the mortars and killed or wounded nearly all the crewmen.

The 2nd Platoon had gone over the center of the ridge and dropped into a long Jap communication trench which was about six feet deep and the same distance below the level of the ridge. From this position a complete view of the entire valley was had as well as the high ridge to our front. Small dug-outs in this trench contained about 10 or 12 sleeping enemy who were quickly disposed of by bayonet or rifle fire. However, tunnels from inside the ridge led into either end of the trench and the enemy soon attempted to force their way upward. At first, surprise was so complete that a Japanese officer and his aide, laughing and talking, came toward us in the trench, walked completely past one of our men and were killed without realizing what hit them.

Enemy knee mortar and rifle squads began popping from caves and attempted to cross from the opposite ridge, but were cut down by second platoon riflemen and two light machine guns. However, in order to do this, the men had to expose themselves considerably and were soon under accurate and deadly machine-gun fire from cleverly hidden enemy positions.

By making use of the tunnels the Nips were soon able to set up knee mortars about 100 yards to either flank and fire systematically from one end of the trench to the other. Each position had two mortars which were firing simultaneously, doing great damage to the earthworks of our line as well as producing heavy casualties in our ranks. Riflemen were blown to bits by these mortars and many were struck in the head by machinegun fire. The blood from wounded was everywhere; in the weapons, on the living, and splattered all around. The dead lay where they fell, in pools of their own blood. Though the platoon medic was wounded early in the morning, he took care of the injured as fast as possible but was unable to keep up and soon his supplies were exhausted.

By 0700 both of our light machine guns had been knocked out, one being completely buried. The few remaining crew members became riflemen and stayed right there throughout the day. During the morning a few Japanese had managed to crawl up from the deep ravine to a line just slightly beneath our position and began hurling grenades upwards at us. Grenades were thrown back and soon the infiltrators were killed or driven backward, but we had suffered too. The battle continued furiously all morning and by noon the 2nd Platoon had suffered heavily, about 50% being killed or wounded. The number of Japs killed had mounted steadily but they were still able to reinforce almost at will and attempted numerous frontal and flanking counterattacks.

Meanwhile the 3rd Platoon had had a steady grenade battle and had repulsed three fixed bayonet attacks by enemy coming from their left flank. However, the men of this platoon had very little cover and were being whittled down man by man until more than half of them were out of action, including their platoon leader. Dead men were pushed hurriedly from the all too small holes in order to make more room for the living. In some cases the firing was so heavy as to even prevent this and the living and bloody mangled dead were as one in their foxholes. By 1800 the first day there were only a handful of men left alive in this platoon and they were clinging tenaciously to the few remaining positions of their own right flank.

The section of heavy machine guns was located on the hill itself, one each in the 2nd and 3rd Platoon areas. These weapons were recognized by the enemy immediately and the Japs proceeded to "polish them off." They did a good job, blowing one gun to fragments as it was being placed on the tripod. The other was smashed beyond use after it had fired one-half of a box of ammunition. The crewmen were nearly all killed and those remaining alive seized rifles of dead comrades.

The platoon of Company C had fared no better than our own 3rd and were in a similar predicament. Machine-gun fire from the right and from the two knolls to the rear had torn these men to pieces. Mortar damage was exceedingly heavy in their ranks, yet they slugged back fiercely at the enemy and repelled several counterattacks against the right front.

During the first day the 1st Platoon had continuous trouble from both flanks and the rear. Deadly fire was delivered on this platoon from the two earthern mounds all day and it was only late in the afternoon that our artillery was able to blast the two knobs and flush the enemy out. When this was done they were picked off and little trouble came from them afterwards. The platoon had suffered heavily in killed and wounded but maintained their perimeter defense, although their ranks had been thinned considerably.

In spite of the terrific pounding we were taking, battle discipline was excellent. It seemed as if the men realized the danger of faltering and each and every man stuck to his allotted position, fighting back savagely while there remained a breath of life in his body. Wounded men insisted on being propped up, given a rifle and another chance to even the score with the enemy. Individual acts of heroism and sacrifice were witnessed continually and many probably went unseen.

In the CP area trouble started early, too. Four enemy were killed in a grenade battle on reaching the site. There were several large crevices in the left edge of this pocket and the Japs were sleeping there when we arrived. They soon started the fireworks and with great difficulty were finally exterminated.

The only communication we had to the outside was by Company E's SCR 300 radio. The artillery observer had two radios along but one was set afire the first day and the other blown to pieces early the second day. Within the company we were able to use SCR 536 radios, but within an hour one was shattered by a mortar shell and the other two had their aerials shot away or blown off.

The first day had been unusually hot, with a burning sun and no breeze at all, so by nightfall our water was gone. No rations were to be had, but provisions and help were expected that night. At 1800 Lieutenant Bell ordered the 2nd and 3rd Platoons to consolidate and withdraw to a perimeter around the CP. It would have been impossible to have tried to hold our original positions even in daylight and suicidal for the night. Wounded were to be moved to the area around the CP and there await evacuation that night.

The withdrawal of the 2nd Platoon began at once with the removal of the wounded. There were six badly mangled men in that position and all had to be carried out. They were placed on ponchos and pulled sled-fashion by the ten remaining men of the platoon. The last four men of the 3rd Platoon acted as protection against two snipers and one machine gun which had zeroed in on a shallow place in our only route of withdrawal. When we were ready to move a man through the exposed area, the four guards would fire steadily and thus enable us to move wounded out one by one. Even in this way one of the wounded was killed by a burst of machine-gun fire and a litter carrier was badly wounded. Some time was taken to destroy equipment we could not use or would not need. Nothing usable was left for the enemy. This movement was finally completed at about 2030 and our defense set for the night.

Our rescue force did not reach us that night as the Japanese had placed an ambush to prevent that. No one slept all night as the bombardment continued constantly. The Jap artillery remained active, mortar fire maintained its tempo, and four "buzz bombs" were dropped on us. Grenades were tossed most of the night but the infiltrating enemy were either killed or driven off. The brilliant light of the flares enabled us to spot many of the enemy before they were completely upon us.

Throughout the first day American M18 self-propelled guns supported us with everything they had and placed fire on pinpoint targets. Many times they had to fire so close to our position that we were showered with rock from the strike, and the noise of the burst was ear-splitting. Their direct fire into bayonet-fixed Japanese squads saved us from numerous fanatical charges into our weakened positions. The Cannon Company commander kept radio contact with us, continually being ready and prompt to fire a mission on request or select his own target of opportunity. Our own long range supporting heavy machine guns aided immensely in breaking up Jap charges and their continuous harassing fire gave the enemy no end of trouble. The mortar support given us, especially in the valley to our front, inflicted countless casualties on the enemy and certainly broke up numerous charges so that we could pick off the stragglers. Finally, we can emphatically testify that in regard to supporting weapons, our artillery did an outstanding job, keeping the enemy under continuous fire plus concentrations delivered promptly on call. The whine of our own shells so close overhead that day and night and the following days was indeed "sweet music" to our ears.

The second day's fighting continued more furiously than the first, the enemy redoubling his efforts to dislodge us. Our fear increased that by overwhelming numbers alone our position would be overrun. Help had not arrived and full realization of our plight soon became apparent. The previous day everyone had been confident of success and far too busy to think otherwise. Because of the strategic importance of this one piece of ground we were ordered to stay "at all costs". When this information came through, Lieutenant Bell quietly but firmly stated "we stay". Though tired, hungry and thirsty, the men determined until the end, prepared for a last ditch death stand. Grenades had long since been exhausted but every spare clip of ammunition was salvaged and the few spare, workable rifles placed in handy positions. Bayonets were taken from scabbards "just in case". The few less seriously wounded made preparations along with the others and all were ready to sell out to the enemy, but only if he were willing to pay a high price in blood. So far it had simply been taken for granted that we would hold, but now a stubborn determination to take the Japanese became our goal. No one had given one inch of ground unless ordered to do so and we were now prepared to hang on in spite of the enemy and his blasting.

Throughout the second day the wounded were in fearful condition, their moans and cries for help being continuous. Medical supplies were exhausted and wounds had to go untreated. In the burning heat the stench of the dead was suffocating and flies collected in great numbers. These things confronted us as the day slowly passed. The enemy pressure increased steadily, particularly in the employment of knee mortars. At one time eight of their weapons, firing in pairs, were pounding us. As the grenades came sailing through the air, men in the line of fire would hurriedly hop into another hole, there to find a moment's safety, only to be driven out again. Some were unfortunate in this type of hide and seek, being caught with their backs toward another Japanese mortar or a sniper.

Our own and supporting fires continually tried to knock out these enemy mortar positions but they were well protected and undoubtedly retreated into caves under bombardment. That afternoon another attempt was made to reinforce us, but by 1600 only five men and the commanding officer of Company C were able to safely cross the bullet-swept plain to our rear. These men immediately found foxholes but their commander was shot through the head while running to our CP, and fell on the parapet of that foxhole.

Late in the afternoon we were notified that a Utter-bearing team of about 80 men would attempt to reach us that night. This was great news as the suffering of the wounded was nerve wracking. Hope of reinforcement was heightened and the men took on new life. After enduring two days of this hell, anything was looked upon as a God-send.

The enemy attack was extremely fierce throughout the day and early evening but slackened a little after dark. Though lessening only slightly, it was heartening to know we would stand a chance to get the wounded out. At about 2200 on 18 May, the first of the littermen began to arrive. As soon as they came in they were taken to a disabled man, who was placed on the Utter and whisked away as soon as possible. There were a few walking wounded and these were sent along with the litter teams. The Japs soon realized what we were doing and opened up with rifle and machine-gun fire. By moving swiftly and ducking flares, all the wounded were evacuated safely from our position in two and a half hours. Eighteen men had been carried out and several others had been able to walk with a little assistance. A great worry was off our minds and those remaining felt better, even though their predicament still seemed hopeless. No one had arrived to strengthen our shaky lines. The rescue party had indeed brought a very limited supply of water and ammunition.

Canteens were thrown from foxhole to foxhole and into the CP, where they were filled and tossed back. Somehow this instilled new life into beaten bodies, even though this was the second sleepless night.

Dawn of the third day found us hanging on only by our finger nails, but there we were and more determined than ever to stay. The battle opened with all its fury again and the enemy threw everything on us for the third consecutive day. Would he never run out of men? Never become short of ammunition? Or never become discouraged by his inability to oust us from the key position of the entire Shuri Line? These questions and many others ran through the minds of the men.

Attacks were steady throughout the day and were repulsed only with the greatest difficulty. Our supporting weapons had our flanks well under cover and kept enemy activity under strict observation. Whenever enemy movement was noted they immediately opened fire. Enemy mortar fire did continue at a fast and accurate rate, and even though our numbers were few, more were either killed or wounded.

Early in the forenoon of the third day we were informed by radio that we were to be relieved that night if at all possible. By noon our radio was so weak that transmission was impossible, so we had no communication outside for the remainder of the time on the hill. The long afternoon wore on, our only thought being whether we could hold on until relief came. Hours seemed endless as afternoon became evening, and by 2100, 19 May, aid had not come. No additional firing was heard to our rear and we began to wonder what had happened. Finally, rifle fire began to increase, a sure sign of some kind of movement, and at 2200 the relief began to come in. These were men from Company L, 306th Infantry.

What a realization that was. The relief CP immediately was established in our old position and then the job of placing the men began. It was very dark and only by knowing where each hole was were we able to set up the defense as ours had been. Only when there was a replacement would one of our men leave, and then they would leave in groups of three and four. A few of our remaining men had been wounded during this last day and they were now taken out by litter teams. Snipers pecked away at us continually, but by 0300, 20 May, all the relief had been positioned and the last six of our group ready to leave. The new commanding officer was told what to expect and where it would come from, and having given this information we prepared to move out.

As we started to leave, a bursting shell to our right rear wounded two of the new men and we decided to evacuate them as we went back. One man was badly torn up and was carried back in a poncho, while the other could walk if able to lean on someone else.

Then the last of our party left Ishimmi Ridge. A white tape had been placed on the route for part of the distance, so we had little trouble in getting back to our Line of Departure, arriving there at 0100 hours. Hot coffee was awaiting us and was eagerly consumed by everyone. Then to curl up in a foxhole and sleep — the first in 70 hours. Shells might fall on us that night but anything over 25 yards distant would be considered miles away compared to previous experience.

Late the next morning the men were counted, and in the final check-up there were 28 men, one NCO, and two officers left of the 129 who had gone up three days before. Of the heavy weapons groups of 17, only 4 returned. The Company C unit's strength of 58 was whittled down to 13 men. Therefore, total casualties, from the original personnel of 204 men, were 156 killed and wounded. By far the greatest percentage of these had been killed. However, this night attack, though costly, was highly successful and their lives were not given in vain. Ishimmi Ridge was the very heart of the Jap defenses before Shuri. The Division line, in fact the entire American front line on Okinawa was at a standstill while Shuri was being crushed, and thus the foothold gained by Company E, and its persistence in remaining there, was the key to the door of "invincible Shuri", the fortress of Okinawa.

Staff Sergeant Alfred C. Junkin, platoon sergeant of the Company C platoon that had accompanied Company E, became platoon leader shortly after the fight started. He later wrote a letter from a base hospital to his battalion commander explaining his actions and those of his men. He brought out one point that was noted by many commanders, and will be noted by others in the future. Speaking of the new men in the platoon, Sgt. Junkin had this to say:

Our 30 replacements showed great courage, but were too new to the job. One of them saw two Nips who got a sergeant 30 feet away, but his finger froze on the trigger. Another saw Japs standing on the horizon and shouted wildly for an older man to shoot them while his own rifle lay in his hands. Another saw enemy a few yards from his hole, aimed and fired an empty rifle. In the excitement, he had emptied his magazine and had forgotten to reload.

Sir, I mean no disrespect by the above comments. The record speaks for itself. Like General Bruce, I am proud to belong to the 77th and especially Company C. But I deplore the necessity of taking green recruits, who hardly know how to load a rifle, into combat. My platoon of 42 men was smashed down to the last two men in the grenade and demolition battles on Pinnacle Rock on May 4th and 5th. With 30 replacements and old men borrowed from other platoons, it happened a second time on May 17th and 18th. I know that you have the interests of the men of our battalion at heart. And I believe you will agree that these teen-age youngsters fight with great courage, but are just too green and inexperienced to do the job.

The sergeant was voicing not only the opinion of enlisted men but officers as well; but there was little else anyone could do. Shortly after the Division was committed on Okinawa, a large number of replacements were received. A training program was instituted and from 5 May to 20 May, 2,092 enlisted men and 28 officer replacements were hastily indoctrinated into the Division way of thinking, fighting and acting. The majority of the replacements were under 25 years of age and had been in the army from 6 months to a year. Few had any unit training after their basic training, but their spirit was good and they were well equipped and in good physical condition. These replacements were given a four-day course, which included explanation of the traditions of the Division; discussions by the Division Psychiatrist, the Chaplain, Medical Officers, and Special Service Officers; terrain appreciation, and a review of the skills of the individual fighting man, infantry-tank-engineer tactics, flamethrowers and special weapons, and unit training in teamwork attacks on fortified positions of all types. Admittedly, this was inadequate, but it was impossible to do more while whole regiments were being decimated at the front.

On the morning of 17 May, the other units of the 307th Regiment were also having their troubles. Companies F and G jumped off at daylight to push to the right along the little ridge line at the head of the main valley, and to make contact with Company E. After an all-day fight, these companies were right where they started. The fire from enemy strongpoints on Ishimmi Ridge and the top of Shuri Ridge was extremely heavy, and the men were unable to move out of their holes without coming under murderous fire.

That night the battalion A and P Platoon, volunteer litter bearers, and a platoon of Company F, pushed off to re-supply Company E and evacuate the wounded. The party was half way to the objective when it ran into a Jap machine-gun ambush. The group was badly shot up and failed to reach the besieged company. The rescue unit got back to the lines with four out of the 16 men from Company F, five out of the 12 from the A and P Platoon, and only a few of the volunteers. The medics were wiped out along with a small group of cooks and drivers who volunteered as bearers.

In Major Ernest Dameron's 3rd Battalion, in the morning of the 17th, the attack was more successful. Company K jumped off at 1000 onto the top of Flat Top (Hill 140), and the valiant Lieutenant Kunze, who had led the attacks the day before, was wounded three more times, the last time fatally. An additional officer sent up during the night took over and was wounded. The battalion S-2, Lieutenant Dethlefs, then took over the company, which consisted of 14 men, counting the officer and the first sergeant. Seven members of the weapons platoon were supporting the attack from a position to the right rear. The fighting continued back and forth across the top of the hill, but the storm of enemy fire still made it an impossible place to hold.

A platoon of tanks tried an enveloping move around the left of the hill, through a gap between the Divisions. The lead tank reached the narrow cut between hills 140 and 150 and was knocked out, plugging the gap. Late in the day, Company K was relieved by Company L.

Company I took the Chocolate Drop this day. The attacks on Flat Top had diverted some of the heavy fire on the position, and units of the company moved out to the left and right and covered flanking enemy positions while the remainder went around the hill and started to work on a huge cave on the reverse slope. The cave was blown almost shut just before dark. Inside this hole were four antitank guns, a field piece, four machine guns, four heavy mortars, and two American 60mm mortars.

The company held on the north slopes of the "Drop" for the night. At 0300, the remaining Japs in the vicinity tried an attack but were beaten off. Twenty Japanese enlisted men and four officers were killed. One Jap officer, a captain, had on his person a sketch which showed the enemy defenses in the area.

The 3rd Battalion of the 305th continued its attack along Highway 5 on 18 May. Prior to 1030, when Companies K and L were to move forward, all the supporting weapons in the regiment and Division, plus corps artillery, brought down concentrations along the highway to soften up the enemy holding the scores of caves and the deep holes dug into the fingers running from the highway ridge. Companies K and L jumped off in time and moved onto the wooded knoll on which Company K had been the day before. The units were astride the highway, L on the left. After reaching the wooded knoll, the advance bogged down. Heavy fire came from the ruins of a small town on the left of the highway and from the left and right fronts. The units sent patrols into the ruins but these were driven back by heavy fire. The knoll was then organized for a night defense.

The 1st Battalion, to the right along the slopes of the ridge marking the regimental boundary, tried to move along the road running off to the west into Dakeshi, but the resistance was too strong. Tanks and M-8s were sent out in the valley to get at the enemy positions along the road, but were held up short of the area by a water-filled ditch. Company C shoved forward to the road at 1800 but withdrew to its former position for the night. The battalion was spread along the base of the ridge running to the south, opposite Dakeshi.

On the Division left, the 307th continued its attacks along the hills and ridges covering the approaches to the main Shuri Line. The 3rd Battalion continued working on Chocolate Drop and Hill 140. Though many enemy had been killed, the two hills were not yet completely captured. Company L continued its back-and-forth fighting across the top of Hill 140. The disabled tank which blocked the narrow cut between Hills 150 and 140, in the gap between Divisions, was removed, the road de-mined, and tanks again pushed forward through the cut, timing their attack with that of the 96th Division unit pushing toward Hill 150. The tanks got through the cut, but a hail of mortar and antitank fire prevented them from going very far forward.

Company I continued cleaning up the reverse slopes of the Chocolate Drop, but opposition from the huge cave and the smaller holes on the south side of the hill, and the heavy fire coming from the ridge line to the south and from the valley just to the front, kept activity down to a minimum.

In the 2nd Battalion sector, along Ishimmi Ridge in the middle of the main valley on the Division Front, Companies F and G were inching forward and to the right toward the embattled Company E, but progress was slow under intense fire. At the end of the day the two companies were still 150 yards short of the Company E position.

Company C, on the right, in the gap between Company E and Highway 5, managed to get five men into the Company E position late in the day. After dark the company moved right and left and made a solid line between Company E and the highway, and sent 90 men with litters forward to help out the weary company. The party moved out at 2200 and was successful in accomplishing their mission of supply and evacuation.

The Division right flank did not move during May 19th. The 1st Battalion of the 305th carried on cave blasting activities along the base of the ridge on the Division right. The 3rd Battalion, 305th, was relieved by the 3rd Battalion, 306th, at noon. This unit had the double mission of relieving not only the three companies along Highway 5, but also positions occupied by Companies C and E of the 307th, on Ishimmi Ridge to the battalion left front. The horseshoe ridge position on Highway 5 was occupied by Companies I and K, and Company L infiltrated into position on Ishimmi Ridge 200 yards to the left front of a semicircular shaped ground formation in the main valley floor, just to the left of Highway 5.

The riflemen of Company L, 306th Infantry, in moving across the open valley from the highway, had to make use of every bit of cover in their crawl to their new positions. Grazing machine-gun fire originating in the ruined village next to the highway, from the left front and right front, stopped the advance just short of the objective at 1600. The men stayed there until 1930, when under cover of darkness, they moved the rest of the way up and relieved what was left of Companies C and E of the 307th. During the night the Japs made a few "half-hearted" attempts to push Company L off the position, but did not succeed.

On the left flank the tanks that had been trying to flank Hill 140 got out a little farther and were successful in bringing down heavy fire along the eastern slopes of the position. They also fired on enemy positions on Hill 166 to the front. Each time the tanks moved through the gap and fired, they reduced by a few rounds the volume of enemy fire which was coming from that sector.

Mopping up continued both on Flat Top (140) and Chocolate Drop. Early in the day, observers on the top of the "Drop" saw three wounded Americans behind the hill to the south. A volunteer group of four men, two of them unarmed, went out and found that two of the wounded had died and the third was delirious. The dazed man had to be forcibly subdued; he thought he was still fighting the Japanese. He and his two buddies had been there since May 17th.

On Ishimmi Ridge Company F, accompanied by two tanks and several bazooka teams, mopped up the area along the battalion front to where Companies E and C had been fighting. The remainder of the 1st Battalion was in the rear, planning a predawn attack for the next day.

Early in the morning of 20 May, a company of Japanese attacked in the gap between the Chocolate Drop and the line of telephone poles in the valley, hitting Companies F and G. The attack was repulsed and about half the attackers killed.

Company L of the 307th completely mopped up Hill 140 (Flat Top) during the day. The action started with a hand grenade barrage by the men on top. Box upon box of grenades was passed up the north slope of the hill by human chain. The men on the top lined up and threw grenades over the south and east slopes as fast as they could pull the pins. Then they followed up and completed the job with satchel charges and flamethrowers.

During the attack on Hill 140, members of Company L, from a position on the left flank, observed a soldier out in front of the forward elements trying to signal to them. Knowing the position of our own troops, they were about to open fire when one observer, using glasses, saw the trapezoid on the soldier's helmet and recognized him as an American soldier. Upon capture of the position, a litter team was able to reach the soldier and it was Private Arthur E. Meyer, who had been reported missing. He had been behind the enemy lines for two days. He was a member of a flanking unit and had been cut off from the main group. During his stay, Private Meyer fought the Japs several times, killing at least four, but they never did do more than throw grenades at him. He was wounded in both legs and had three wounds about the chest. Upon evacuation, he was in high spirits and although suffering severely from the wounds, he was proud that he was a member of the force that cracked this enemy fortification.

Tanks had come all the way through the gap between Hills 150 and 140 during the day and were responsible for polishing off many of the stronger enemy positions on the lower slopes of the hill.

The Chocolate Drop was also completely taken during the day. The huge cave on the south slope of the hill was closed and the remaining Japs on the ridges to either side of the position were wiped out.

All heavy weapons of the regiment now concentrated on Tom Hill (Hill 166), which lay 900 yards to the south of Flat Top and which had been the thorn in the side of the 77th and the 96th Divisions in their attacks toward Shuri Ridge. This high, conical position dominated the entire valley in front of the main Shuri Ridge and the enemy on it had been responsible for the heavy fire which had made Flat Top and Chocolate Drop fights so tough.

During the previous five days, the mortars of Companies H and M had dropped more than 30,000 rounds of 81mm ammunition on the enemy. The companies had each fired more than 1,000 rounds of 60mm to the front. In addition, the daily artillery quota on the battalion front had been 4,000 rounds.

The 1st Battalion, 305th on the Division right flank, moved about 200 yards forward along the road running south and east toward Shuri during the day (20 May). Company A, supported by tanks and M8s, moved onto a small knoll near the head of the valley to the left. Another move was tried in the afternoon but rifle fire from positions to the right front prevented it. The attack was held up then until the 1st Marines on the right could move forward and protect the right flank.

Company K of the 306th jumped off along Highway 5 at 0730 and had moved 600 yards by the end of the day. This put the company just short of where the highway joined the road, coming in from the right boundary. This piece of terrain was just short of the gap that led through Shuri Ridge into the town. A high hill to the right was still in enemy hands, making movement farther forward very risky. Company I moved behind Company K, mopping up caves, and occupied the position vacated by that company.

Company L, on Ishimmi Ridge to the left front, remained in place under heavy enemy fire. Smoke screens had to be used to cover the evacuation of the wounded, and supplies were brought up at night. The valley leading to the company position was swept by fire from the commanding terrain in the Marine sector and the high ridges to the front.

Another set of pre-dawn attacks was launched by the Division on the 21st — this time on both flanks.

The 1st Battalion, 307th, was to initiate a simultaneous, two-pronged attack on the "Three Sisters," three hills forming a triangle in the open ground 350 yards to the south of Flat Top. Company A moved through the 3rd Battalion at 0300 and started through the gap between Hills 140 and 150, in an effort to swing around to the left of the base of the three-sister triangle. As the company moved into the gap, riflemen of an adjoining regiment of the 96th Division opened fire on them, giving the attack away. The enemy picked up this mistake and also dropped mortar fire into the narrow cut.

The 307th, during the preceding two days, had taken elaborate precautions to prevent such a slip as this. Personal visits to the friendly regiment had been made by the battalion S-3 who had informed that command of the plans for that move. Other officers of the battalion and regiment had taken the precaution of warning the 96th, and the regimental liaison officer from the neighboring sector had been fully informed of the plans. It is evident that someone just forgot to give the front line men on Hill 150 the warning to be on the alert for a friendly unit coming through off their right flank.

Not only was the whole attack plan given away but the fire caused trouble within Company A. This was the first action of any kind for 88 replacements who had joined the unit just a few days before. The replacements had had two days of unit training. When the rifle and machine-gun fire from the friendly unit, later mixed with Jap mortar fire, hit the company, their replacements scattered.

The First Sergeant, bringing up the rear of the company, managed to gather many of the new men together again, but held them in the valley north of the cut until daybreak. The point of the company, less one man killed and three wounded, pushed on to the left of the two hills that made up the base of the Three Sisters. This unit consisted of one platoon and a squad from another platoon. The men dug in on the northeast slope of the hill, with their backs to an open valley through which ran the Kochi-Shuri road.

The remainder of the company gathered together at dawn, moved through the cut, past the unit holding the base of the two hills, up on the side of the third hill. This platoon was allowed to move through the open valley leading to the third hill and was just at its base when the Japanese opened up with all types of weapons from the left front, right front, and right rear. In the first burst of the surprise fire, three men were killed and four wounded. One of the four died later. The platoon withdrew to the company position on the left of the two base hills. The platoon sergeant, acting platoon leader, made three attempts to bring in the bodies of the three men killed, but was prevented from doing so by rifle and mortar fire.

Company B moved out before dawn in a column of platoons, three men abreast, crossed the open valley to the right of Chocolate Drop, guiding on a line of telephone poles, veered left 150 yards south of the "Drop" and ran into a Jap unit occupying a small hill 200 yards short of the objective. A hard fight ensued and the north slopes of the hill were cleaned out and occupied.

The enemy to the right front of the Company B position covered the approaches to the right of the two base hills of the "Sisters" with grazing fire, and no further forward movement was made. In this fight, Private first class Desmond T. Doss, medic hero of the Escarpment and other fights, was wounded and evacuated, thus ending his long period of superior service to the men of his company.

At the end of the day, the 1st Battalion, 307th, had Company A on the slopes of the left of the two base hills of the group. Company B was bottled up in the valley to the rear of the two hills, and Company C was dug in behind Company B.

The predawn attack in the 305th sector along Highway 5 by the 3rd Battalion, 306th (attached), was more successful and Company I reached the base of the high hill guarding the gap that led into Shuri Town. Company I jumped off at 0415 in a column of platoons. After advancing 300 yards, the point men heard a platoon of Japs to their left, in column, going in the same direction. At first the men thought the column was a friendly unit and shouted to them. Only Japanese words came back, so the company opened fire and killed many of the enemy. The rest of the enemy bolted through the middle of the company and cut off the CP group and part of the weapons platoon from the main body. By dawn, however, the major part of the company had reached the slopes of the high hill guarding the cut leading to Shuri. The CP group infiltrated into the company position at 0800. Throughout the day the riflemen carried on a rifle and grenade fight with the enemy below the crest of the ridge.

Company K advanced behind I, cleaning up by-passed enemy positions. By 1600 the company had destroyed 70 caves and killed 147 Japs.

At 1600, Company L, to the left front on Ishimmi Ridge, was hit by a counterattack. Platoon leaders on the ridge top first saw about 50 Japanese crawling up the south slope. Artillery and mortar fire was called in and decimated the attackers. A half-hour grenade battle ensued, with the enemy taking the worst of the fight. The action ended suddenly and those attackers remaining got up and ran away, only to be cut down by rifle and machine-gun fire.

The situation of the Japs holding Shuri was desperate. Their left, at the entrance to Shuri Town, was in danger of being penetrated at any time. The center of the line just forward of Ishimmi and the Three Sisters was under direct fire and was the last strongpoint in the defense of the whole line. On the enemy right, the 96th Division had taken Conical Hill, the key terrain feature of the entire Jap defense.

There was only one thing in the Japs' favor. The weather had closed in the day before and it rained incessantly. U. S. supply routes to the front lines disappeared in the mud. Tanks could not move at all and evacuation of the wounded became a problem. This increased the burden on Lt. Col. L. C. Fairbanks 302nd Engineer Battalion, which was responsible for maintenance of Highway 5, the central supply route to the Okinawa front. The 1118th Engineer Group had remained on Ie Shima, but the 302nd, utilizing the extra equipment "accumulated" from various sources, worked desperately, efficiently and effectively in the mud. A soldier news reporter of the 302nd Engineers described the work in the following words:

"We thought we had mud on Guam and Leyte, as well as the usual problems in operation and vehicle repair, but conditions on Okinawa have put us into low-gear and we're winning the battle of roads by mustering every man, machine, and field expedient for the fight," said T/4 Fran O'Hanlon, vehicle dispatcher with the 302nd Engineer Combat Battalion. 'The continual rains have played havoc with the roads," he continued, and keeping the MSR open puts a terrific strain on both men and machines.

Our line company and battalion motor sections, both repairmen and operators, are working long hours with very little rest, irregular meals, and the added discomfort of being wet and muddy all the time. The men who work beneath trucks and dozers almost float in mud and silt — and if anything is more miserable than ten or twelve hours of that, I'm sure that I can't flunk of it."

Master Sergeant Tate Townsend, who works with the heavy equipment section, added, "Our carry-alls, shovels, trucks and dozers have been working on a 24-hour basis lately so that the roads can be kept open. Along with keeping the roads open for regular evacuation and supply traffic, we've had to move lots of heavy equipment up near the front where it would be more accessible to our place of operation. We brought a power shovel up from the beach the other night during a storm and under blackout conditions. It took us 16 hours to get to our destination, and at one time we were using three bulldozers and a four-ton wrecker — either pushing or pulling that shovel and trailer; when it takes that much horsepower to move a piece of equipment, you're really in mud."

The slogan in the battalion shop-truck states emphatically, "If we don't have it — well make it!" This threat has been fulfilled in many instances by WOJG Lawrence Gunderman, motor officer; T/4 Louis Krouza, welder; and T/4 Virgil Clerico, machinist. On Leyte they welded a clutch plate to a transmission shaft — a job that wasn't successfully completed by a higher echelon — by arranging a true alignment of the two parts in a lathe and doing the welding job. When asked if the heat from the welding torch didn't damage the lathe, T/4 Clerico replied, "No, because we used an old Jap lathe for that land of work — we don't do things like that with our own equipment — it's too hard to replace." Just about any machinist will tell you that a stripped worm gear is an item for the junk pile, but here on Okinawa when the worm on the shaft of a blade-elevator was stripped on a sorely-needed grader, Clerico and Krouza did a rebuilding job by sheer ingenuity and craftsmanship. Clerico ground the worm tooth down to a good base and tapped holes for ¼" bracer-bolts, while Krouza built up the missing worm with his welding torch. Regular shop equipment doesn't include a standard grinder for worm gears, but this didn't stop the engineer machinists: they took a diamond-point cutting tool and shaped a circular emery stone so that it would have the proper contour to fit between the spiral tooth. This type of Yankee originality gets engineer equipment back on the job, while if it were necessary to wait for a new part, a machine might be idle for weeks.

The engineer motor sections no longer wait for vehicles to be hauled back to the motor pool for minor repairs. Instead, they have developed a streamlined repair section that moves out anytime during the day or night to repair damaged vehicles that have become stalled along the road. Although major repair jobs cannot be done in this manner, the system saves time, keeps slow-moving traffic off the road, and gets the equipment back into service sooner.

"On Guam and Leyte," said T/5 Ernest Noyce, carry-all operator, "we had clean coral to work with, but this stuff on Okinawa seems to be half clay. When we have graded a good road bed and covered it with coral, the continual rain mixes with the clay and the first thing we know our vehicles are getting bogged down again. We can't do much about the rain or the coral, so we just have to keep plugging along — making repairs wherever needed."

The problem of mines, while not severe on either Guam or Leyte, has been a hazard on Okinawa. Here, the heavy equipment operators and truck drivers are often endangered by mines which have escaped detection. Although several mines have been detonated by engineer equipment, casualties have been light which makes everyone happy. However, a mine explosion usually damages a vehicle considerably and the engineer motor sections have that work in addition to their repairs on regular breakage.

The battle with the demon mud continues, and the men responsible for the operation and upkeep of the equipment that must function to make way for the important supply and evacuation traffic, have disregarded many factors of personal comfort and safety to accept the challenge of the roads.

This willingness to work long hours and to utilize incredible field expedients was equally evident in the Division's other Service Units: the 777th Ordnance Company, 77th Quartermaster Company and 77th Signal Company.

Because of the weather and the difficulty of supply and movement, activity along the Division front remained at a virtual standstill. The units of the 307th on Hill 140 and Chocolate Drop supported by fire the 1st Battalion units at the base of the Three Sisters. The 2nd Battalion, holding Ishimmi Ridge from the Chocolate Drop right to the road held by the 3rd Battalion, 306th, had Company G on a small hill in the Ishimmi Valley to protect the rear of the units attacking the Sisters and the front of the units to the right. Company E took over from G, holding the ridge in the center of the valley. Company F moved into reserve behind the Chocolate Drop and was replaced by Company E, 306th.

The 305th, which had pushed along Highway 5 and the Division right flank into the outskirts of Shuri, was relieved by the 306th on the 21st of May. Company G of the 306th relieved the 1st Battalion, 305th, on the Division right.

The only attack along the whole front on the 22nd of May was made by Company F on the east side of a semi-circular ridge lying 300 yards to the left of Highway 5 in the open valley to the rear of Company L. The 1st Platoon got onto the left side of the mass, but the 3rd Platoon was held up by heavy machine-gun fire which covered the approaches to the right side of the hill.

As the attack developed, the Japanese defending the position yelled for help and 50 of the enemy moved out from the Ishimmi draw to the right front of Company L. The Japs moved on the double toward the semi-circular ridge, but most of them were cut down by automatic riflemen from the Company L positions. After a day of snap-shooting at the disorganized Japs, the company was relieved by Company G at 1600. This position was the one which had been held by Company E, 307th, during its valiant three-day fight.

The activity along the Division front on 23 May consisted of combat patrolling. Any large-scale attacks would have been useless in the sea of mud that made up the front. Company B of the 307th tried sending combat patrols onto the right of the two base hills of the Three Sisters, but hand-to-hand fighting resulted each time. Several attempts were made to take the position, but though the patrols reached the top of the hill, they could not hold it for long.

Captain Frank L. Vernon, directing Company B, 307th Infantry, was killed on the 25th by enemy mortar fire while his company was in the attack on Three Sisters. Captain Vernon was the last of the original company commanders in the regiment who had fought through Guam, Leyte and Okinawa without relief at any time.

The 1st Marines had reported during the last two days that they occupied the large hill to the right front of the 3rd Battalion, 306th, but this was obviously incorrect because fire from that hill continually harassed the 306th and patrols from the 306th had been driven off this same hill.

Inclement weather continued to hold up the Division attack to take Shuri Ridge. The ground was too fluid for any vehicular movement. Units along the front continued to probe at enemy positions but no ground was taken. Supply problems during this period of heavy rains were acute, and much of the front line re-supplying was done by back-packing over the last 500 to 1,000 yards to the front lines. Highway 5 and the Kochi-Shuri road were both impassable.

King Mud continued to rule on 25, 26 and 27 May. On the 28th Company E, 306th, moved from its positions on the ridge line just north of the town of Ishimmi onto a hill that looked into the town. The position was taken after a fierce grenade fight. This ridge, like all the rest, was a maze of interlocking trenches and caves. Many satchel charges were used in blasting these shut. The position was consolidated and the men dug in by noon. An enemy counterattack in the afternoon was repulsed.

It had become apparent in the past few days that the Japs were evacuating the Shuri-Yonabaru ridge defenses and moving to the south coast for a last stand. The Jap units in front of the 77th Division, however, remained where they were, on orders to stay there until the whole line had been evacuated, then to withdraw on the 29th and 30th. Those Tap units never got out.

On the 29th the Marines made a highly publicized move into Shuri Castle area. They pulled out of their positions on the 77th's right, swung around to the west and the south and onto the evacuated, blasted stronghold. Their withdrawal from the hills on the Division right left the Division flank exposed and Japanese remained active on those ridges in the Marine sector. The 77th was not notified until the Marines were on the Shuri Castle Hill, which was in the 77th's zone. The 77th had called an air strike and heavy artillery bombardment of that position, and was barely able to avert the called strikes in time. Nevertheless, the 77th's men were happy to know that the Shuri positions had been enveloped.

On 30 May the Division pushed through the opposition to its front, took the Three Sisters, Tom Hill, Shark Head (high ground to immediate east of Shuri), and the left side of the gap into the town.

On the Division left, the 307th 1st Battalion launched an attack to gain control of the Three Sisters. The Company A and B units moved on to the two base hills of the group, then around to both flanks of the base, mopping up the south slopes after a two-hour fight. Company B sent a patrol to the right toward the third hill and Company A sent a platoon to the left toward the same position. The Company A men reached the base of the hill and crawled on all fours to the top. A base of fire was formed by the platoon to help the remainder of Companies A and B clean out the area inside the three hills. In the mopping-up operations during the afternoon, 365 Japanese were killed and many caves burned out and sealed.

The 2nd Battalion left Company G to the right rear of the Three Sisters to neutralize any fire holding up the advance of the 1st Battalion. Companies E and F moved around the left, through the gap between the 96th and the 77th and advanced 600 yards south to occupy Tom Hill with little trouble.

The 3rd Battalion, 307th, attacked Dorothy Hill (Hill 133) and took it after a hard fight. Company I from Chocolate Drop ridge, Company L from Hill 140, and Company K in reserve, moved out in column in the order, I, L and K, crossed the line of departure at the line of telephone poles in the middle valley and moved across the open Ishimmi Valley toward the hill.

Dorothy Hill consisted of a jagged cliff which rounded out on either side to form a dome-shaped position. The rear of the hill was a mass of caves, level upon level of them dug through the hill. The advance through the valley was contested by scattered mortar fire, but no men were hurt. Company I, with two platoons of 14 men each, got onto the base of the rough ridge and one platoon was pinned down by heavy fire from the top and sides of the position. In this fire the platoon leader and all the non-coms were wounded. The 2nd Platoon, on the left of the hill, crossed to the front and consolidated with the first. The consolidated unit moved to the right toward the top of the hill, and got about a squad on the top. Company L moved up from the rear to the right of the hill by this time and worked onto the top and reverse slopes. Three levels of caves, about four or five to a level, were found on the south slope of the position.

The two companies started to work methodically, began at the top left and worked across the face of the slope, cleaning out that series of caves and tunnels. Then the men dropped down a level and repeated the process. By nightfall the battalion had occupied the top and reverse slopes of the hill. During the night 15 Japanese were killed as they wormed out of caves carrying satchel charges and grenades. None of them carried rifles.

The 306th launched an attack on 30 May to occupy the ridge line which formed the eastern rim of the bowl holding Shuri Town. The 1st Battalion made the initial assault on the gap between the ridges flanking Highway 5, while the 2nd Battalion attacked Ishimmi town and Shark's Head 400 yards farther south.

In the 1st Battalion zone, every effort to take Hill 110.5 on the right, covering the highway gap leading into the town, was repulsed. On the left of the gap, however, Company B moved ahead without much opposition and took the ridge overlooking Shuri.

The 2nd Battalion attacked at 1100 and by 1230 had taken Ishimmi without much trouble. At 1330 the battalion jumped off, and moved 400 yards to take Shark's Head Hill at 1400.

The Japs remaining in the Shuri Line had evacuated dining the night, leaving only a handful to make a last stand. The enemy holding Hill 110.5 in the Marine zone of action were stubbornly holding out, however, and continued to fire on our troops.

At 0800 on May 31st, the 1st Battalion of the 305th again attacked this Marine objective and cleared it by noon, thus ending all organized resistance in the area.

The 307th attacked at 0900 and advanced against negligible resistance to the Corps boundary. The 305th Infantry took over the Division front late in the day. For the next few days, the 305th mopped up behind the Corps line in the Division zone and prepared to advance behind the 96th Division as it pushed to the south coast of the island.

In this drive, the strongest line of defense yet encountered in the Pacific was broken. The 77th, bucking the center of the fortifications, killed approximately 14,000 Japs in order to advance 3,500 yards on a 1,000 yard front. It took 32 days to do it. The 7th, 27th and 96th Infantry Divisions, the 1st and 6th Marine Divisions all faced the same type defenses. The Japs had defended well and with plenty of everything, but somehow the stronghold had been crashed.

Chapter 27: The Last Three Hills

WITH the collapse of the Japanese main line of defense from Naha to Yonabaru, the Shuri Line, the enemy established his troops for a last stand on high ground in southern Okinawa.

The 96th, 7th and 77th Infantry Divisions, and the Marine Divisions advanced south from the Shuri Line to the southern and eastern coast of the island in a slow methodical mop-up of the scattered outposts of Japs in that sector. The enemy established himself initially on the Yuza-Dake escarpment, and when driven from there made his last organized stand on Hills 79 and 85, north of Makabe.

During this pursuit and final clean-up, the troops had a little more time to give voice, in their letters and their comments, to their opinions concerning the Okinawa show. They believed that a remarkable supply job had been done that they might have food, water, and ammunition up front. But there were many justifiable complaints at the way in which rations destined for the Division had been looted of the more desirable food items by Army and Navy Service troops, a practice as universal as the war. The mail service, however, had been the best in their combat experience, and the rest camps, movies just behind the combat zone, and Red Cross facilities dining battle had been unusual.

There was a good deal of sarcastic comment concerning the press releases and war reporting. Combat veterans who remembered seeing Howard Handlemen, Mac Tohnson and others up front at Guam, remembered watching Sam Blumenfeld, Bill Alcine, Al Dopkins and Henry McLemore hit the beach at Ormoc, remembered watching Grant McDonald and Warren Moscow ride an LVT over the reef on the Yakabi assault and meeting Ernie Pyle with the cave-mopping patrols on Ie Shima, remarked at the absence of war correspondents north of Shuri. The soldiers weren't calling any names but they wondered. There was also bitter joking over the fact that Tenth Army announced the capture of many objectives from one to three days before they, the fighting men, finally secured such objectives. "We can't keep up with the communiques," was a common remark of unit commanders.

Some soldiers, more money conscious, criticized the Army order which limited them to 10 dollars' worth of Okinawa Invasion Currency on departure for Okinawa, which currency was not accepted at Ship's Stores en route, and at the fact that they were not paid for three months. Of course, there was little opportunity to spend money anyway, but it seemed a needless and arbitrary restriction.

The ordinary soldier or officer was too busy trying to do his job and stay alive to ponder over questions of higher tactics. However, from early May forward, the men and the leaders of lower units frequently asked, "Why don't we land a division behind those Japs?" And when the usual problems of poor beaches and isolation were raised, some unshaven, dirty platoon sergeant would answer, "We could have done it. It wouldn't be as dangerous as Ormoc was."

However, the Division did not talk away the month of June. It worked at mopping up, cleaning areas, building roads and improving camps.

The war was not ended and the dangers not past. There were still stray Japanese to fight, and there were plenty of mines. This danger was highlighted by the deaths, on June 1st of Major W. W. Kreis, S-2 of the 307th Infantry, and Pfc. Leonard H. Kraft, and the wounding of Major W. K. Bennett, S-3 of that regiment, by a land mine. They were members of a party that had gone forward to inspect terrain recently captured and just turned over to the relieving 305th Infantry.

During the period June 1st to June 17th, the 305th followed in the rear of the advancing 96th Division, mopping up by-passed enemy positions and consolidating the ground. The regiment had the task of protecting the corps right rear. During this period it rained heavily, and transportation was extremely difficult. For the first two weeks in June, the roads were almost impassable, and many of the supplies were transported on men's backs for 3,000 and 4,000 yards.

On June 1st, the 305th came from Division reserve to take over responsibility of the Shuri area, charged with the final cleaning out of the few individuals left and of protecting the corps right rear. All three battalions moved into the area on June 1st. The 1st was on the right in Shuri Town and its western environs, the 3rd was on the left on the high ground east of Shuri, and the 2nd Battalion was two thousand yards to the front in the Haibaru-Mura, moving immediately to the rear of the 96th Division.

By June 6th, the 2nd Battalion had moved to Kamizato, the 1st Battalion, which had crossed in front of the third, was in the Chan area, and the 3rd Battalion was on the southern outskirts of Shuri.

During this period, new replacements were trained in combat patrolling. These new men found from experience how to blow caves, bring in prisoners, locate and mark mine fields, and handle civilians. It was a daily hill-by-hill scouring for any live enemy left. A large amount of intelligence material was found and sent to the rear, and many ammunition, food and medical dumps were seized.

The men did not engage in heavy fighting during this period. Most of the work was done with grenades and satchel charges. An average rifleman did not expend a clip of ammunition in a week.

On June 10th, the regiment was placed in corps reserve and on June 11th, assembled north of the Urasoe Mura escarpment. During the period until June 15th, the regiment sent platoon-strength patrols daily to the Chan, Tera, Kamizato area by truck.

The regiment received orders to send one battalion to Kamizato to give depth to the Corps sector, on 15 June, and the 2nd Battalion was dispatched at 0900 to a bivouac area near Inasomi, arriving there at 1300. The remainder of the regiment joined the 2nd Battalion on the 16th, and at noon on that day was attached to the 96th Division.

The 2nd Battalion of the 305th was attached to the 381st Infantry on 18 June and moved to Marvel Hill with orders to wipe out a pocket of resistance by-passed several days before by the 96th. At 1100 the battalion moved from the hill to the vicinity of Yuza Town. The company commanders were oriented on the situation, namely that the enemy had re-occupied the unit's assigned position. The commanding officer assigned the right flank of the battalion position to Company E. This was the southeastern slope of the ridge which jutted out 900 yards to the northwest from Hill 167 at Yuza-Dake. The left flank was given to Company F. This position was on the northeastern slopes of the ridge. Company G was placed in reserve. The battalion left flank was tied in near the top of the high escarpment to the left front with the right flank of Company E, 382nd Regiment.

At 1330 the battalion was informed that the 2nd Battalion of the 382nd had moved forward 600 yards, compelling the battalion of the 305th to place two platoons of Company G on the left flank protecting the area vacated by the friendly unit.

Each company was ordered to send platoon-strength patrols to investigate the assigned positions on the top of the hill they surrounded. The patrol from Company E reached the crest of the ridge and ran into intense machine-gun and rifle fire from coral and concrete emplacements to the front. The company committed a second platoon with the mission of contacting the right flank of Company F and placing fire on the enemy holding up the first platoon. Company F's right flank was contacted but not physically tied in. This created a gap in the Company E front.

A request for tanks to relieve the pressure from the top of the objective was granted by the 382nd Regiment, and at 1445 a section of medium tanks was sent around Company Es right to knock out the opposition, between the two platoons. After the tanks fired into this position, the two platoons attacked and captured the objective. The assault had been confined to a 20-yard area, but in the fight three enemy pillboxes and 12 Japanese defenders were eliminated.

Companies F and G moved up on their objectives with little opposition. This put the battalion on the leg of an L-shaped ridge formation, facing a series of small knolls on lower ground to the front, on the slopes of the shaft of the L.

At 1800 the commanding officer of the 382nd issued an order to the battalion to attack at 08i00 the next day. The drive was to be south and southeast to the front, to destroy a pocket of resistance among the knolls that divided the 1st and 2nd Battalions of the 382nd.

The plan of attack for 19 June was issued at 0630 that morning. Company G was to attack to the left, F echelon to the right, and E remain in reserve.

The mission of Company G was to clean up the base of the escarpment to the left front, to facilitate Company Fs attack across the open valley to the front. Company F was to seize a small ridge 400 yards southeast (7661 S4), the battalion objective.

The objective ridge, which lay in the angle formed by the L-shaped ridge formation, consisted of three small knolls on a small plateau which extended about 20 feet above the valley floor. A second and higher hill lay several hundred yards to the south. This position was the objective of the 1st Battalion, 382nd Infantry.

At 0750, 19 June, the 60 and 81mm mortars of the battalion laid down a ten-minute concentration on the objective. Artillery could not be used because of the proximity of friendly troops. The 2nd Battalion, 382nd

Regiment, was 600 yards forward and to the left of the attacking troops, on the high escarpment looking down on the objective. The 3rd Battalion of that regiment was 1,000 yards forward of its 2nd Battalion.

At 0800 the 2nd Battalion, 305th, launched its attack with Company G in the assault, supported by a platoon of heavy machine guns. The rough terrain limited the use of tanks, which had to cross the fronts of Companies E and F, destroying small pockets of enemy resistance as they went.

Company G's initial advance was limited to 50 yards by machine-gun fire from the high escarpment to the left. Two medium tanks and one flamethrowing tank joined Company G's assault at 0820 and neutralized enemy fire to such an extent that the riflemen were able to move forward with satchel charges and flamethrowers and destroy three pillboxes which had dominated the open terrain in front of Company F. The enemy, in his many small positions in the jumbled rocks, continued to resist strongly and the company was held up.

At 1035 Company F launched its assault to make physical contact with the Company G right flank. After advancing approximately 30 yards, the company encountered an enemy pillbox which held a mortar and a light machine gun. A flamethrowing tank, with infantry support, moved forward and burned out the position. The attack was continued, but was again held up by heavy fire. The enemy position was located by the tank liaison officer in the battalion OP, the chain of communications went into operation, and the tanks advanced and wiped out the resistance.

Again the company moved forward, and was halted by very heavy mortar and rifle fire from the high escarpment to the left front. In this situation of receiving fire from almost inaccessible positions on high ground to the front, the two assault companies were ordered to hold while Company E moved out from the right to secure the enemy positions to the right of the two companies. This was on the flank of the battalion objective.

At 1300 Company E, supported by a section of medium tanks, attacked. The force moved across the valley basin and ran into heavy fire from a well fortified position to the front of the objective. Tanks fired a number of long-range missions, then closely supported the company in an advance that led them to the forward slope of the objective ridge. Fifteen pillboxes were destroyed in this advance. The company was then ordered to tie in with the flank of the 1st Battalion, 382nd, to the right front.

The positions of Companies F and G had not changed by 1800, and Company F, in an unfavorable position for the night, was ordered to move back to Company E's former position. Company G, with one platoon of F, was to hold in place for the night.

Company F began its movement back at 1815 but was held up by machine-gun and mortar fire from the high escarpment to the front. Smoke was laid down to the front and the company was successful in pulling back to their position for the night.

Company G started to dig in for the night, but the men were harassed by enemy fire and were unable to do much digging. Again smoke was dropped in, and under its screen the company dug in, set up their defenses and were ready for the night. Under cover of darkness, the company was supplied with food, water and ammunition.

Company E, which had pushed across open ground and occupied the forward slopes of the objective, tied in with the 1st Battalion, 382nd Infantry, at Ozato, and dug in for the night. A 400-yard gap existed between the neighboring battalion and Company E. At 2000 Companies E and F received a warning order to be prepared to attack the next morning at 0900. During the day the battalion had killed 18 known and 80 probable enemy, but lost four Americans killed and 13 wounded.

During the night 18 Japs were killed while attempting to infiltrate the battalion lines. At 0630 the battalion commander issued the order for the day. Company E was to attack east, into the right end of the battalion objective. Company F was to attack southeast and contact Company E's left flank, seizing the left part of the objective. A platoon of medium tanks and one flamethrowing tank were to support the Company F assault. Company G was to remain in reserve and support the attack by fire. One platoon of the company was to mop up the area between Yuza and the top of the escarpment, in the battalion rear and left.

On June 20th, the battalion took its objective, removing one of the principal hindrances in the way of the 96th Division. Due to the enemy defensive setup, it was decided to carry on a short period of pin-point mortar and tank fire to reduce as far as possible the enemy strongpoints. At 0800 the mortars began firing on designated targets on the objective. Medium tanks also pin-pointed positions on the escarpment overlooking the objective.

From 0840 to 0900, the 60 and 81mm mortars, machine guns and tanks laid down an intense concentration on the fortified area around the objective hills. The battalion attack was delayed 20 minutes while the 1st Battalion, 382nd, laid mortars on the 305th's objective.

The 81mm mortars screened the high escarpment with smoke at 0920 and the battalion began a rapid advance toward the objective. At 0930 contact was established between Companies E and F on the eastern slopes of the objective. Company E at this time was receiving intense machine-gun fire from pillboxes on top of the knoll dominating the objective, and called for tanks.

The tanks arrived at 0945 and Company E moved forward to engage in bitter close-in fighting. Several times enemy soldiers dressed in U. S. uniforms and carrying satchel charges were killed during their attempts to destroy tanks.

From 0930 to 1200, all available weapons were employed in neutralizing the enemy mortars holding up Company F's advance. The mortar position was located, but an overhanging ledge covering it prevented the 60mm mortars from gaining effective results. In a quick change-over, the battalion commander, in the OP to the rear, directed fire of Company E mortars and the target was eliminated.

The close proximity of troops to the enemy positions, and the tricky terrain, called for much ingenuity in laying in effective mortar fire without endangering our troops. One section leader, noting how easy it was to follow the descent of the 60mm mortar shells, requested permission to adjust his fire on shells on which the safety pins had not been pulled by watching the spot where the dud-shells fell. The idea was utilized and worked admirably.

Company E occupied its half of the objective at 1200, and immediately placed automatic weapons in position to support Company F coming up from the left rear. One platoon of Company F moved forward but was stopped halfway to the objective by heavy fire coming from a fortified tomb. A flamethrowing tank burned out the position and the platoon reached the objective at 1335.

This gave the battalion control of the position and the commanding officer of the 382nd RCT was notified of this. The battalion was ordered to occupy and defend the position. Companies E and F occupied the three knolls making up the objective, and Company G occupied a reserve position on the battalion right rear.

During the day, wounded had been evacuated under white phosphorus smoke screens delivered by grenades. In the fight, 40 pillboxes were destroyed, 30 caves sealed, and 250 enemy killed. Our casualties were one killed and four wounded.

At 1800 the battalion was notified it would revert to 305th control the next day and was subsequently to move to Tomui.

During the night a band of Japs, armed with heavy demolition charges, machine guns, rifles and knee mortars, infiltrated around Company F's left and attacked Company G and the battalion CP. The attack was repulsed after two hours of close-in fighting. In the morning, 70 dead Japanese were counted. None of the battalion men was hurt.

At 0630, June 21st, the battalion moved to Tomui, arriving at 0900. The unit occupied an assembly area 1,000 yards south of Nakaza. The battalion was placed in regimental reserve for the attacks to the south in the next few days. It was to be prepared to attack south to the Corps boundary on order.

The 1st and 3rd Battalions of the 305th had moved from Inasomi to an area near Tomui on June 20th, and late that day had received orders from the 96th Infantry Division, to which the 305th was attached, to pass through its 381st Regiment in an attack on Hills 79 and 85 the next day. The move was to be from an assembly area 1,000 yards southeast of Medeera (7858KIMN) to the northwest. This attack was to clear all Jap resistance in the 96th zone of advance.

This meant that the regiment had to move its entire team about five miles over narrow roads, set up fire-support plans, orient and issue orders to all commanders, and launch a coordinated assault by noon.

Late the afternoon of the 20th, the commanding officer of the regiment sent his S-2 on a road reconnaissance for a route to the assembly area. The S-3 went along to look over the terrain. The S-4 set up his plans, which included an initial ammunition distribution point just behind the line of departure. This meant that the necessary ammunition would have to be trucked from the 96th Division dump about 12 miles to the rear, over bad roads, under a schedule that would have to work.

Early in the morning of the 21st, the regimental commander and his S-2 and S-3 left the bivouac area near Tomui, moved ahead of the troops through friendly country and set up an observation post southeast of Medeera, looking toward the objective hills. The 1st and 3rd Battalions, partially motorized, left the bivouac area near Tomui and arrived at the assembly area southeast of Medeera at 0830. The 2nd Battalion followed on foot and arrived at 1200. The mobile ammunition distribution point was waiting for the troops at the assembly area, and as the battalions moved out in column toward the LD, the men passed the distribution point and obtained the necessary ammunition.

After studying the terrain from the OP, the regimental commander ordered all weapons of the regiment placed in support of the attack. Four platoons of heavy machine guns fired not only overhead fire but also pinpoint fire along the flanks of the advancing companies. The 81mm mortars were massed by battalion and fired in battery. Each mortar platoon leader was assigned a definite sector of fire.

Three battalions of 105mm howitzers and a company of 4.2 mortars began the preparation on Hill 79 at 1135. Two platoons of M-8 SP 75mm guns simultaneously began firing on caves and pillboxes on the forward slopes of the objective. A company of medium tanks, supplemented by a platoon of flamethrowing tanks, moved into position to support the assault companies.

At 1150 all mortars in the regiment opened up at the rate of 15 rounds per minute, and the heavy machine guns started working on previously selected targets. The 60mm mortars and light machine guns contributed to the mass of fire power. Because of the terrain and the narrow frontage, the plan of attack called for an advance in column with the 1st Battalion in the assault. At 1200 the battalion jumped off toward Hill 79 under an extremely heavy curtain of protecting fires by the regiment. Assault units of the battalion advanced 400 yards before coming under enemy machine-gun fire, which slowed down but did not stop the advance. By 1600 the battalion had advanced to within 150 yards of the top of the wooded, gently sloping hill.

The enemy maintained a heavy volume of machine gun and rifle fire against the 1st Battalion, but by 1630 the battalion had elements on the very top of Hill 79. Due to the lateness of the hour, and to effect a better defense, the forward elements on the top of the hill were pulled back about 100 yards into a battalion line of defense across the northeast slopes of the hill. The 3rd Battalion had moved behind the 1st and went into a night defensive position about 200 yards to the rear, in contact with the 1st Battalion, 184th Infantry.

The attack was successful, the 1st Battalion was in possession of Hill 79, and the 3rd Battalion was ready to pass through the 1st the next morning in an attack on Hill 85. The 2nd Battalion was in reserve near the regimental CP 1,500 yards east of Hill 79.

During the day the 1st Battalion and supporting units killed 235 Japanese, captured three prisoners and 34 civilians, and destroyed or captured two medium tanks, four heavy and five light machine guns, one knee mortar and four 150mm artillery pieces. In addition, 12 caves had been sealed. Our own casualties were one officer killed and three wounded, and 20 enlisted men wounded.

The attack order for the 22nd was issued orally to all battalions at 211900. Time of the attack was set at 0830, with the 3rd Battalion passing through the 1st to secure Hill 79, the 2nd to move into an assembly area on the right flank of the 1st, prepared to attack Hill 85 on order. The objective, though it looked like one peak on the map, was actually four knolls in line.

Company I advanced to within 400 yards of the top of the hill and was slowed to a crawl by heavy fire coming from the second of the four knolls on the top of the hill. Wire and crossed grazing machine gun fire at the base of the knoll made it almost impossible for the company to continue its advance. Company K, in the meantime, advanced over Hill 79 and took the first knoll with little resistance. Most of the enemy defenders had been entrenched in the southwest side of the two knolls, and had been flanked by the advance of Company F. Much of the opposition encountered by Company I had come from the knolls taken by Company K.

Both Companies I and K were ordered to take the dominant peak, the third in line, at 1545. This was overrun by the two companies in less than half an hour. A base of fire was formed on this knoll, and the last one was taken with little trouble. In the mopping up of the entire position, it was found that many U-shaped caves had been constructed in 10-foot wide fissures, some of which were 40 feet deep. These had originally been set up to cover Medeera to the north, but the attack had come from the east. These deep crevices were blown by dropping or lowering satchel charges. A few prisoners, dazed and wounded, came out of the caves before they were closed.

Although both Hills 79 and 85 had been taken, it was reported by the two companies that extensive mopping up would have to be carried out the next day. In this fighting, 313 Japanese were killed, nine captured, 70 estimated killed, and nine field pieces destroyed. Our casualties were two men killed and 41 wounded.

A deep draw between Hills 81 and 85, 250 yards to the front of Company I, was blasted with previously registered mortar fire throughout the night, and many of the enemy trying to evacuate the Hill 85 caves were killed.

On June 23rd, Company L moved up arid cleaned out the last of the Japs on the fourth knoll on Hill 85, then moved farther west to contact the Marines on Hill 81. While going through the draw between the hills, the company counted 350 dead Japanese and killed eight more, to complete the mopping-up of the area. A search of the dead in the draw revealed one colonel, one lieutenant colonel, three majors, two captains, one 1st lieutenant, 12 2nd lieutenants, eight sergeant majors, two sergeants and one corporal. This indicated that a high headquarters had been located in the vicinity, probably in a cave which connected Hill 81 and Hill 85. It was later discovered that two lieutenant generals, who had committed suicide, were buried in the vicinity.

The 96th Division was contacted by a Company K patrol in Medeera. At 1520 the regiment received a warning order from higher headquarters to be prepared on order to relieve the 307th Infantry on outpost duty along the Naha-Yonabaru road, east of Route 5 to the coast. This relief was to be made position by position in order to fulfill the mission of containing all the Japs on the southern end of the island. At 1325 the 3rd Battalion was relieved by a battalion of the 96th Division and moved to Kakazu.

The entire 305th was assembled in a bivouac area north of Shuri by 25 June, the day on which Okinawa was declared secure, and readied itself for a move south for outpost duty. During the next three days the 3rd Battalion carried on extensive patrolling missions in the ridges flanking the main Shuri Valley, stopping enemy attempts to infiltrate to the northern end of Okinawa.

The 305th received high praise from the 96th Division and others for its efficient performance in South Okinawa. The last attacks were in effect demonstrations of the latest battle-tested techniques in infantry tactics conducted by experts.

The 77th Division held the dearly bought distinction of being the first ground organization to attack the Ryukyus, and the last to engage an organized enemy position there.

On Okinawa proper, the Division killed 16,127 Japs and took 58 prisoners. Its losses were 873 killed, dead of wounds and missing, and 3,076 wounded. Although the battle was a frontal assault on the strongest defenses in the Pacific, the 77th killed 18 Japs for each American killed, or 4 Japs for each American battle casualty of any sort.

The Division cemetery on Okinawa, neat and beautiful like the others at Agana, Ipil, Valencia, Zamami and Ie, was soberingly populous. To those rows of crosses and the many surviving comrades who came voluntarily to the dedication ceremony, Brigadier General Edwin H. Randle said:

We are gathered to pay our last respects to those of our comrades who have fallen on this island, so far from home and from all those persons and places they held most dear.

Throughout our history as a nation we have always been fortunate to have such men, sometimes only a few, more often many.

Those who have fallen in other wars have seemed to us legendary heroes of whom we read in history books. But the men who lie here are very real to us. We knew them personally and intimately. We lived with them. We have fought with them, and we have seen them die. We know that they had the same hopes and fears, the same love of country, and the same pride of which the rest of us are possessed.

Like us, they hoped one day to return to their homes and friends and loved ones, to the large or small communities from which they sprang.

But here they lie buried on hostile soil, far from all they held most dear. They learned, as all of us have learned, that the price of liberty is, to some generations, even more than eternal vigilance.

They take their place among the immortal band which made similar sacrifices at Lexington and Concord — Lundy's Lane and Cerro Gordo; and with those who also looked death in the eye and met it without shirking at Gettysburg and in the Argonne.

In every period our country has had strong, courageous men who have been willing to give their all to defend their ideal of a free country. We must not grow cynical because we hear of unnecessary and unwarranted strikes, self-seeking chiselers, phonies, crooks and fools. They are always present in a free country and are testimony to its freedom. Rather must we remember that there is a great and vast majority of honest men who stand always ready to defend with their lives the simple freedoms impressed so deeply within themselves. Such were these.

And so we must dedicate ourselves to carry on the task they have forwarded thus far. As Chief Justice Holmes said years ago, on a similar occasion:

"At the grave of a hero we end, not with sorrow at the inevitable loss, but with the contagion of his courage; and with a kind of desperate joy we go back to the fight."

And through the years to come we must, as a sacred duty, keep their memories ever fresh before us and before those at home, who, because they have not seen with their own eyes, cannot fully understand the things that these men have, in their strong faith, endured for them and for their own ideals.

If those who now lie here could speak, they might say with the poet:
"Here dead we he because we did not choose
To live and shame the land from which we sprung.
Life, to be sure, is nothing much to lose;
But young men think it is, and we were young."

Even before Okinawa was secured, the 77th was alerted for a move to the Philippine Islands where it was to re-equip, train and prepare for a part in the invasion of Kyushu. The 77th was the only Division of the Okinawa veterans to be slated for the next operation. General Bruce departed about 20 June for Guam, still hoping to get the Division diverted to Oahu where better rehabilitation and supply facilities were idle. A small advance party followed by air on the 24th. The troops loaded into LSTs soon thereafter and sailed south.

Part VII: Mopping Up After the War

BRIEF: The Division returned to the Philippine Islands early in June 1945 with the mission of hastily rehabilitating, re-equipping and planning for a part in the November invasion of Kyushu. As usual, the 77th had to build its own rest camp, this time near Danao on the east coast of Cebu. By exerting effort and ingenuity the troops worked themselves out of the mud and into reasonably comfortable quarters.

An extensive recreation program was instituted which included games, swimming, sailboat racing, nightly movies, and dances. The Red Cross and local societies assisted. Into the midst of the program fell the news of peace. The 77th did not indulge in riotous celebration. The men remembered Okinawa, considered what Kyushu would have been, and were quietly thankful.

From 26 August through September the Division without incident took the surrender of 5,543 Japanese troops on Cebu.

The 77th was ordered to prepare for occupation duties in North Honshu or Hokkaido. Winter clothing was issued and plans were made to operate under cold weather conditions. General Randle and a small advance party departed on 16 September.

The Division, combat loaded, left Cebu on 26 September and arrived off Hakodate, Hokkaido early on 4 October. The Division Artillery headquarters and the 306th Combat Team landed there. The remainder of the Division sailed to Otaru and disembarked on the 5th and 6th of October. Division Headquarters, Division Troops, and the 307th Combat Team occupied the Sapporo area. The 305th Combat Team proceeded by rail and road to the inter-mountain city of Asahigawa.

This was an orderly, peaceful occupation. The Japanese caused no trouble either initially or subsequently. The Japanese Army and Naval Forces had been almost entirely demobilized prior to the occupation so the 77th merely collected and disposed of the military equipment. The only difficulties developed in quieting and repatriating thousands of Chinese and Korean laborers and prisoners. From Hokkaido the combat veterans of the 77th returned home via the "point system." New officers and men took their places and carried on their duties. During the long, cold, snowy winter they worked and played as well disciplined occupation troops in this strange land.

The 77th closed out its military affairs, transferred its property, personnel and responsibilities to other units, and was inactivated in Hokkaido on 15 March 1946. It had served four years, fought about 200 days in three campaigns, had killed 43,651 Japanese and had suffered almost 14,000 casualties. Its work was done.

Chapter 28: Cebu: Rehabilitation and the Jap Surrender

TO COLONEL TANZOLA, late commander of the 305th Combat Team, is attributed the quip, "My men can fight another campaign but I'm not sure they can stand another rehabilitation period." He referred to the fact that the 77th and most combat divisions usually found it necessary to build their own rest camps in less than desirable locations, and to move away from such camps about as soon as completed. Cebu was no exception.

The Division came south on LSTs (landing ship, tank). People back home may have considered LSTs to be homely, practical, nautical monstrosities but the troops liked the things. LSTs plodded along slowly and surely with terrific rolls but then there was nothing to do and no one was in a hurry. Men could lie around on deck all day — reading and "shooting the bull" — and when time came to eat, the chow line was not too long. There were relatively few Navy men aboard and these were usually friendly because they had carried many a load of GI's to enemy beaches. They'd do anything for them. So when our troops loaded up from Hagushi Beaches into the yawning jaws of the LSTs they were fairly contented. If they weren't going to Oahu, at least Cebu had one large city to offer. Word had got around that Cebu City wasn't too badly damaged. Men made plans which included plenty of beverages and senoritas.

By the time the Division reached the Philippines, General Bruce and the advance party had selected a camp area just south of Danao, Cebu, and had made preliminary arrangements for the disposition of troops. Although not ideal, this area along the beach was certainly better than the alternative location which was Leyte. No one wanted to return to the mud of Leyte. Cebu offered a good harbor, some stretches of real concrete road, relatively good recreational facilities and some fresh food.

General Bruce took an active interest in the development of the camp. He personally designed many of the native style buildings and contributed ideas for decorations and furnishings. He chose sites for the four enlisted men's recreation centers before the rest of the camp was laid out in detail. He was determined that the 77th should have a pleasant camp and an enjoyable stay on Cebu.

As the troops came from the LSTs at Danao and moved into their palm-shaded camp areas, they decided that it was better than they had anticipated. Then came the rains, and practically everything in the Division went under water. Everyone was digging, draining, releasing dams, and moving madly to higher ground. This mud was bad all right — but still not as bad as Leyte. Soon the men in the regiments were so hard at work trying to build a decent camp that they forgot Okinawa, Cebu City, Oahu, and everything else. It wasn't long before you could hear some GI gripe, "Wish I was back in combat!" As soon as the mud was partially under control, the building program started. The Civil Affairs Section, headed by Lieutenant Colonel Albert E. Hallett, hired hundreds of easy-going native laborers and purchased tons of bamboo. Before long the Division bristled with dozens of well constructed, concrete-floored, bamboo buildings.

Each company built, a bamboo kitchen with concrete floor and screened sides. Next to the kitchen was a large, airy mess hall with wooden tables and benches, a nipa shingled, roof and woven palm-leaf sidewalls. Officers and men lived in pyramidal tents that were raised up off the ground on bamboo supports and furnished with all types of impromptu bamboo furniture. Other buildings and raised frame tents were prepared for offices in the various headquarters. Tons of brush and litter were hauled from the area, and tons of stone, gravel and sand hauled in. Roadside signs went up. What had been a stretch of brushy, weedy woods, occupied here and there by ramshackle camps of refugees, became an orderly, well policed military camp.

All this took planning, work and time. The pre-fabricated buildings, shower heads, Coca-Cola machines, ice cream freezers, reefers, pianos, barges, baseballs and other items did not automatically descend on the Division like manna. Neither did these come in answer to ordinary requisitions. Only through the activities of several officer scouts and "expediters'* who combed the Philippines, through aggressive effort, and through friendship with the Navy and the Air Corps, were these various luxuries assembled.

While permanent structures were still going up, temporary facilities were used to great advantage. On 19 July, two days after the rear echelon landed, movie projectors were operating for men who sat on coconut logs and gazed at a screen stretched between two palms by the water's edge. This was not too comfortable — but definitely picturesque! By skillful swapping, Lieutenant Colonel Robert Adair, athletics and recreation officer, managed to get a minimum of five new films each week, and these movies were shown in each of seven motion-picture theaters operating in the Division area. These theaters, as well as other major installations, were named in honor of fallen comrades.

On 23 July, just 13 days after the Division had moved ashore, the first USO show, "Victory Varieties," was presented to the men of the 305th Infantry. This was the beginning of a long series of top flight USO shows. The Cabbie Theatre at Division Headquarters, the Silver Theatre of the 307th and 306th, and the Doogan Theater of the 305th Infantry were packed at every showing of "Variety Days," "Oklahoma," "Comedy Caravan," "Melody Parade," "Three Men On A Horse," "Kay Kyser," "Plenty Potent," and all the other shows. On the 31st of July, Special Service presented Dick Jergens "All Marine Band" with a show that was both smooth and fast, and it made a hit. One of the brightest spots of the entertainment series was a World Premiere of "Week-End at the Waldorf — an MGM show with an all-star cast.

In order not to be too far outdone by the professionals, each regiment organized a show of its own that played the Division circuit. Troops saw the "Oak Leaf Revue" of the 305th, the "Clear the Way Revue" of the 307th, the "On the Ball Caravan" of the 306th, and "Liberty Varieties" of Division Artillery and Special Troops. There were impromptu entertainments, at many of which someone sang one of the numerous parodies on Cole Porters "Don't Fence Me In," the most popular being a parody entitled "Don't Send Me In" by Bernard Bryer of 292d Joint Assault Signal Company. To the veterans of several severe beachheads, there was ironic humor in the words:

Let me float in the boat till the enemy's remote,
Don't send me in.
Let me land on the sand with the generals and the band,
Don't send me in.
Send me back to the farm raising pigs and pullets
I don't mind guns but I can't stand bullets,
Leave me at the galley washing pots and skillets
Don't send me in.
Just let me dally in the galley, while the reef and beach is under fire
On my back in my sack it seems a racket, but you know how fast I tire
It's a lie, I'm not shy, but I'm much too young to die
Don't send me in.

I'll volunteer for a mission to the rear
Don't send me in.
You can have my souvenirs, I ain't got many
You can keep all your medals cause I don't want any
All I want to carry backs a healthy fanny,
Don't send me in.

Each company used its mess hall as a day room, but the "indoor" recreational activities centered about four recreational clubs, located so as to be available to the greatest number of troops and adjacent to the theatres and chapels — one in each regimental area and one for the Special Troops and Artillery. Care was taken in clearing these sites to maintain a balance of shade and sunlight. Three of the clubs were located on sandy beaches, and rafts were anchored about 100 feet off shore. Umbrellas and split bamboo lounge chairs brought a bit of "Stateside" atmosphere.

Each club was designed to provide certain facilities; the concrete floor was finished smooth for dancing, and an orchestra platform was raised at one end of the main room. In addition, there were a reading and writing room, a hobby shop, PX facilities, and a snack bar for the coffee, doughnuts, and "coke." Rest rooms were provided for guests. Tables and chairs were constructed of bamboo, and ping pong tables of plywood. Each club had a radio and a record player. Recreation ran the gamut from chess to dancing, through bingo, checkers, bridge, puzzles, art, photography, fishing, and hobby shows; and there were Filipino women to take care of that chore of sewing on patches and stripes. Two Red Cross girls were on hand in each club to supervise the activities and to handle the many inquiries for reports on relatives — a Red Cross service of great value to troops.

As soon as the recreation buildings were furnished, dances were held. The distribution of girls, orchestras, door prizes, "coke" and ice cream was carefully adjusted to give a fair share to all units. The transportation of girls, the provision of chaperones, and other planning problems were so well handled that practically everyone had more than one chance to do some fancy foot warming and to relax in the pleasant atmosphere of music and girls. The Filipino guests, though always outnumbered, paid the compliment of requesting a later curfew for dances. The various bands and orchestras did a superb job of stirring memories and making these festivities some of the best remembered of the stay overseas.

Four officers' club buildings were also erected just as complete as the recreation centers but lacking the "supervision" of Red Cross girls. Officers' dances were arranged. On the 25th of August, an official reception and dance in honor of the Governor of Cebu was held at the Division Headquarters Club. Later a series of officer dances featured an airborne invasion of American girls. These were nurses, WAC officers and Red Cross workers "borrowed" from Leyte and flown to Cebu by courtesy of the Army and Navy Air Corps.

A Division fresh from combat is lucky to inventory one baseball and a fish hook. The 77th was no exception, but requisitions were rushed by air to Base "S" in Cebu City and unit officers went to work to make facilities for baseball, softball, volleyball and horseshoes available for all. Finding the space for baseball was a problem. Camp areas and motor pools inevitably took the better clearings (for Cebu was either coconuts, corn, paddy or undergrowth) and engineer equipment was tied up with road building. The 305th and 306th Infantry had to play major games away from home at the 307th or Division Artillery fields, but this inconvenience was outweighed by the presence of 28 softball diamonds and 15 softball leagues within the Division. Of six basketball courts, two were regulation size. Despite the tropical climate, men did play basketball and a few worked out at boxing. However, volleyball, with its nearly perfect flexibility in respect to numbers and space, was naturally the second most popular campside exercise of the soldiers — next to bunk fatigue.

There were many tight, hard-fought games, such as those of softball between the 76th Field Hospital and the 77th Signal Company, or the hardball games in which the 306th led the island champions, the 388th Port Battalion. In volleyball, the 603rd Medical Clearing Company played through the season undefeated.

The 77ths amphibious training and experiences may have had something to do with the number of men who turned seaward for sport. Where the reef was a hindrance to low-tide swimmers, channels were blasted; rafts and piers were provided near all areas. The water was usually warm, and although the currents occasionally brought in curious "needling" jelly fish, the sun tan addicts were out there every day. At low tide, the study of sea life and the capture of it was of absorbing interest. Other officers and men went in for water craft of all sorts. The native sailing canoe with bamboo outriggers was the standard vessel. Queen of the Division fleet was the 307th's See Boo Queen, a large sailing outrigger which presided in a motherly way over several regattas. The business men of Cebu were no different from practical traders the world over and would lend a boat for the season provided some salvage canvas sails appeared eventually on the vessel.

Would-be deep-sea fishermen tried their luck with varying success from the decks of the 77th Division fleet, which consisted of three powered pontoon barges and later included an "F" Boat capable of carrying about 60 tons of cargo. This F8, because of its buxom lines, was nicknamed the SS Squatting Duck. These craft flew the Statue of Liberty flag and even made a trip to Mindanao for fresh pineapple for the Division messes.

The troops were not on Cebu long before they realized that their dreams of a big city were just a little premature. They wondered how the fight in the city had happened to destroy all the large modern buildings but left intact all the little bamboo shacks. The dock area was just one long line of hollow shells that once had been warehouses and offices, and the entire business district was a shambles. However, the GI's did not find Cebu City a total loss. Base "S" operated Club Cebu (Red Cross) for enlisted men visiting the city and, across the street, a snack bar where they could buy sandwiches and a real, live carbonated Coca-Cola. There were several GI movie theaters scattered about and boxing matches were occasionally held on the tennis courts next to the CIC building.

Most of the GI's went to the town for entertainment provided by the Filipinos. From some of the more substantial buildings, there came at all hours the wild beat of American jazz as interpreted by a native band. Somehow or other, the Filipinos knew the latest hits and their renditions, if a little different from ours, were nevertheless rhythmic and exciting.

Few parties were dry, for the local liquor was everywhere available and the U. S. beer ration was liberal. However, there was a curfew at 2200 in the city and the men had to be on their way home by that hour or discuss conditions in the guardhouse with Base "S" MP's.

These Cebu City adventures were shared with men of the Americal Division, veterans of Guadalcanal and Bougainville who had invaded Cebu the same day the 77th hit Kerama Retto (26 March, 1945). Veterans of the two divisions found much to discuss between beers.

There was more to the tour of Cebu than camp building and recreation. The Division drew some new equipment, repaired the old, painted everything and, in general, worked to get back in trim. There was training directed at assimilating the replacements into the fighting teams.

The Sixth Army Training Program called for three weeks of amphibious training. The 77th was excused from this requirement on the basis that its numerous successful assault landings constituted proof of competence.

Finally there was planning. Most of the troops sensed that the 77th was slated for a part in the first invasion of Kyushu to come off in the Autumn. General Bruce and his staff worked on detailed plans for several possible employments, and there were frequent conferences with staff officers from IX Corps on Leyte. All the machinery of planning was in motion. Top Secret documents, maps, models, and orders were moving about.

Then came the atomic bomb! And on 8 August, Russia declared war. Then the reports of the atomic bombing of Nagasaki were followed by the first peace offer. The men of the 77th waited. They believed the end was near but they had been so many times disappointed that they were not optimistic. The news of the Japanese surrender was not greeted with wild, riotous gunfire as at Okinawa, or by breaking windows and looting as at other places. The men of the 77th cheered a little but for the most part they just listened. Perhaps, in a way, they listened to the silence of November 1, 1945, a day that would have been noisy with gunfire and red with blood. Actually, the veterans could not make themselves believe the peace. They had by continued combat reached the stage where war had become normal.

Soon after Japan surrendered, the Americal Division, which was tactically responsible for Cebu, established contact with leaders of Japanese forces in the mountains of Cebu and made arrangements for the local surrender. Actually, several days of negotiations were required to convince the Japs that the news was true. Once convinced they hurried to comply. On the 28th of August at Ilahan, Cebu, the Commanding General of the Americal Division took the surrender of 2,600 Japanese troops. The Japanese, including nurses and "comfort girls," marched in at daybreak, stacked their arms and equipment and formed into units. A battalion of armed Americans formed opposite them. At 1000 the surrender was finished and the enemy climbed into American trucks for the trip to the stockade at Cebu City.

The 77th was represented in two ways at this affair. As the column of prisoner-laden trucks stood by the roadside, the Antitank Company, 307th Infantry, out on practice march with their M18 self-propelled guns quite coincidentally passed along the road. Japanese officers and men alike leaned soberly from the trucks and stared in amazement at the column of mechanical monsters. The second representation was planned. After the ceremony, Colonel Aubrey Smith, Commanding Officer, 306th Infantry, Lieutenant Colonel Henry Koepcke, Division G-3 (Operations Officer), and Lieutenant Colonel Max Myers, Division G-2 (Intelligence Officer), conferred with Lieutenant General Fukue, Major General Majone, and Admiral Harada concerning the surrender arrangements for 5,000 additional Japanese on Cebu. This conference, which was held in a near-by house, was necessitated by the impending departure of the Americal Division. Colonel Smith, representing the 77th, designated assembly points at Balembon, Asturias, Tuberon and Carmen. The Japanese commanders were told to bring their forces to these places between the 28th and 31st of August. General Fukue did not mention that he was surrendering to the Division which helped to destroy his 102nd Japanese Division on Leyte.

During the last days of August and the first week of September the 306th Infantry, with the 77th Reconnaissance troop attached, received, disarmed and convoyed to Cebu City, 5,543 Japanese who had been hiding on Cebu. This was done without incident or accident. The enemy forces were well disciplined and eager to surrender. Japanese officers were anxious to obey orders to the letter. The Americans participating were all combat veterans, alert for tricks but not excitable.

The Americans were impressed by the poor health of the Japanese and by the brutality of their officers. Many had malaria and all were undernourished. The sick had to limp or crawl because their officers would not permit them to be carried. The nurses carried heavy packs and were treated as roughly as the men. Soldiers were slapped and kicked just as a matter of course.

On the 9th of September, President Osmena's birthday, the whole island of Cebu celebrated V-J Day. These people had seen the last of their detested enemies corralled in the Base "S" stockade and they were in a real mood to celebrate. They had each and every one suffered in the occupation, and even on this day of thanksgiving they bore the Japanese an unswerving hatred that more fortunate peoples found difficult to understand. As they looked about their once beautiful city of Cebu, they could see the ruins where once there had been white buildings of which they had been proud. But this day marked a new era and if they had to start all over at the bottom, at least they could choose their own way and be free of the restraining hand of the oppressor. They cheered the Americans because they had a genuine sense of gratitude for the deliverance of their country.

So at 1430 that Sunday afternoon there was wild cheering as a parade came marching down Jones Avenue toward the Capitol. First in line were the small, brown men of the 43rd Filipino Regiment, then representatives from the American Naval Air Base on Mactan Island, and finally a motorized combat force from the 77th.

Later, Filipinos and American soldiers gathered before the steps of the Capitol to hear speeches by the Mayor of Cebu, Lieutenant Colonel Baura, Acting Commander of the 43rd Filipino Infantry Regiment, Colonel Rattan, Commander of Base "S," and Fructuoso B. Cabahug, Governor of Cebu. General Bruce made a short congratulatory talk and the ceremony was closed with the reading of a message from President Osmena. The occasion will be best remembered by the 77th for the gala dance that was given that night at the Osmena fountain. Filipinos and Americans danced happily until late that night on the semi-circular cement walk to the tunes of a native dance band. At the same time a huge crowd was dancing in the street near the Capitol where the "Doughboys" of the 305th Infantry furnished music.

That the 77th was scheduled for occupation duty in Japan became common knowledge, but the guesses as to "where" competed with the point system for a place in public discussions. Soon rumors mentioned Hokkaido more often than any other locale.

Actually, General Bruce and his staff had been alerted and briefed early in August by Major General Ryder, IX Corps Commander, concerning a plan for occupation of northern Honshu and Hokkaido. As soon as Japan surrendered, these plans crystallized and the Division prepared as if for another combat operation.

For the troops the preparations included lectures on cold weather clothing and orientation courses on how to behave in an occupied country, saluting, brass-polishing, and all the details of guard duty. Each man was re-equipped to the best of the ability of the Quartermaster. Vehicles were painted and in general the entire Division got a face-lifting. It was going to put on an impressive show for the Nips. There was some question as to the probable Jap reaction to the five little flags, labeled "Guam," "Leyte," "Kerama Retto," "Ie Shima" and "Okinawa," which were painted on each Division vehicle.

The 77th, under IX Corps, had to be prepared to land behind the 81st Division at Aomori on North Honshu or to land independently on Hokkaido. On 9 September, the mission was clarified with orders to land at

Otaru, Hokkaido, on 5 October. The next day these orders were modified to include a landing by one combat team at Hakodate, Hokkaido.

General Randle and a small advance party departed on the 16th to accompany the 81st Division by ship to Aomori, then by air to Hokkaido.

Loading, which commenced on the 18th, was difficult because the shipping became available in a piecemeal manner. But Division Supply Officer, Lieutenant Colonel Henry O'Brien and the veteran Transport Quartermaster Team, led by Lieutenant Colonel Earl P. Schlotterbeck, untangled snarled red tape day by day and the ships were loaded by 2000, 23 September.

The Division, combat loaded "just in case," departed Cebu on 26 September, 1430, en route, via Leyte, for the Tsugaru Straits between Honshu and Hokkaido.

Chapter 29: The Occupation of Hokkaido

THE CONVOY that bore the 77th north toward Hokkaido included 17 transports. One day out of Leyte it was joined by five additional ships which had sailed from Manila with supplies and engineer troops. At first glance one would have thought that this task force was headed for a landing on a hostile shore, but to the experienced eye there were several differences. The escort, for example, was only two destroyers. There were no assault destroyers, control craft, no carriers, and no heavy fighting ships. However, no fighting ships were needed. There were no dangers except for drifting mines and the weather.

Aboard these occupation-bound ships were men who had lived, sweated and bled through three tough Pacific campaigns. Their thoughts were not too completely on the task before them, although most men lapsed into a resigned "let's finish the job" attitude. They felt that they had done their work out there in the endless Pacific, and many wanted to know why they couldn't go right home as victorious soldiers of other wars had done. To them the system of discharging by points, which were credited for almost everything but days of actual combat, was somewhat unfair. Some of these men felt sorry for their own plight and were not averse to voicing their sentiments. However, the state of the sea was soon to push this situation into the background.

For three days the convoy dodged a typhoon but finally was caught by the tail of it and there were some seasick soldiers — and sailors. By all their traveling over the waves on their invasions, the soldiers of the 77th had become more accustomed to the rolling sea than many an apprentice seaman. The sun seemed to follow the convoy persistently, no matter how far north it journeyed. Men with the "crud" and the heat rash despaired of feeling the relief they had been expecting. Men who had been suffering for long months under the moist heat of the tropics thought longingly of using blankets once more and of drinking water that wasn't hot and chlorinated. The convoy traveled with lights at night and combat veterans found it difficult to adjust themselves to such a "dangerous" and startling practice. To them the ships seemed unduly and riskily exposed.

To the delight of officers as well as enlisted men, there was some easing up of the usual pre-combat discipline. Chores aboard ship were few, and the only restricting duties were attendance at hour-long lectures conducted once or twice a day. These talks turned out to be quite informative to the occupation troops, as they concerned the morals and customs of the Japanese and instructions as to how the victorious American soldiers should deal with the defeated Oriental enemy. The 77th's earnestness to make good was evidenced by the many men who launched themselves on a course of study in the Japanese language with the aid of Nisei interpreters and the military phrase book. To break the monotony of the daily rock and roll of ship life came the broadcasts of World Series baseball games and the daily announcements concerning the changes in the point system.

In the early morning of 4 October, the ships steamed single file through a marked, mineswept channel in Tsugaru Strait. Off Hakodate an American naval task force waited. The ships carrying the Division Artillery headquarters and the 306th Combat Team moved in toward the harbor while the Otaru Force proceeded west.

The Hakodate Force landed and Brigadier General Ray Burnell assumed command ashore. Troops occupied billets previously selected by Lieutenant Colonel Marion Williams of the Advance Party. The Japanese stolidly, almost indifferently, surveyed the landings and caused no trouble.

The remainder of the Division was off Otaru by 0600 on 5 October. As Navy cruisers and destroyers stood by, landing craft were lowered immediately and took billeting parties in past the breakwaters toward the concrete piers. Officers and men stared at the coaling docks and cranes, the crowded wharf areas, and decided that Hokkaido must be at least partly civilized. The first comers climbed ashore in an almost deserted waterfront, but were met by Brigadier General Randle, Assistant Division Commander, whose party included local governmental and military officials.

The Advance Party had spent several days traveling about Hokkaido, receiving full cooperation everywhere from the Japanese. Therefore, the troops, as they landed found trains waiting, route markers in English along the roads, and guides for everyone. Numerous Japanese policemen, easily recognized by gold braid and chromium plated swords, directed traffic along these roads.

By 0730, a Division Information Center and the Shore Party Command Post had been established on Pier One at Otaru. The plan followed was to land the 307th Combat Team on 5 October and the 305th Combat Team on 6 October. Harbor facilities were used to the very maximum, which permitted the unloading of 12 ships at piers at one time. Rail transportation arrangements had been made and were so scheduled as to accommodate all units as they debarked.

In accordance with these plans, the 307th RCT commenced unloading at 0800, 5 October. Troops were marched directly from ships to trains which were dispatched hourly. These were the first trains many men had seen for 15 months. Despite the smaller gauge tracks and the miniature cars, many men began to get that "Stateside" feeling. The desire for comfort overruled the inquisitive nature so only a few of the American passengers took time to examine the many differences in the Japanese railroad trains. The occasional Japanese who could speak English was a great curiosity.

Vehicles were unloaded, assembled and moved in convoys over the roads to Sapporo, the capital city of Hokkaido and the new home of the 77th Division Headquarters and Special Troops. Combat drivers who had pushed Army vehicles through tropical lands and over invasion beaches gloated over the almost modern highways. Bulk cargo was unloaded and temporarily stored in pier warehouses for future movement to troop areas. Concurrently with the 307th landing, elements of Special Troops were unloaded and dispatched to their billets. By 0100 October 6th, the entire 307th had unloaded and was en route to Sapporo. The 77th Reconnaissance Troop reconnoitered the principal roads and towns in the Sapporo area.

As soon as berthing space was vacated by RCT 307, ships lifting RCT 305 were brought into the piers. Some cargo was loaded concurrently with that of the 307th, but the bulk of unloading both personnel and equipment commenced at 0700, 6 October. A speedy discharge was effected in a manner similar to that of the 307th. Troops were moved from Otaru by train to Asahigawa and vehicles and cargo moved by road thereto. By 2200 that night, unloading of the 305th and the remainder of the Division Special Troops was completed.

Division Headquarters and Division Troops occupied various previously selected buildings in Sapporo which they found to be a relatively modern city with wide paved streets, public utilities and modern but almost empty department stores. The 307th Combat Teams took over the Japanese Army barracks at Tsukisappu just outside the city. The 305th Combat Team plus the 154th Engineer Battalion closed in at Asahigawa, an intermountain city 85 miles northeast of Sapporo on 7 October. These troops fell heir to a large Japanese army winter training post. At Hakodate, the Hakodate task force was disposed in various buildings and installations within the city.

All units immediately tackled their parallel tasks of getting settled in their new quarters, establishing alert plans, instituting the U. S. Military Government control, and collecting and disposing of Jap military arms and equipment. Two additional tasks developed quickly — dealing with the thousands of restless Chinese and Koreans, and sending half the Division home on points. Everything was to be done at once, but obviously everything could not be done at once. So everyone from the Commanding General down, plugged ahead with the skill and patience developed by wartime practice in similarly confusing situations. One by one the missions were accomplished.

The Division Military Government Section, headed by General Randle, supervised dealings with the Japanese Prefectural Government. The 77th did not bother with individual Japanese or small agencies on governmental matters. It told the Prefectural Government to get the desired jobs done by a definite date and left the headaches to the Japanese.

However, Military Government had to deal with the thousands of Chinese and Koreans who had been brought to operate the coal mines and farms during the war. These people, who had been worked almost as slaves, seldom paid and kept in undesirable living conditions, became restless at the wars end. There were some instances of rioting and looting and the laborers refused to work the coal mines. However, they continued to occupy the mine barracks so Japanese miners could not be brought in. This caused further critical coal shortages in Japan.

The Military Government Section of the Division sent officer teams to critical areas. These officers met with Chinese, Korean and Japanese leaders, outlined steps being taken for repatriation of the displaced persons, instructed Japanese to provide these people shelter, clothing and food equivalent to Japanese allotment, and instructed the displaced persons to wait peaceably in their present locations. In most instances such arrangements checked the trouble.

Units and patrols fanned out over Hokkaido to collect Japanese military equipment and serve notice on the population that the victors had arrived. The 1st Battalion, 307th Infantry, occupied the port city of Muroran on 13 October. The 305th sent strong patrols to Wakkanai, Obihiro, Kushiro and Nemuro. Smaller patrols checked through the numerous towns and villages. Later, the zones of responsibility were shifted and the 307th occupied a portion of eastern Hokkaido.

Everywhere the U. S. troops received implicit obedience and cooperation. At first the people remained indoors and children and women ran when Americans were sighted. Civilians wore drab, dark and threadbare clothing. However, they soon learned that the Americans were not there to loot, kill and rape. Then the people came out in their best, bright clothes, and went on living. Members of families which had moved their belongings to escape the falling American bombs began to tread their way wearily back to their homes. Some cities had been smashed and rehabilitation of people, towns and homes was slow and painful. Despite all this, the Japanese children learned to say "Good Morning" and to seek "Chocoretto." Business men moved rapidly to supply the souvenir trade and the demand for kimonos, tea sets, and assorted Oriental goods. Only the demobilized Jap soldiers remained an intangible element left stranded and uncertain by a war they had not known was lost.

In order to occupy much of the leisure time afforded the Americans, athletic programs were instituted and Japanese college gymnasiums and fields were put to use. Even the Japanese caught the spirit of American competition, and before long they had formed a few choice teams of their own to challenge the Americans. Each regimental Red Cross Director and Field Director set up his own area club where toiletries and difficult-to-get sweets and tobaccos were dispensed. Ping-pong tables and even billiard tables were made available. Movies were the order of the evening in all bivouacs. In Sapporo a huge Japanese theatre was requisitioned by the American command and dedicated to the memory of Colonel Douglas McNair. Here men of the Division and IX Corps enjoyed daily shows including a huge all-service musical and fun revue. Later the replacements were to whistle at a real geisha girl show and other Japanese stage shows with preponderantly female casts.

Highlight of the Division's first days in Hokkaido was the visit of Lieutenant General Robert L. Eichelberger, Eighth Army Commander, who arrived at Chitose Air Base at noon on October 16th. General Eichelberger had engineered the Division's reactivation and early training at Fort Jackson, and had always claimed a strong attachment for the Liberty Patch wearers. Therefore, although his visit was an official inspection tour, it was also somewhat in the nature of a homecoming for the General. The 3rd Battalion of the 307th Infantry formed an honor guard for him upon his arrival and music for the occasion was furnished by the Division Band. A detailed inspection of many units in the Sapporo area occupied the time until Gen. Eichelberger's departure for Eighth Army Headquarters on the evening of the 17th.

During October and early November, six thousand enlisted men and six hundred officers were sent home on the Readjustment Program. These men were eager to go, of course, and yet it was a definite wrench to break away from associations and friendships which had been welded under fire. They went south by train to Yokohama, thence by ship or plane to the States.

As the Golden Gate Special trains departed from Hokkaido stations, they were sent off not only by their soldier comrades but also by newly found Japanese friends. The appearance at the stations of these Japanese families with flowers and little farewell gifts was an indication of the ability of the American GI as an ambassador.

Thousands of replacements arrived from the United States and new men hastily assumed the duties of the homeward-bound veterans. The 77th carried on with the job.

Although the Division's personnel had come from the northeastern and southeastern states, and the 77th had been publicized as a metropolitan New York outfit, the new men, mostly from the west, midwest and far west caught the spirit of the great Lady Liberty. They began to boast of her battles almost as if they themselves had taken part in them. Most of the new men who were to complete the occupation job had trained in Infantry Replacement Centers and had not been previously assigned to any division to which they could attach themselves, either mentally or physically. Now they had the great Statue of Liberty Patch to sport before admiring eyes in Japan. Like General Bruce, they too were "proud to belong."

To occupy much of the occupation soldier's time, entertainment units from organizations throughout the Division were formed and put on a run of the Division circuit. Study centers were opened in the various areas. Here men interested in advancing their educational background or preparing themselves for future study could undertake USAFI courses, either by correspondence or in classes. First priority was given these classes, and class attendance was watched by First Sergeants almost as avidly as by a truant officer with a class of first graders. Despite a lack of books and equipment, this educational program was beneficial, especially to those soldiers whose schooling had been interrupted by the war and who were anxious to continue their studies. For many men it was an opportunity to review previous work and afforded them the chance of learning; new skills.

Occupation duties consisted mostly of guard duty and the construction of better shelters and living facilities. With the coming of winter, men of the 77th who had sweated it out in the Philippine coconut country began to regret their warm weather gripes. The cold and snow of Hokkaido for many was unlike any winter they had experienced in the States. Snow fell for 23 out of 31 days in January, and 21 out of 28 days in February. In Sapporo it reached a depth of 10 feet by the end of February. To uncover roads and homes, snow plows, tractors, graders and trucks of the 302nd Engineers were brought into play. Officers, non-coms and privates were employed as supervisors to instruct the Japanese laborers in the task of clearing their homeland from the flaky covering. Although the temperature hovered in the vicinity of zero, most men confessed that the cold of Japan was not as biting as the cold of the United States. The winterized clothing about which so much had been heard prior to leaving Cebu, really came into use.

In early January, certain outfits instituted 15-mile hikes under full field packs in foot-deep snow, but these were not rated too high in popularity. In fact, the hikes were discontinued when two men were hospitalized from foot injuries caused by the heavy rubberized boots they wore. Winter sports were popular and almost every area had its own ski and sled run. Skiing became the favorite outdoor sport of the Liberty Patch wearers. Trucks were available on schedule to take men up the incline, and skis were available for hire. The 306th Infantry stationed at Hakodate was the proud possessor of an 800-yard ski run equipped with a cable tow operated by a marine engine. However, ping pong was rated as the most widely patronized garrison sport.

Basketball came into the limelight with the opening of such buildings the Martin O. May Fieldhouse, nicknamed "The Little Madison Square Garden" where nightly basketball games were staged. The Division basketball team, angling for a shot at the title contest to be played in Hawaii, reached the finals in the Tokyo Olympics but was beaten for the Crown by the 41st Division five, 48-38. A dark horse throughout the tourney, the 77th team successively defeated clubs rated much better than themselves.

Boxing shared the spotlight laurels, for the best record the Eighth Army Olympic boxing quarter finals was set by the 77th when Dick Miller and

Leon Mauch of the 306th and 307th Infantry respectively, captured the feather and welterweight crowns at Sendai, Japan. The three-man 77th Division team came through with two champions and placed one man in the semi-final round.

During the Divisions stay in Japan men continued to be returned to the States. Men in the 60 to 70 point brackets were eligible for shipment prior to 27 November. On 1 December, one hundred 60-pointers were shipped out, and on Tuesday, 4 December another one hundred departed. On 17 December another two hundred fifty men of the 77th Division with between 55 and 60 points were shipped out for the 4th Replacement Depot for transport home.

An outstanding event took place in the 77th on the first of December, 1945 when the practice of wearing the helmet liner was discontinued because of cold weather. So went the second of the four "Ls" that had characterized 77th men since their early training days. First "L" to fall by the wayside had been the legging which was discarded midway in the battle for Leyte when combat boots became available "landscape" work and light packs remained to the end.

Some of the old timers may be happy to know that the old gripes about slow mail service and poor chow remained with the occupation troops until deactivation. However, in comparison to the unheated barracks met by the initial occupation force, the infantrymen began to enjoy steamheated quarters or rooms heated by stoves burning diesel oil.

On 19 December the first untoward incident to come about in the occupation of Hokkaido occurred when an 18-year-old Japanese named Kataunori Tamura was charged with the murder of an American sentry doing guard duty in Sapporo.

With the advent of the first peacetime Christmas after four years of fighting, troops of the 77th thought back to a year before when they were in the midst of the battle for Leyte. They remembered MacArthur's announcement that the 77th had given America a really cheering gift in the form of a successful landing at Palompon. But in 1945, the 77th Division men were also thinking of the poor people over whom they were victorious. Officers and enlisted men of the division tendered two parties for 1,500 school children of Sapporo at the McNair Theatre. Throughout the Division there were Christmas parties and carol singing sponsored by the Red Cross. But most interesting were the Christmas dinners of fresh food and turkey with all the trimmings. All Division mess halls were decorated with Christmas trees, Santa Clauses and various kinds of decorative material. Several of the mess halls had been newly renovated with fresh coats of paint. With fresh flowers unobtainable, artificial flowers made very attractive substitutes on many tables. All phases of the activities in Hokkaido showed that the troops were determined to make this Christmas Day away from home as homey and American as possible. However, on the day after Christmas, fire destroyed a 305th barracks. Two soldiers were burned to death.

Throughout the cold months, recreational activities were featured. Enlisted men as well as officers had their night clubs, with beer on sale and dancing partners available. Post exchanges blossomed into garrison-like shops that featured photographers, snack bars, souvenir counters and well stocked shelves. The Red Cross sponsored daily trips to the ski run, bingo contests in the evening, amateur entertainment contests, spelling bees, hobby shops and light snacks. Late film attractions could be seen at the theatres nightly. Periodically each area was favored with a visit by one of the various variety shows that represented the Division's many units. Talented Japanese acrobats and "carney" men armed with the few remaining animals put together a circus that played every 77th show place. Dance recitals and stage shows by Japanese entertainers were also presented. An educational as well as interesting feature was offered the 77th soldiers when Japanese guides volunteered their services to conduct weekly visits to Shinto shrines in the vicinity of camp areas. On the athletic front, both participants and spectators were satisfied with the nightly games at the field houses where boxing, basketball and track were featured.

Then on 1 February, when a lot of latrine rumors had everyone confused, it was officially announced that the 77th was to be inactivated on 15 March. In February also, the 77th lost all enlisted men with 42 and 44 points. Instead of receiving replacements, the Division began to transfer more low point men to other units. On the 28th General Bruce, who had joined the 77th in the heat of the Arizona desert in May, 1943 and piloted it through three major campaigns in the Pacific and over most of the occupation route in Japan, was assigned to command the 7th Infantry Division stationed in Korea. General Randle, Assistant Division Commander since he joined the 77th after the North African campaign, commanded the Division from 29 February to Inactivation Day, 15 March 1946.

A division is a complex organism and its passing, like its birth, involves time, planning and effort. Therefore, during the closing week of February and the first fifteen days of March 1946, there was much to be done. One by one the functions and activities ceased or were transferred to other commands. Piece by piece the property was inventoried, shipped, or transferred. Personnel strength totals dropped steadily as men departed to new assignments, and the constantly diminishing remainder worked harder to complete the policing of the installations.

The issuance on 15 March, of General Order Number 77 inactivating the organizations and units which composed the 77th Infantry Division, was only an official recognition of an accomplished fact. The praises of Secretary of War Robert Patterson, General Douglas MacArthur, General Robert Eichelberger, and Major General Bruce were for work finished. Almost four years old and a half a world from home, the 77th was done with this war. The Liberty Patch was shifted to the right shoulders of those in service, and to the hearts and memories of those gone home.

Chapter 30: Mission Accomplished

THE 77th did its work well. Those quiet men who lived to wear all its campaign stars are not likely to enter into futile discussions as to whether the 77th or some other division was "best." They know that in war there are too many variables to permit precise measurement of ability in men or in divisions. But they and everyone can be proud of the 77ths record.

The 77th was in active service almost exactly four years and spent one-half of that time in rigorous training and the other half overseas. It was activated in South Carolina, U. S. A., and inactivated in Hokkaido, Japan, on the other side of the world. Between those two places the Division travelled more than 25,000 miles and spent a total of 90 days aboard ship.

During its five operations, in three campaigns, 200 days were spent fighting and killing Japanese. Another 180 days were lived on land where hostile enemy were occasionally encountered. At least 70 of the days at sea were days within reach of Japanese submarines or aircraft.

It killed 43,651 enemy. That total may err a thousand either way; there was little time or inclination for precise counting. It took in battle only 488 enemy prisoners but, later, it officiated at the surrender of 5,543 Japanese on Cebu.

Two thousand of the 77th's men won't come home, ever; 6,282 were wounded, and many more were non-battle casualties. However, the enemy paid with 22 dead for each 77th man killed. Five Japanese were killed or captured for each 77th Division battle casualty.

The 77th men know that they were fortunate in that they were never called upon to fight a losing campaign, or to fight in the snow. Those however, are the only battle tests they missed. They tried and succeeded at amphibious assaults, shore to shore operations, jungle fighting, open and mechanized warfare, attacks on fortifications, cave blasting, night attacks, mountain warfare, reconnaissance, and defensive jobs. Qualified observers told them that the 77th was one of three Army divisions in the Pacific considered competent for any assignment, any time, any place. Theater and Army commanders requested the 77th's services. No other division was kept busier.

The Division was formed and trained to fight. It did that. But it performed well in other ways. Throughout its career it built a reputation as a neat, courteous organization. It left behind it a string of clean camps and maneuver areas. It caused few disturbances. It had a low disease rate. It established and maintained cordial relations with the Marine Corps and the Navy. In its occupation area, Hokkaido, there were no uprisings, no major black markets, and no mass protest meetings of American soldiers. Commendatory letters accumulated in the Division files.

The job was done well.

A NOTE TO THE READER

WE HOPED YOU LOVED THIS BOOK. IF YOU DID, PLEASE LEAVE A REVIEW ON AMAZON TO LET EVERYONE ELSE KNOW WHAT YOU THOUGHT.

WE WOULD ALSO LIKE TO THANK OUR SPONSORS **WWW.DIGITALHISTORYBOOKS.COM** WHO MADE THE PUBLICATION OF THIS BOOK POSSIBLE.

WWW.DIGITALHISTORYBOOKS.COM PROVIDES A WEEKLY NEWSLETTER OF THE BEST DEALS IN HISTORY AND HISTORICAL FICTION.

SIGN UP TO THEIR NEWLSETTER TO FIND OUT MORE ABOUT THEIR LATEST DEALS.

Made in the USA
Monee, IL
20 June 2021